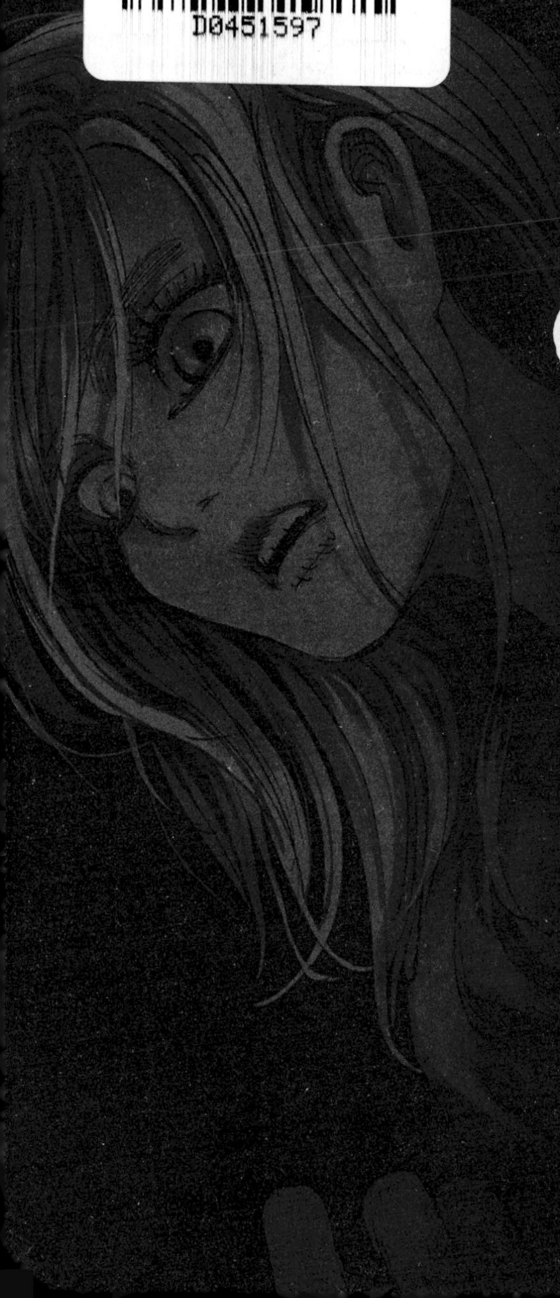

ATTACK ON TITAN 16

HAJIME ISAYAMA

"Attack on Titan" Character Introductions

104th Corps

raduated at
ne top of her
raining corps,
ikasa is a
ighly talented
oldier. Her
arents were
urdered
efore her
yes when she
as a child,
ut Eren saved
er life. Since
hen, she has
ade it her
ission to
rotect him.

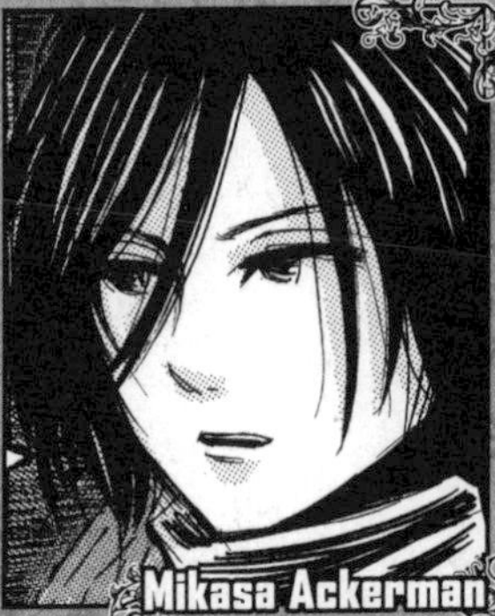

Mikasa Ackerman

Eren joined the Survey Corps out of his longing for the outside world and his hatred of the Titans. He has the power to turn himself into a Titan, but its origins are unknown.

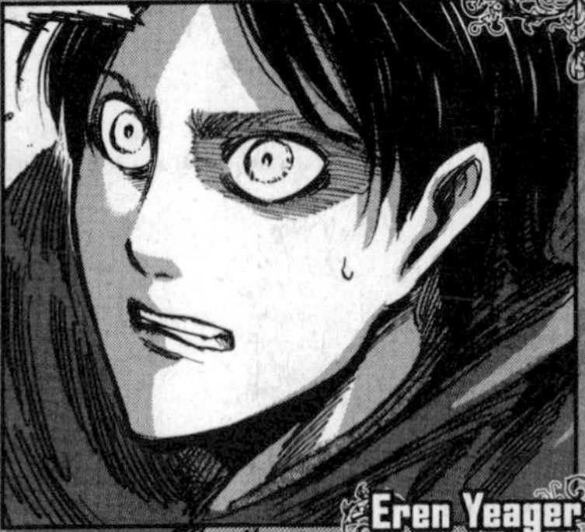

Eren Yeager

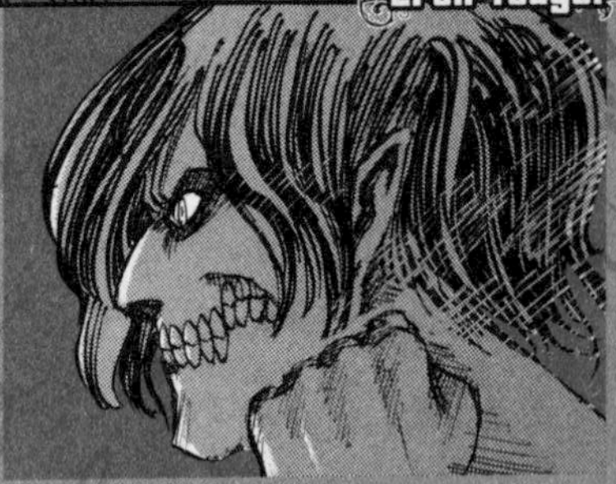

ren and Mikasa's
hildhood friend.
hough Armin isn't
thletic in the least,
e possesses both
harp observational
owers and keen
sight, and he
xhibits an
xtraordinary ability
o develop
trategies.

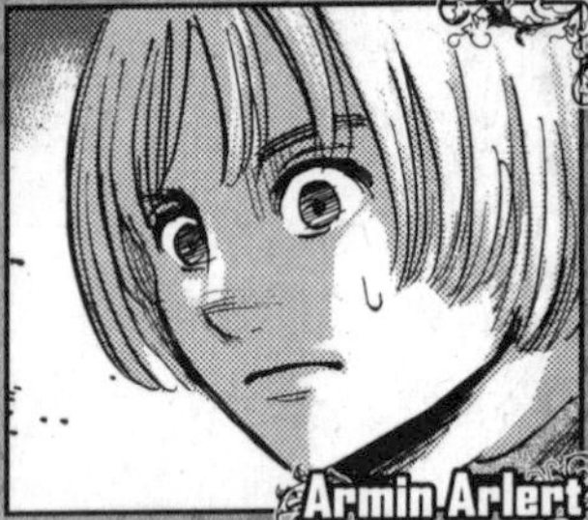

Armin Arlert

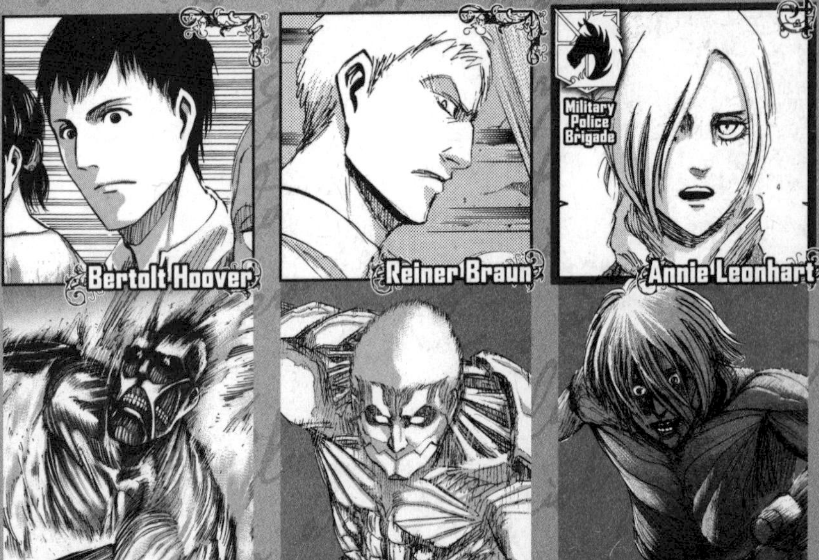
Military
Police
Brigade

Bertolt Hoover

Reiner Braun

Annie Leonhart

The Colossus Titan

The Armored Titan

The Female Titan

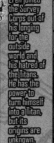

Survey Corps

Soldiers who are prepared to sacrifice themselves as they brave the Titan territory outside the walls.

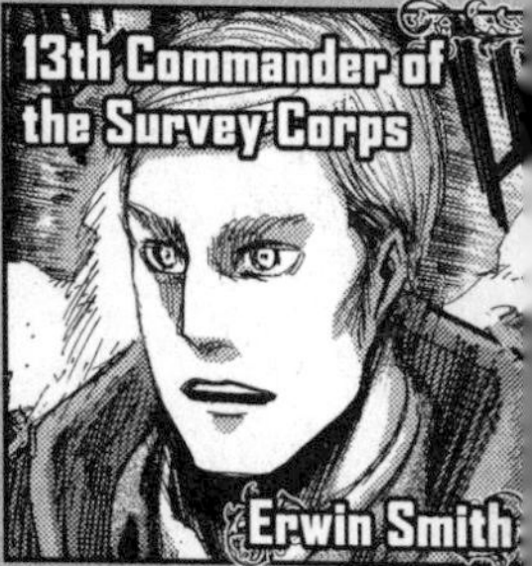
13th Commander of the Survey Corps
Erwin Smith

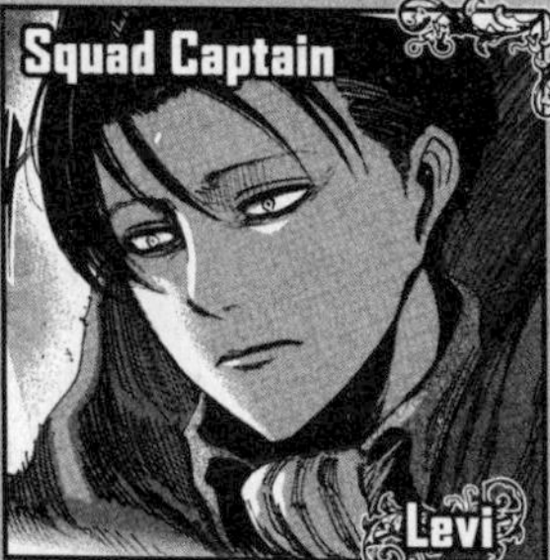
Squad Captain
Levi

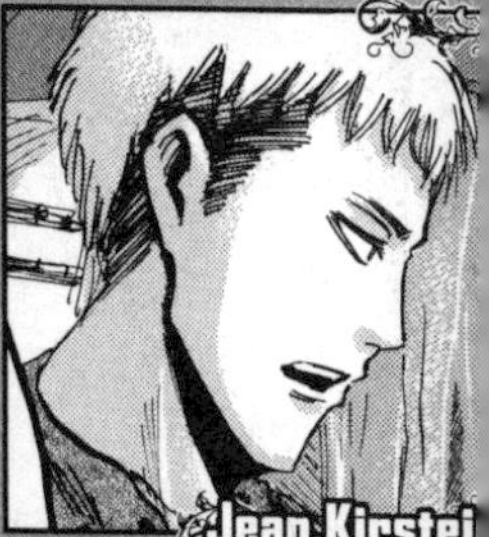
Jean Kirstei

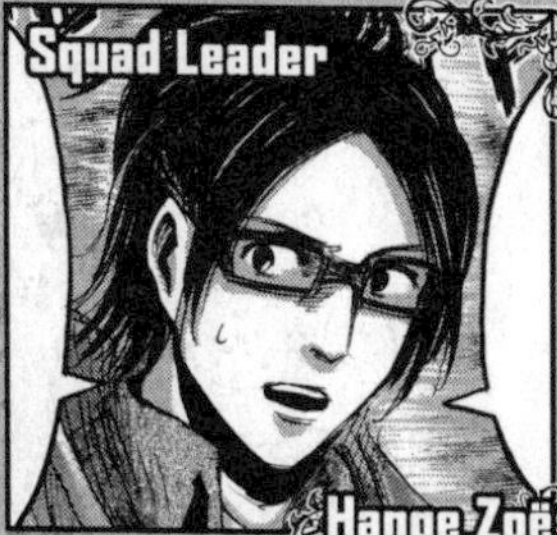
Squad Leader
Hange Zoë

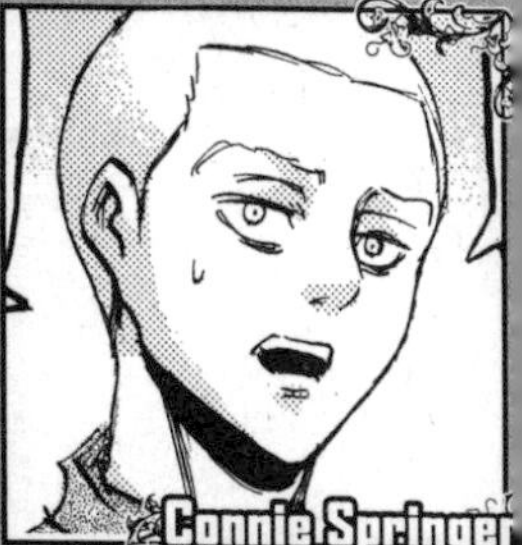
Connie Springer

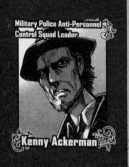

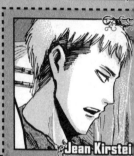

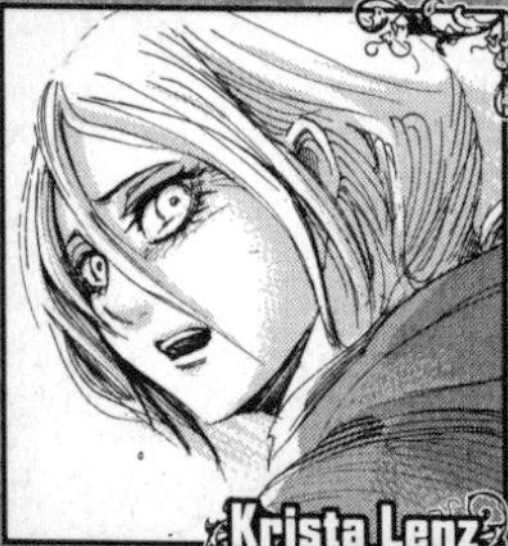
Krista Lenz
(Historia Reiss)

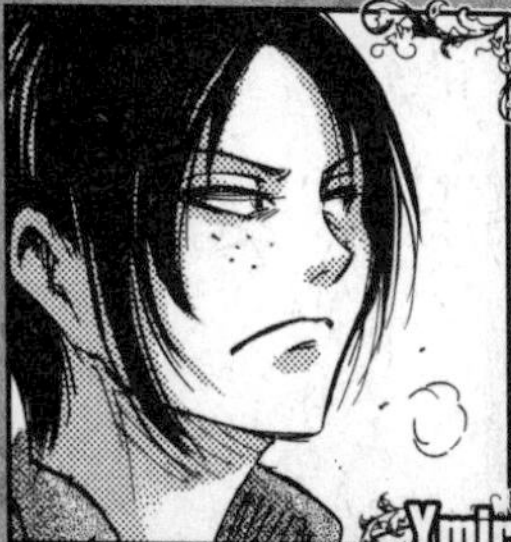
Ymir

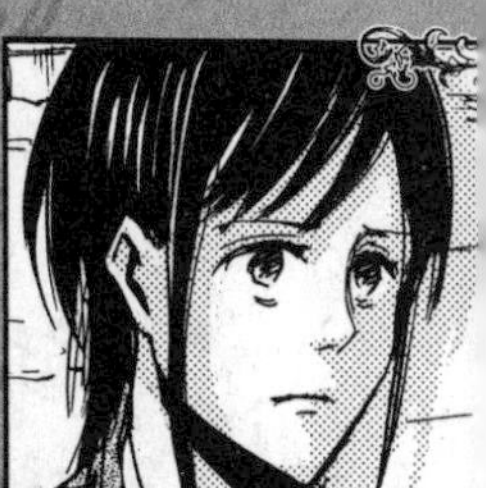
Sasha Blous

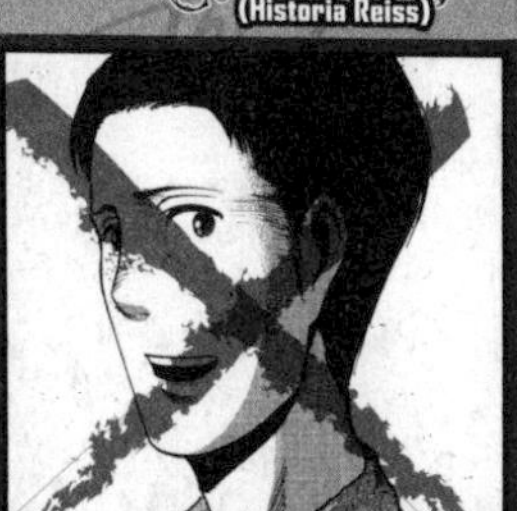
Marco Bott

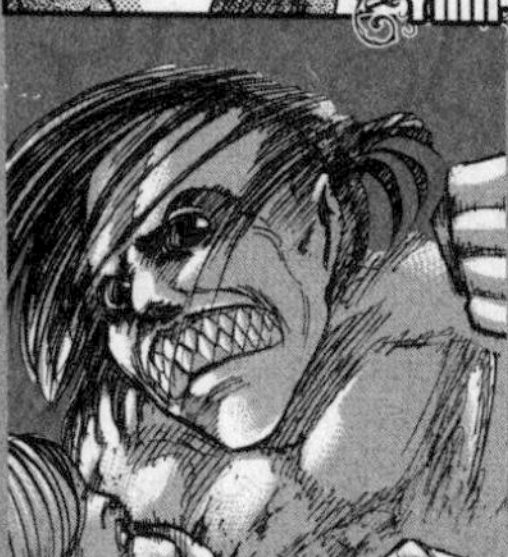

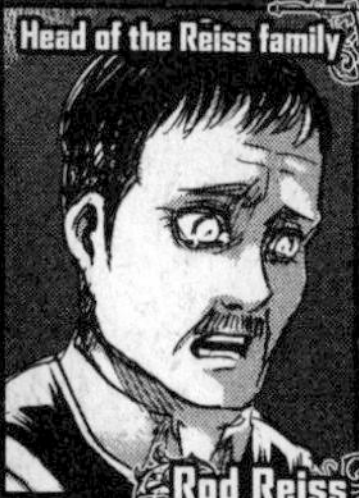
Head of the Reiss family
Rod Reiss

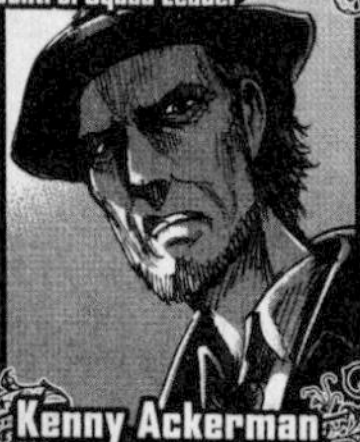
Military Police Anti-Personnel Control Squad Leader
Kenny Ackerman

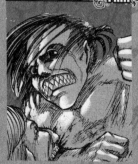

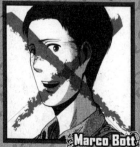

ATTACK on TITAN

Episode 63: Chains

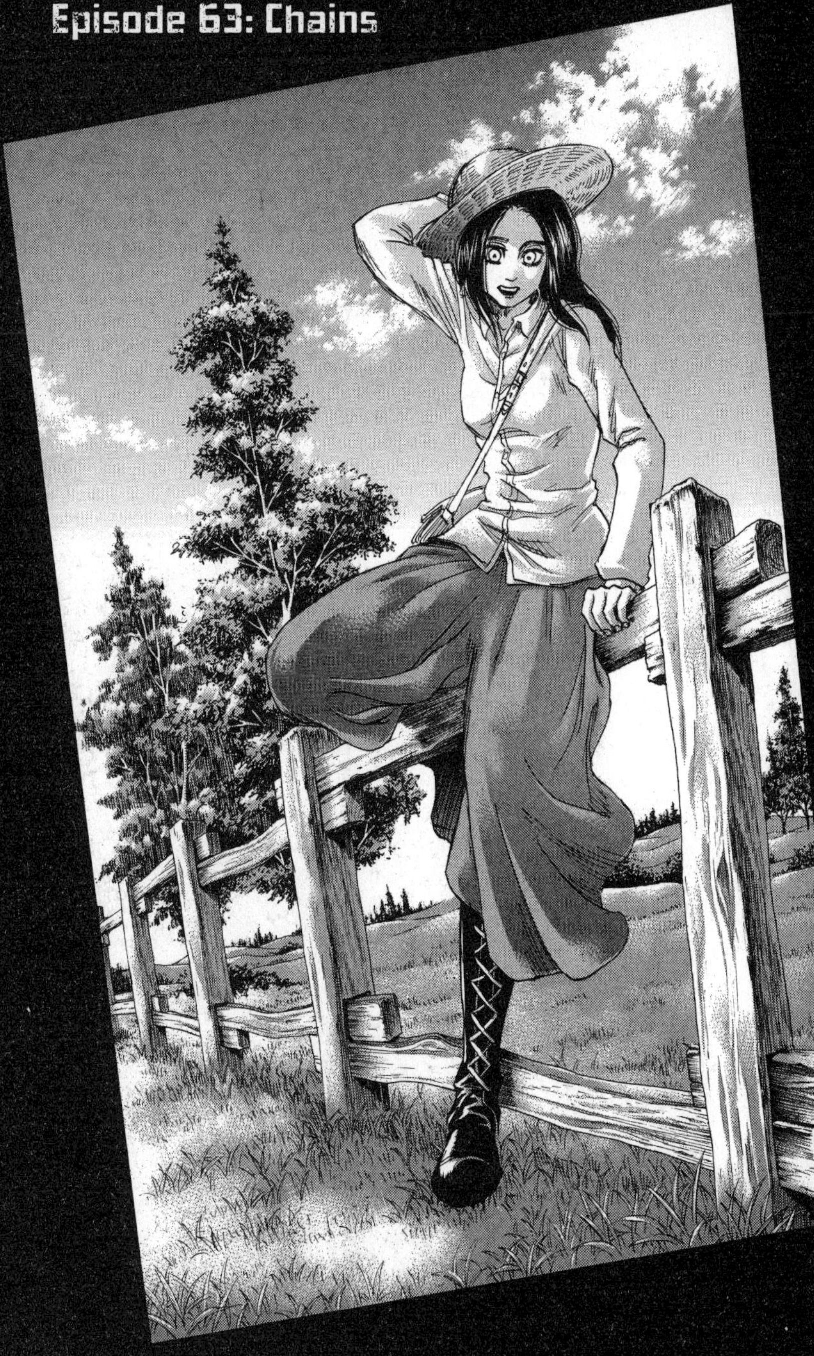

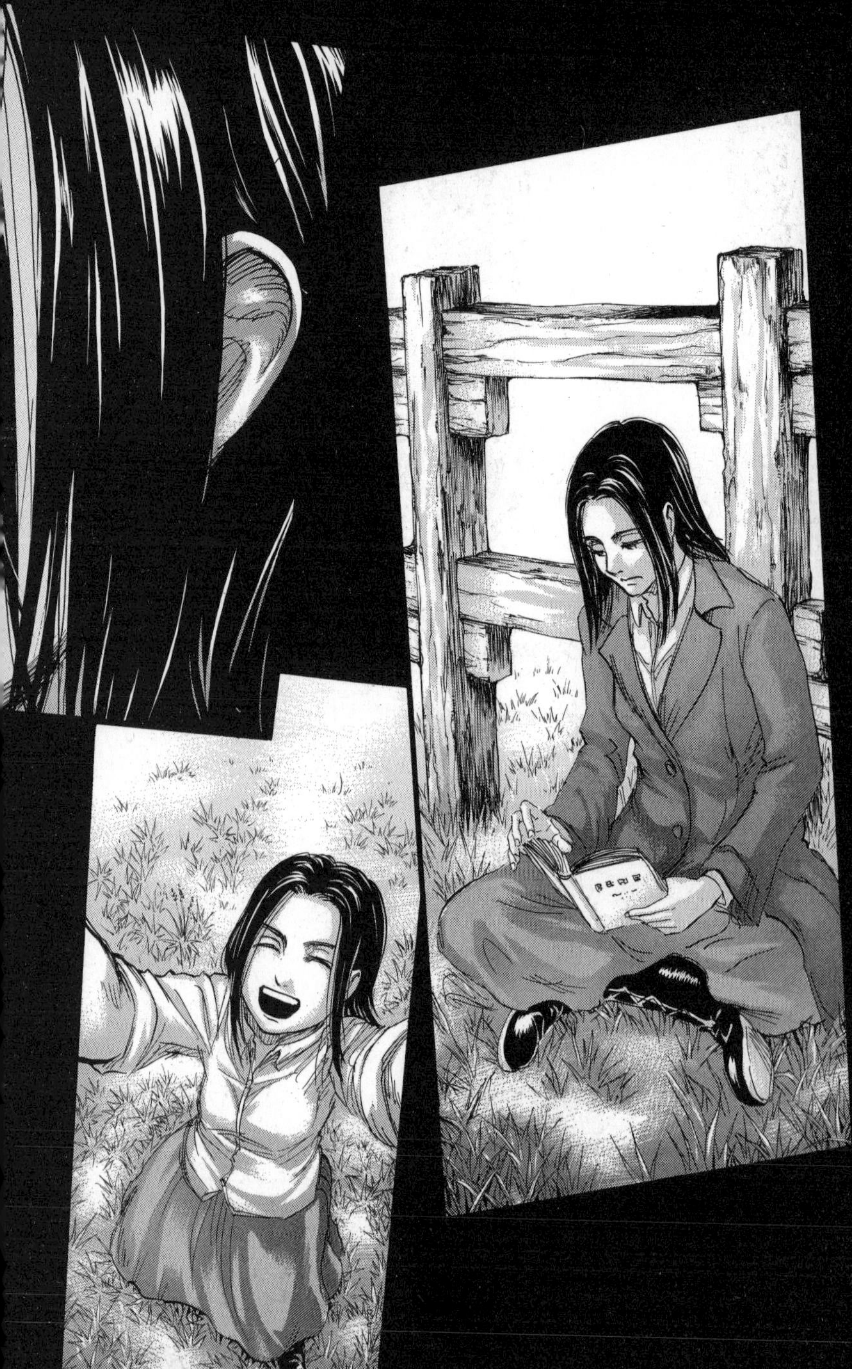

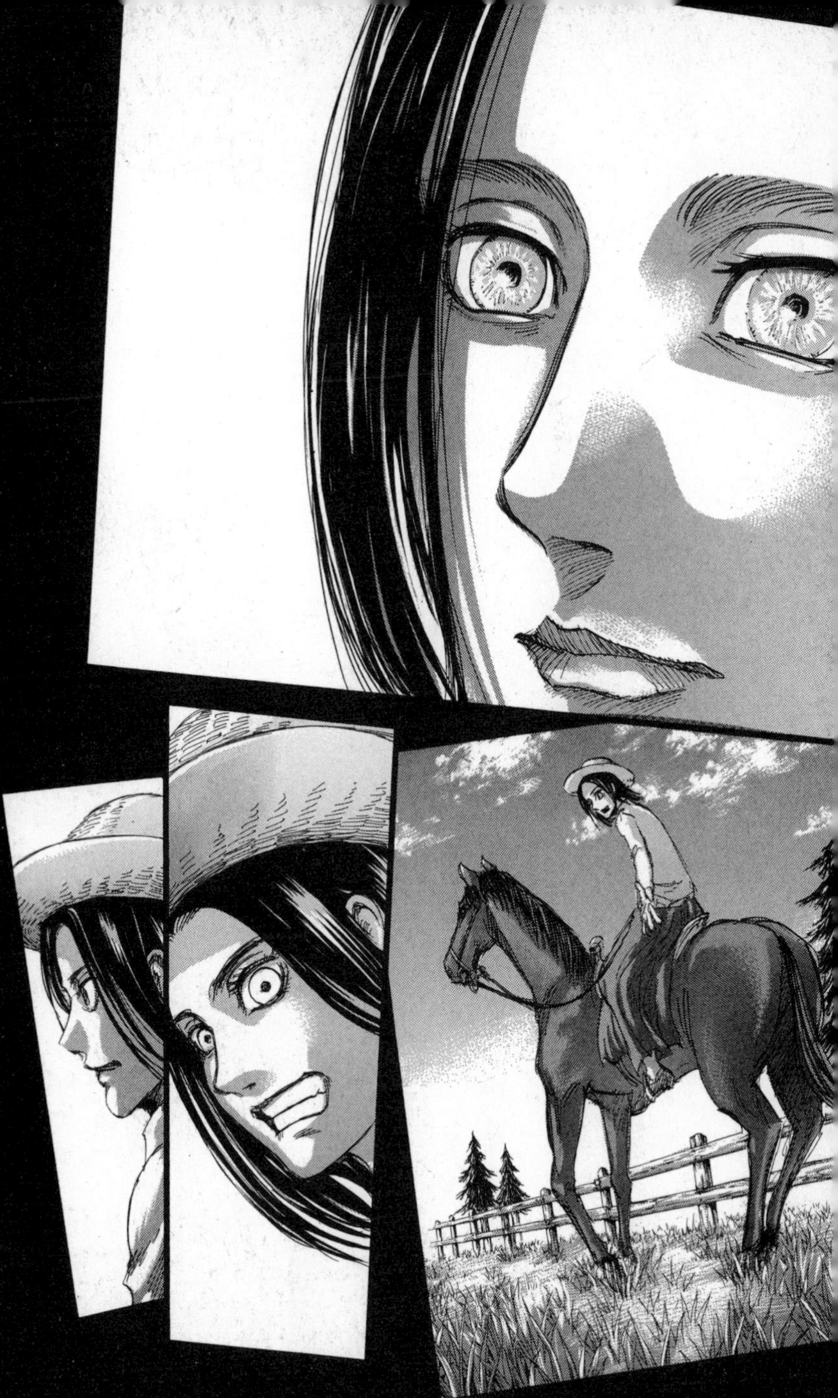

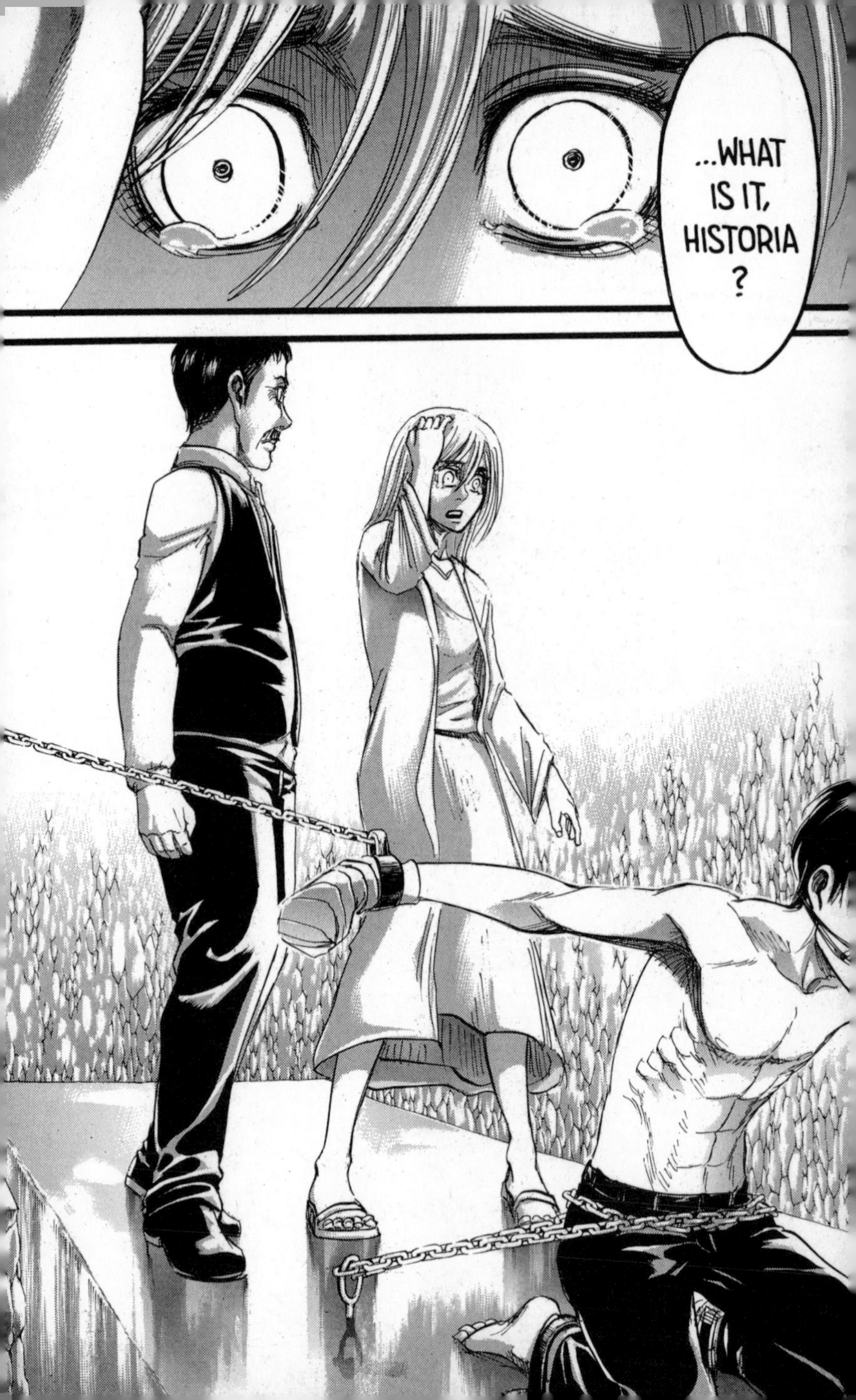
...WHAT IS IT, HISTORIA?

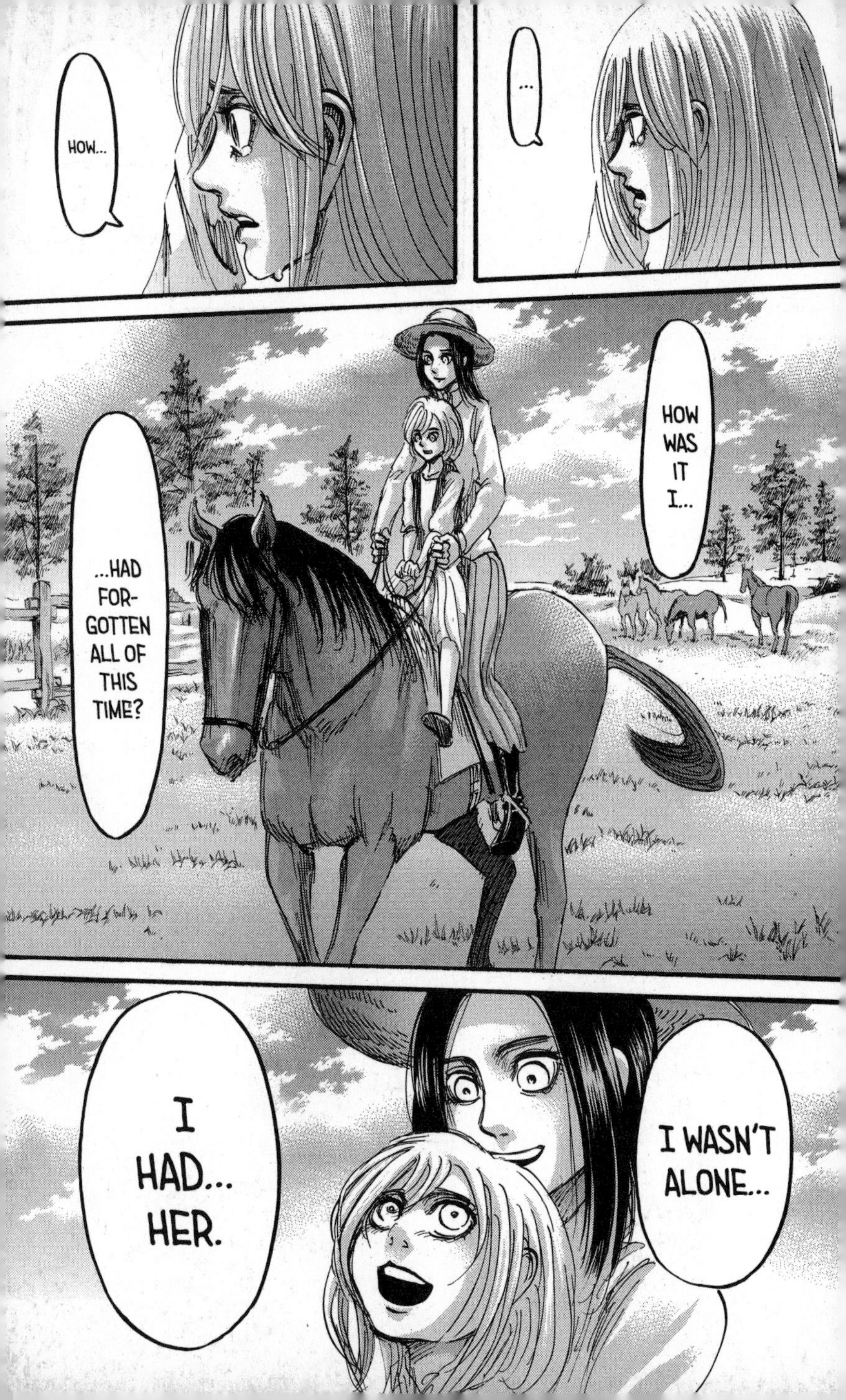
...
HOW...
HOW WAS IT I...
...HAD FOR-GOTTEN ALL OF THIS TIME?
I WASN'T ALONE...
I HAD... HER.

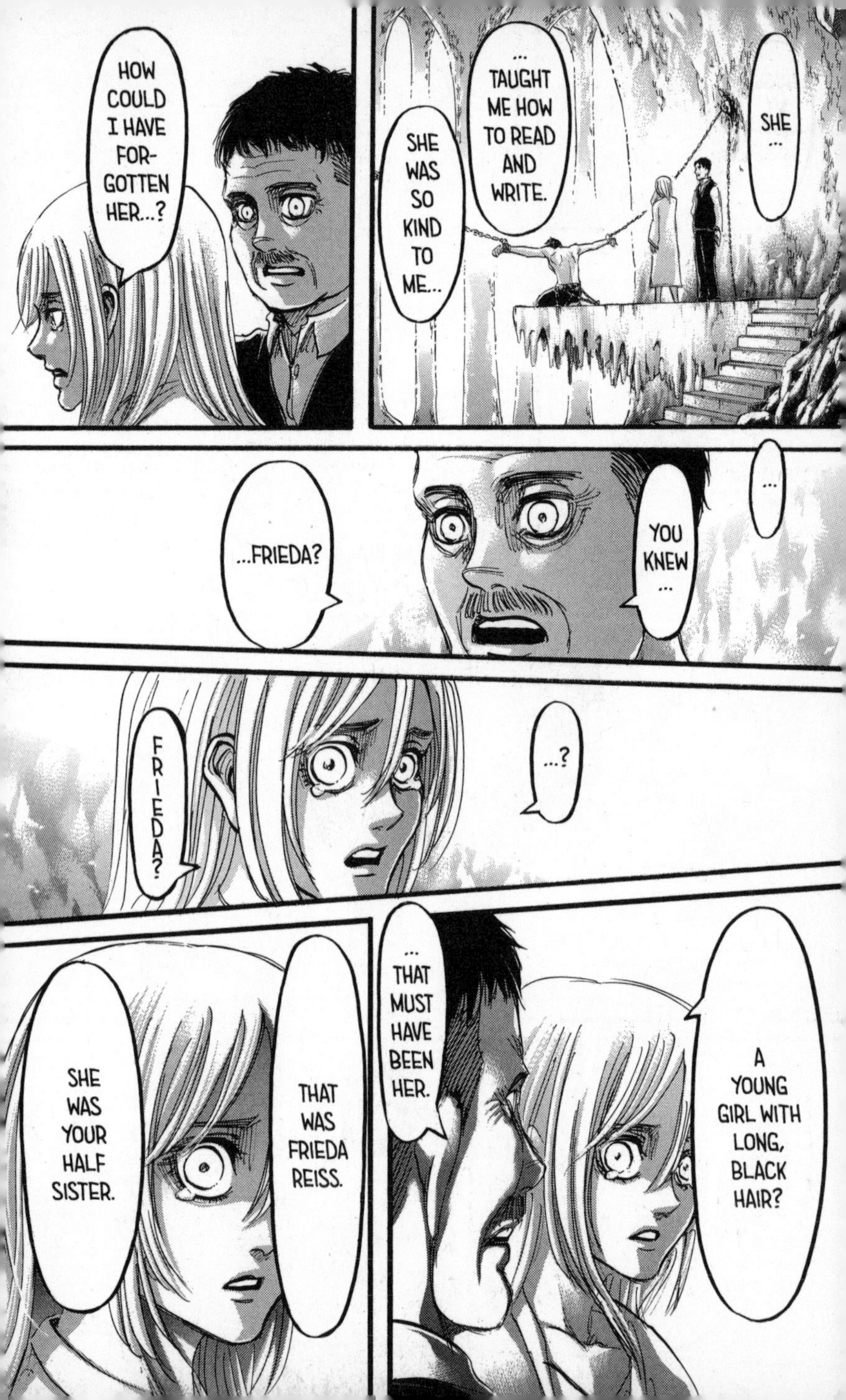

SHE ...
... TAUGHT ME HOW TO READ AND WRITE.
SHE WAS SO KIND TO ME...
HOW COULD I HAVE FOR-GOTTEN HER...?
...
YOU KNEW ...
...FRIEDA?
...?
FRIEDA?
A YOUNG GIRL WITH LONG, BLACK HAIR?
... THAT MUST HAVE BEEN HER.
THAT WAS FRIEDA REISS.
SHE WAS YOUR HALF SISTER.

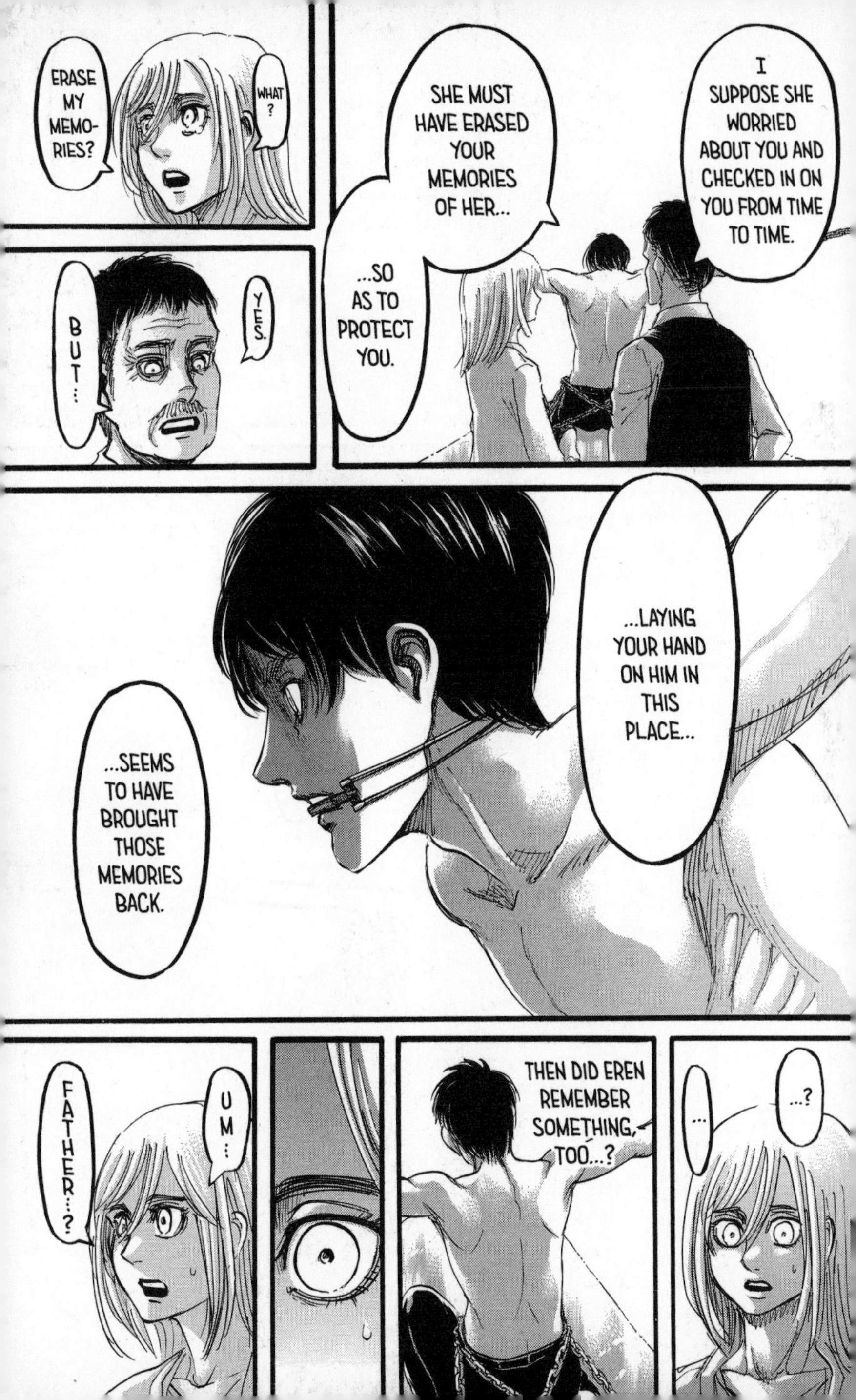
I SUPPOSE SHE WORRIED ABOUT YOU AND CHECKED IN ON YOU FROM TIME TO TIME.
SHE MUST HAVE ERASED YOUR MEMORIES OF HER...
...SO AS TO PROTECT YOU.
WHAT?
ERASE MY MEMORIES?
YES.
BUT...
...LAYING YOUR HAND ON HIM IN THIS PLACE...
...SEEMS TO HAVE BROUGHT THOSE MEMORIES BACK.
...?
...
THEN DID EREN REMEMBER SOMETHING, TOO...?
UM...
FATHER...?

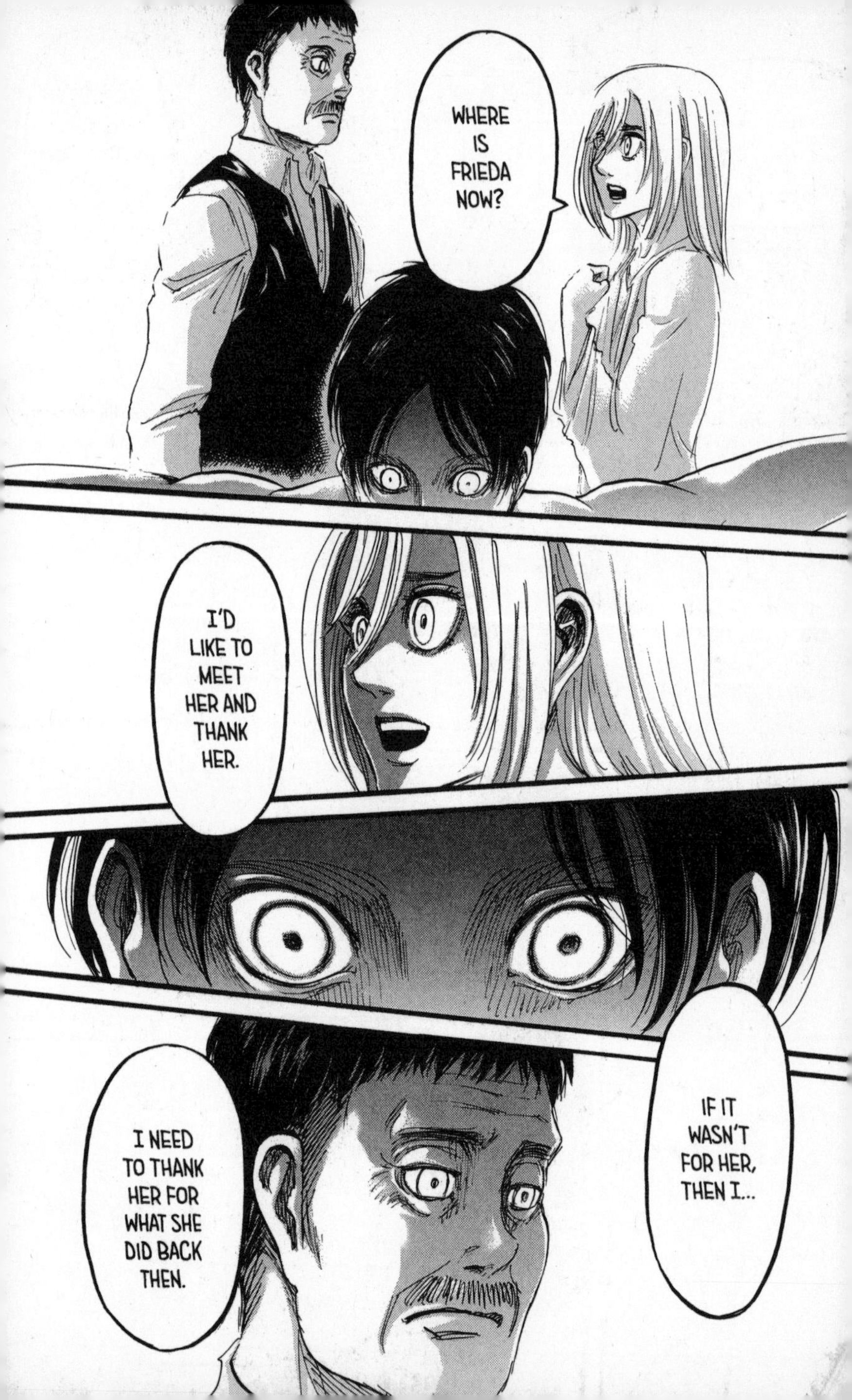
WHERE IS FRIEDA NOW?
I’D LIKE TO MEET HER AND THANK HER.
IF IT WASN’T FOR HER, THEN I...
I NEED TO THANK HER FOR WHAT SHE DID BACK THEN.

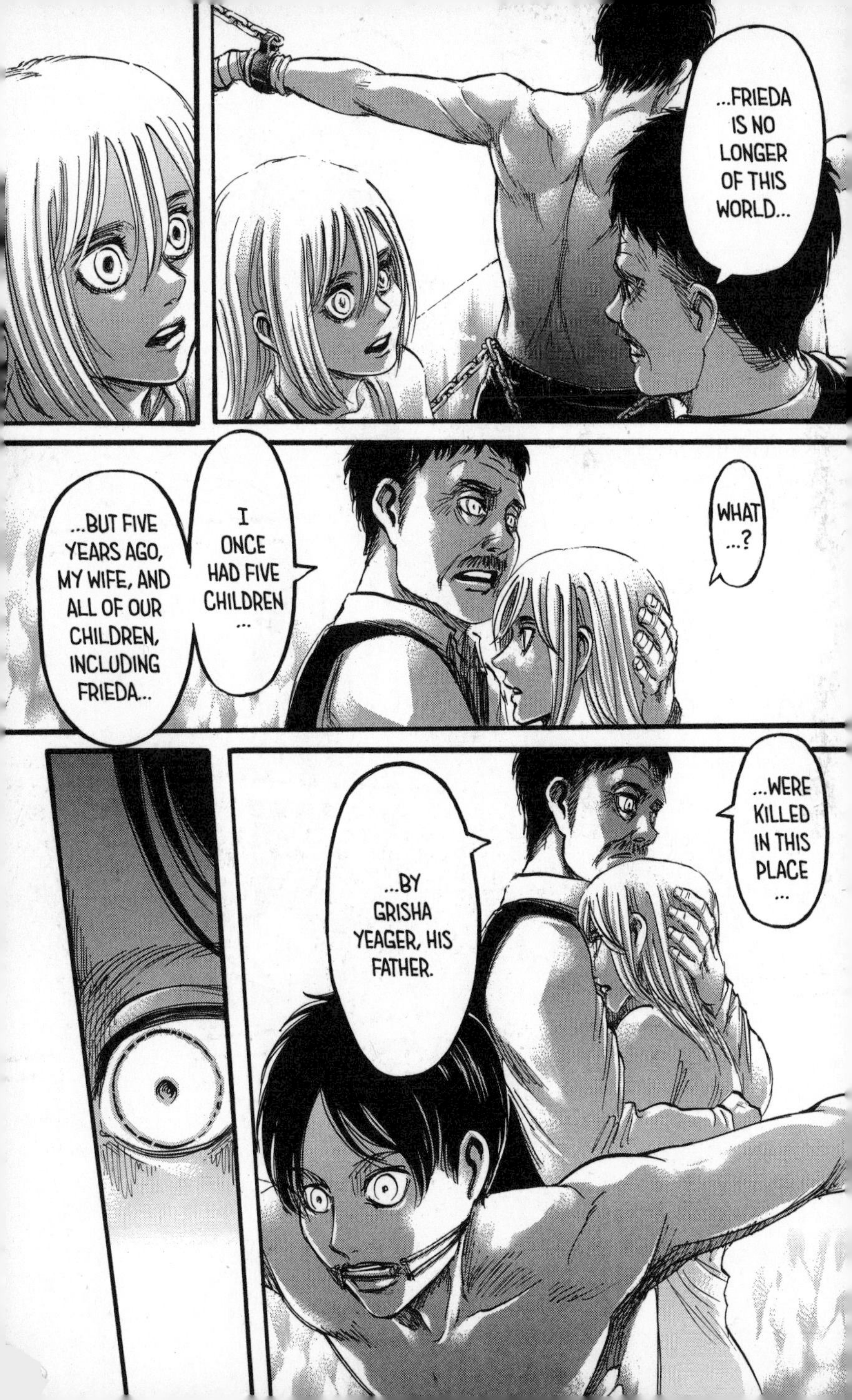
...FRIEDA IS NO LONGER OF THIS WORLD...
WHAT ...?
I ONCE HAD FIVE CHILDREN ...
...BUT FIVE YEARS AGO, MY WIFE, AND ALL OF OUR CHILDREN, INCLUDING FRIEDA...
...WERE KILLED IN THIS PLACE ...
...BY GRISHA YEAGER, HIS FATHER.

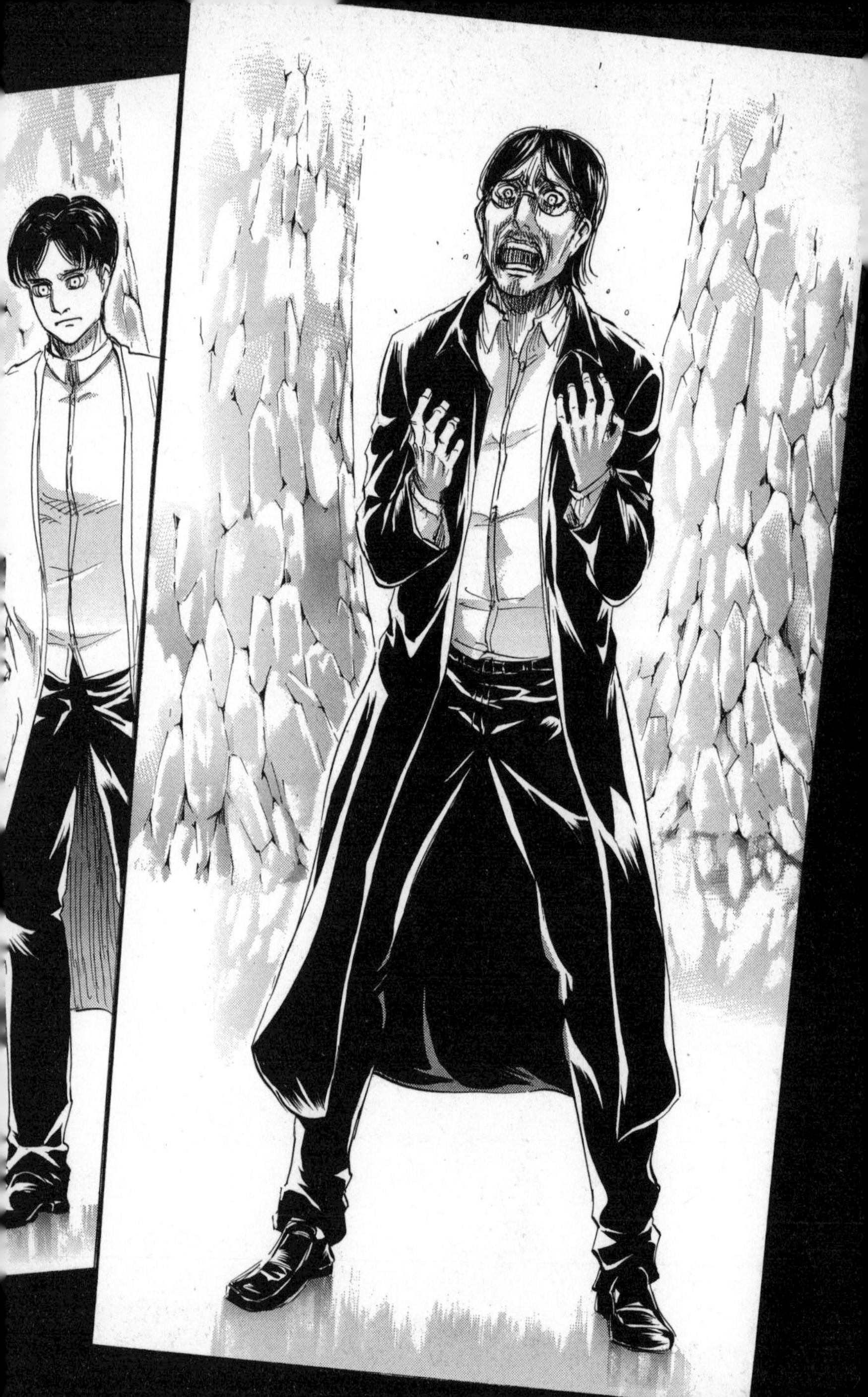

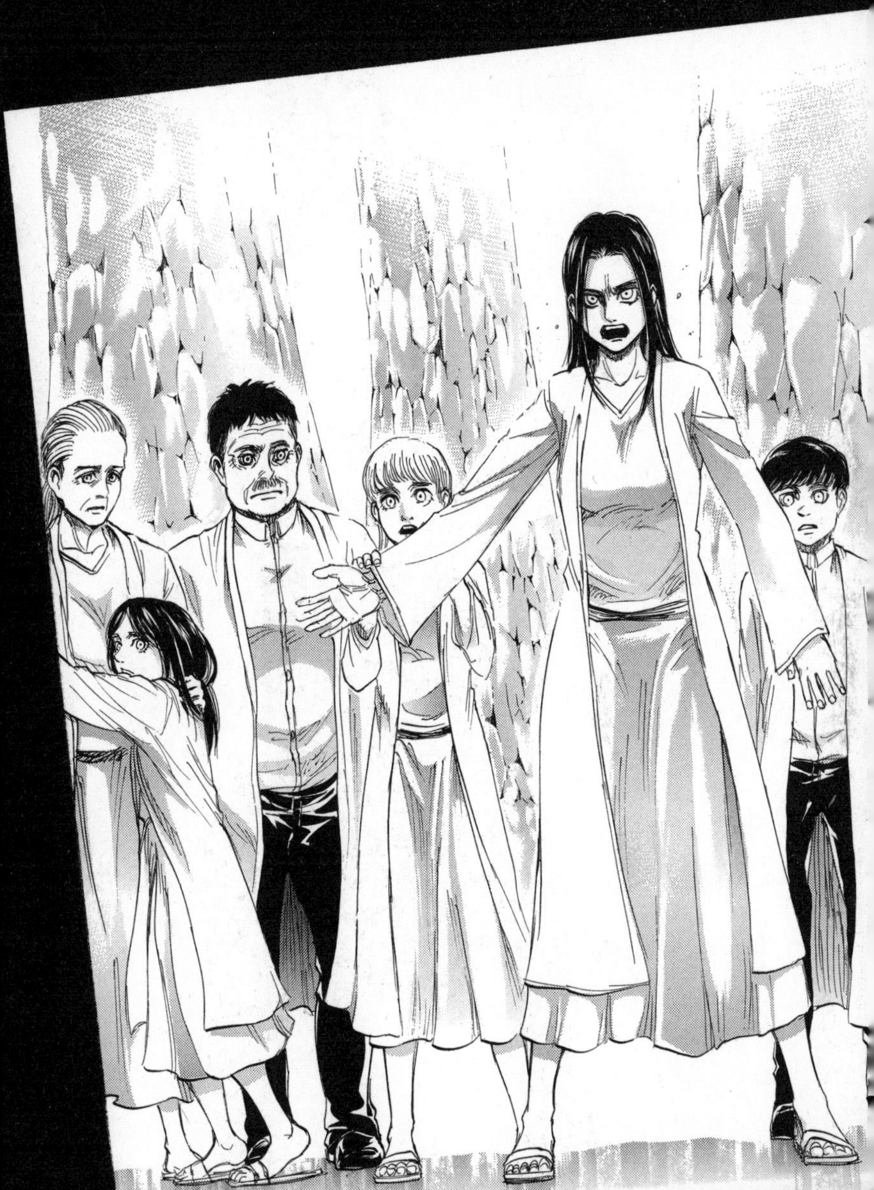

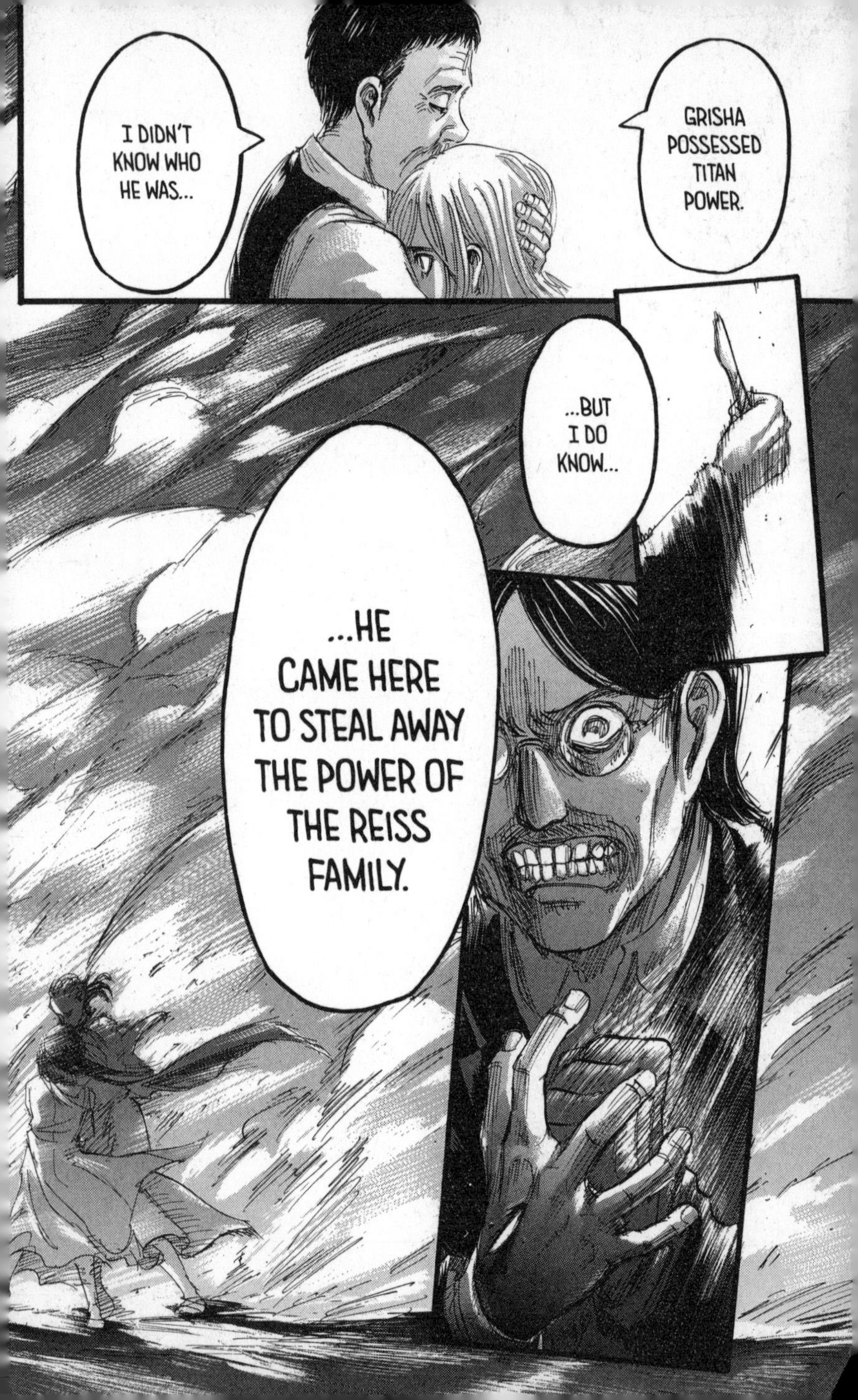
GRISHA POSSESSED TITAN POWER.
I DIDN'T KNOW WHO HE WAS...
...BUT I DO KNOW...
...HE CAME HERE TO STEAL AWAY THE POWER OF THE REISS FAMILY.

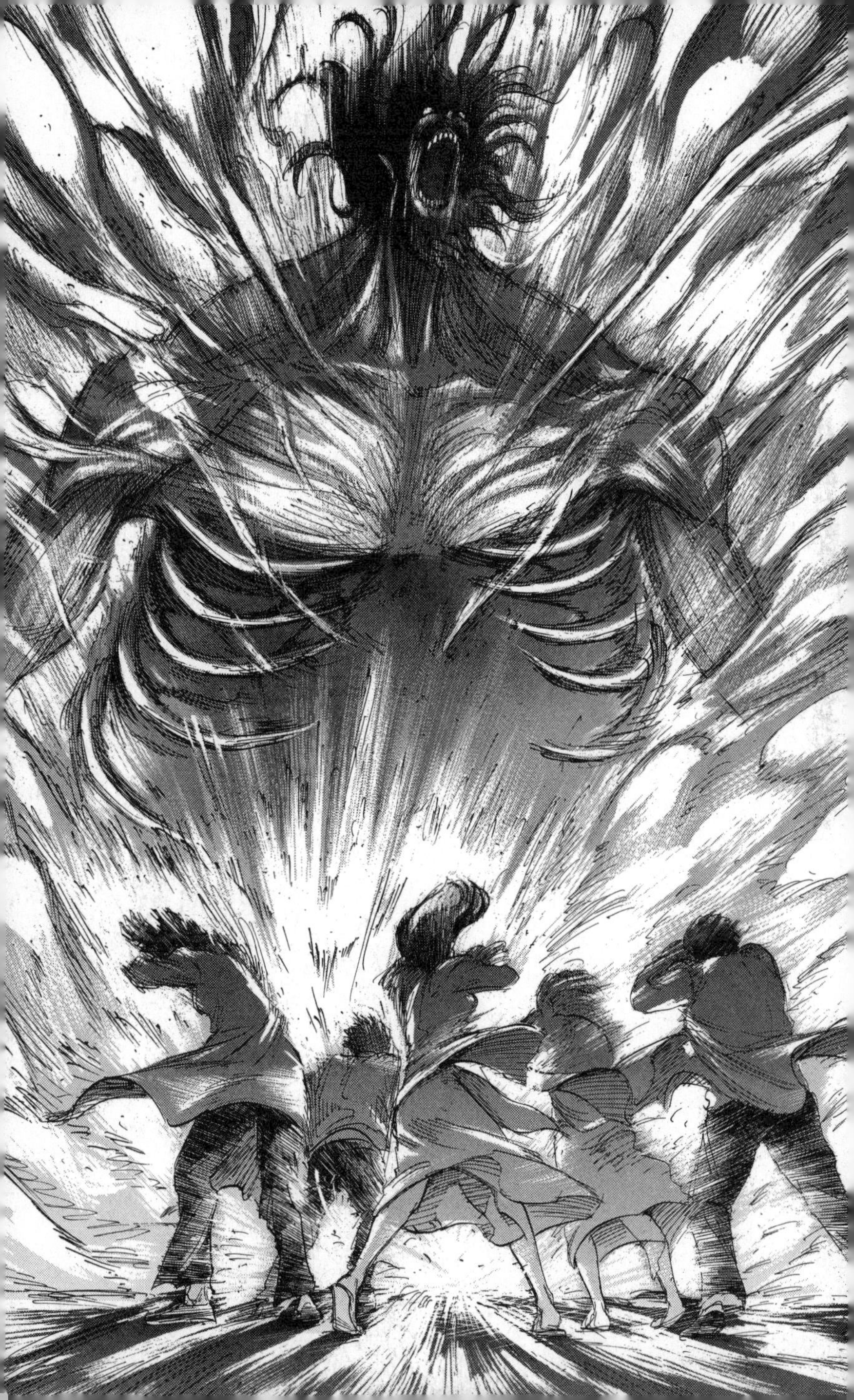

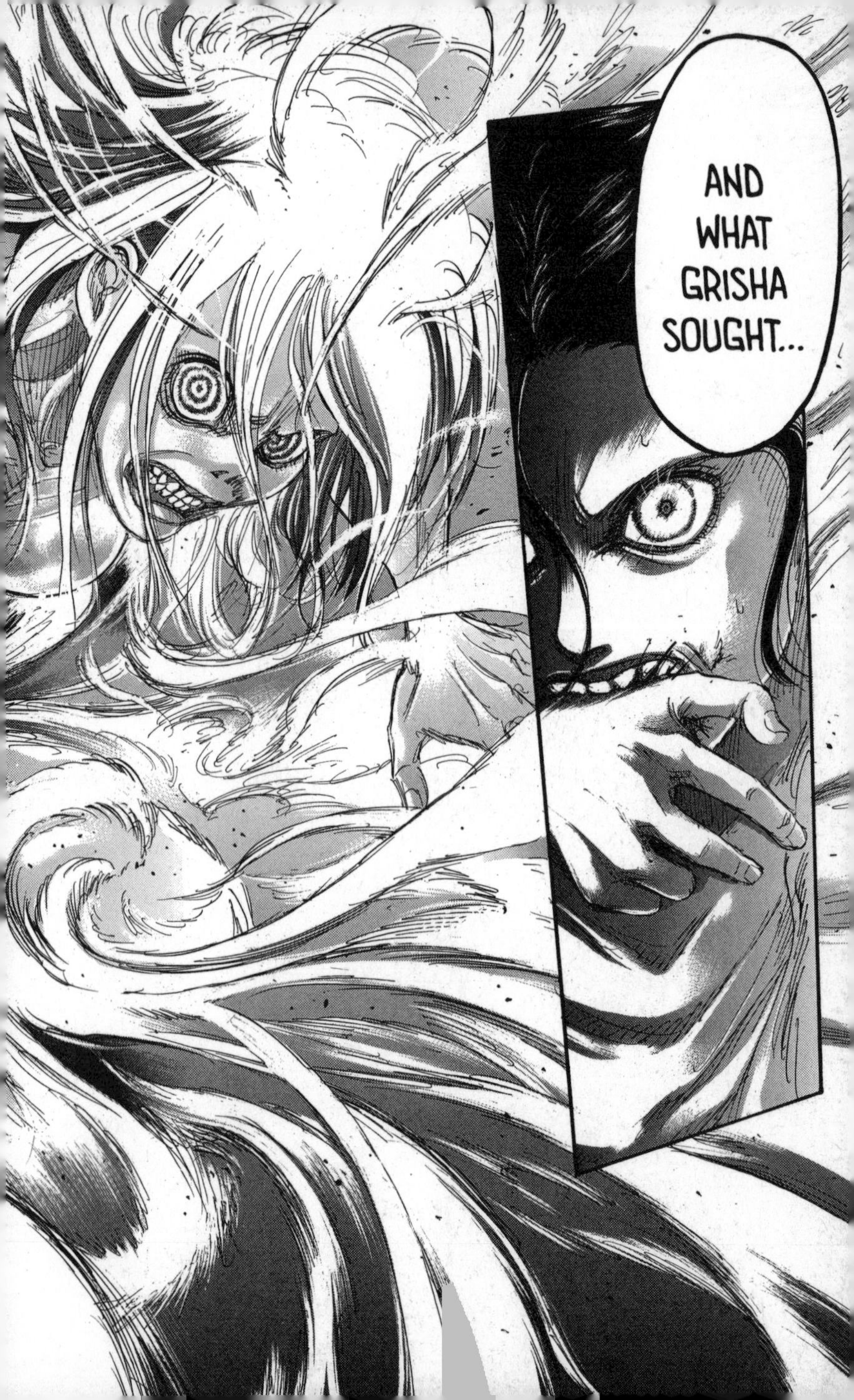
AND WHAT GRISHA SOUGHT...

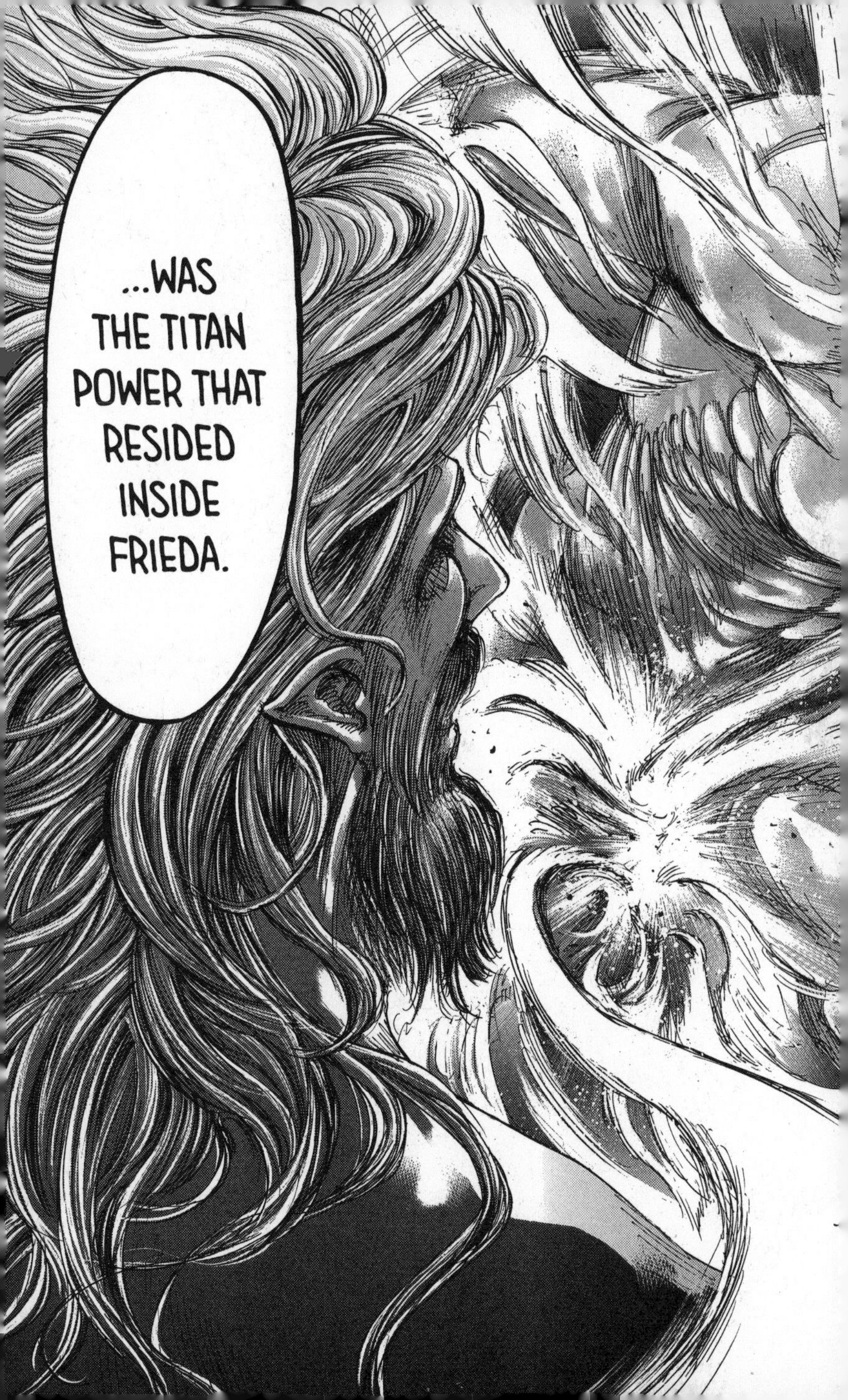
...WAS THE TITAN POWER THAT RESIDED INSIDE FRIEDA.

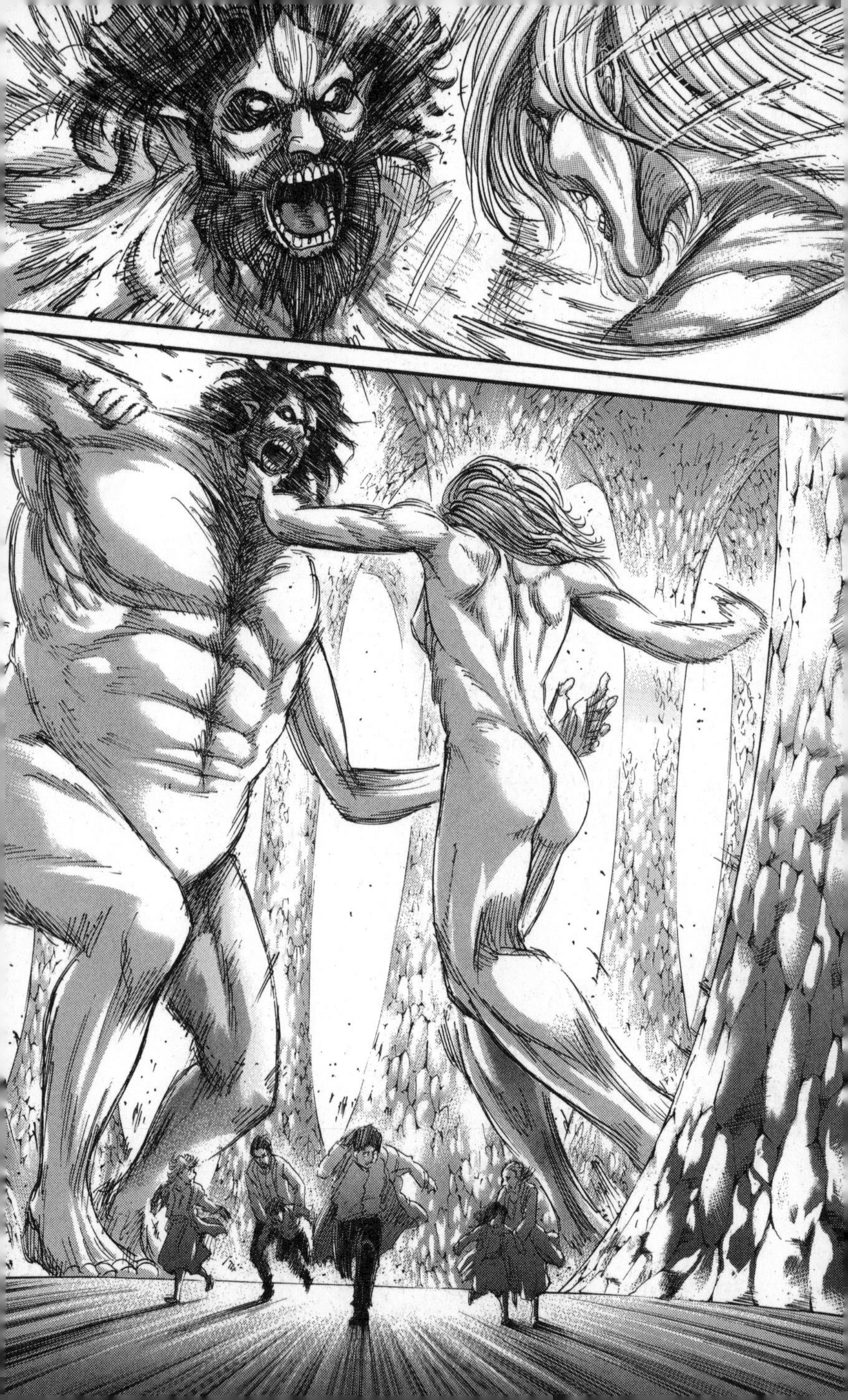

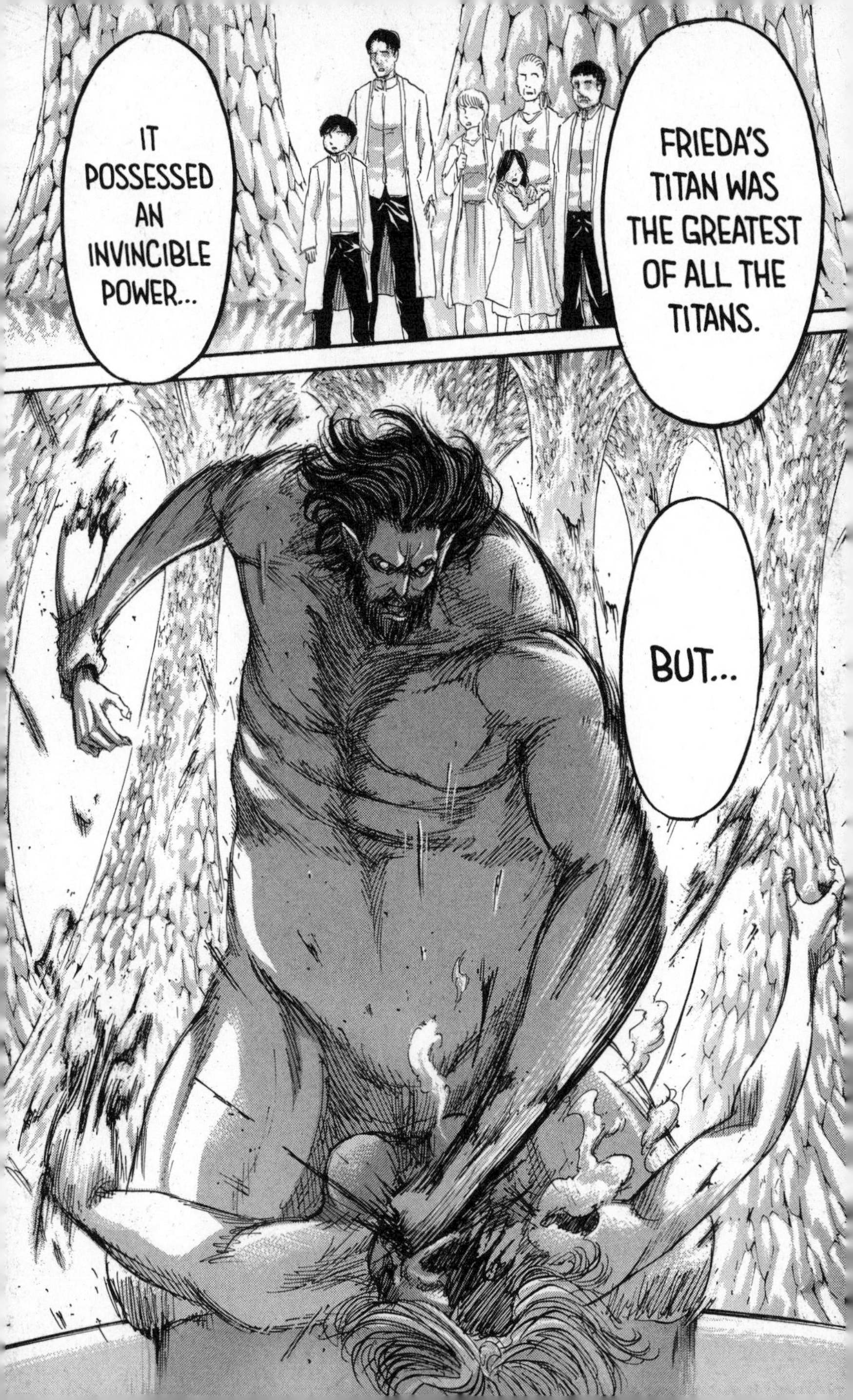
FRIEDA'S TITAN WAS THE GREATEST OF ALL THE TITANS.
IT POSSESSED AN INVINCIBLE POWER...
BUT...

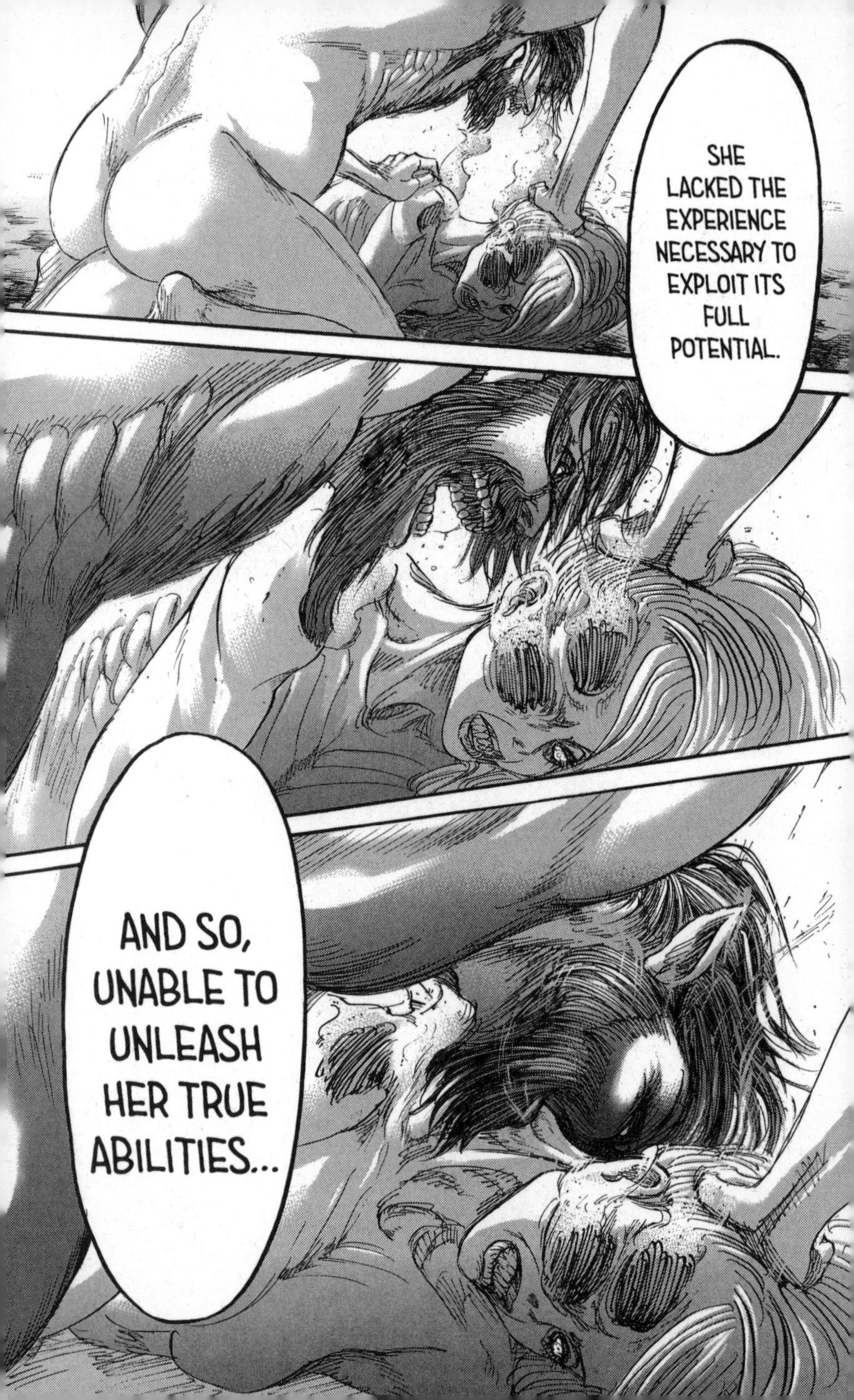
SHE LACKED THE EXPERIENCE NECESSARY TO EXPLOIT ITS FULL POTENTIAL.
AND SO, UNABLE TO UNLEASH HER TRUE ABILITIES...

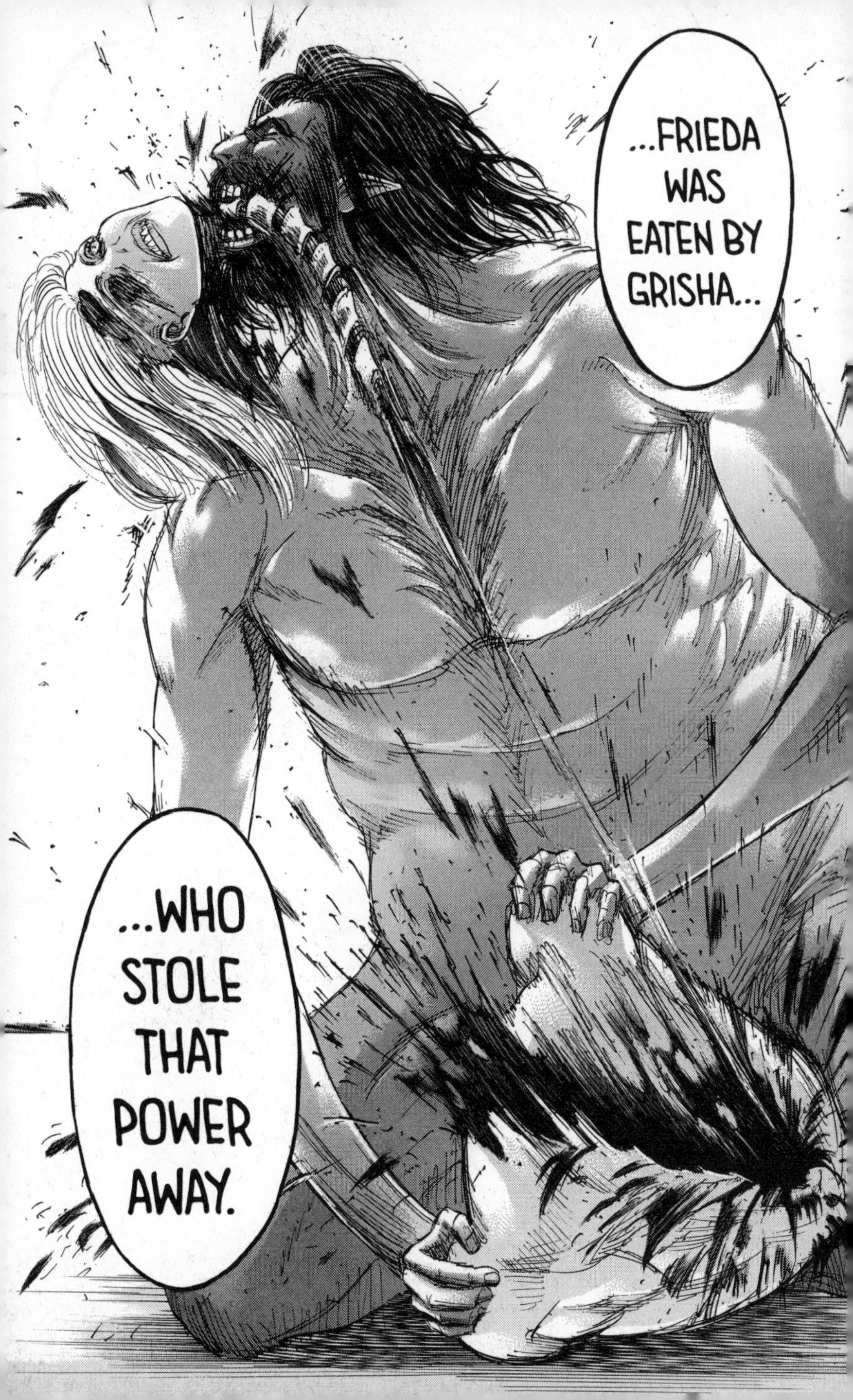
...FRIEDA WAS EATEN BY GRISHA...
...WHO STOLE THAT POWER AWAY.

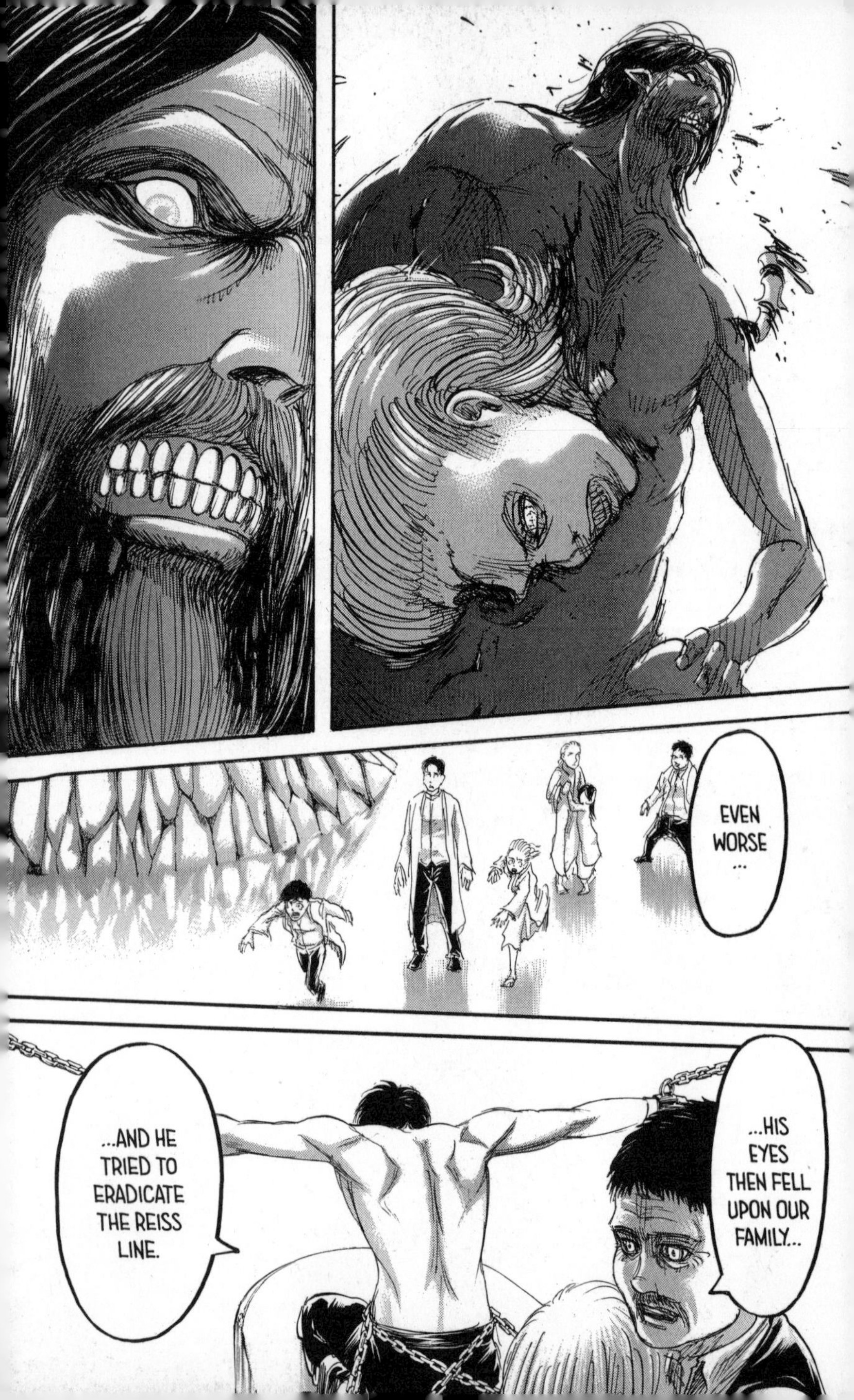
EVEN WORSE ...
...HIS EYES THEN FELL UPON OUR FAMILY...
...AND HE TRIED TO ERADICATE THE REISS LINE.

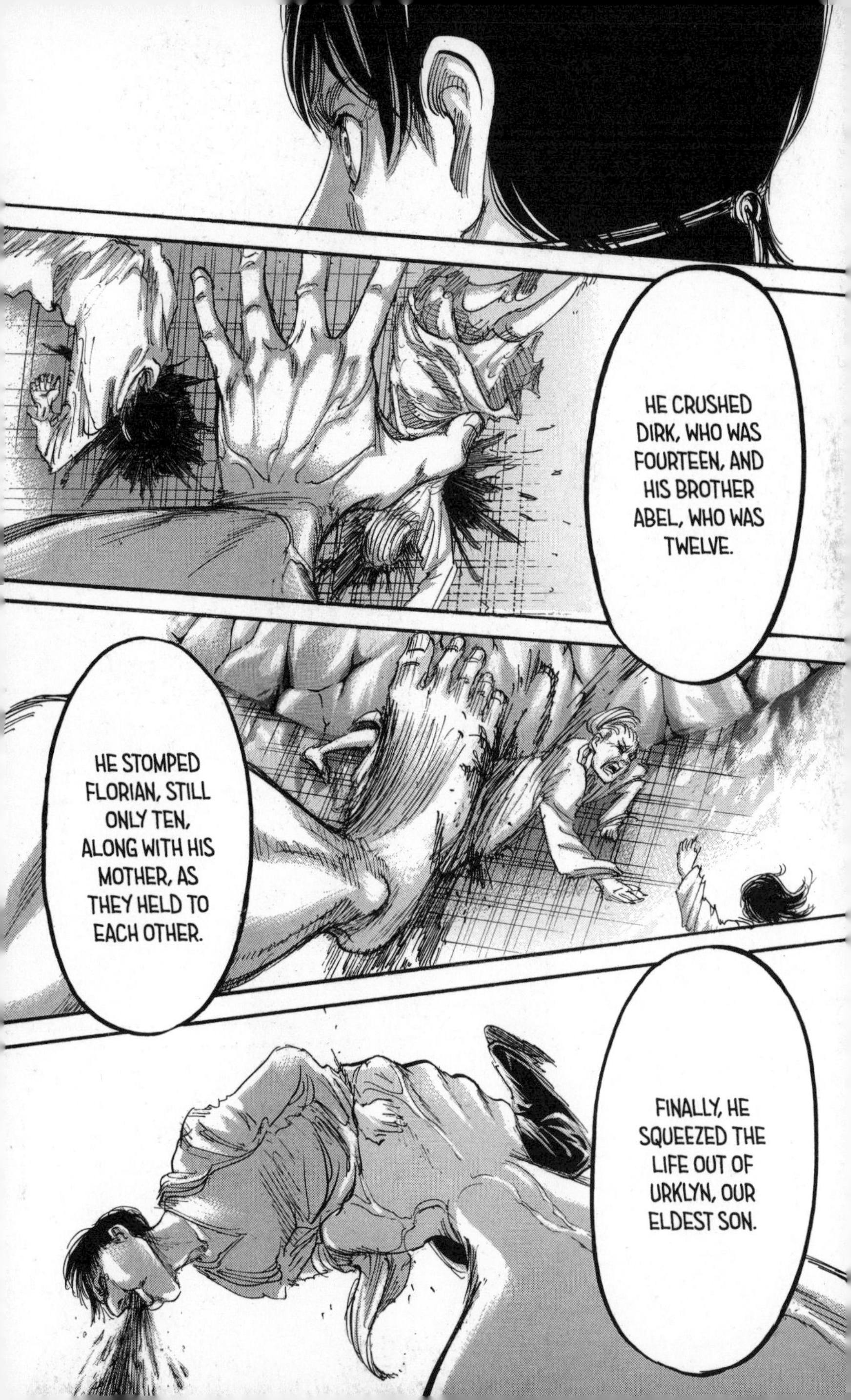
HE CRUSHED DIRK, WHO WAS FOURTEEN, AND HIS BROTHER ABEL, WHO WAS TWELVE.
HE STOMPED FLORIAN, STILL ONLY TEN, ALONG WITH HIS MOTHER, AS THEY HELD TO EACH OTHER.
FINALLY, HE SQUEEZED THE LIFE OUT OF URKLYN, OUR ELDEST SON.

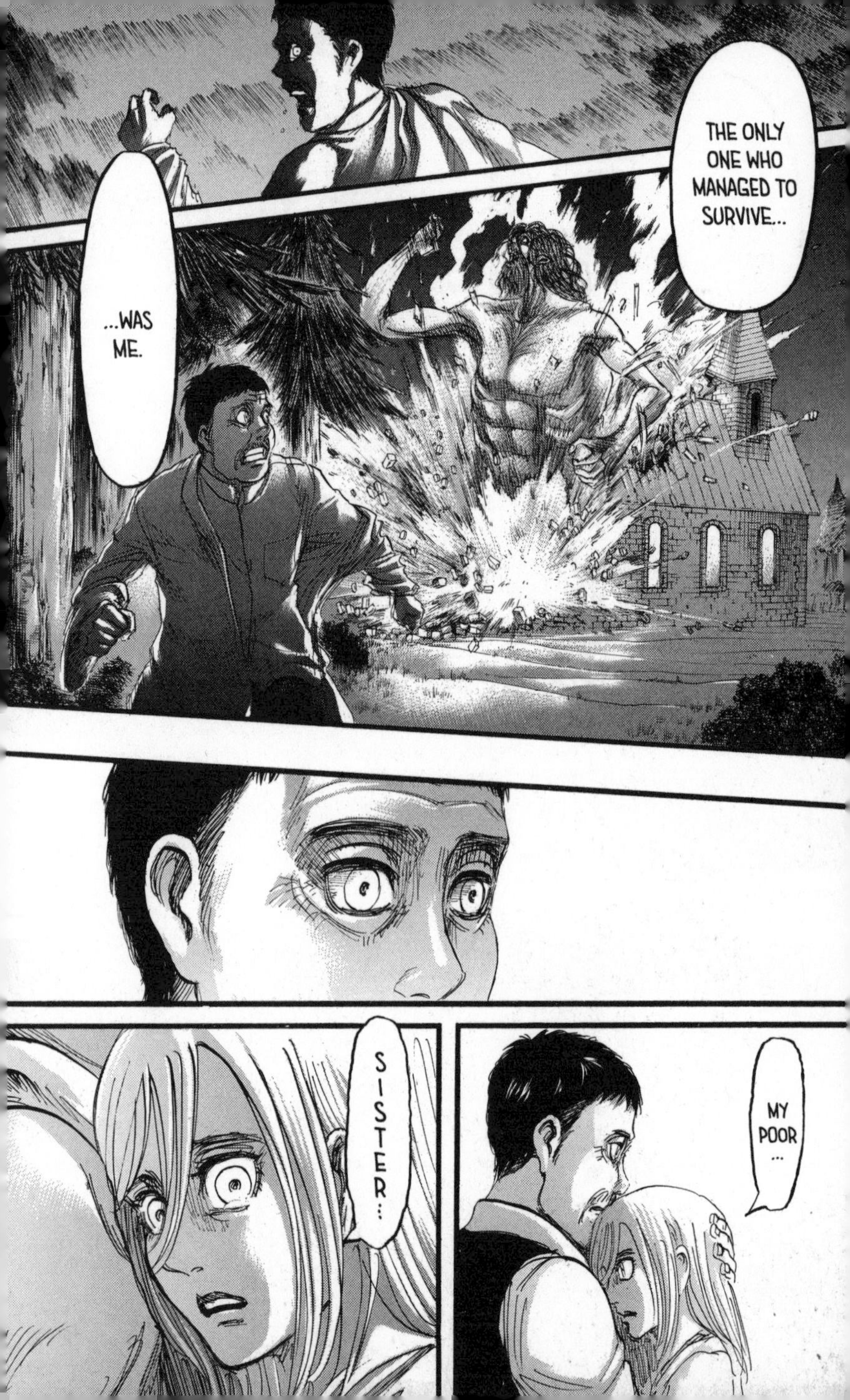
THE ONLY ONE WHO MANAGED TO SURVIVE...
...WAS ME.
MY POOR ...
SISTER...

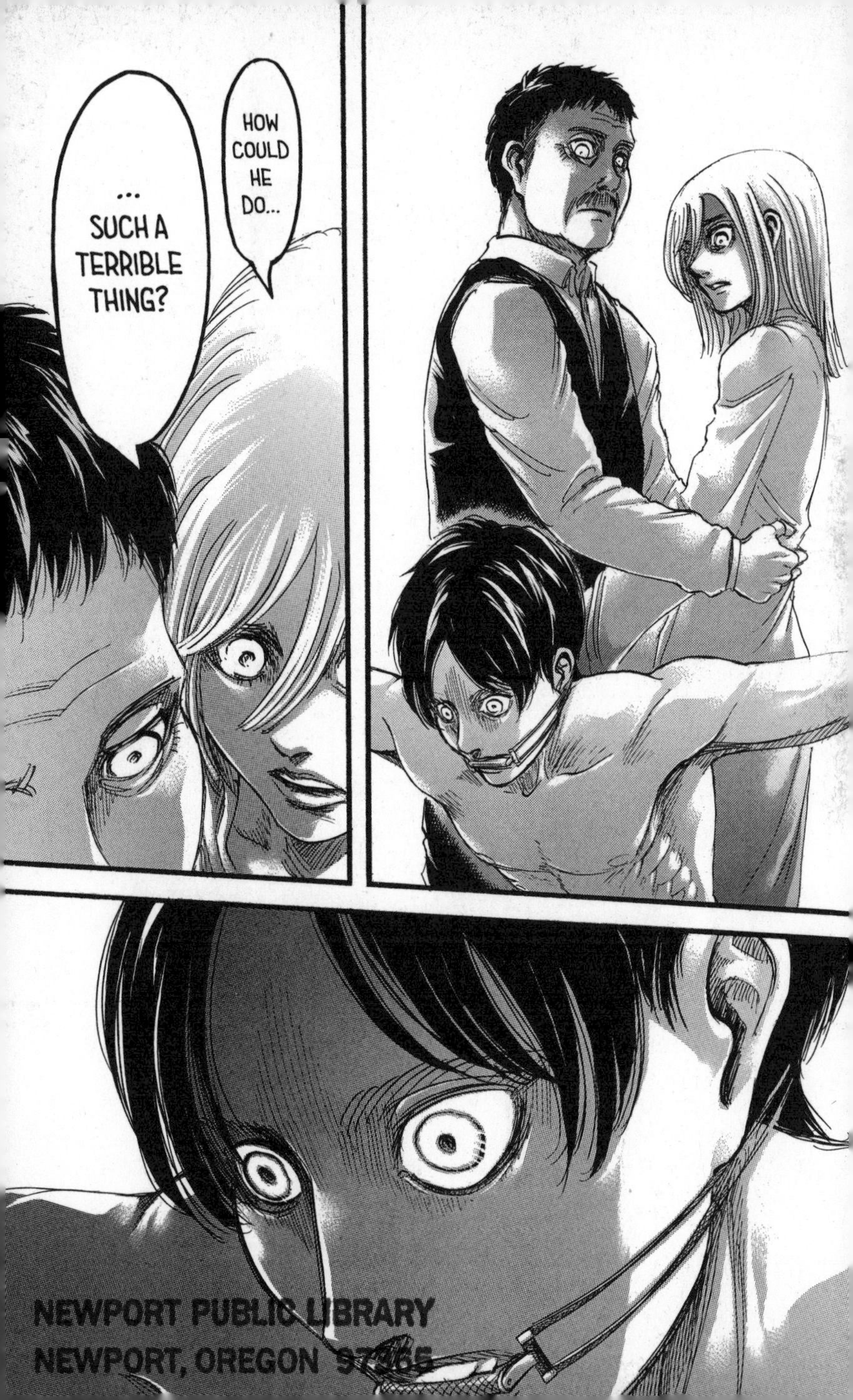
HOW COULD HE DO...
... SUCH A TERRIBLE THING?

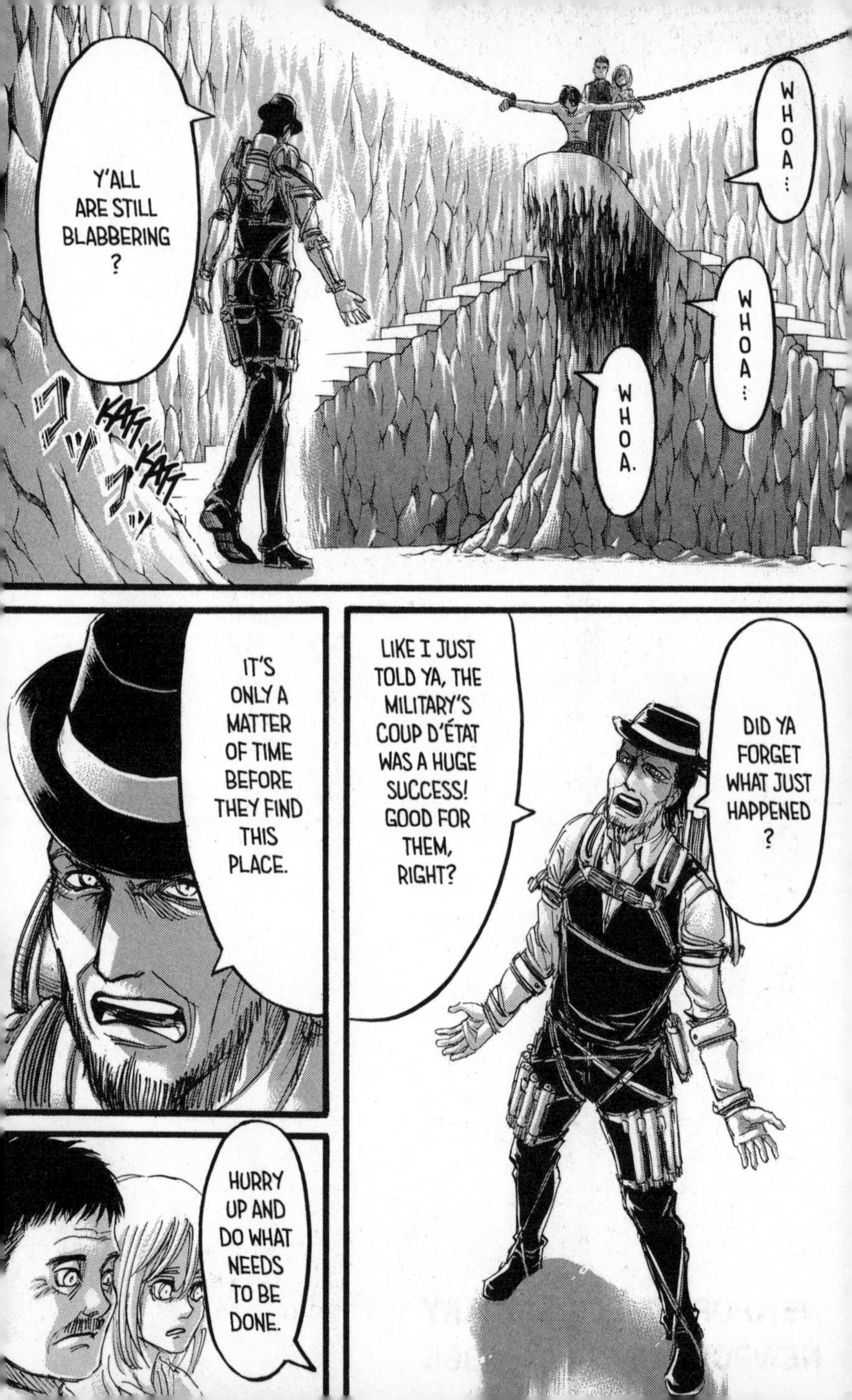
WHOA...
WHOA...
WHOA.
Y'ALL ARE STILL BLABBERING?
KAKT KAKT
DID YA FORGET WHAT JUST HAPPENED?
LIKE I JUST TOLD YA, THE MILITARY'S COUP D'ÉTAT WAS A HUGE SUCCESS! GOOD FOR THEM, RIGHT?
IT'S ONLY A MATTER OF TIME BEFORE THEY FIND THIS PLACE.
HURRY UP AND DO WHAT NEEDS TO BE DONE.

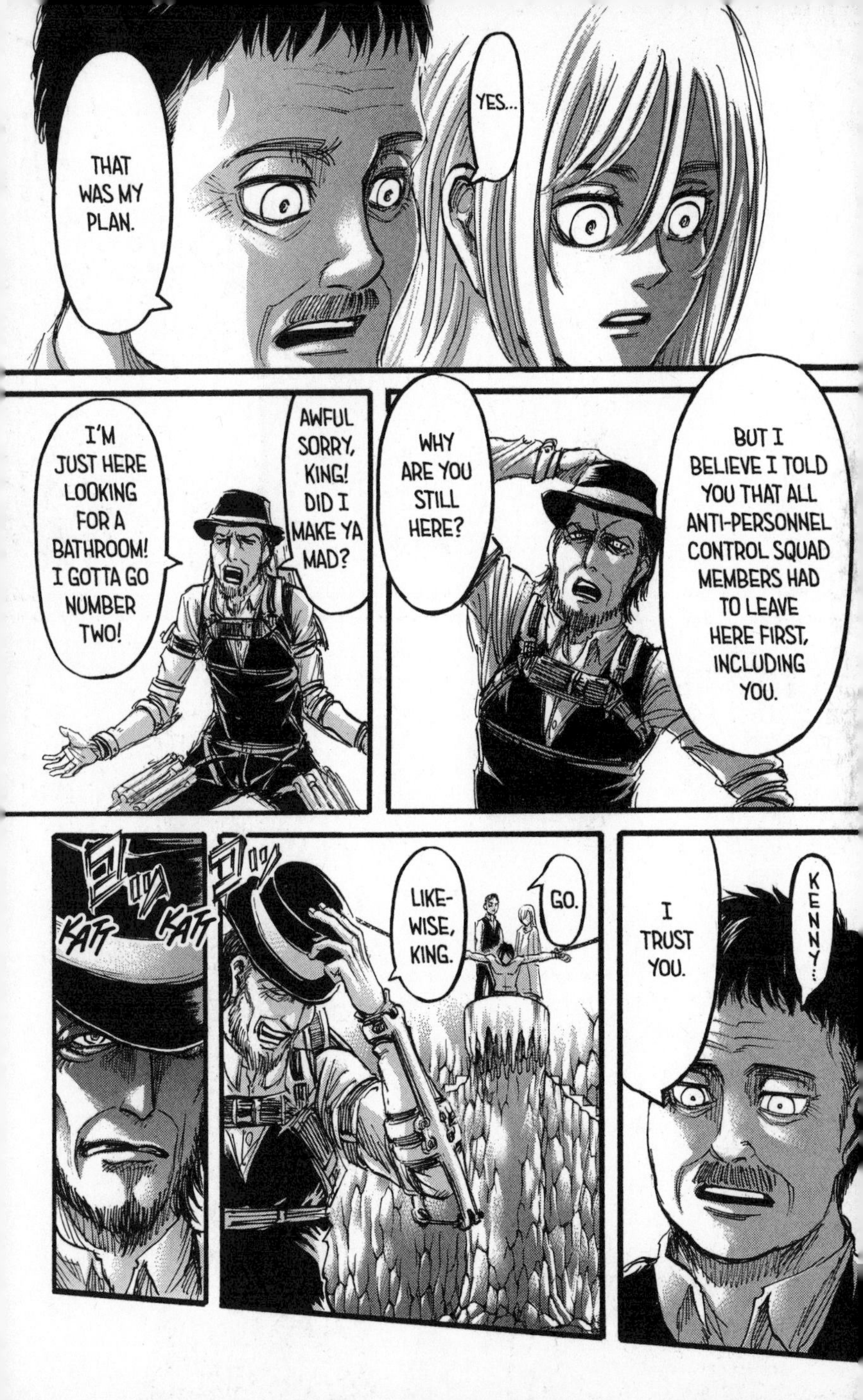
YES...
THAT WAS MY PLAN.
BUT I BELIEVE I TOLD YOU THAT ALL ANTI-PERSONNEL CONTROL SQUAD MEMBERS HAD TO LEAVE HERE FIRST, INCLUDING YOU.
WHY ARE YOU STILL HERE?
AWFUL SORRY, KING! DID I MAKE YA MAD?
I'M JUST HERE LOOKING FOR A BATHROOM! I GOTTA GO NUMBER TWO!
KENNY...
I TRUST YOU.
GO.
LIKE-WISE, KING.
KATT
KATT

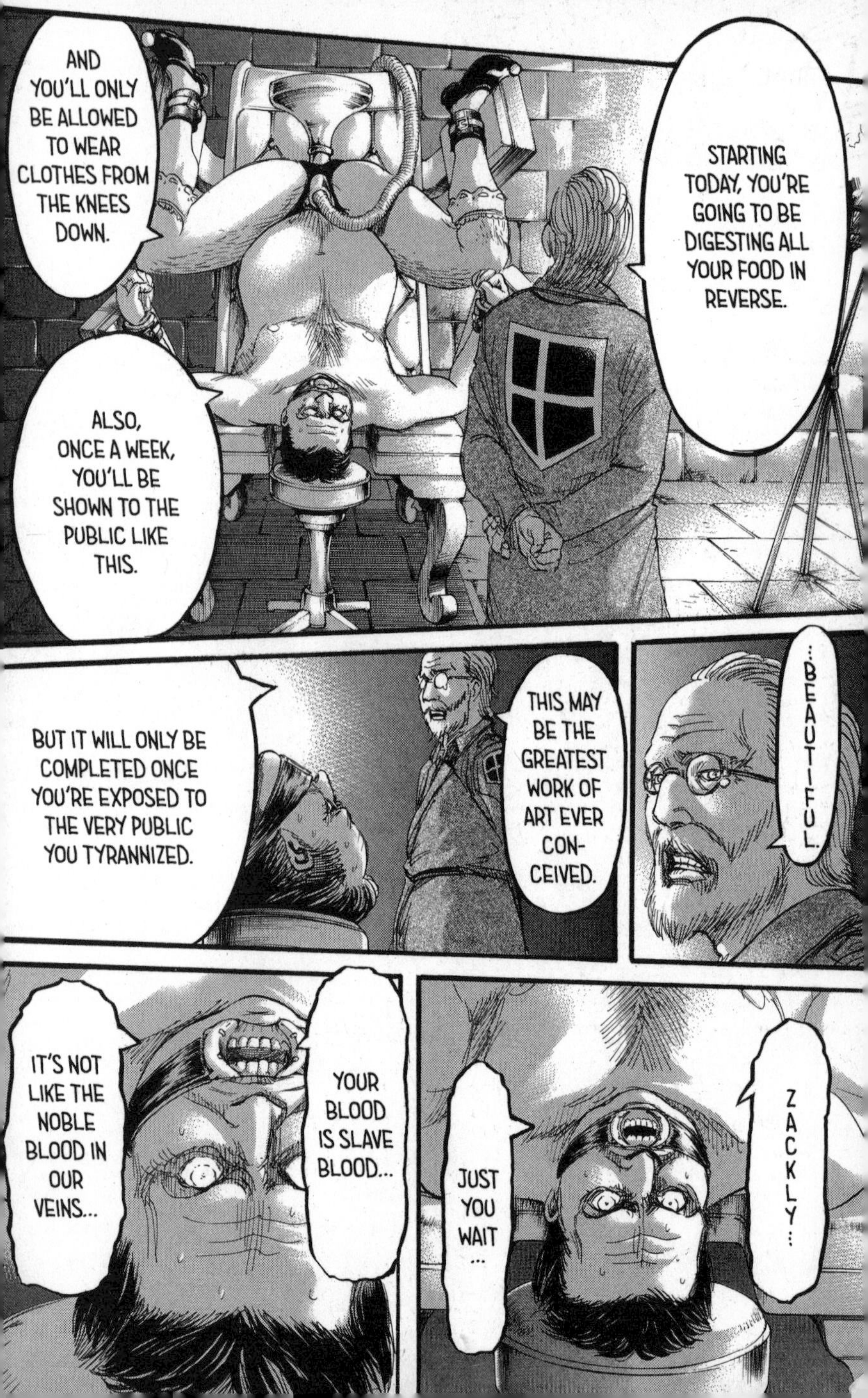
STARTING TODAY, YOU'RE GOING TO BE DIGESTING ALL YOUR FOOD IN REVERSE.
AND YOU'LL ONLY BE ALLOWED TO WEAR CLOTHES FROM THE KNEES DOWN.
ALSO, ONCE A WEEK, YOU'LL BE SHOWN TO THE PUBLIC LIKE THIS.
...BEAUTIFUL.
THIS MAY BE THE GREATEST WORK OF ART EVER CON-CEIVED.
BUT IT WILL ONLY BE COMPLETED ONCE YOU'RE EXPOSED TO THE VERY PUBLIC YOU TYRANNIZED.
ZACKLY...
JUST YOU WAIT...
YOUR BLOOD IS SLAVE BLOOD...
IT'S NOT LIKE THE NOBLE BLOOD IN OUR VEINS...

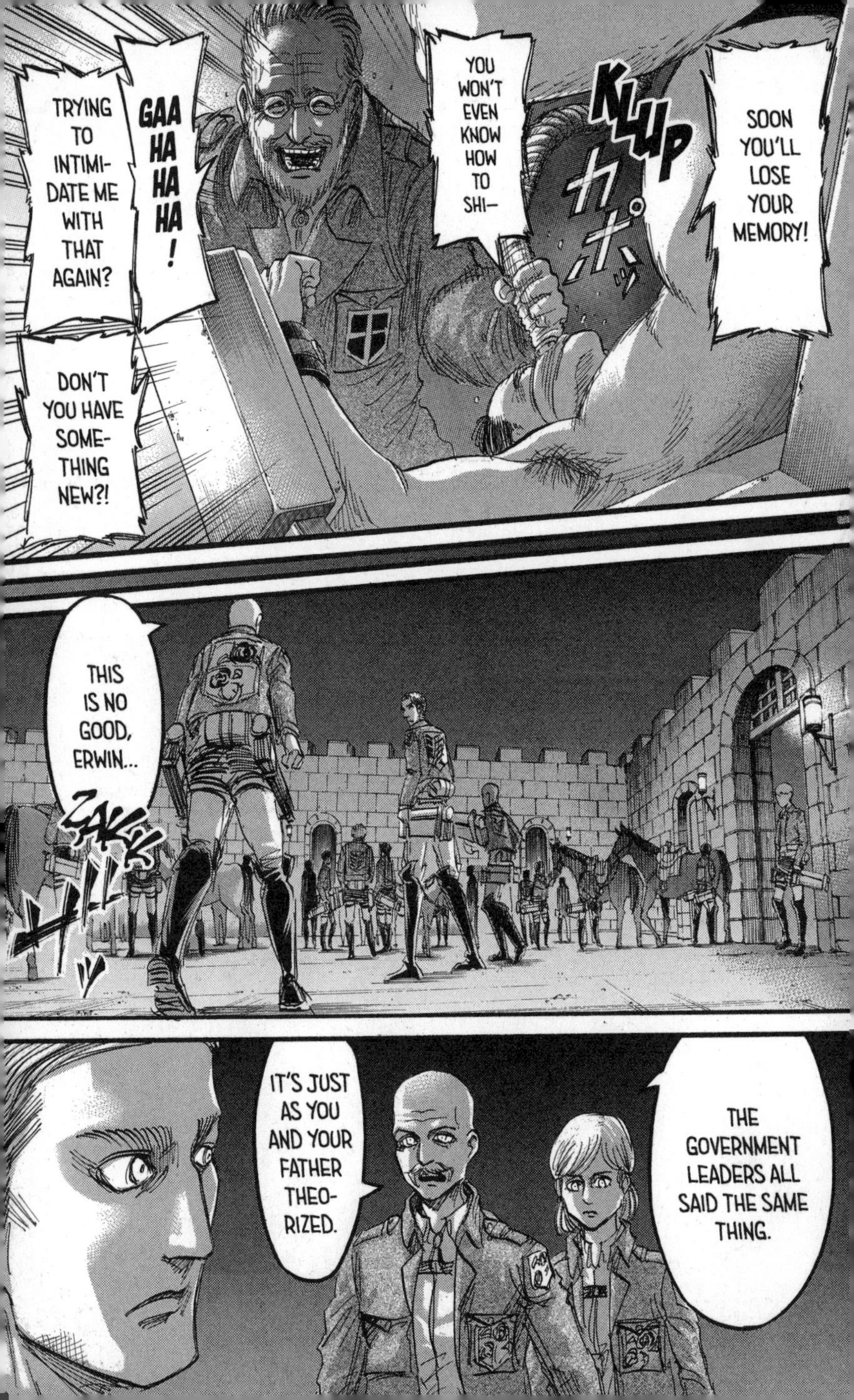
SOON YOU'LL LOSE YOUR MEMORY!
KLUP
YOU WON'T EVEN KNOW HOW TO SHI—
GAA HA HA HA!
TRYING TO INTIMIDATE ME WITH THAT AGAIN?
DON'T YOU HAVE SOMETHING NEW?!
THIS IS NO GOOD, ERWIN...
THE GOVERNMENT LEADERS ALL SAID THE SAME THING.
IT'S JUST AS YOU AND YOUR FATHER THEORIZED.

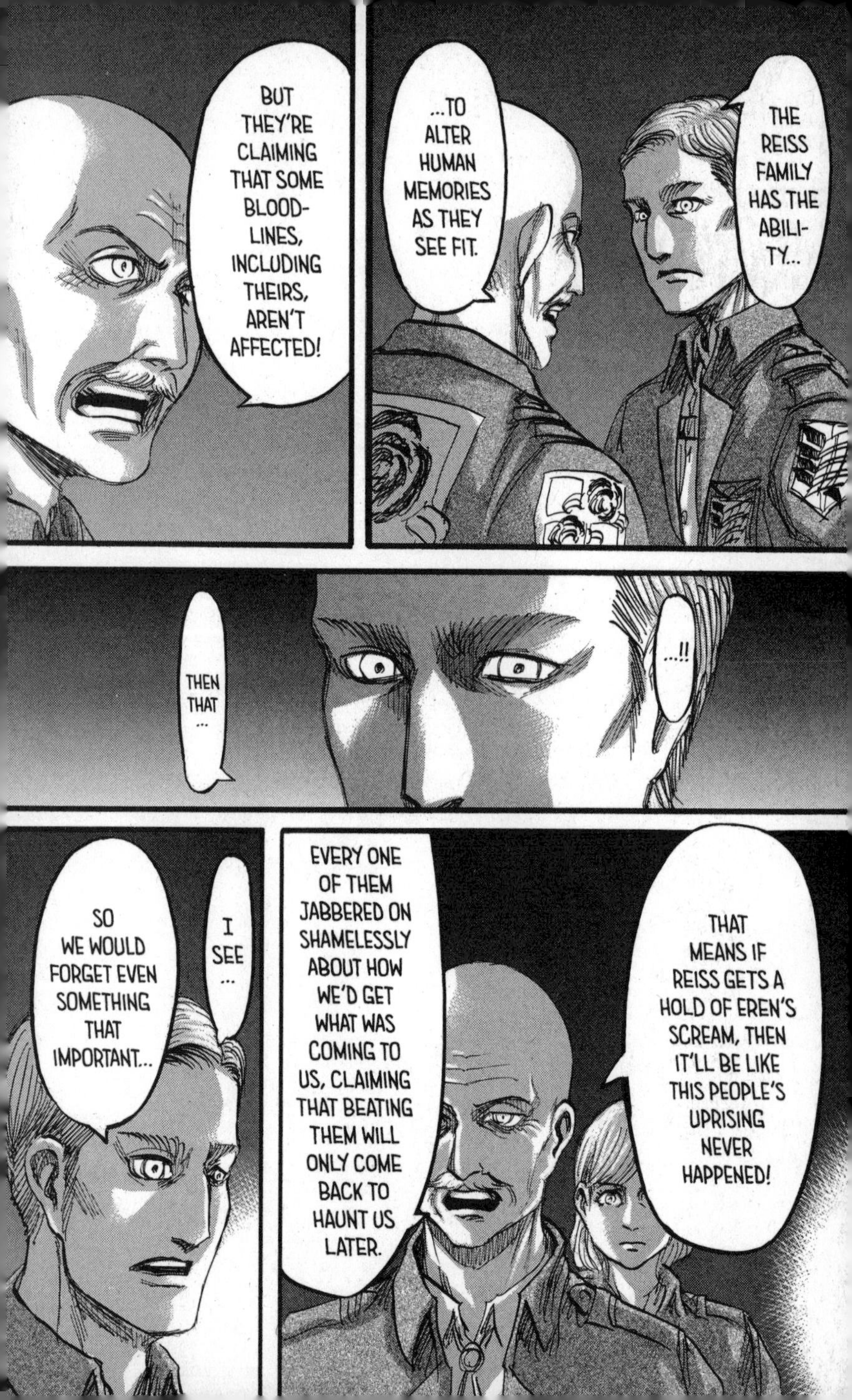
THE REISS FAMILY HAS THE ABILITY...
...TO ALTER HUMAN MEMORIES AS THEY SEE FIT.
BUT THEY'RE CLAIMING THAT SOME BLOODLINES, INCLUDING THEIRS, AREN'T AFFECTED!
...!!
THEN THAT...
THAT MEANS IF REISS GETS A HOLD OF EREN'S SCREAM, THEN IT'LL BE LIKE THIS PEOPLE'S UPRISING NEVER HAPPENED!
EVERY ONE OF THEM JABBERED ON SHAMELESSLY ABOUT HOW WE'D GET WHAT WAS COMING TO US, CLAIMING THAT BEATING THEM WILL ONLY COME BACK TO HAUNT US LATER.
I SEE...
SO WE WOULD FORGET EVEN SOMETHING THAT IMPORTANT...

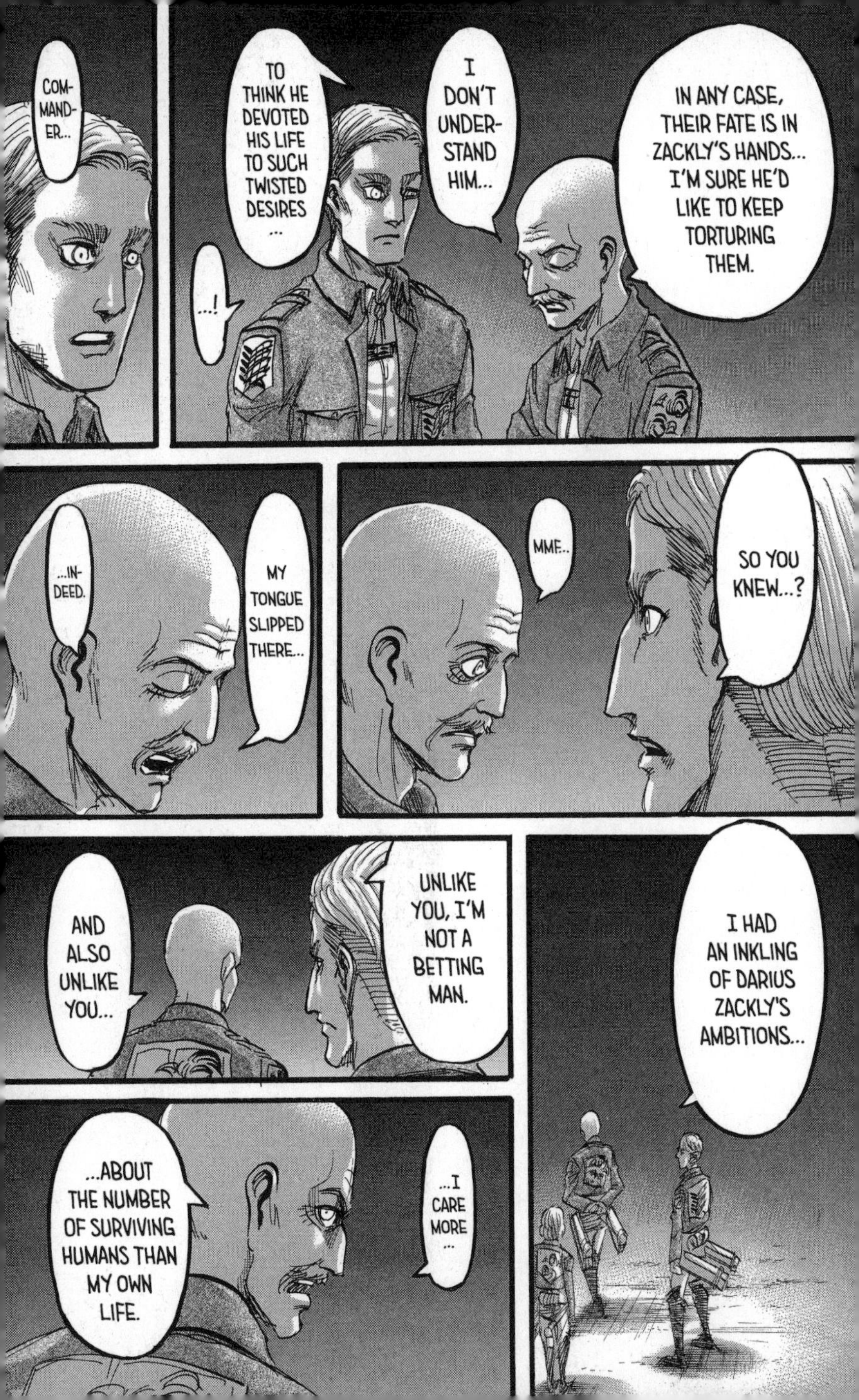
IN ANY CASE, THEIR FATE IS IN ZACKLY'S HANDS... I'M SURE HE'D LIKE TO KEEP TORTURING THEM.
I DON'T UNDER-STAND HIM...
TO THINK HE DEVOTED HIS LIFE TO SUCH TWISTED DESIRES ...
...!
COM-MAND-ER...
SO YOU KNEW...?
MMF...
MY TONGUE SLIPPED THERE...
...IN-DEED.
I HAD AN INKLING OF DARIUS ZACKLY'S AMBITIONS...
UNLIKE YOU, I'M NOT A BETTING MAN.
AND ALSO UNLIKE YOU...
...I CARE MORE ...
...ABOUT THE NUMBER OF SURVIVING HUMANS THAN MY OWN LIFE.

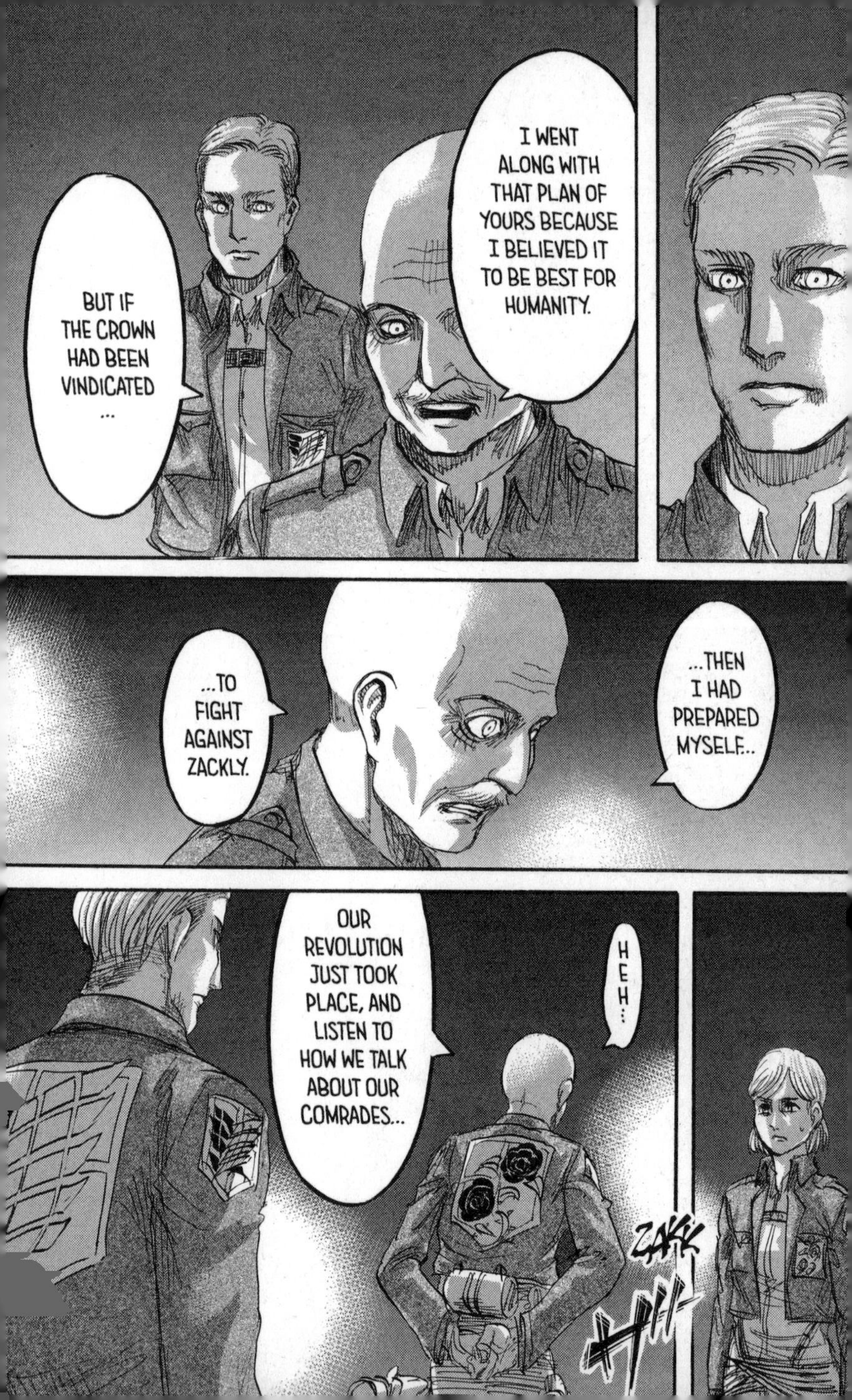
I WENT ALONG WITH THAT PLAN OF YOURS BECAUSE I BELIEVED IT TO BE BEST FOR HUMANITY.
BUT IF THE CROWN HAD BEEN VINDICATED ...
...THEN I HAD PREPARED MYSELF...
...TO FIGHT AGAINST ZACKLY.
ZAKK
HEH...
OUR REVOLUTION JUST TOOK PLACE, AND LISTEN TO HOW WE TALK ABOUT OUR COMRADES...

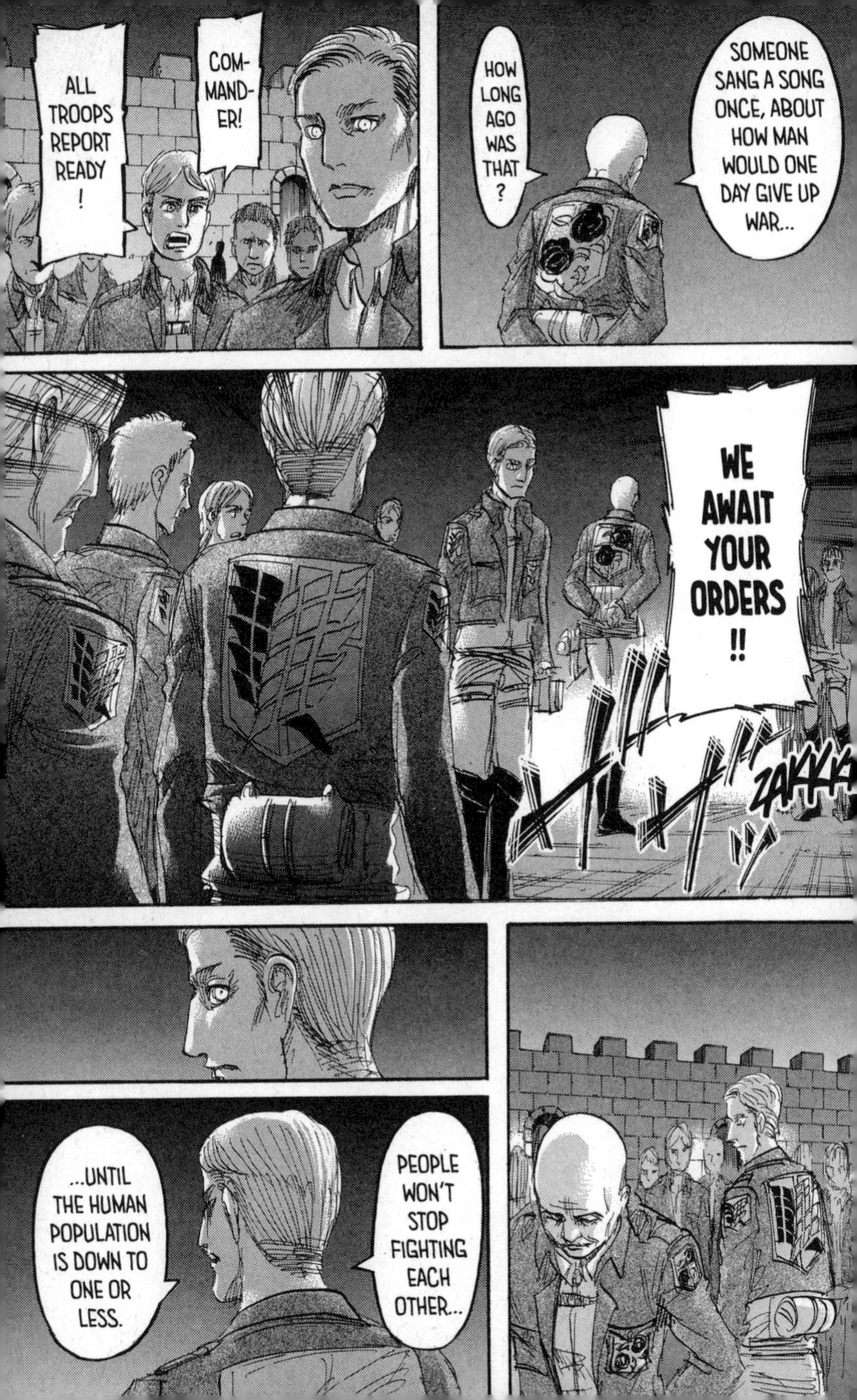
SOMEONE SANG A SONG ONCE, ABOUT HOW MAN WOULD ONE DAY GIVE UP WAR...
HOW LONG AGO WAS THAT?
COMMANDER!
ALL TROOPS REPORT READY!
WE AWAIT YOUR ORDERS!!
ZAKKA
PEOPLE WON'T STOP FIGHTING EACH OTHER...
...UNTIL THE HUMAN POPULATION IS DOWN TO ONE OR LESS.

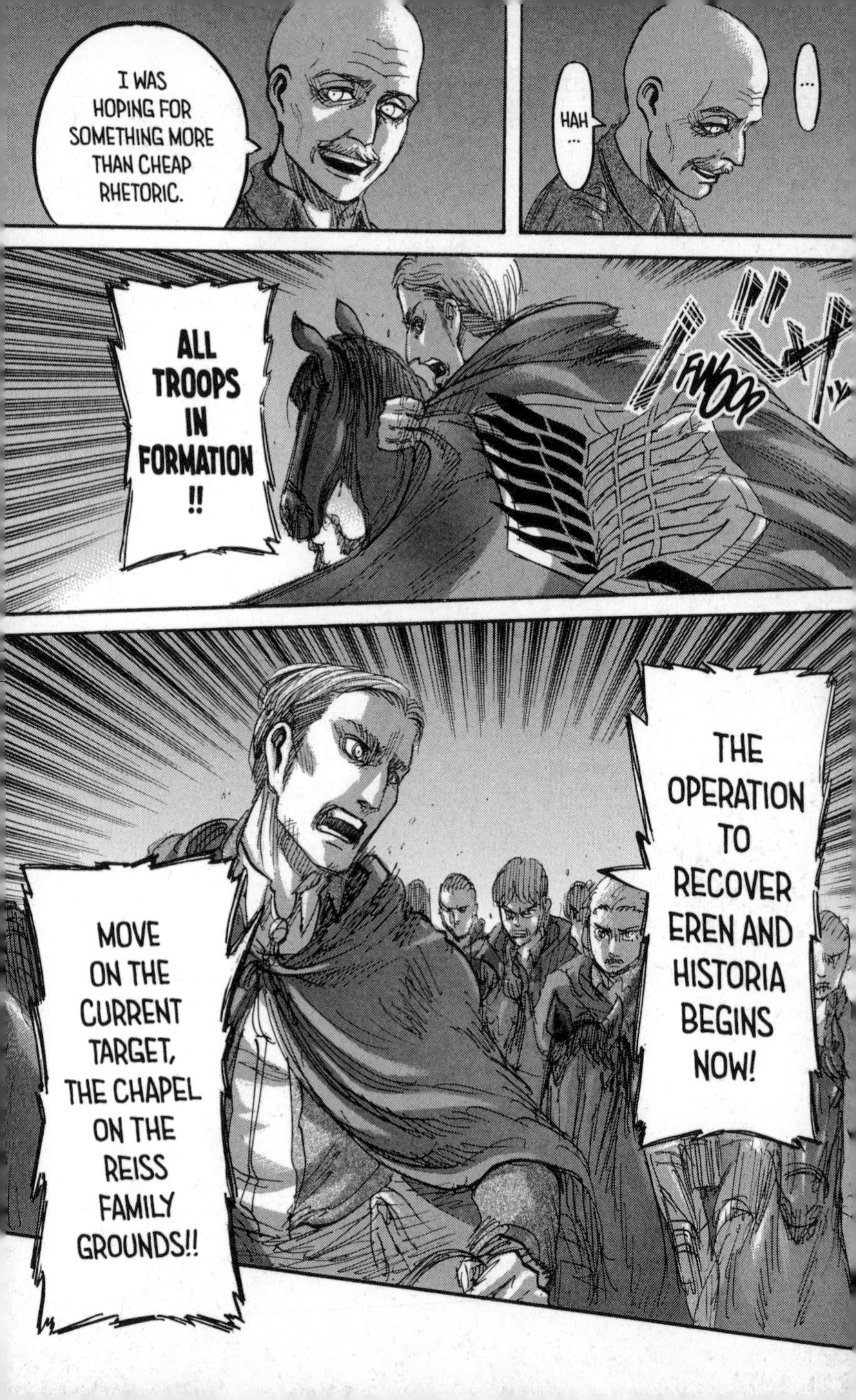
...
HAH ...
I WAS HOPING FOR SOMETHING MORE THAN CHEAP RHETORIC.
FWOOP
ALL TROOPS IN FORMATION !!
THE OPERATION TO RECOVER EREN AND HISTORIA BEGINS NOW!
MOVE ON THE CURRENT TARGET, THE CHAPEL ON THE REISS FAMILY GROUNDS!!

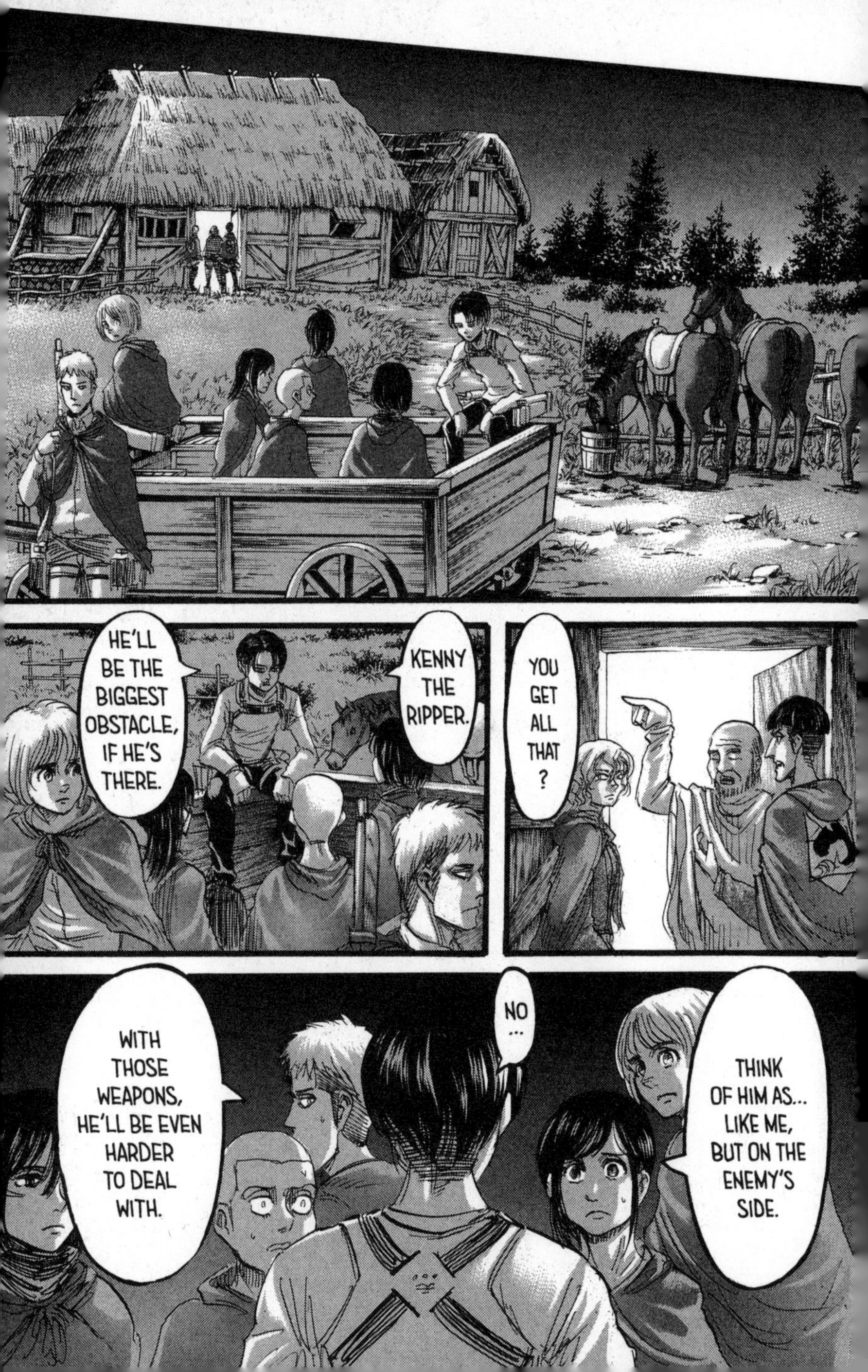
YOU GET ALL THAT?
KENNY THE RIPPER.
HE'LL BE THE BIGGEST OBSTACLE, IF HE'S THERE.
THINK OF HIM AS... LIKE ME, BUT ON THE ENEMY'S SIDE.
NO ...
WITH THOSE WEAPONS, HE'LL BE EVEN HARDER TO DEAL WITH.

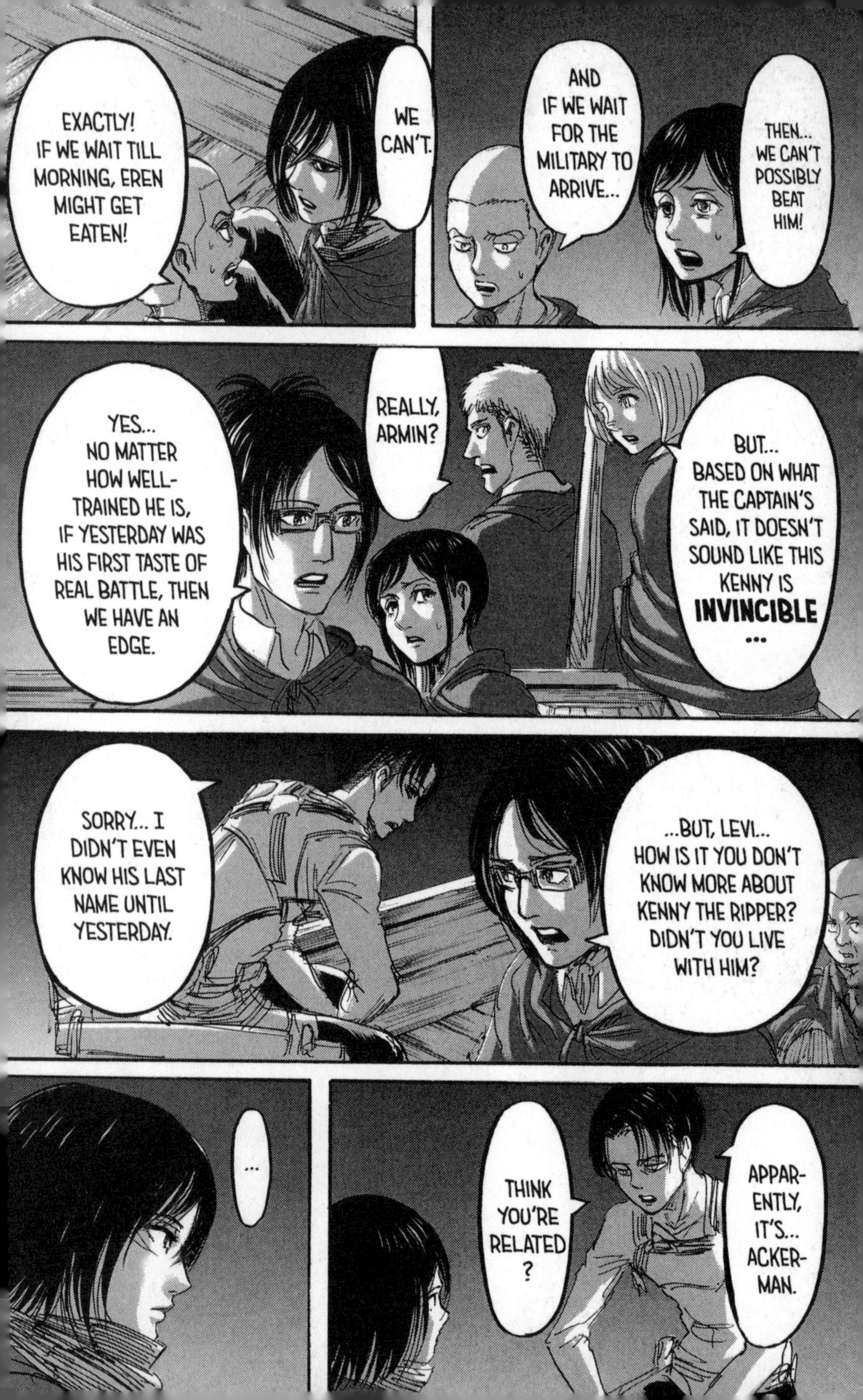
THEN... WE CAN'T POSSIBLY BEAT HIM!
AND IF WE WAIT FOR THE MILITARY TO ARRIVE...
WE CAN'T.
EXACTLY! IF WE WAIT TILL MORNING, EREN MIGHT GET EATEN!
BUT... BASED ON WHAT THE CAPTAIN'S SAID, IT DOESN'T SOUND LIKE THIS KENNY IS **INVINCIBLE**...
REALLY, ARMIN?
YES... NO MATTER HOW WELL-TRAINED HE IS, IF YESTERDAY WAS HIS FIRST TASTE OF REAL BATTLE, THEN WE HAVE AN EDGE.
...BUT, LEVI... HOW IS IT YOU DON'T KNOW MORE ABOUT KENNY THE RIPPER? DIDN'T YOU LIVE WITH HIM?
SORRY... I DIDN'T EVEN KNOW HIS LAST NAME UNTIL YESTERDAY.
APPARENTLY, IT'S... ACKERMAN.
THINK YOU'RE RELATED?
...

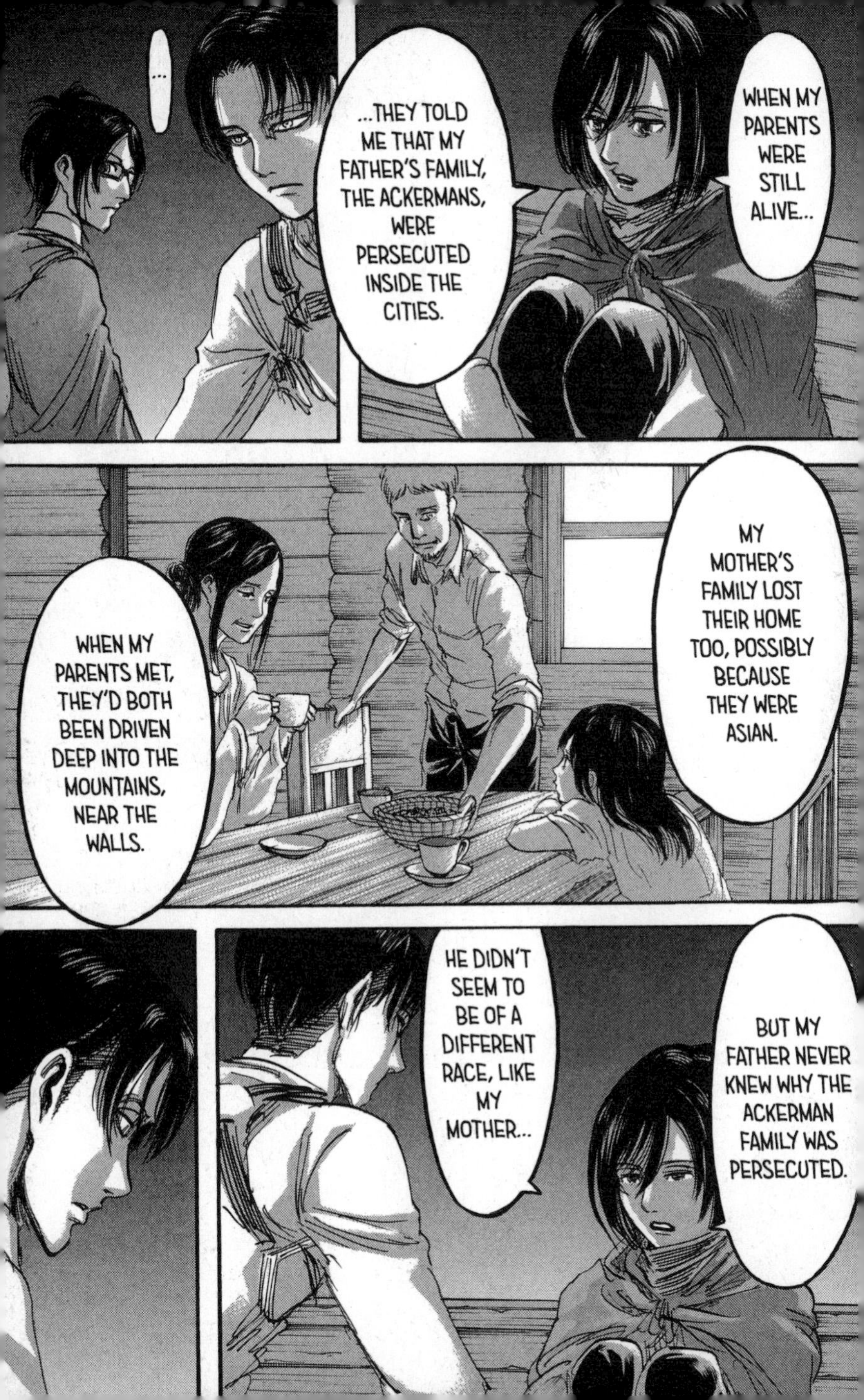
WHEN MY PARENTS WERE STILL ALIVE...
...THEY TOLD ME THAT MY FATHER'S FAMILY, THE ACKERMANS, WERE PERSECUTED INSIDE THE CITIES.
...!
MY MOTHER'S FAMILY LOST THEIR HOME TOO, POSSIBLY BECAUSE THEY WERE ASIAN.
WHEN MY PARENTS MET, THEY'D BOTH BEEN DRIVEN DEEP INTO THE MOUNTAINS, NEAR THE WALLS.
BUT MY FATHER NEVER KNEW WHY THE ACKERMAN FAMILY WAS PERSECUTED.
HE DIDN'T SEEM TO BE OF A DIFFERENT RACE, LIKE MY MOTHER...

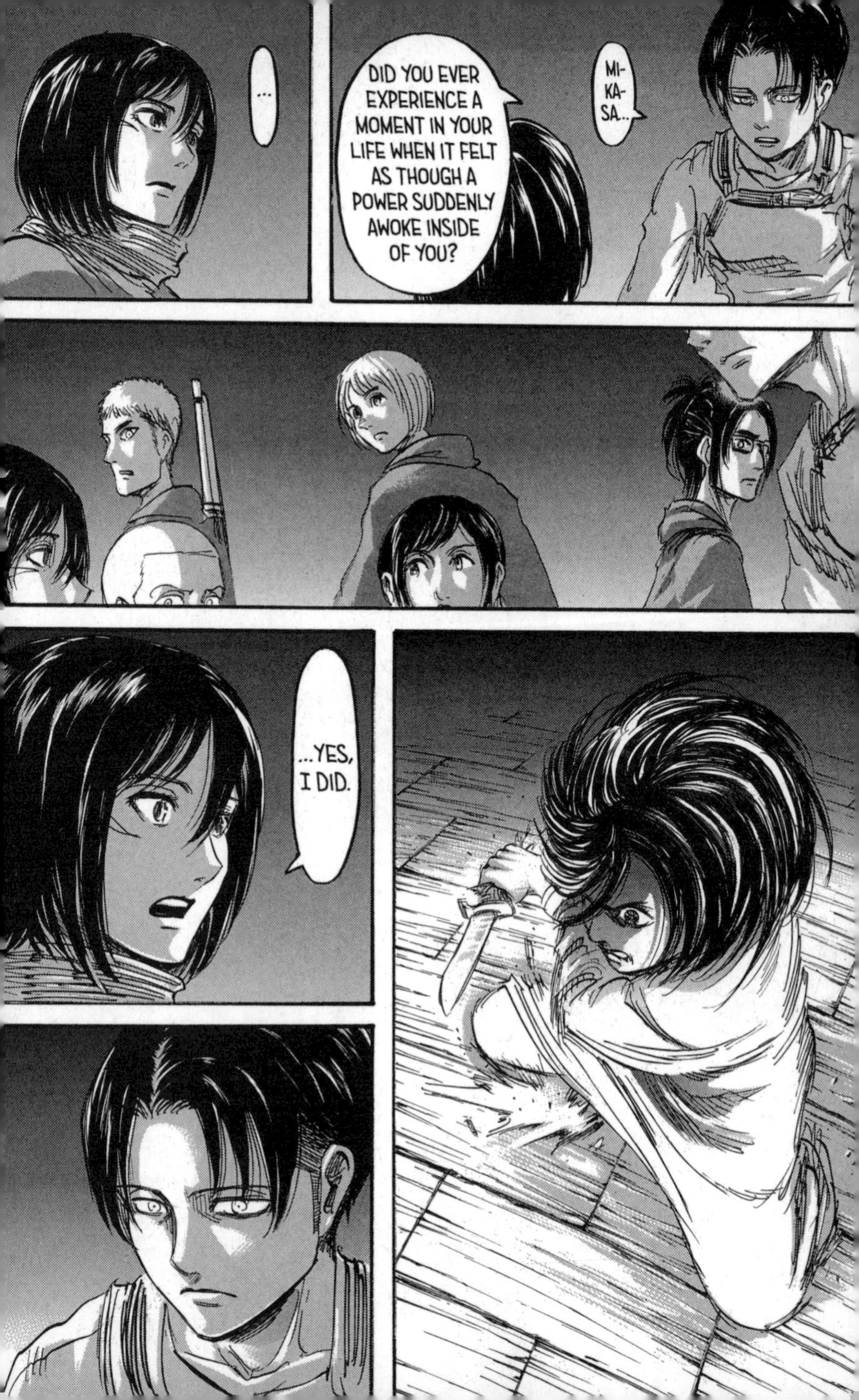
MI-KA-SA...
DID YOU EVER EXPERIENCE A MOMENT IN YOUR LIFE WHEN IT FELT AS THOUGH A POWER SUDDENLY AWOKE INSIDE OF YOU?
...
...YES, I DID.

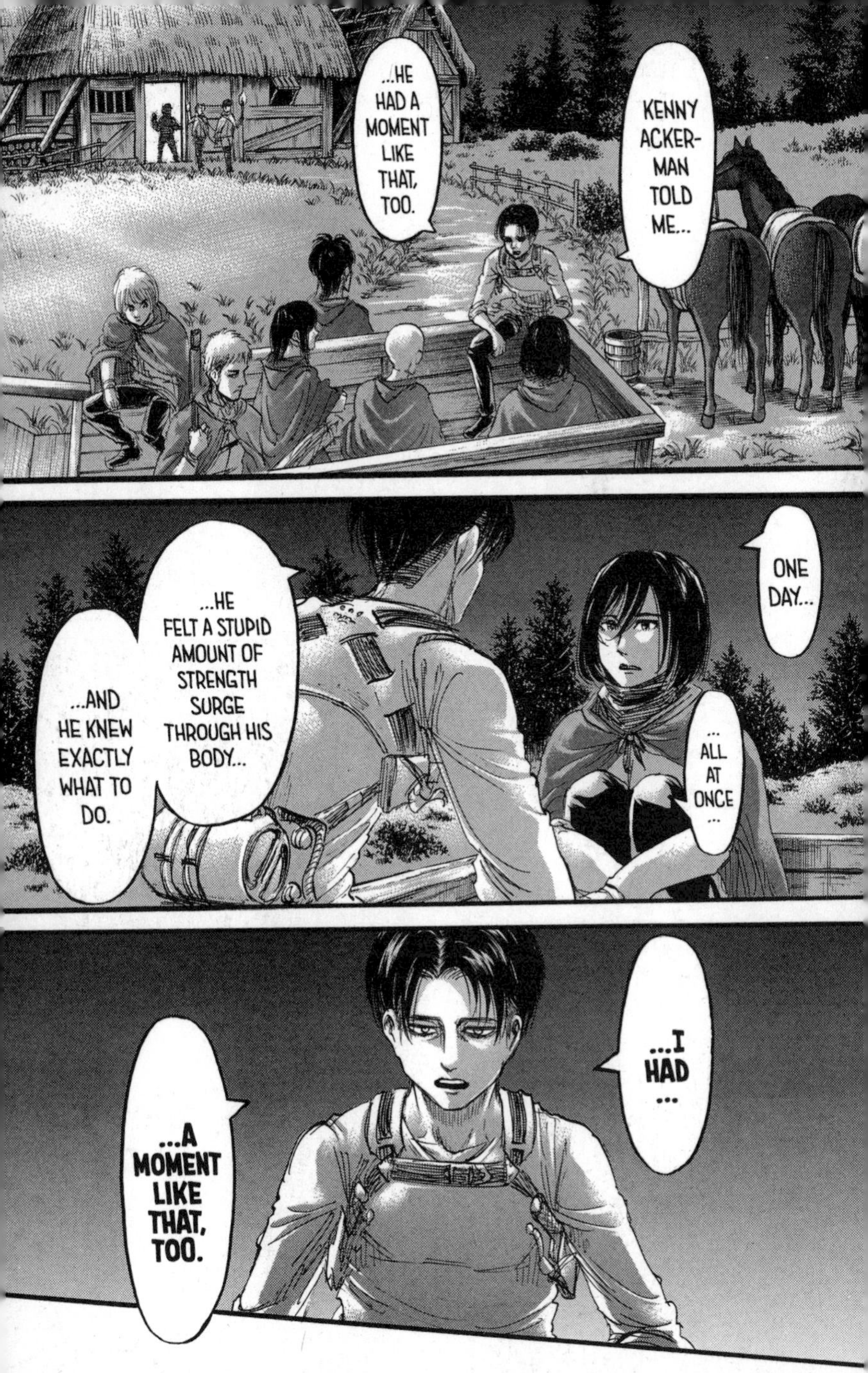
KENNY ACKERMAN TOLD ME...
...HE HAD A MOMENT LIKE THAT, TOO.
ONE DAY...
...ALL AT ONCE...
...HE FELT A STUPID AMOUNT OF STRENGTH SURGE THROUGH HIS BODY...
...AND HE KNEW EXACTLY WHAT TO DO.
...I HAD...
...A MOMENT LIKE THAT, TOO.

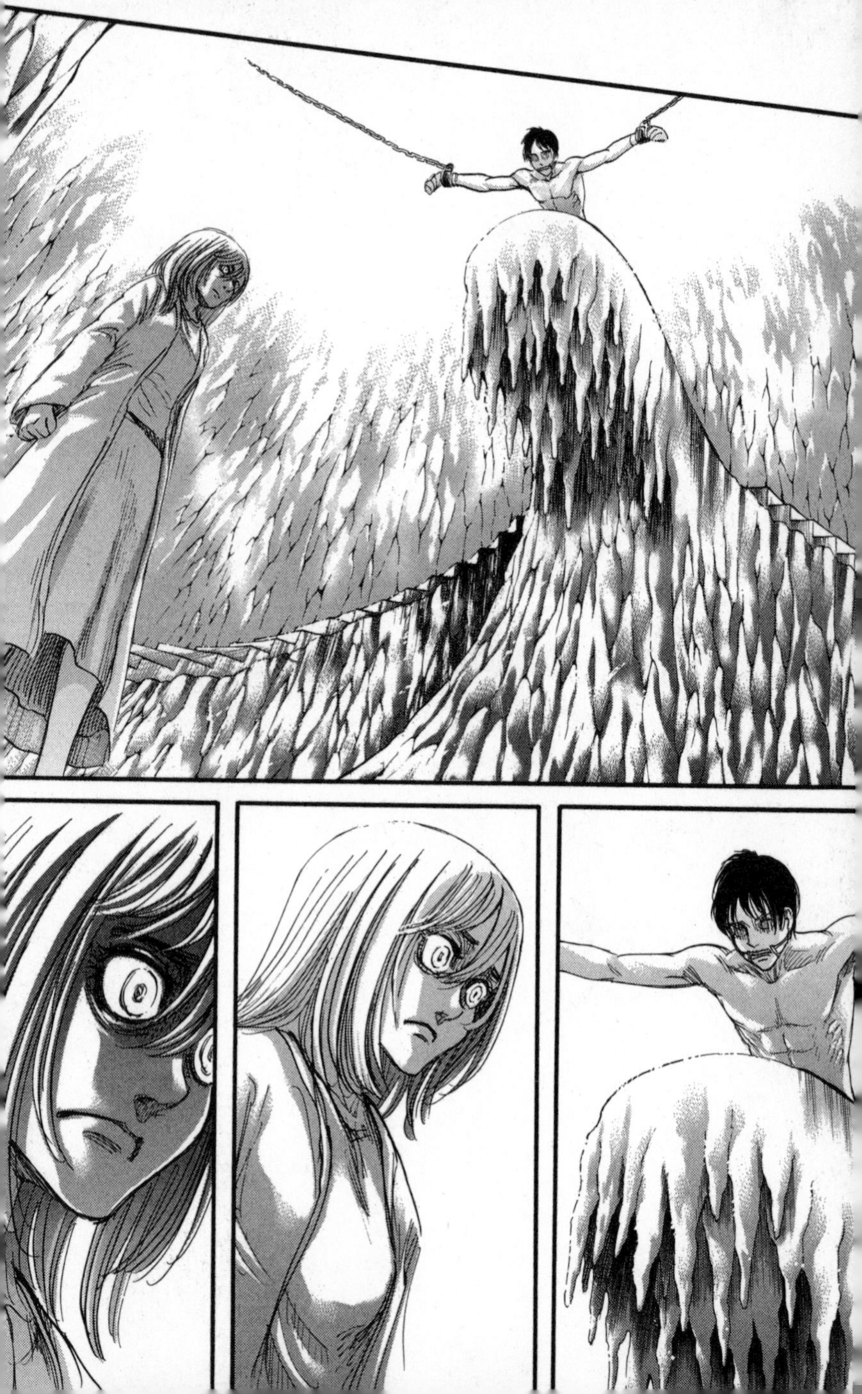

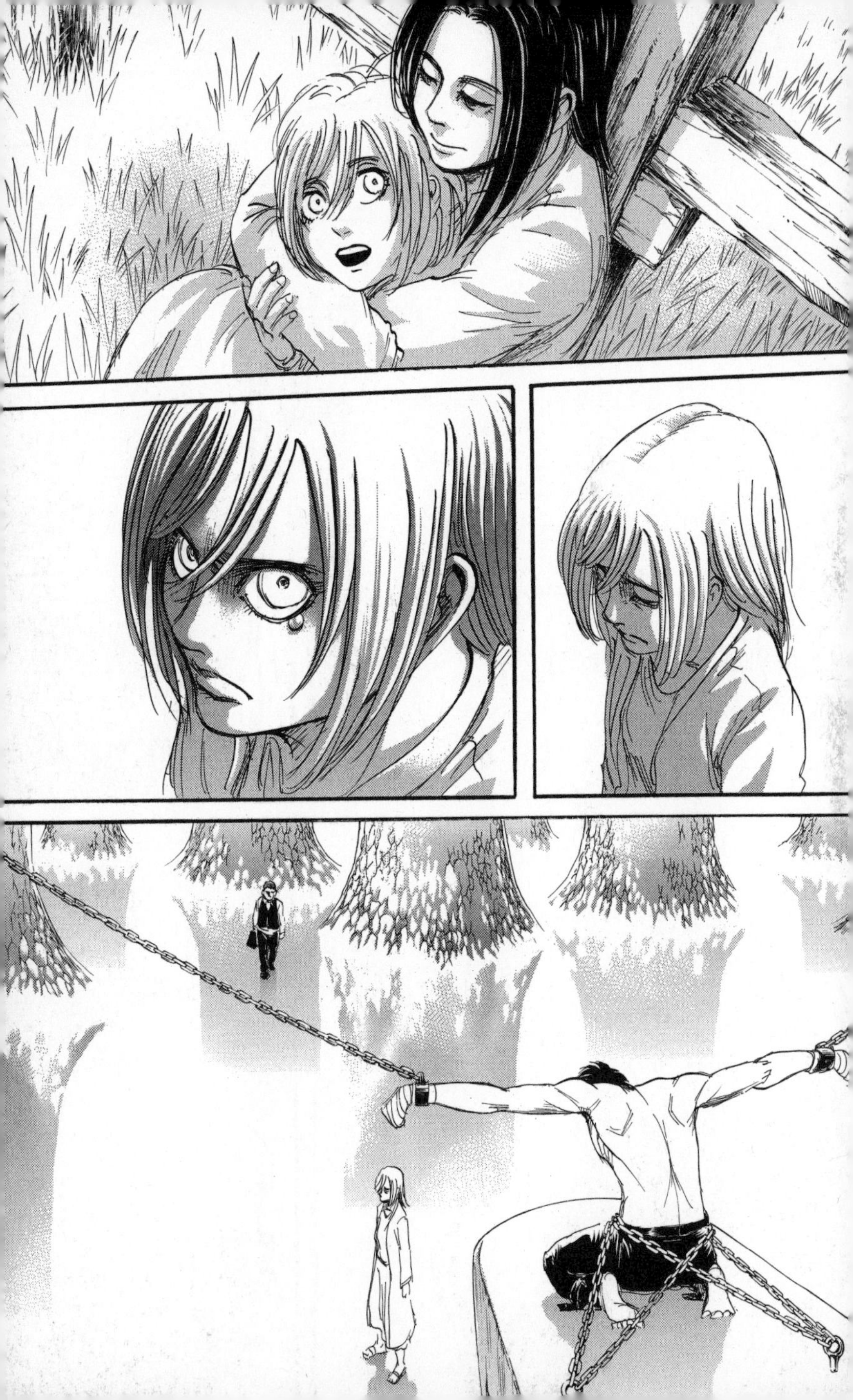

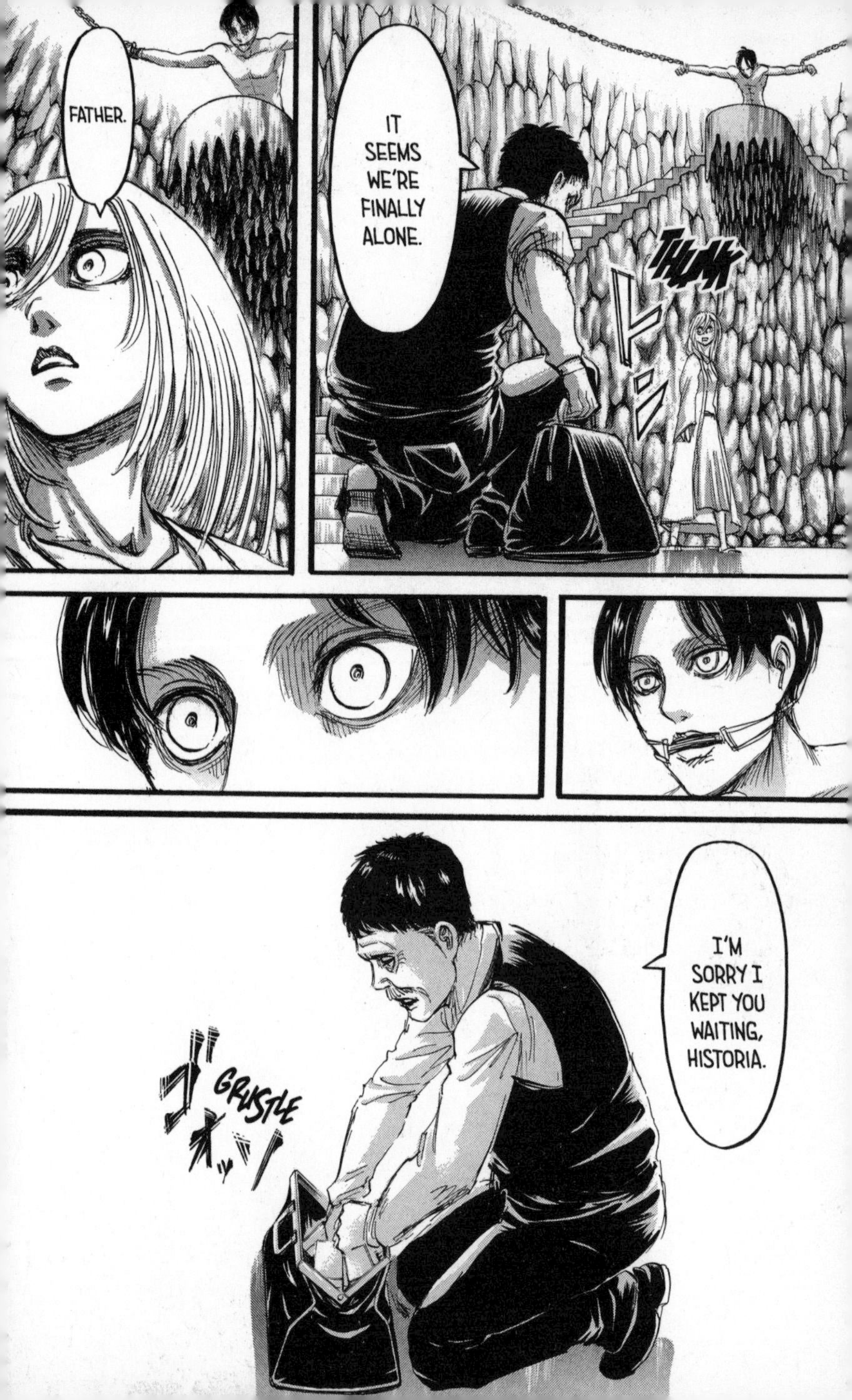
IT SEEMS WE'RE FINALLY ALONE.
THUMP
FATHER.
I'M SORRY I KEPT YOU WAITING, HISTORIA.
GRUSTLE

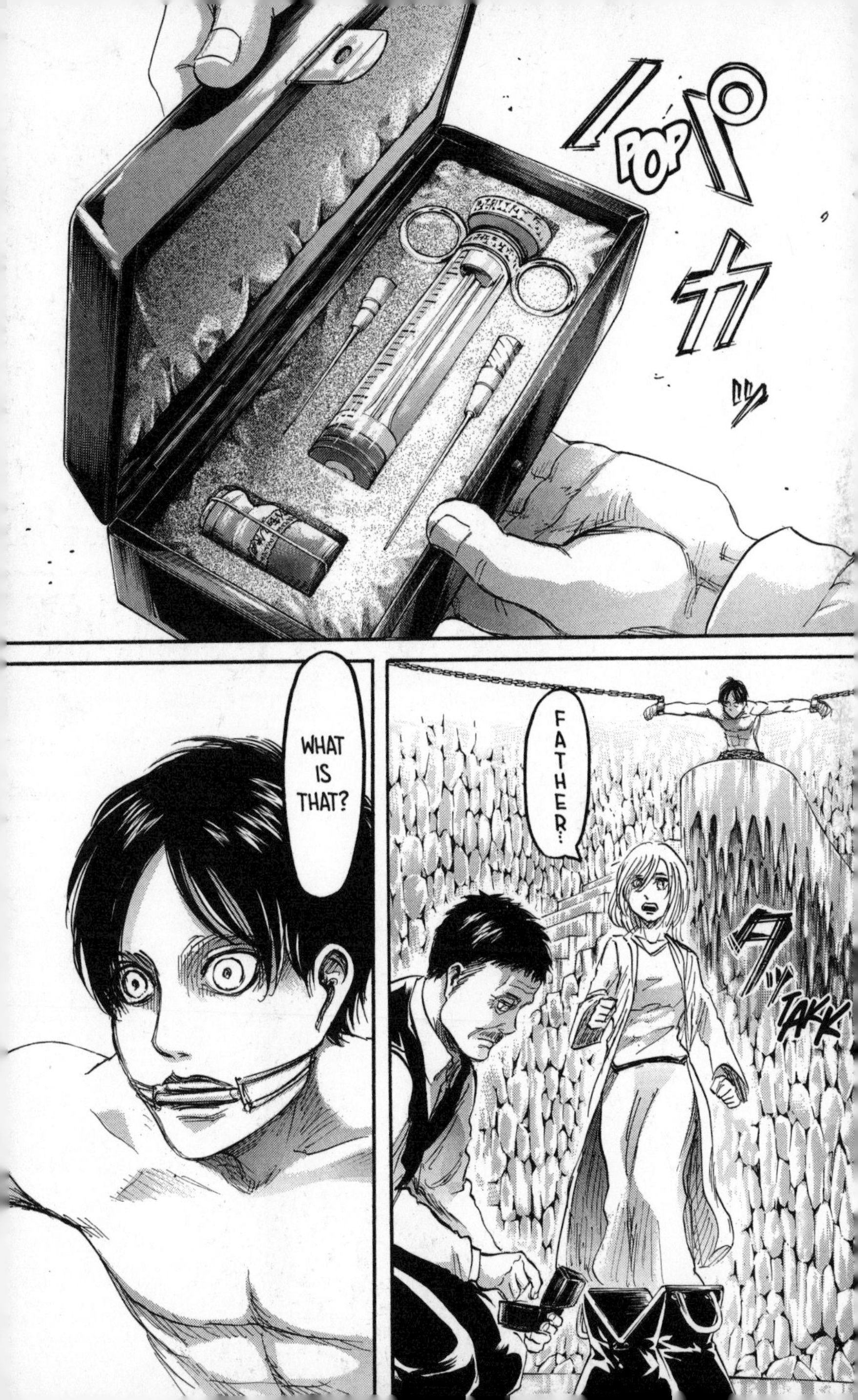
パカッ
POP
FATHER...
タッ
TAKK
WHAT IS THAT?

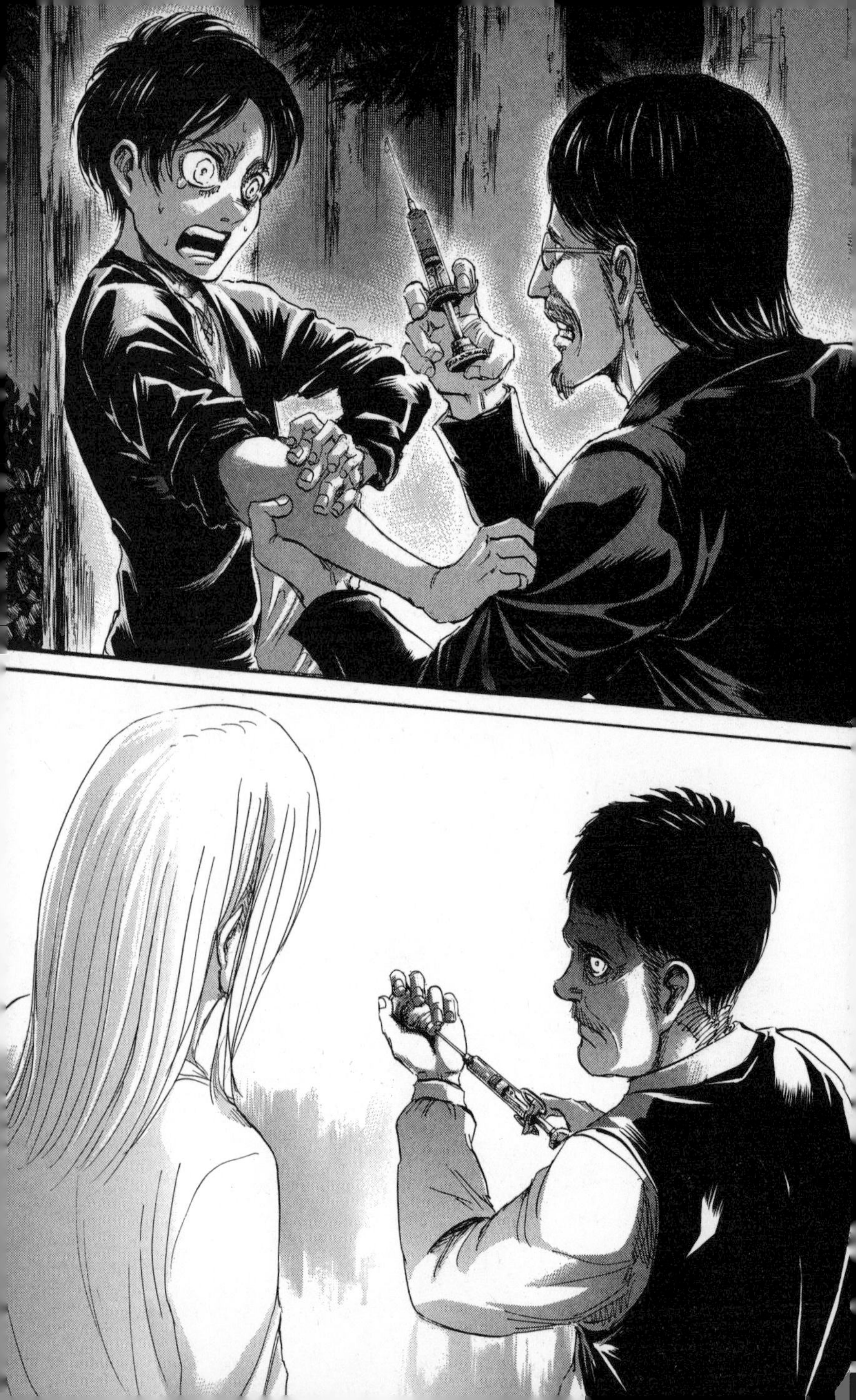

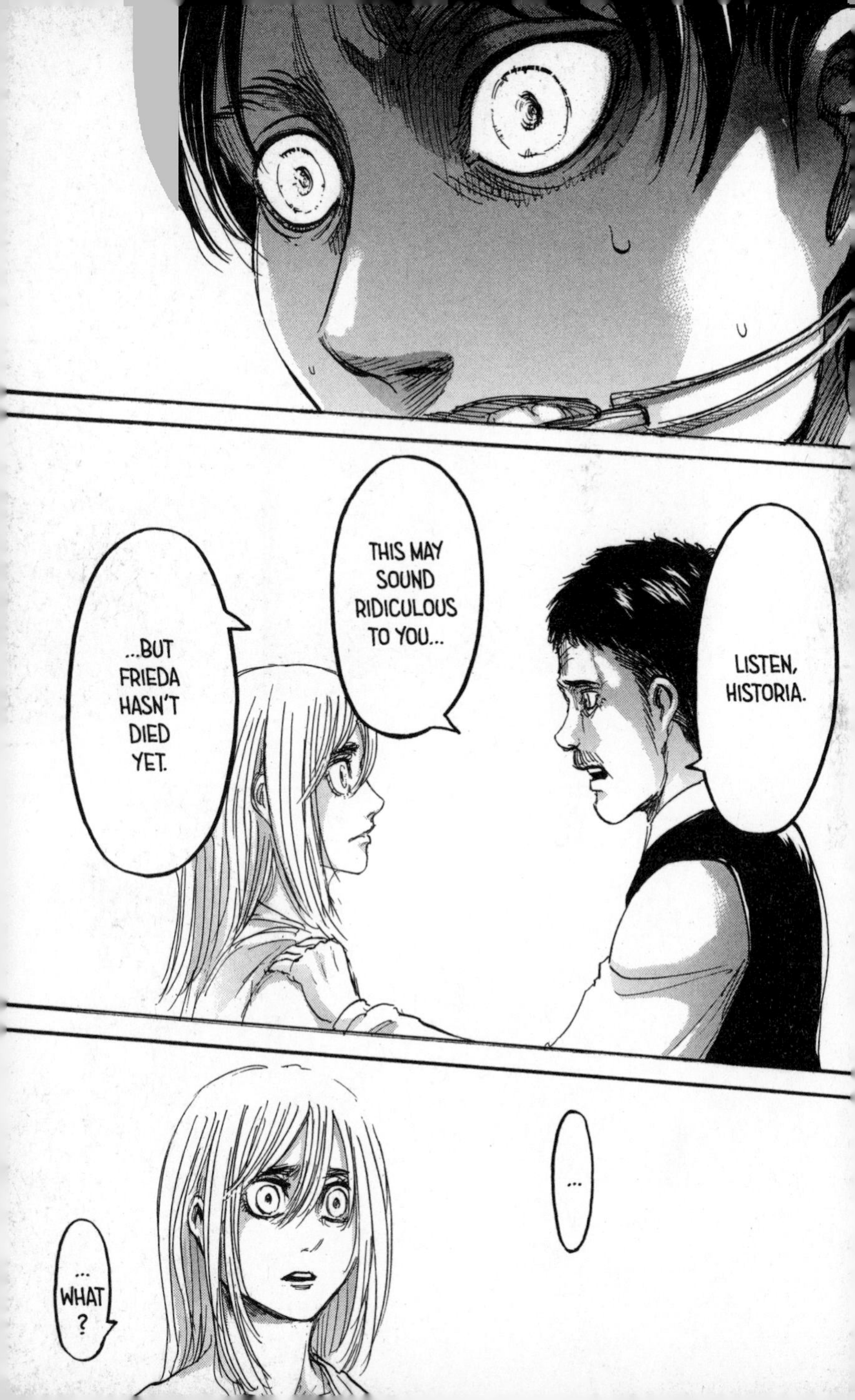
LISTEN, HISTORIA.
THIS MAY SOUND RIDICULOUS TO YOU...
...BUT FRIEDA HASN'T DIED YET.
...
...WHAT?

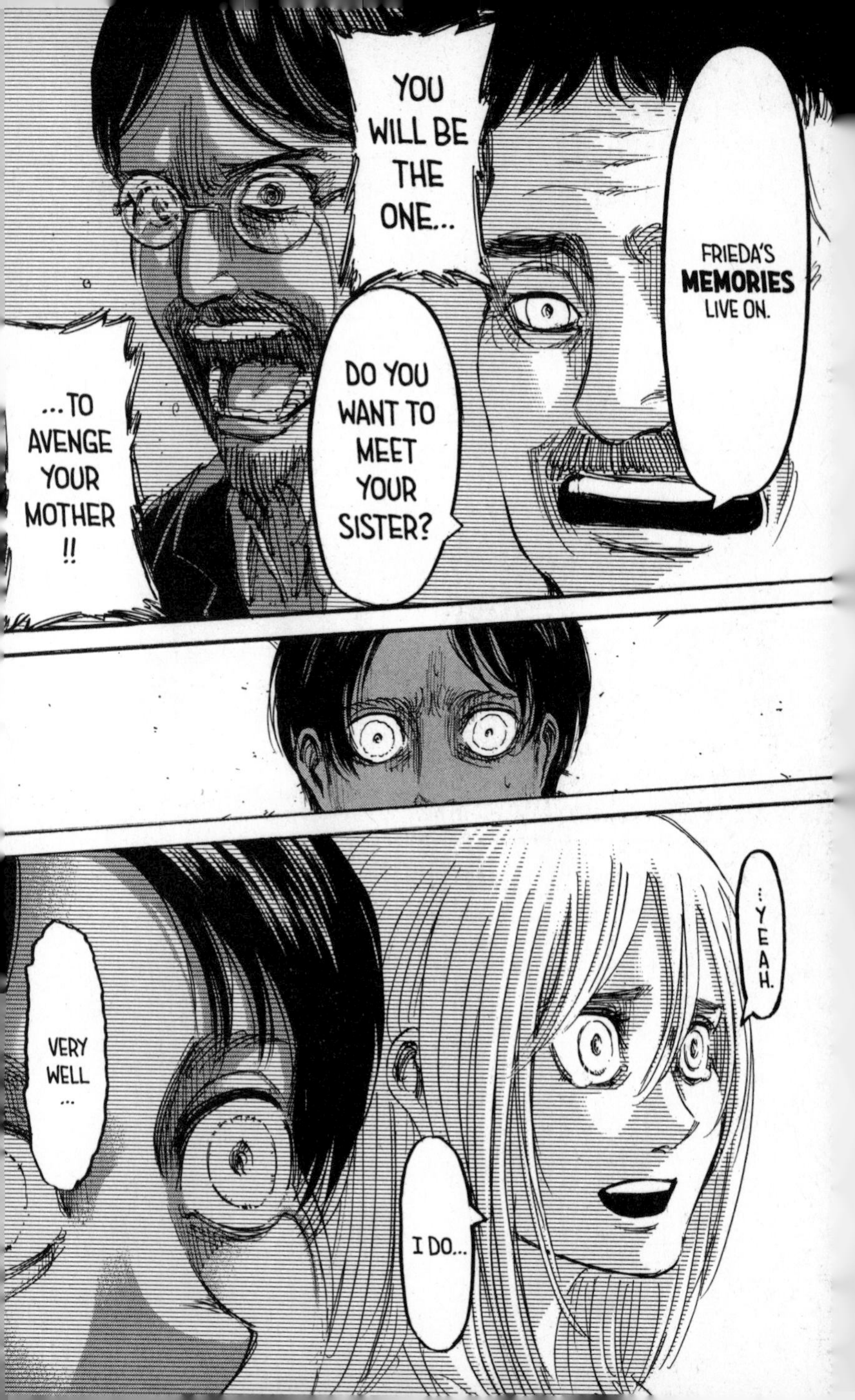
FRIEDA'S **MEMORIES** LIVE ON.
YOU WILL BE THE ONE...
DO YOU WANT TO MEET YOUR SISTER?
...TO AVENGE YOUR MOTHER !!
...YEAH.
I DO...
VERY WELL...

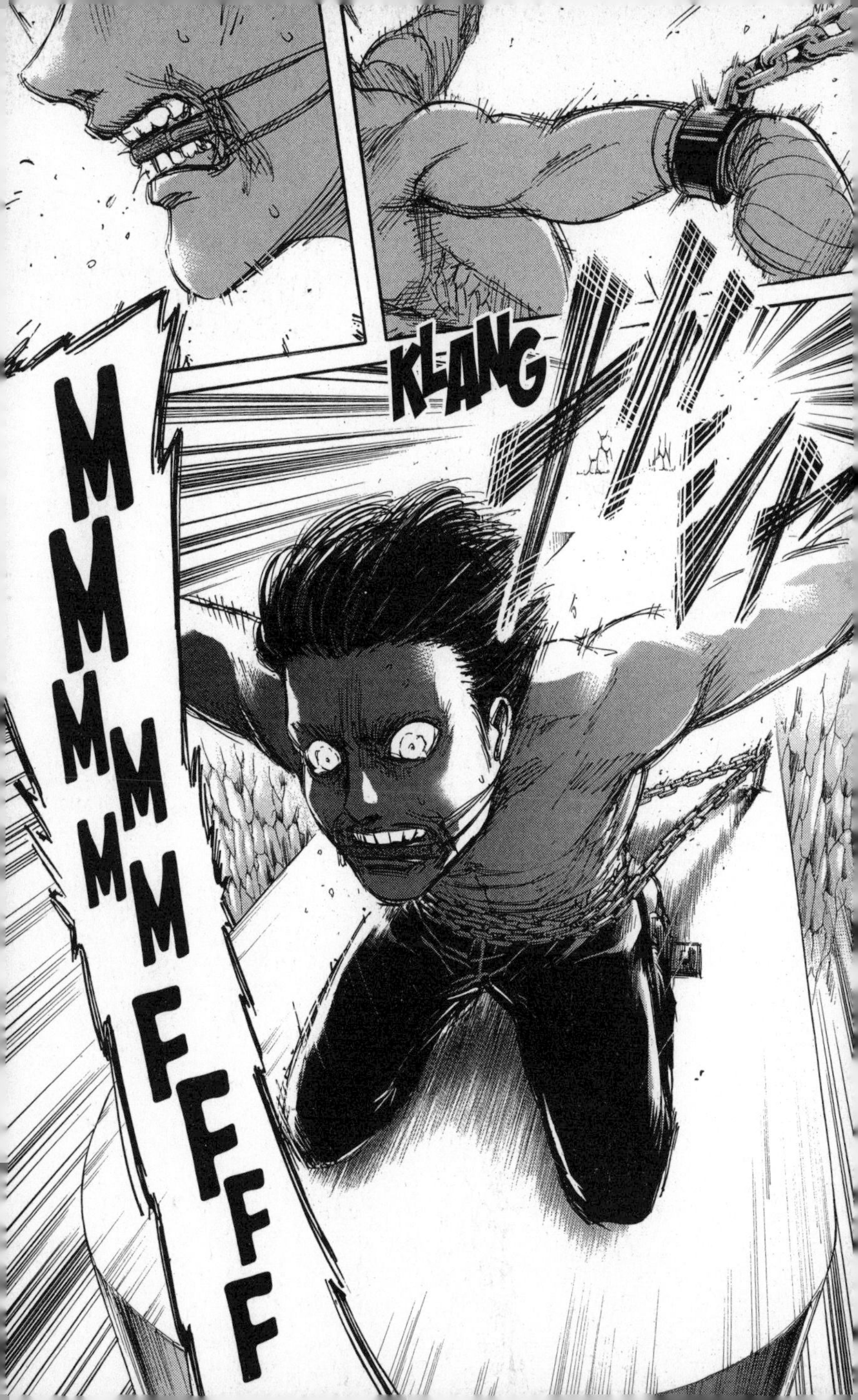
KLANG
MMMMMMFFFFF

ATTACK on TITAN

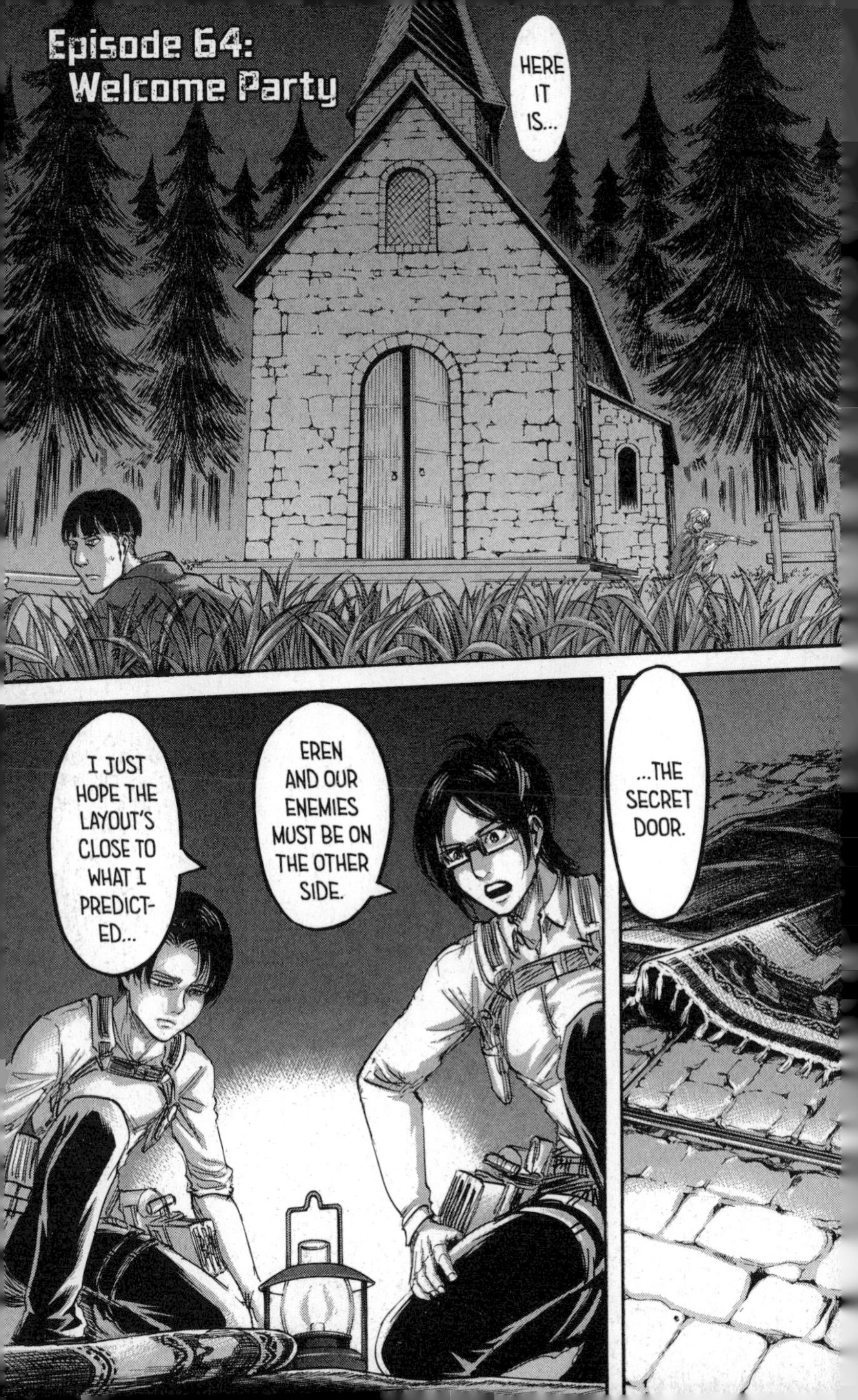
Episode 64: Welcome Party
HERE IT IS...
...THE SECRET DOOR.
EREN AND OUR ENEMIES MUST BE ON THE OTHER SIDE.
I JUST HOPE THE LAYOUT'S CLOSE TO WHAT I PREDICT-ED...

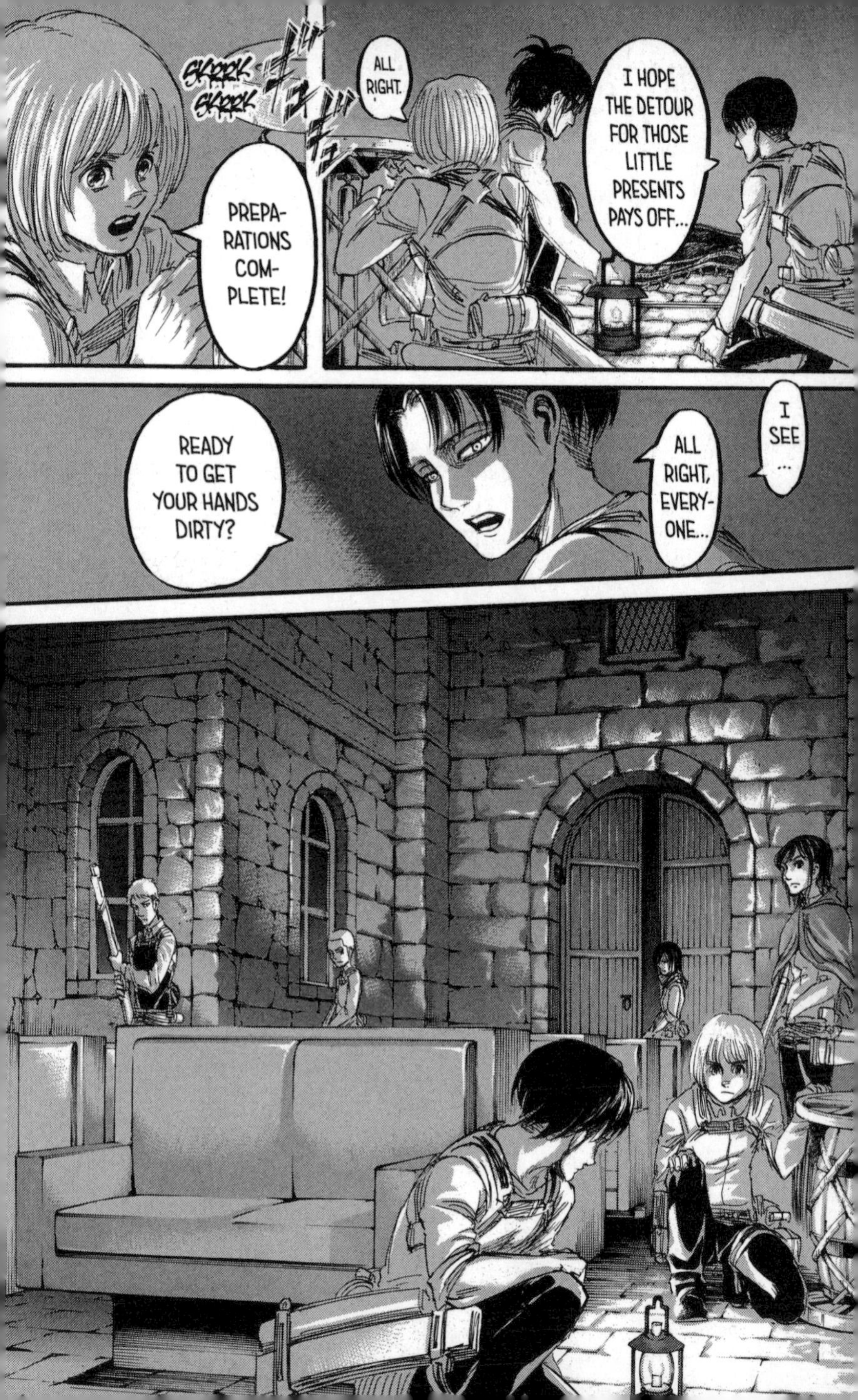
I HOPE THE DETOUR FOR THOSE LITTLE PRESENTS PAYS OFF...
ALL RIGHT.
SKRRK SKRRK
PREPARATIONS COMPLETE!
I SEE ...
ALL RIGHT, EVERYONE...
READY TO GET YOUR HANDS DIRTY?

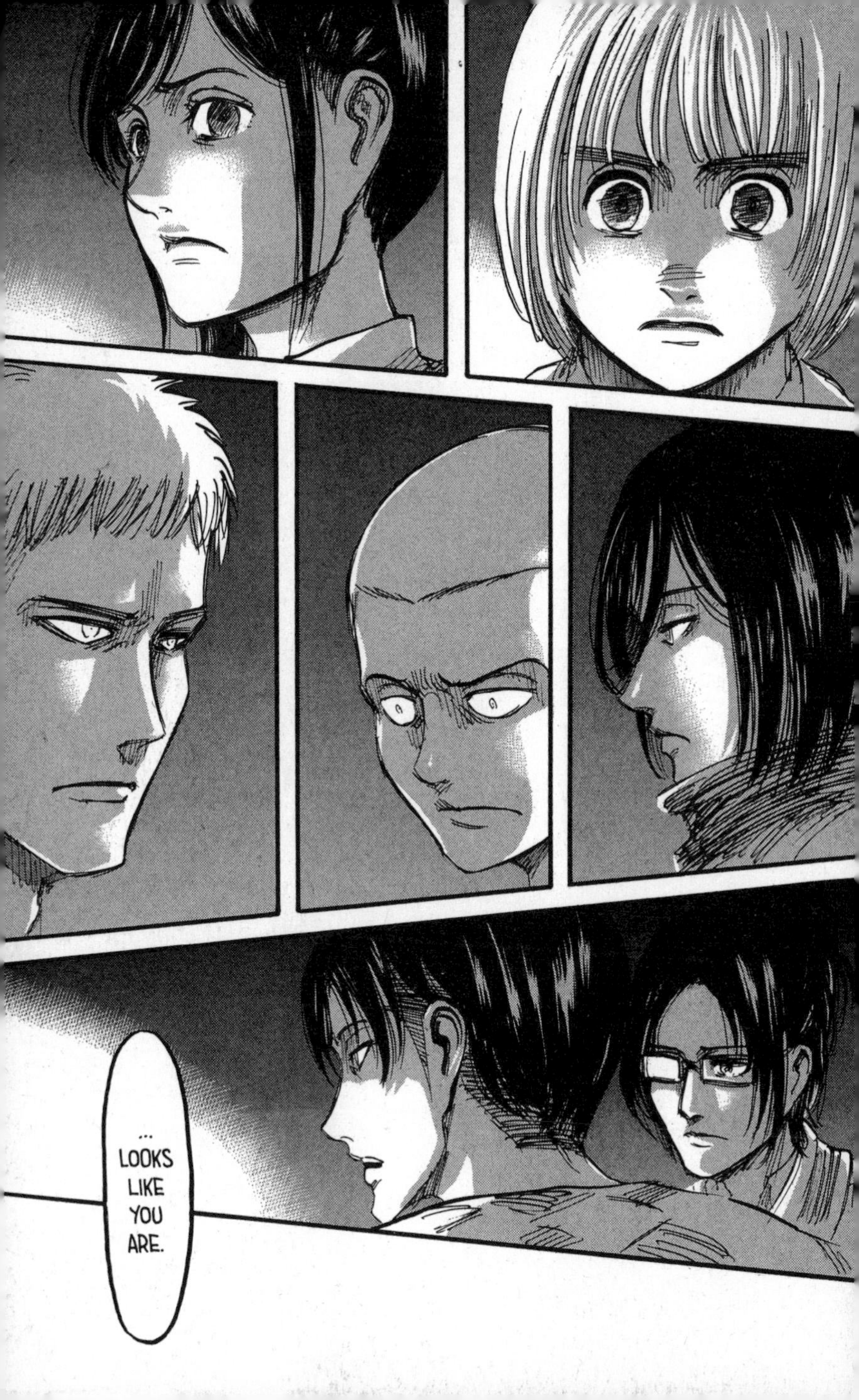
...
LOOKS LIKE YOU ARE.

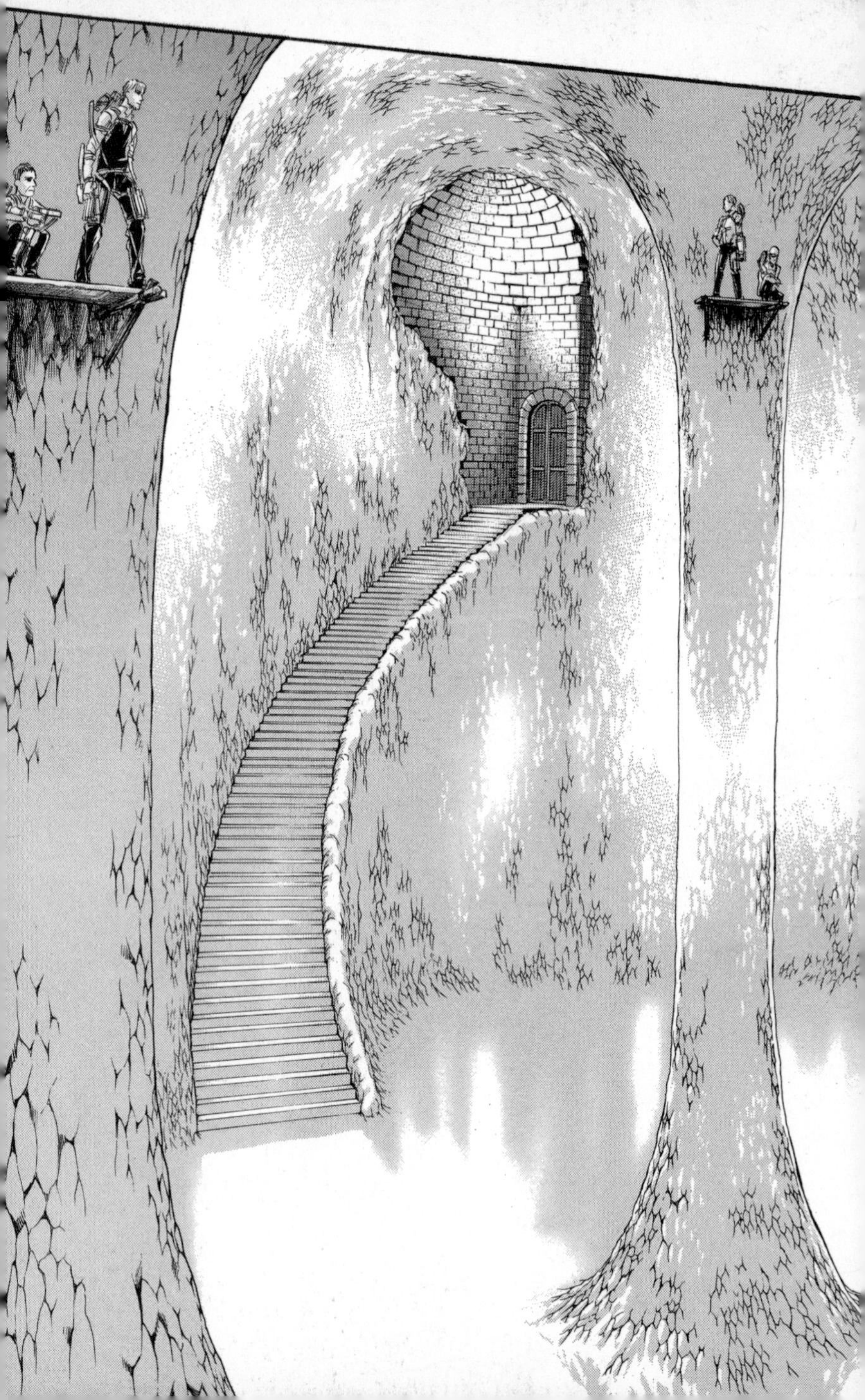

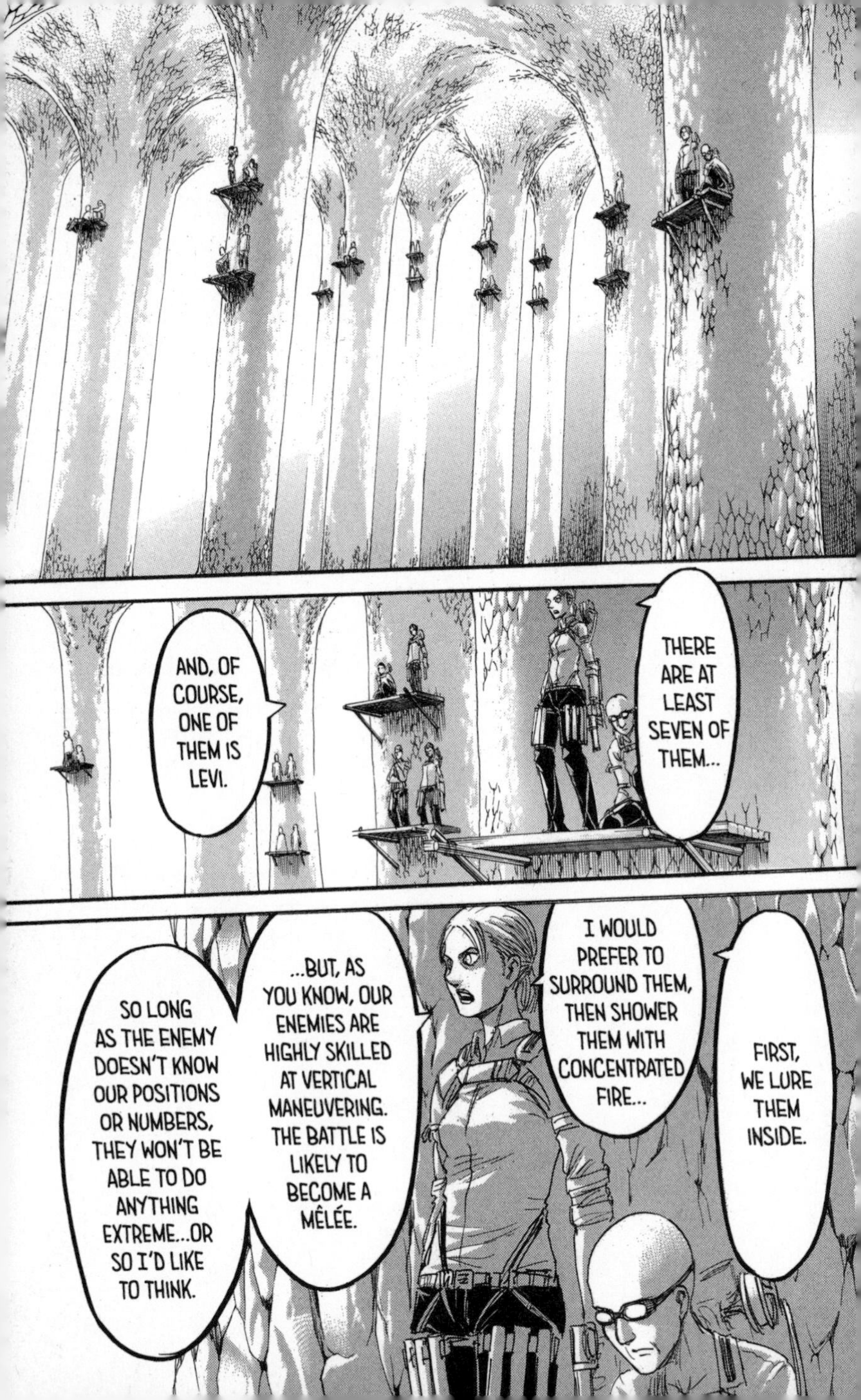
THERE ARE AT LEAST SEVEN OF THEM...
AND, OF COURSE, ONE OF THEM IS LEVI.
FIRST, WE LURE THEM INSIDE.
I WOULD PREFER TO SURROUND THEM, THEN SHOWER THEM WITH CONCENTRATED FIRE...
...BUT, AS YOU KNOW, OUR ENEMIES ARE HIGHLY SKILLED AT VERTICAL MANEUVERING. THE BATTLE IS LIKELY TO BECOME A MÊLÉE.
SO LONG AS THE ENEMY DOESN'T KNOW OUR POSITIONS OR NUMBERS, THEY WON'T BE ABLE TO DO ANYTHING EXTREME...OR SO I'D LIKE TO THINK.

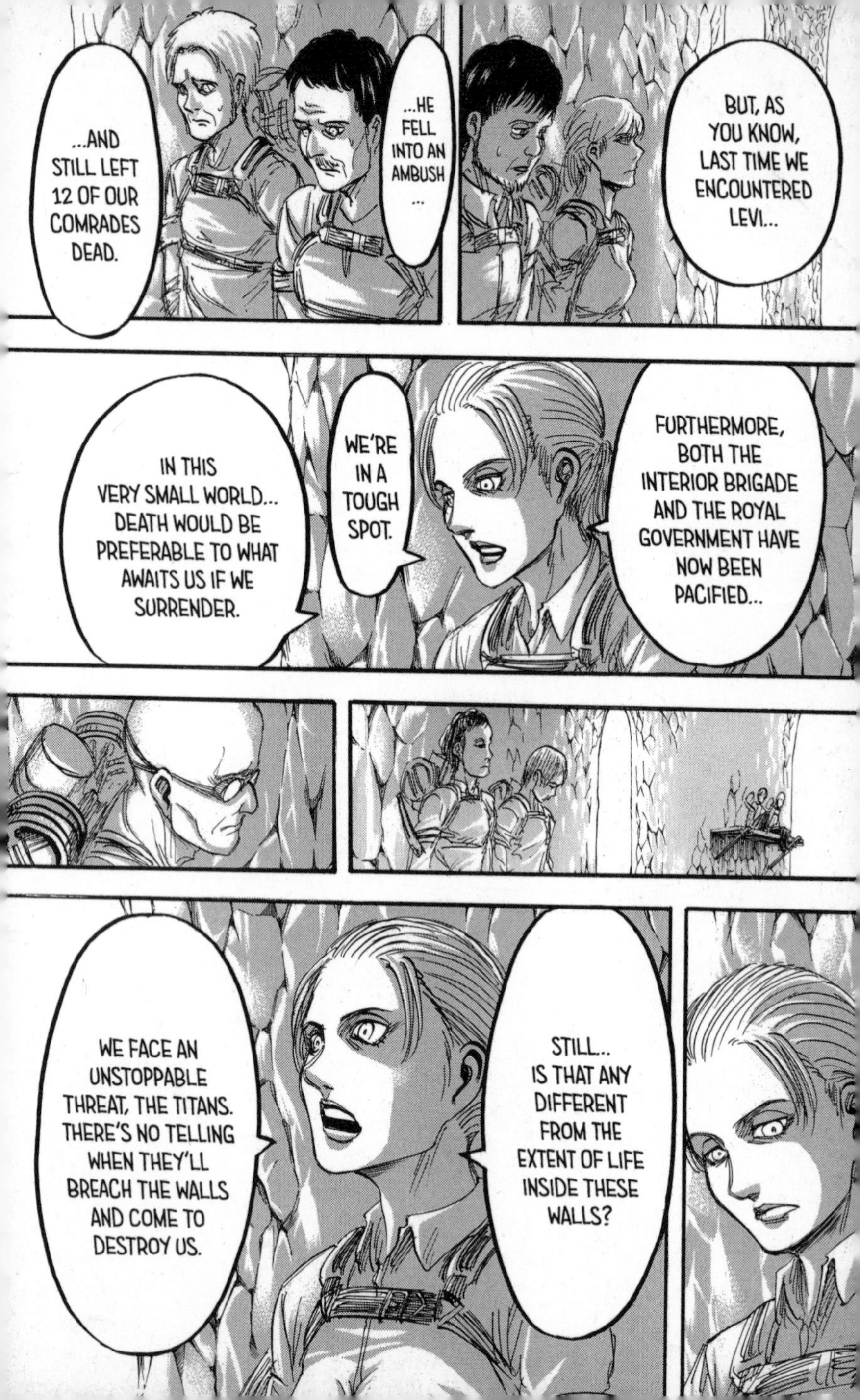
BUT, AS YOU KNOW, LAST TIME WE ENCOUNTERED LEVI...
...HE FELL INTO AN AMBUSH ...
...AND STILL LEFT 12 OF OUR COMRADES DEAD.
FURTHERMORE, BOTH THE INTERIOR BRIGADE AND THE ROYAL GOVERNMENT HAVE NOW BEEN PACIFIED...
WE'RE IN A TOUGH SPOT.
IN THIS VERY SMALL WORLD... DEATH WOULD BE PREFERABLE TO WHAT AWAITS US IF WE SURRENDER.
STILL... IS THAT ANY DIFFERENT FROM THE EXTENT OF LIFE INSIDE THESE WALLS?
WE FACE AN UNSTOPPABLE THREAT, THE TITANS. THERE'S NO TELLING WHEN THEY'LL BREACH THE WALLS AND COME TO DESTROY US.

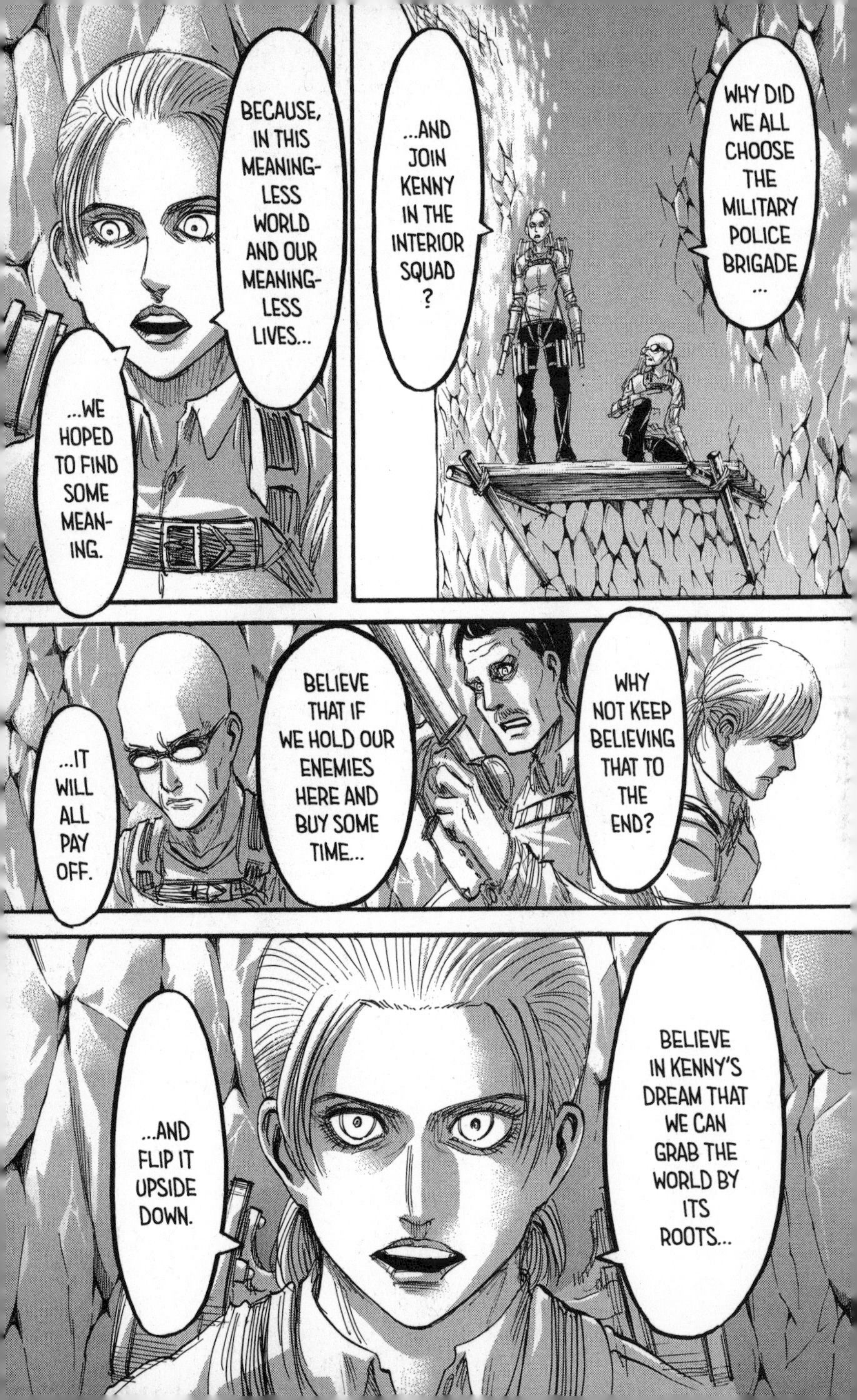
WHY DID WE ALL CHOOSE THE MILITARY POLICE BRIGADE...
...AND JOIN KENNY IN THE INTERIOR SQUAD?
BECAUSE, IN THIS MEANING-LESS WORLD AND OUR MEANING-LESS LIVES...
...WE HOPED TO FIND SOME MEAN-ING.
WHY NOT KEEP BELIEVING THAT TO THE END?
BELIEVE THAT IF WE HOLD OUR ENEMIES HERE AND BUY SOME TIME...
...IT WILL ALL PAY OFF.
BELIEVE IN KENNY'S DREAM THAT WE CAN GRAB THE WORLD BY ITS ROOTS...
...AND FLIP IT UPSIDE DOWN.

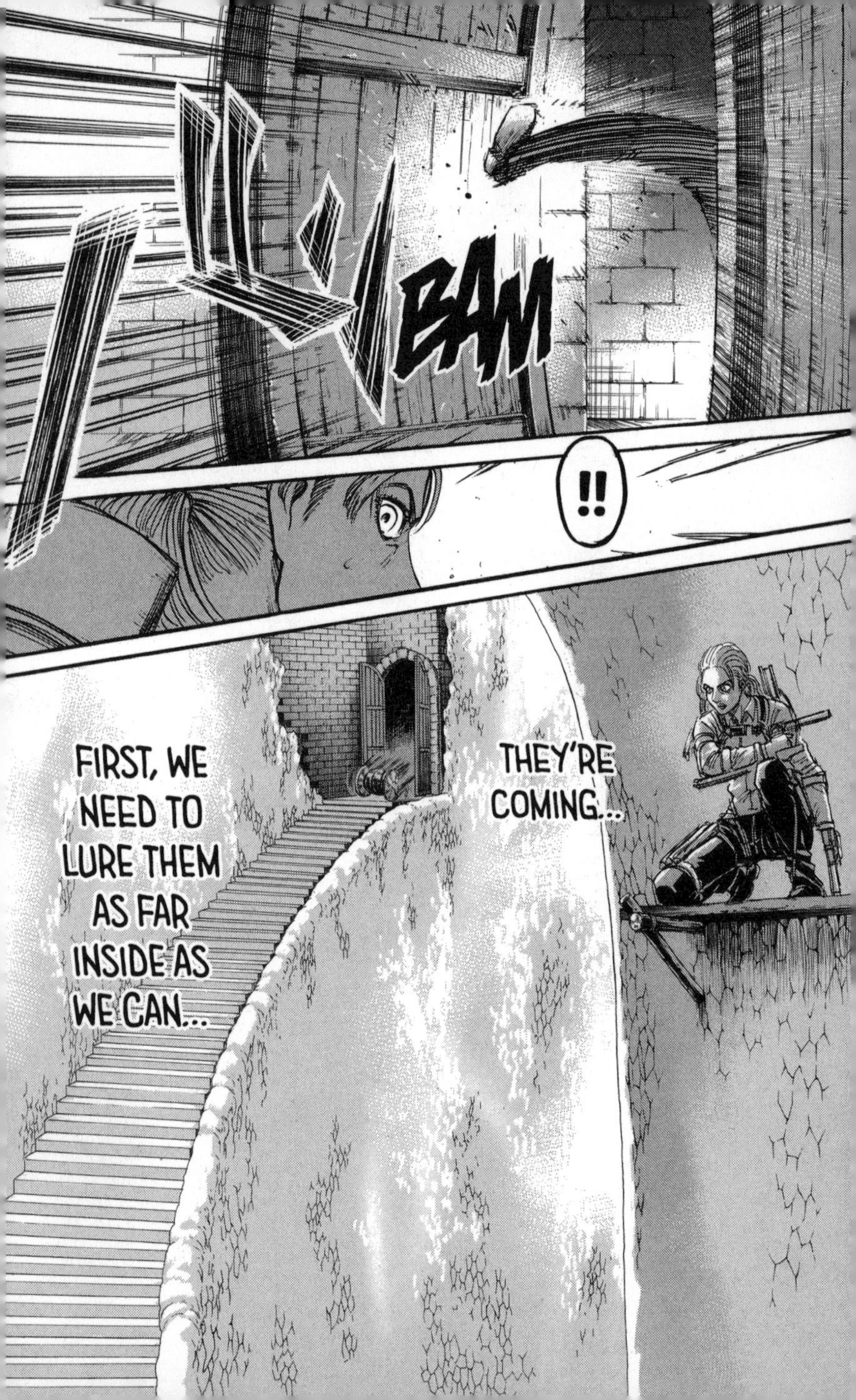
BAM
!!
THEY'RE COMING...
FIRST, WE NEED TO LURE THEM AS FAR INSIDE AS WE CAN...

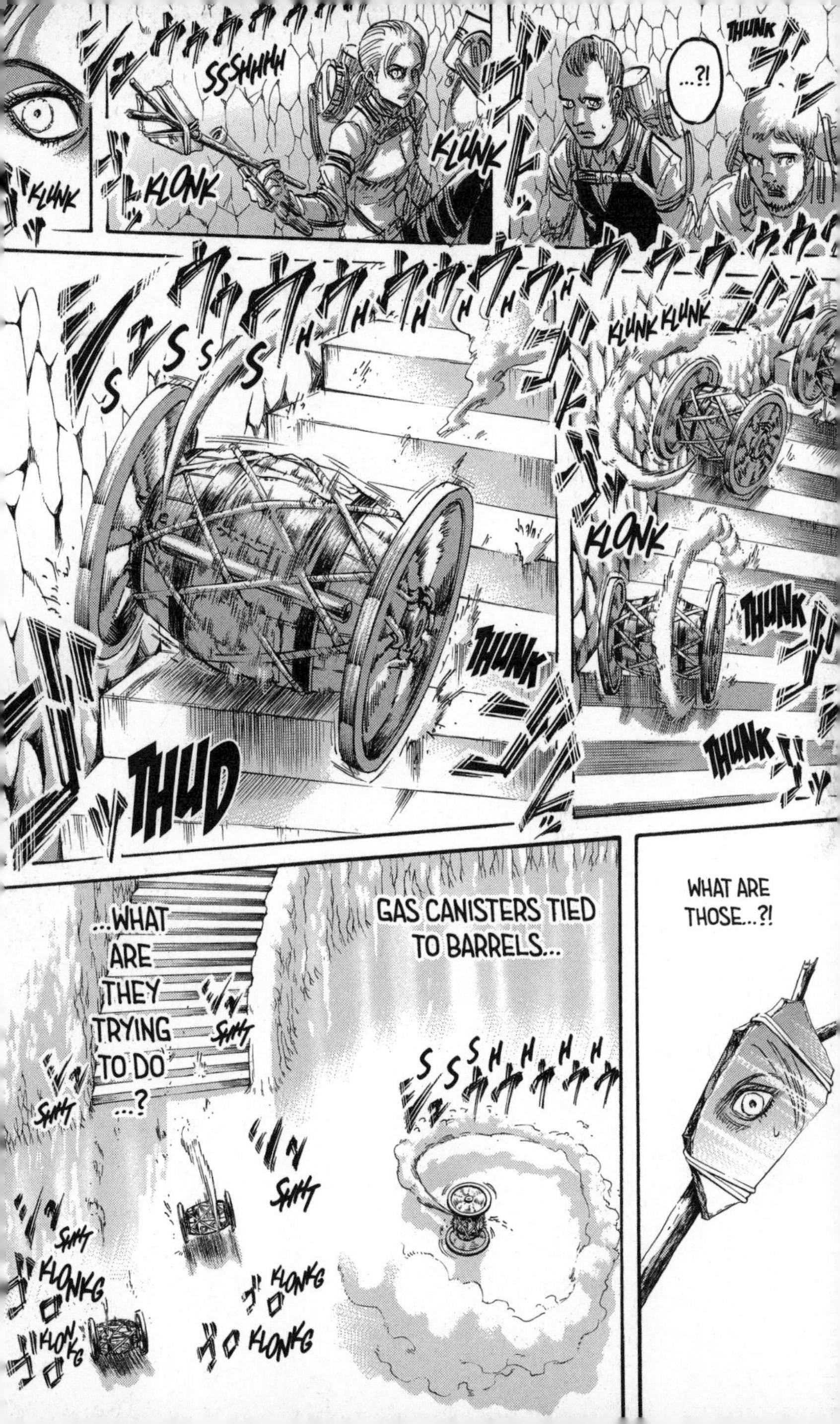
THUNK
...?!
KLUNK
SSSHHHH
KLONK
KLUNK
KLUNK KLUNK
KLONK
THUNK
THUNK
THUNK
THUD
WHAT ARE THOSE...?!
GAS CANISTERS TIED TO BARRELS...
...WHAT ARE THEY TRYING TO DO...?
SSSHHHHH
SHH
SHH
SHH
SHH
KLONKG
KLONKG
KLONKG
KLONKG

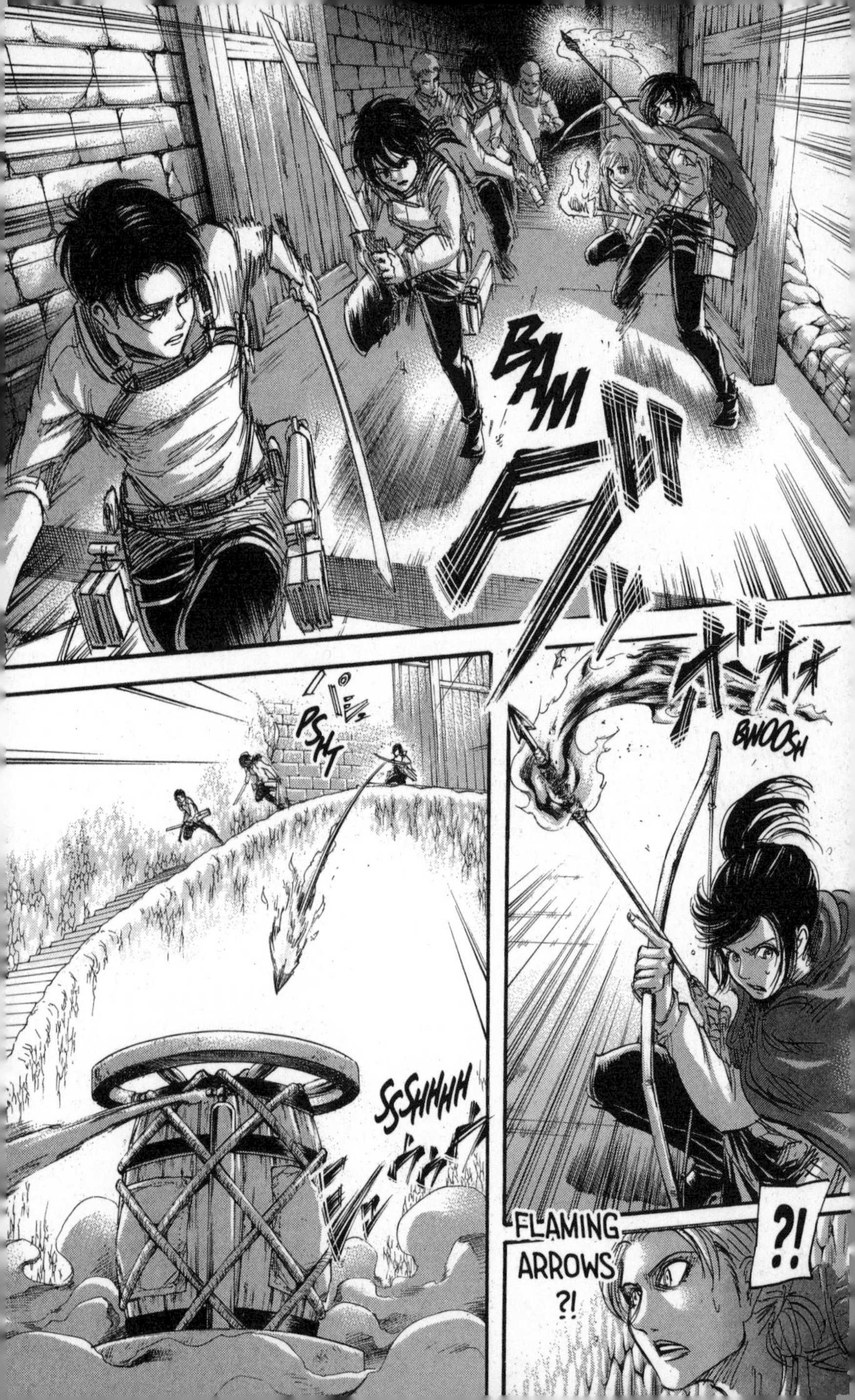
BAM
BWOOSH
PSHT
SSSHHHH
FLAMING ARROWS ?!
?!

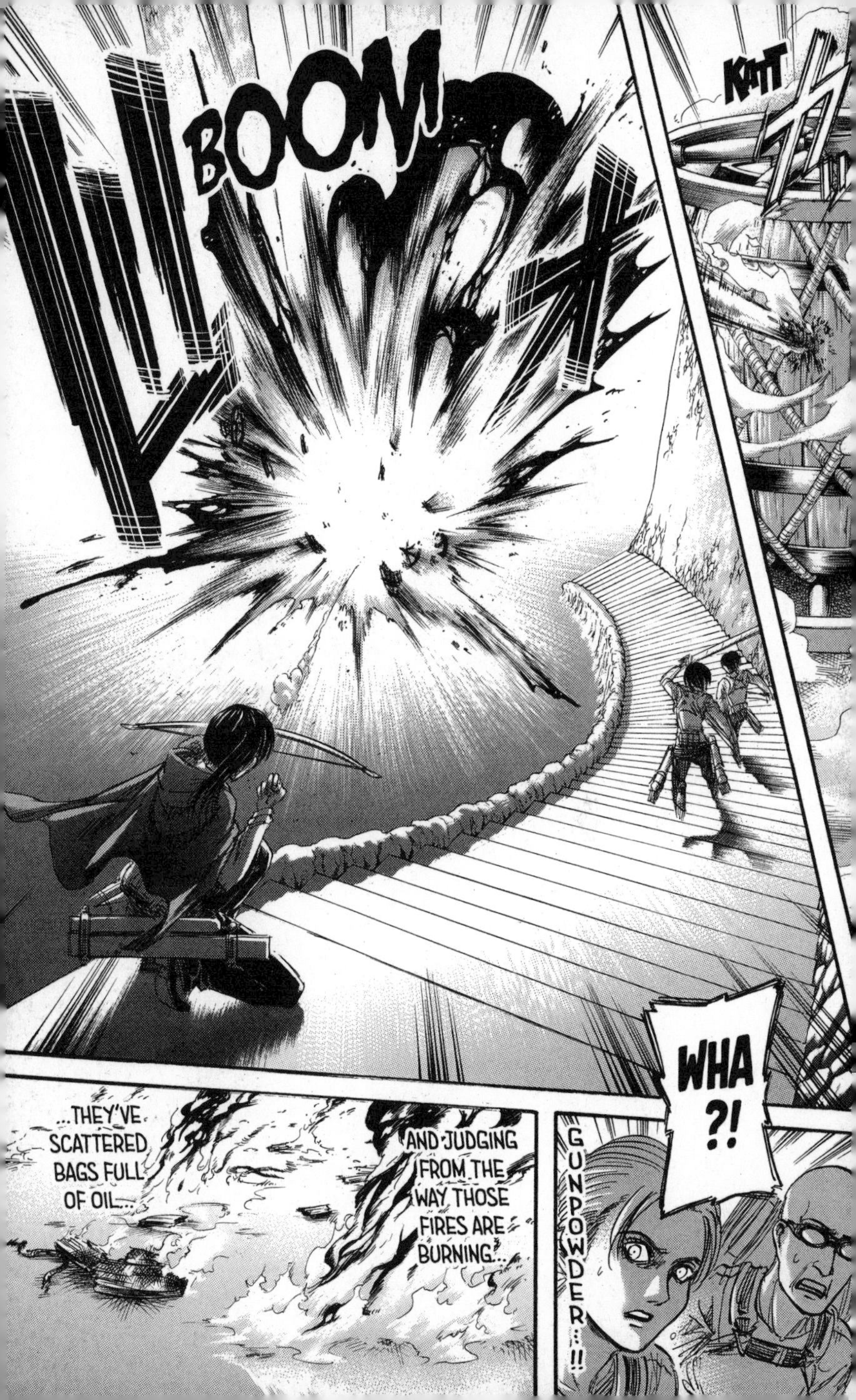
KATT
BOOM
WHA ?!
GUNPOWDER...!!
...THEY'VE SCATTERED BAGS FULL OF OIL...
AND JUDGING FROM THE WAY THOSE FIRES ARE BURNING...

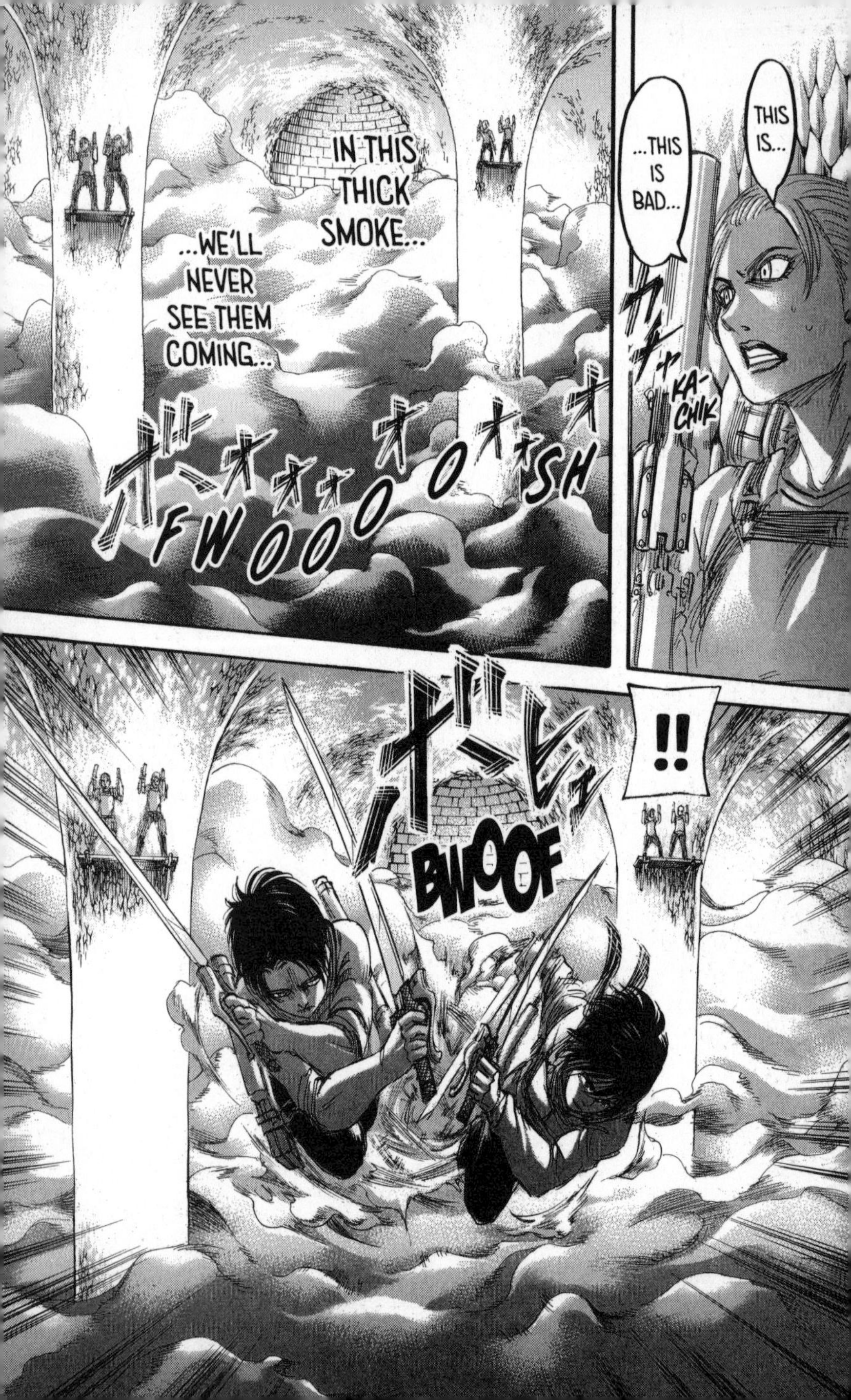
THIS IS...
...THIS IS BAD...
KA-CHIK
IN THIS THICK SMOKE...
...WE'LL NEVER SEE THEM COMING...
FWOOOOSH
!!
BWOOF

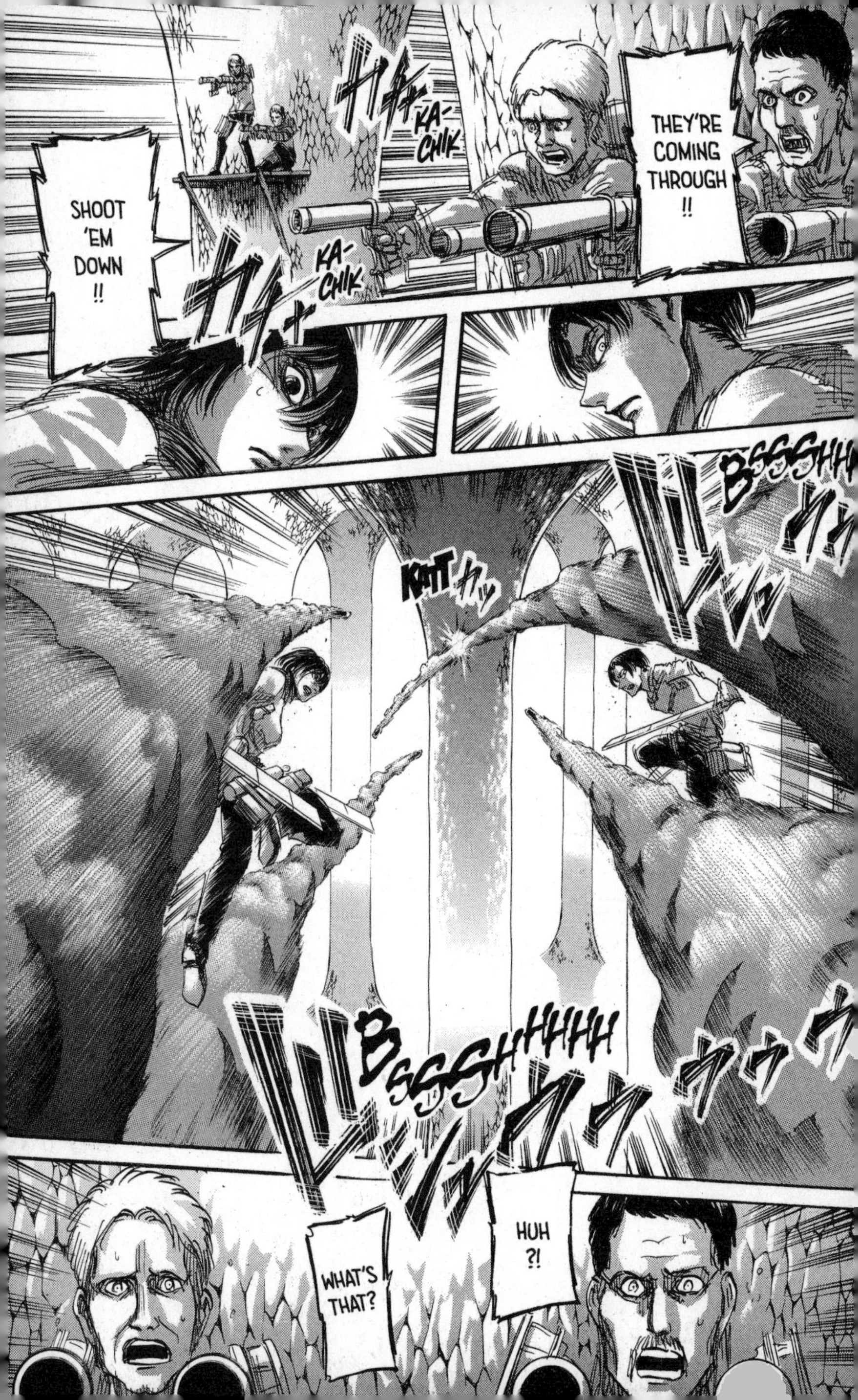
THEY'RE COMING THROUGH !!
KA-CHIK
KA-CHIK
SHOOT 'EM DOWN !!
BSSSHH
KATT
BSSSHHHHH
HUH ?!
WHAT'S THAT?

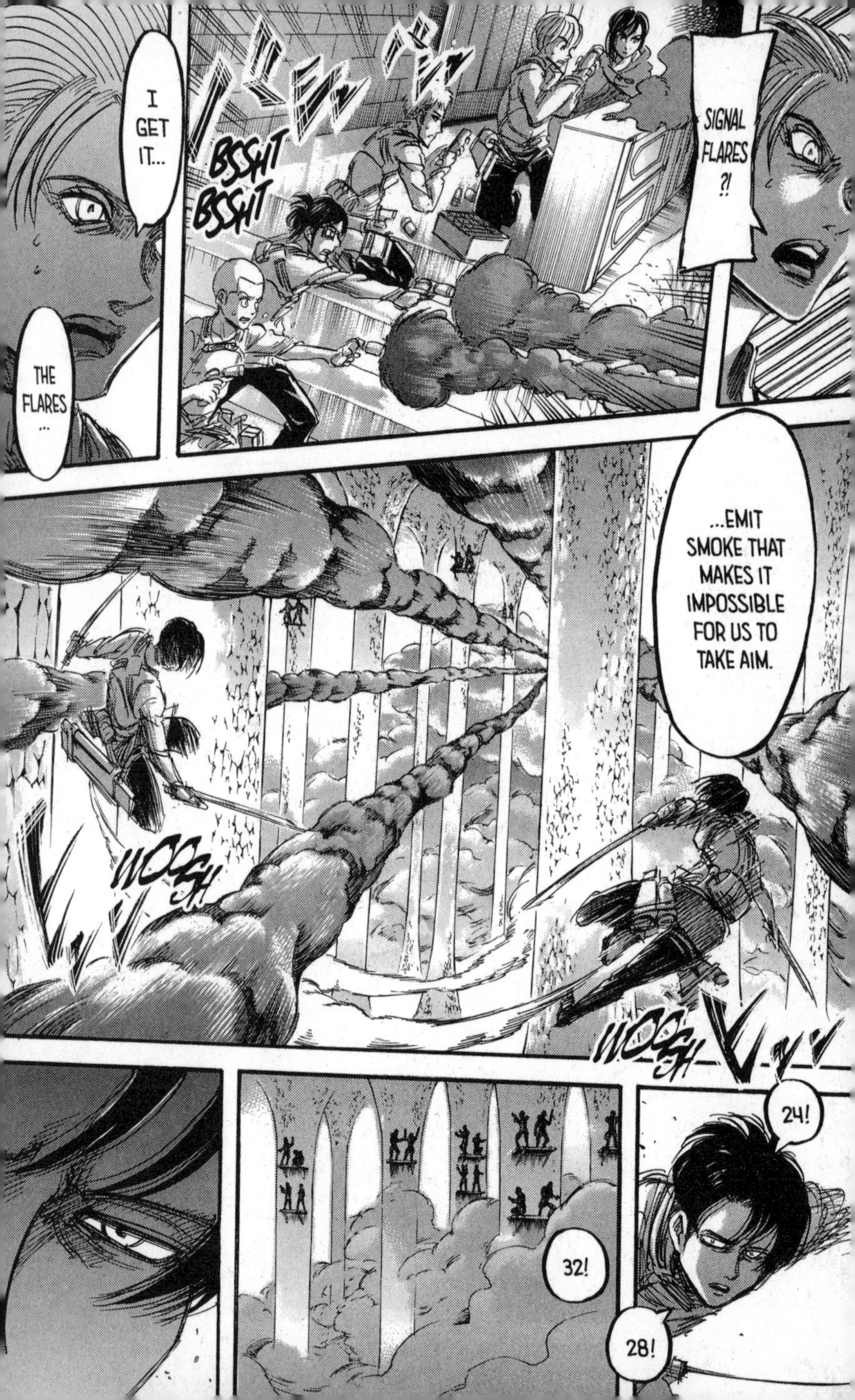
SIGNAL FLARES ?!
BSSHT
BSSHT
I GET IT...
THE FLARES ...
...EMIT SMOKE THAT MAKES IT IMPOSSIBLE FOR US TO TAKE AIM.
WOOSH
WOOSH
24!
28!
32!

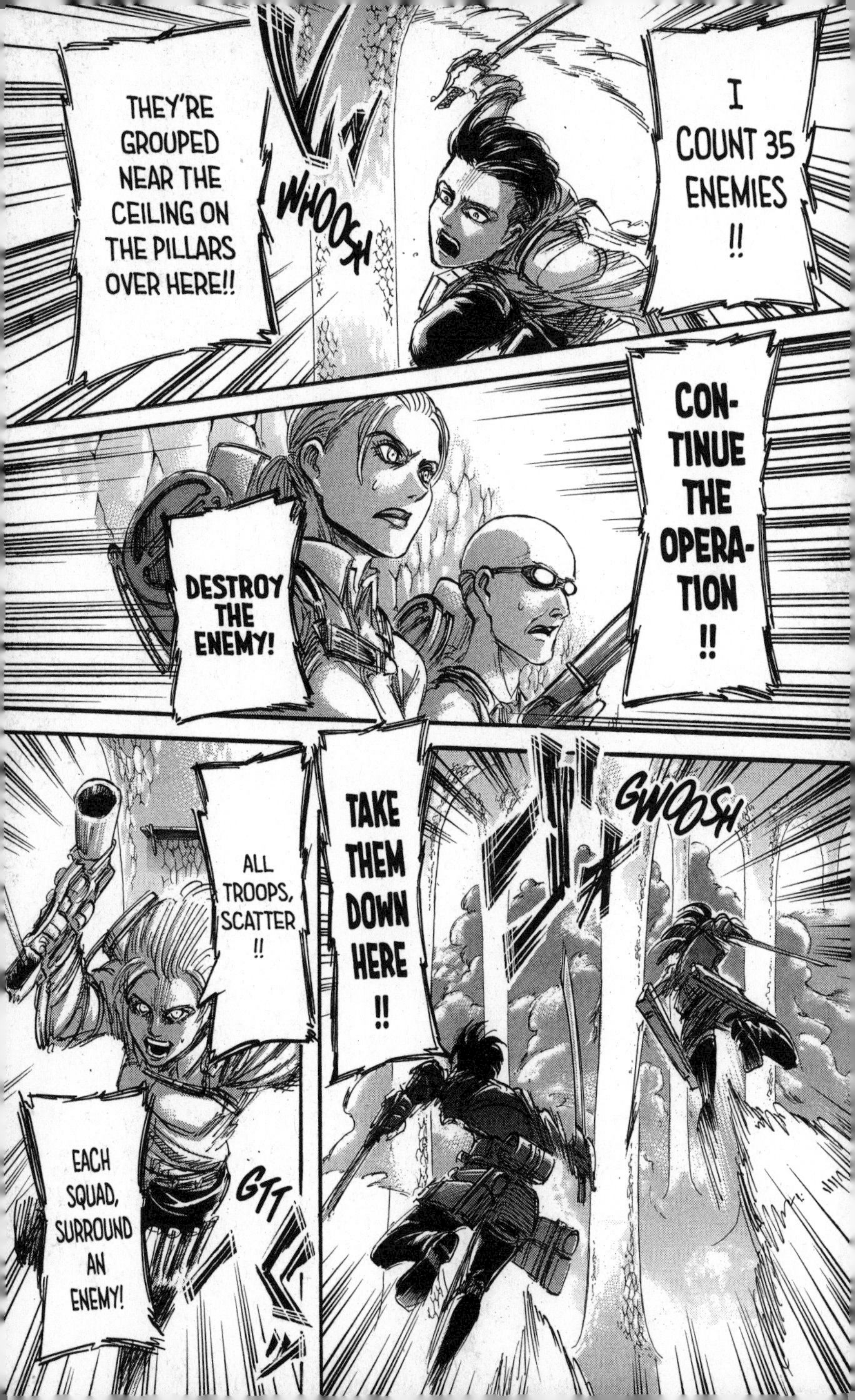
I COUNT 35 ENEMIES!!
WHOOSH
THEY'RE GROUPED NEAR THE CEILING ON THE PILLARS OVER HERE!!
CON-TINUE THE OPERA-TION!!
DESTROY THE ENEMY!
GWOOSH
TAKE THEM DOWN HERE!!
ALL TROOPS, SCATTER!!
GTT
EACH SQUAD, SURROUND AN ENEMY!

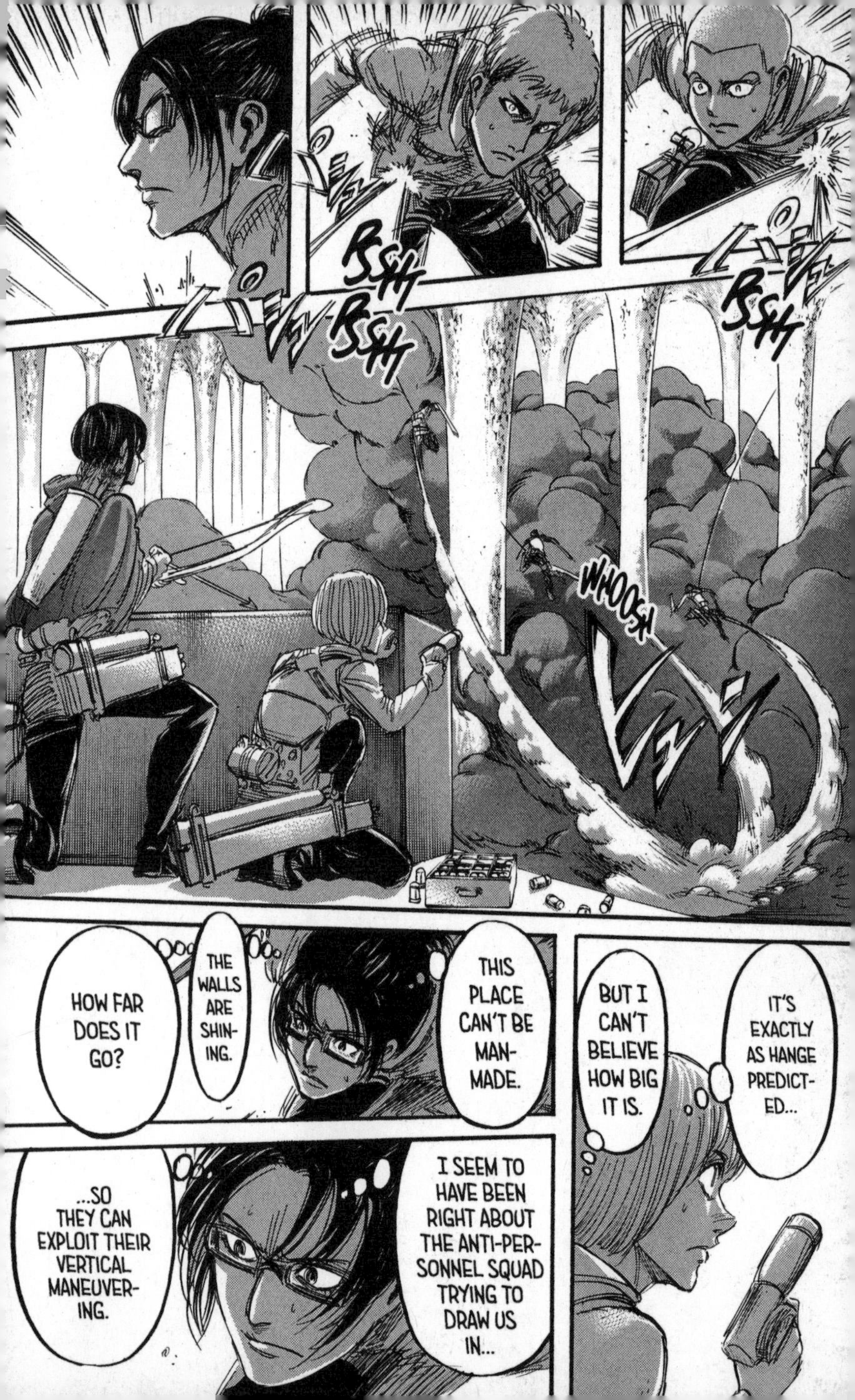
RSSH
RSSH
RSSH
WHOOSH
IT'S EXACTLY AS HANGE PREDICT-ED...
BUT I CAN'T BELIEVE HOW BIG IT IS.
THIS PLACE CAN'T BE MAN-MADE.
THE WALLS ARE SHIN-ING.
HOW FAR DOES IT GO?
I SEEM TO HAVE BEEN RIGHT ABOUT THE ANTI-PER-SONNEL SQUAD TRYING TO DRAW US IN...
...SO THEY CAN EXPLOIT THEIR VERTICAL MANEUVER-ING.

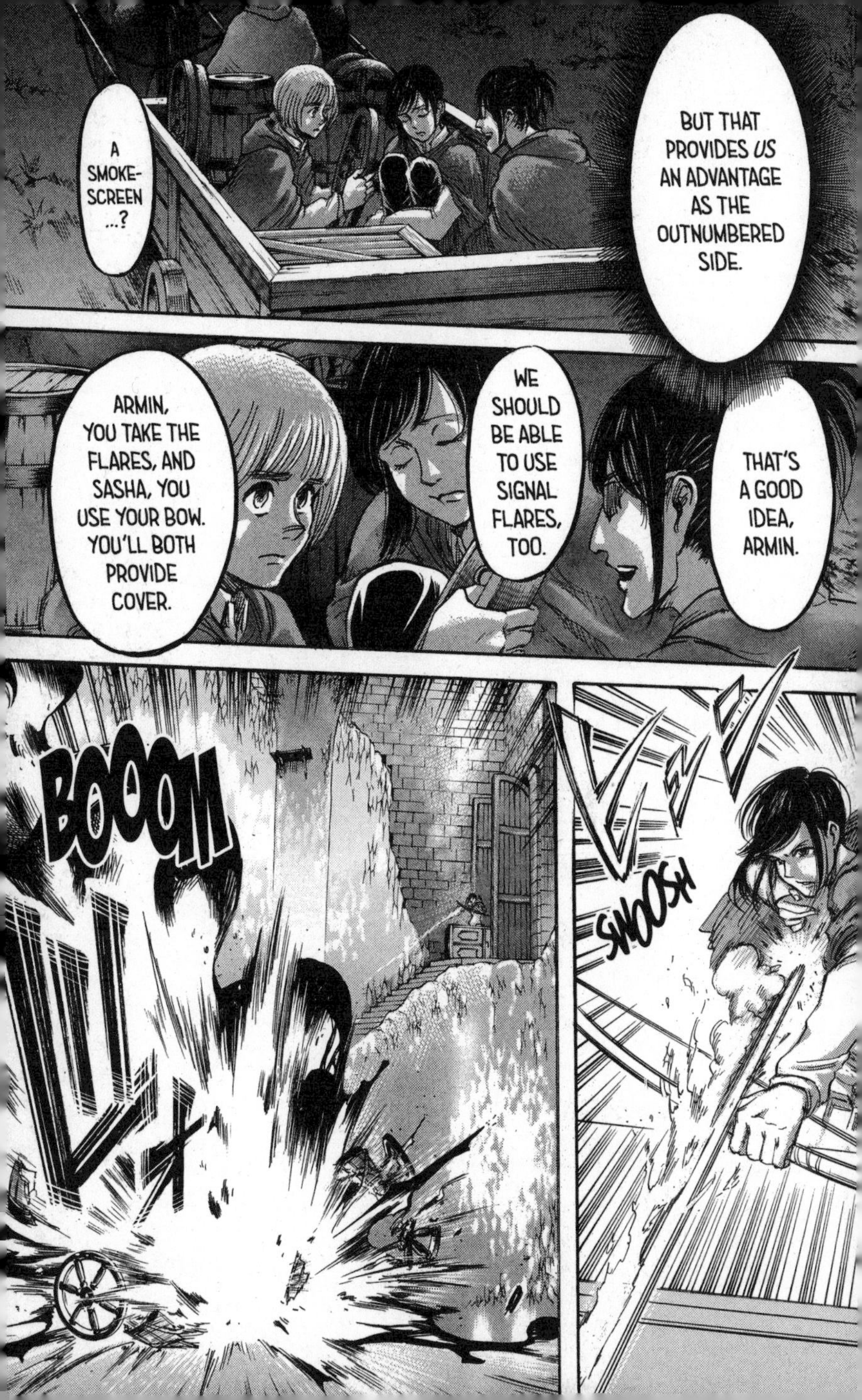
BUT THAT PROVIDES *US* AN ADVANTAGE AS THE OUTNUMBERED SIDE.
A SMOKE-SCREEN ...?
THAT'S A GOOD IDEA, ARMIN.
WE SHOULD BE ABLE TO USE SIGNAL FLARES, TOO.
ARMIN, YOU TAKE THE FLARES, AND SASHA, YOU USE YOUR BOW. YOU'LL BOTH PROVIDE COVER.
SWOOSH
BOOOM

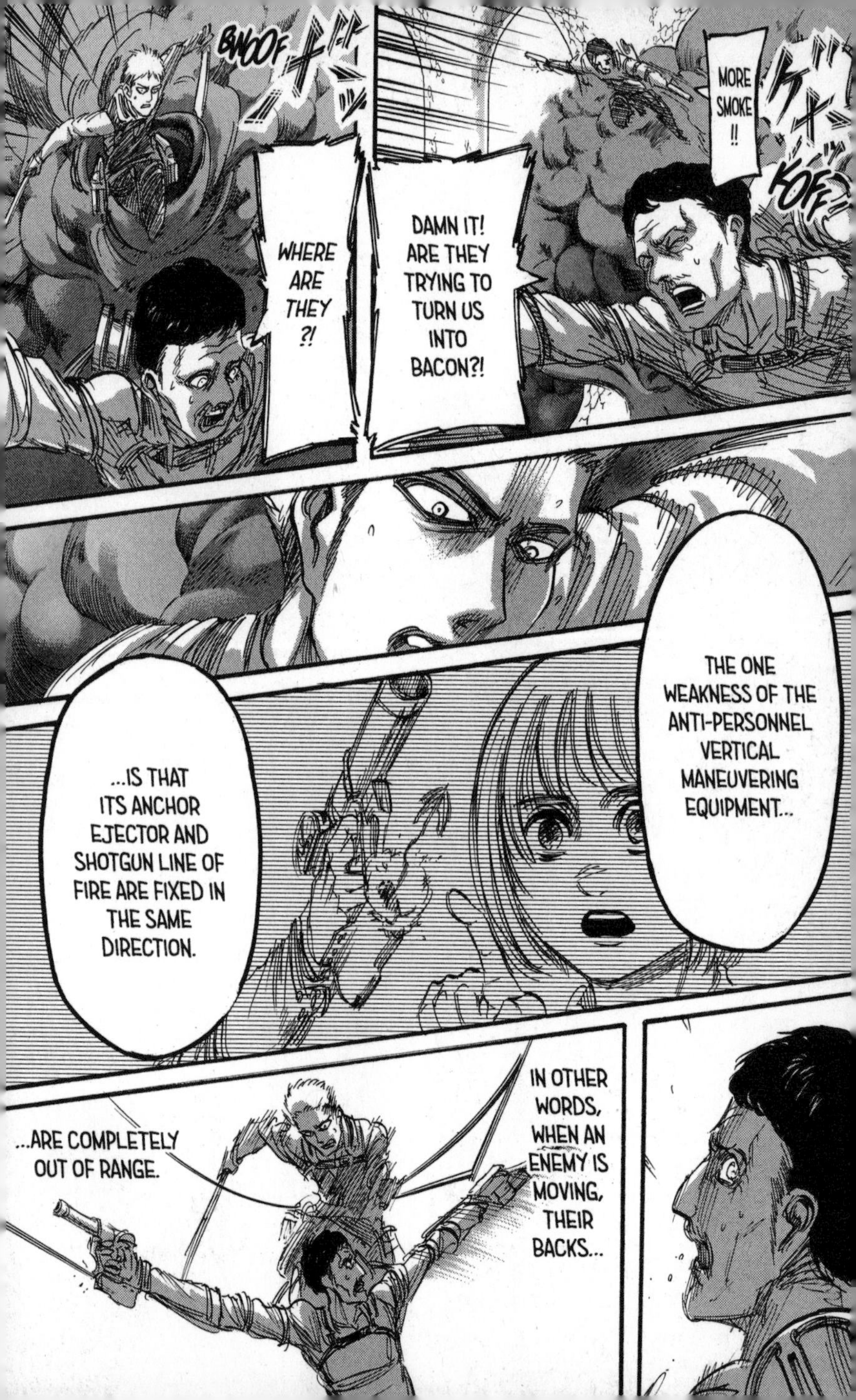
MORE SMOKE!!
KOFF
DAMN IT! ARE THEY TRYING TO TURN US INTO BACON?!
WHERE ARE THEY?!
BWOOF
THE ONE WEAKNESS OF THE ANTI-PERSONNEL VERTICAL MANEUVERING EQUIPMENT...
...IS THAT ITS ANCHOR EJECTOR AND SHOTGUN LINE OF FIRE ARE FIXED IN THE SAME DIRECTION.
IN OTHER WORDS, WHEN AN ENEMY IS MOVING, THEIR BACKS...
...ARE COMPLETELY OUT OF RANGE.

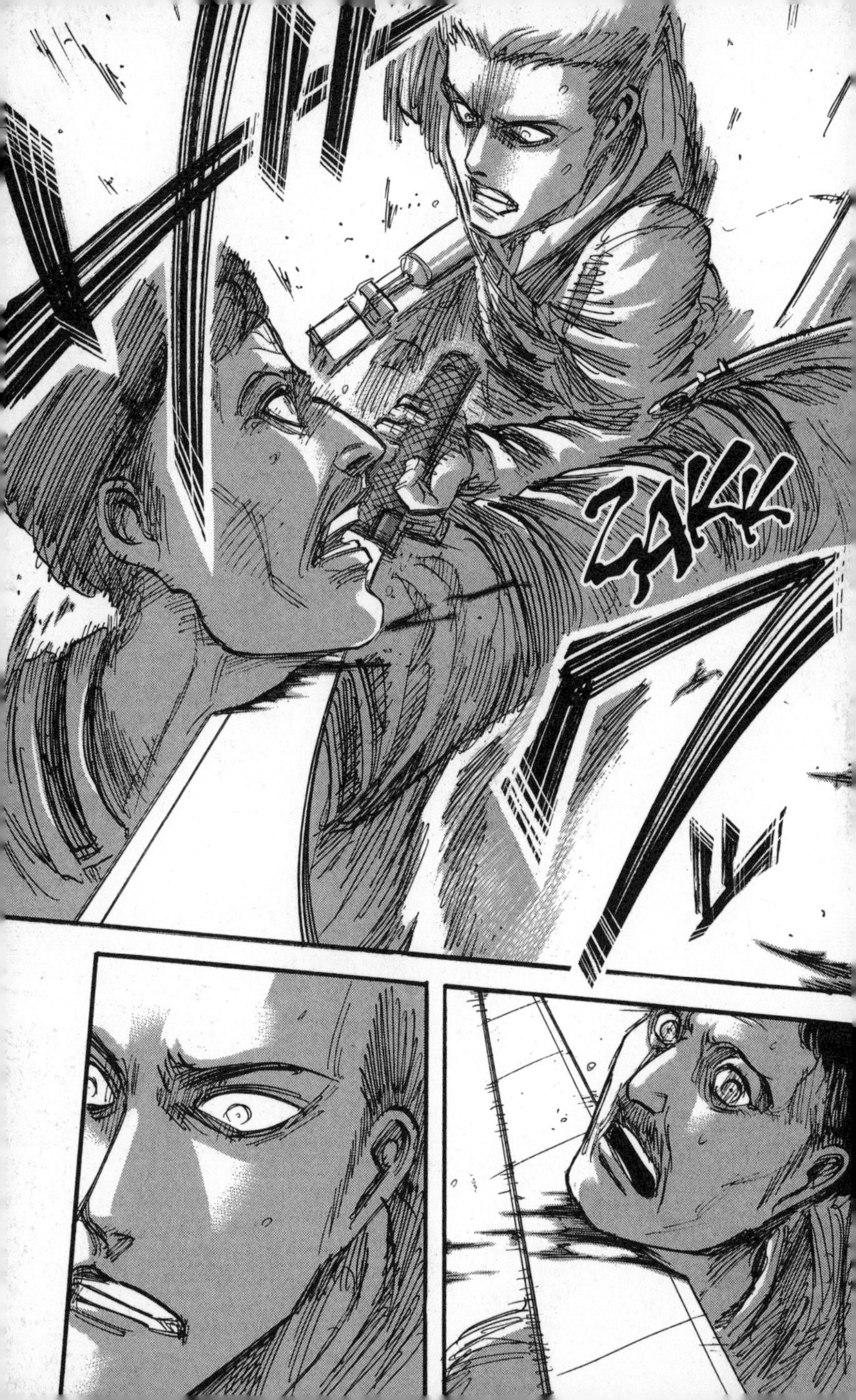
ZAKK

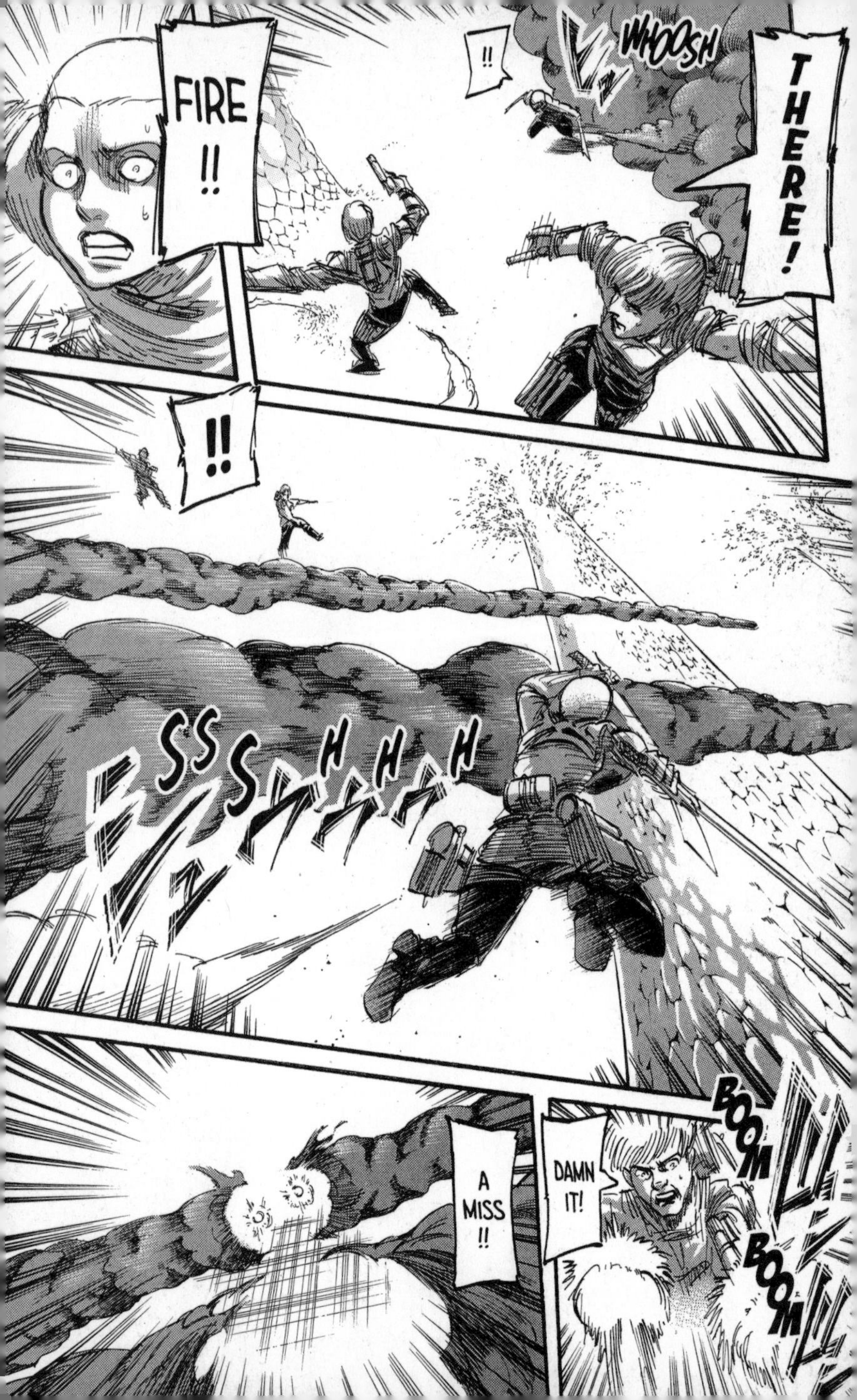
THERE!
WHOOSH
!!
FIRE !!
!!
SSSHHHH
BOOM
BOOM
DAMN IT!
A MISS !!

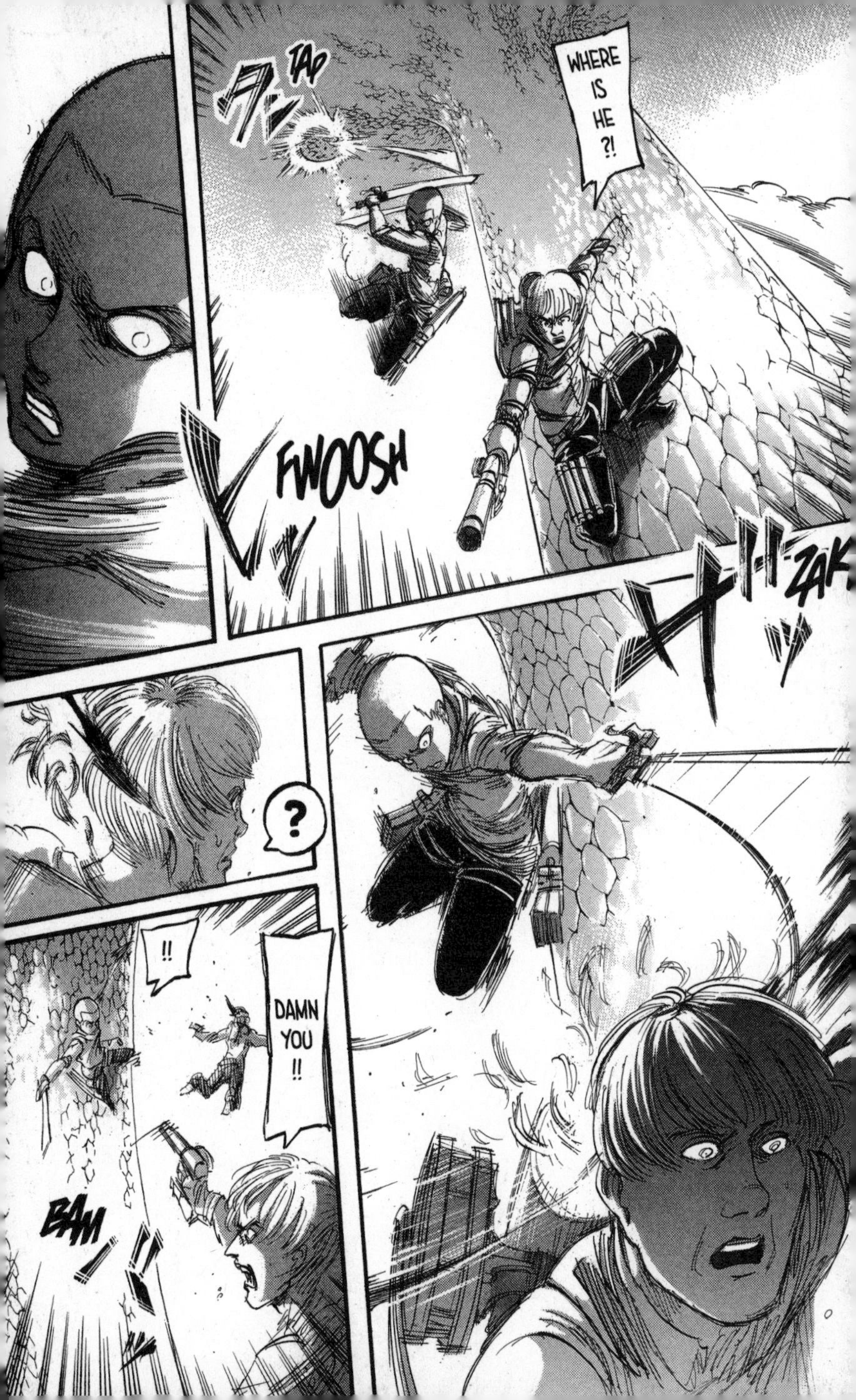
WHERE IS HE ?!
TAP
FWOOSH
ZAK
?
DAMN YOU !!
!!
BAM

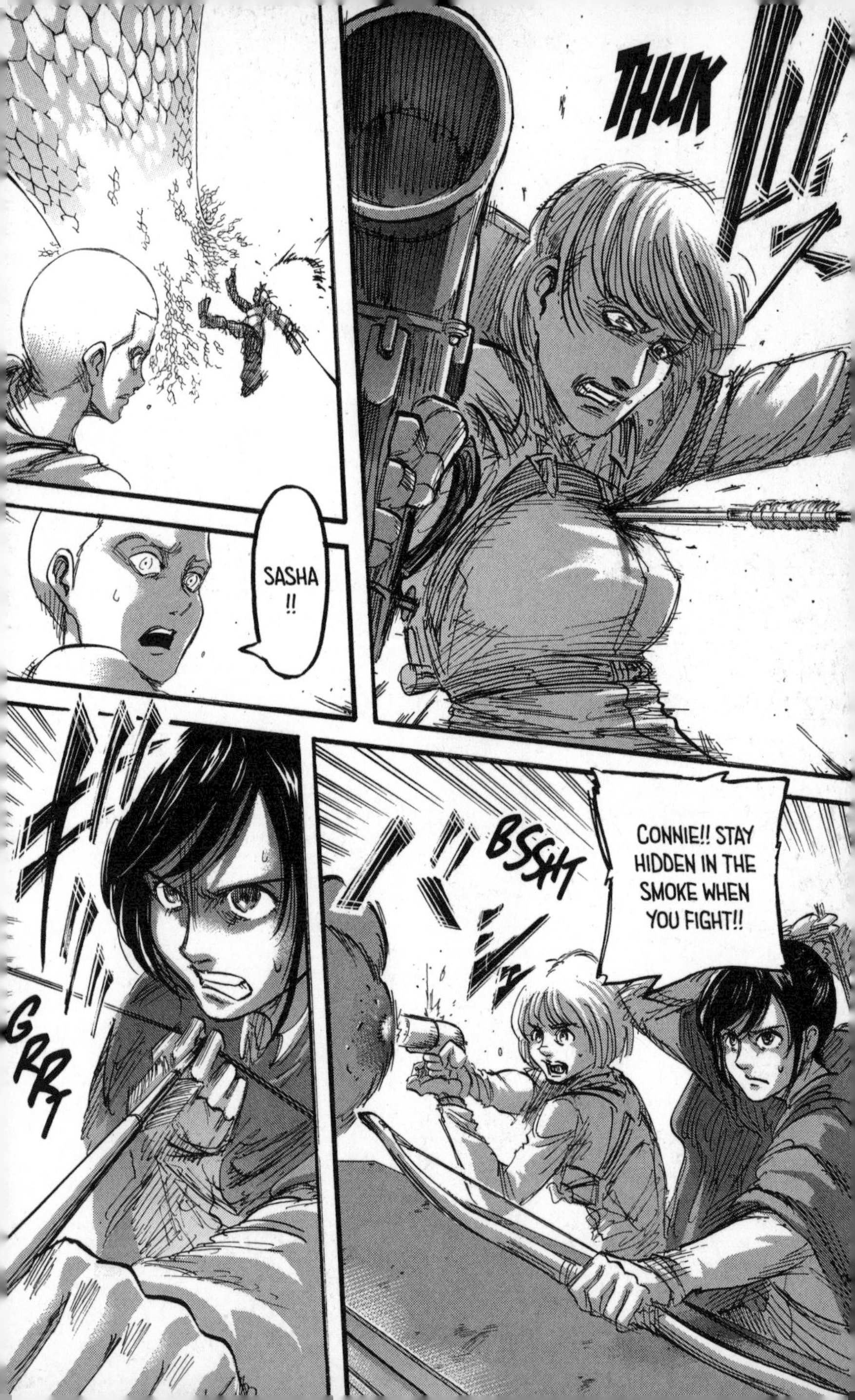
THUK
SASHA !!
BSSHT
CONNIE!! STAY HIDDEN IN THE SMOKE WHEN YOU FIGHT!!
GRR

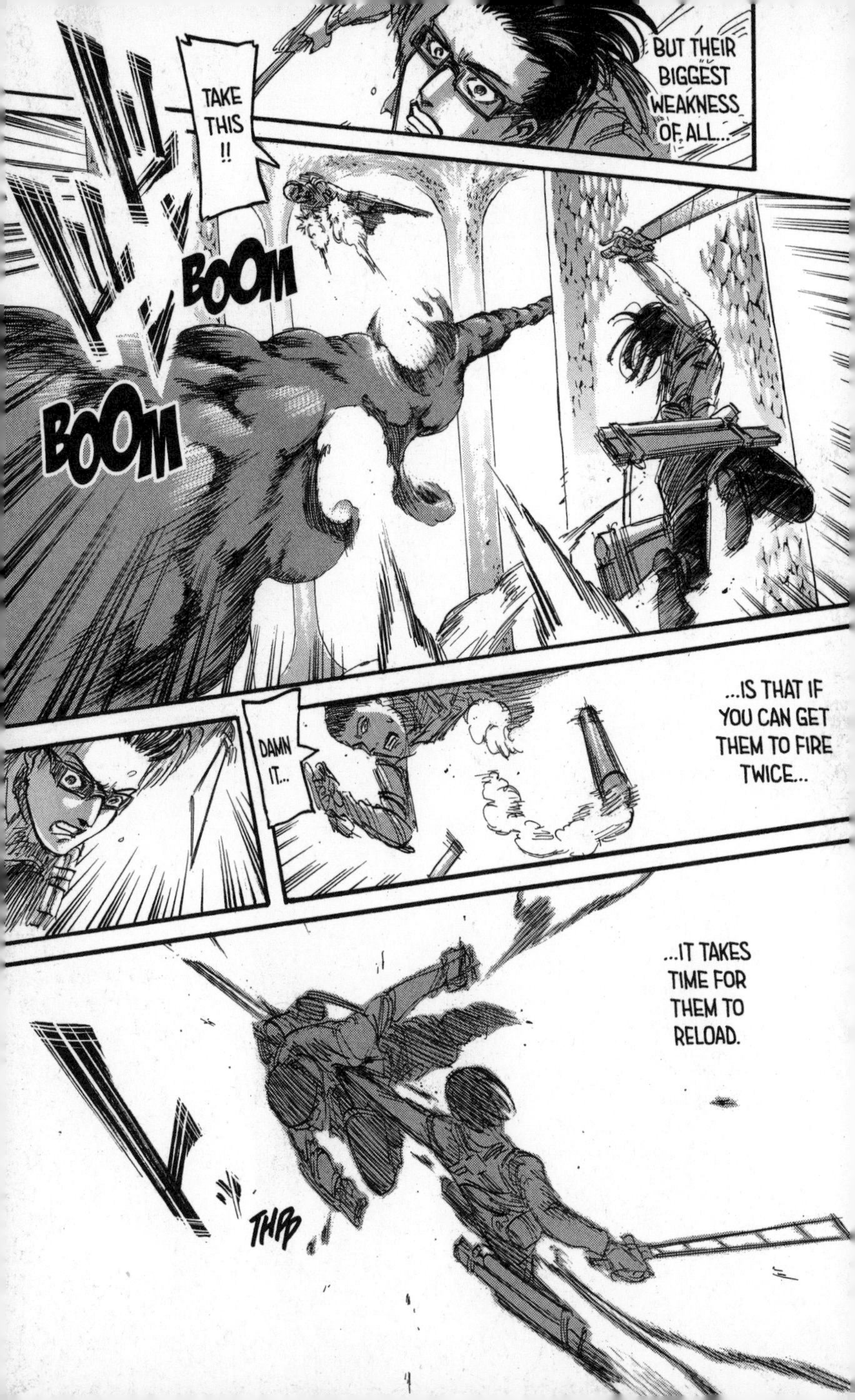
BUT THEIR BIGGEST WEAKNESS OF ALL...
TAKE THIS!!
BOOM
BOOM
...IS THAT IF YOU CAN GET THEM TO FIRE TWICE...
DAMN IT...
...IT TAKES TIME FOR THEM TO RELOAD.
THPP

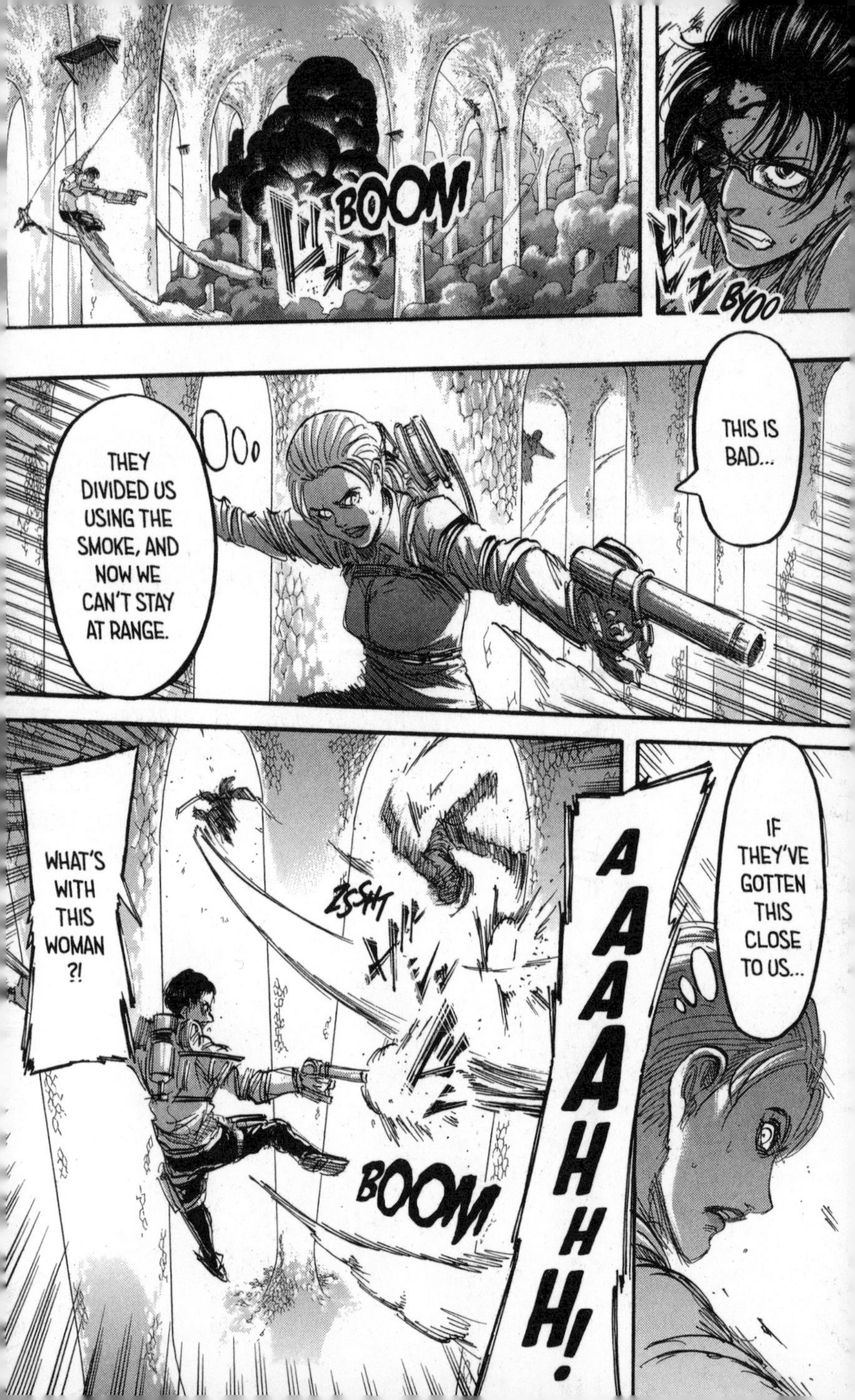
BYOO
BOOM
THIS IS BAD...
THEY DIVIDED US USING THE SMOKE, AND NOW WE CAN'T STAY AT RANGE.
IF THEY'VE GOTTEN THIS CLOSE TO US...
AAAAAHHHH!
ZSSHH
BOOM
WHAT'S WITH THIS WOMAN ?!

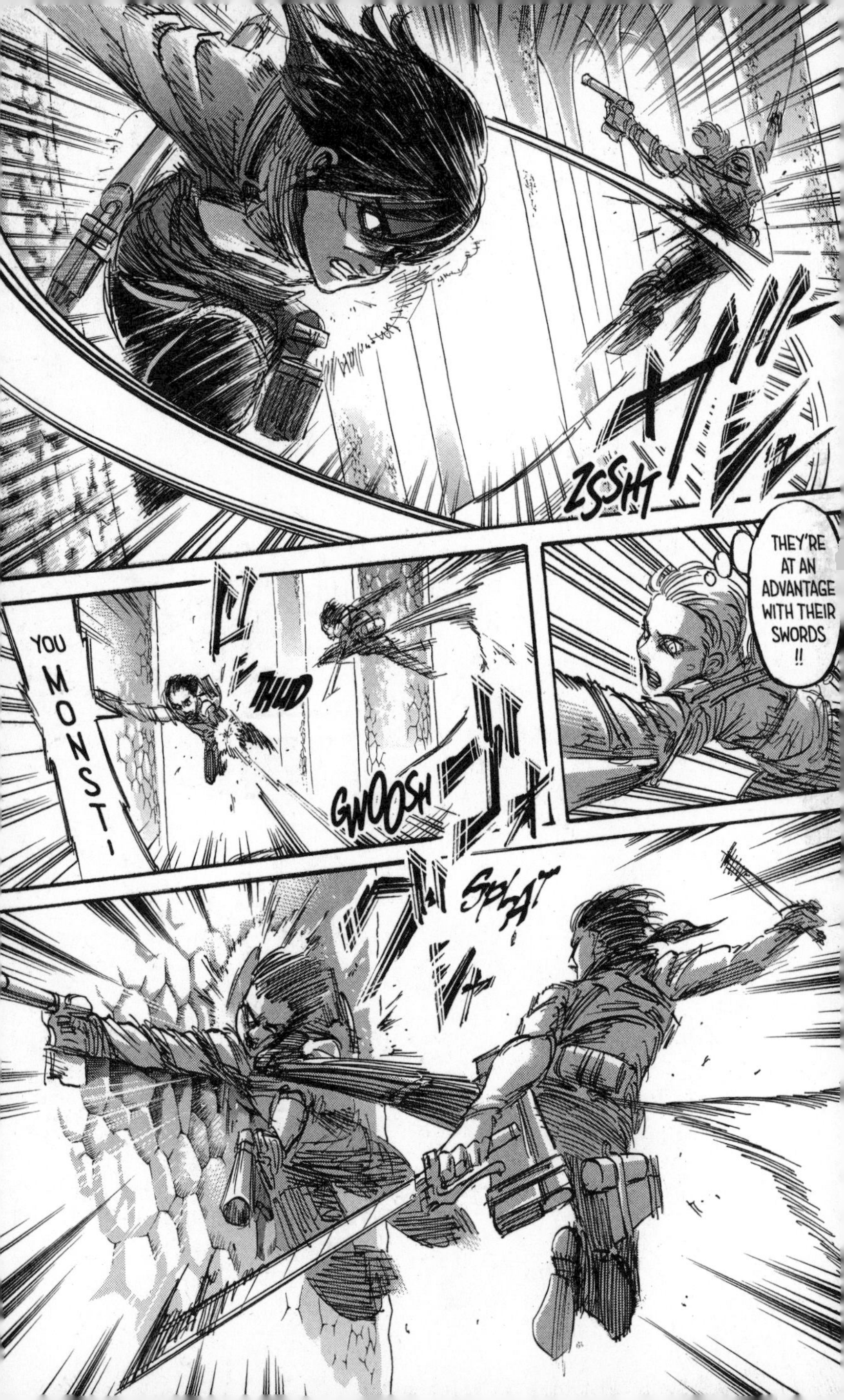
ZSSHT
THEY'RE AT AN ADVANTAGE WITH THEIR SWORDS !!
THUD
YOU MONST-
GWOOSH
SPLAT

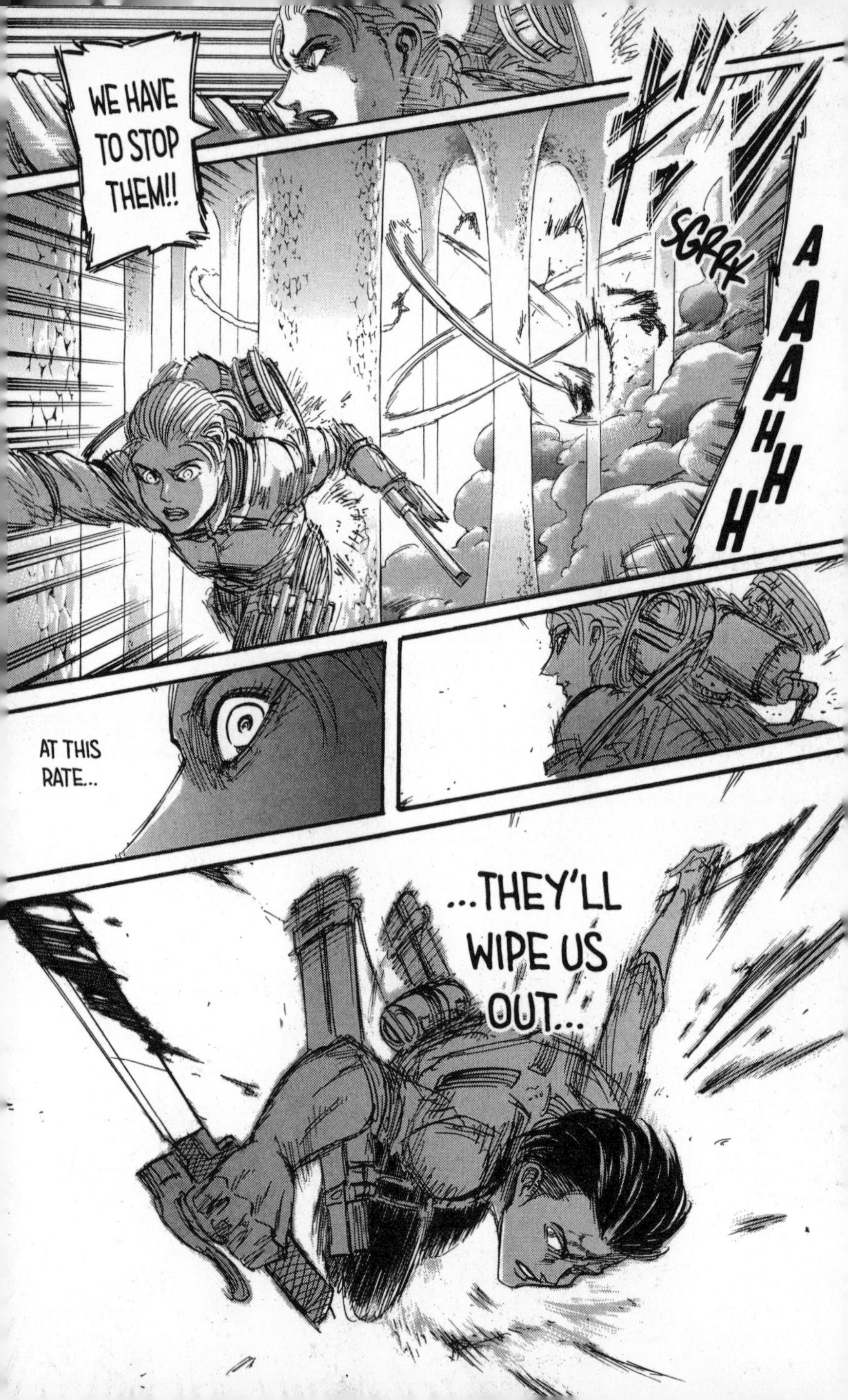
WE HAVE TO STOP THEM!!
SGRAK
AAAAHHHH
AT THIS RATE...
...THEY'LL WIPE US OUT...

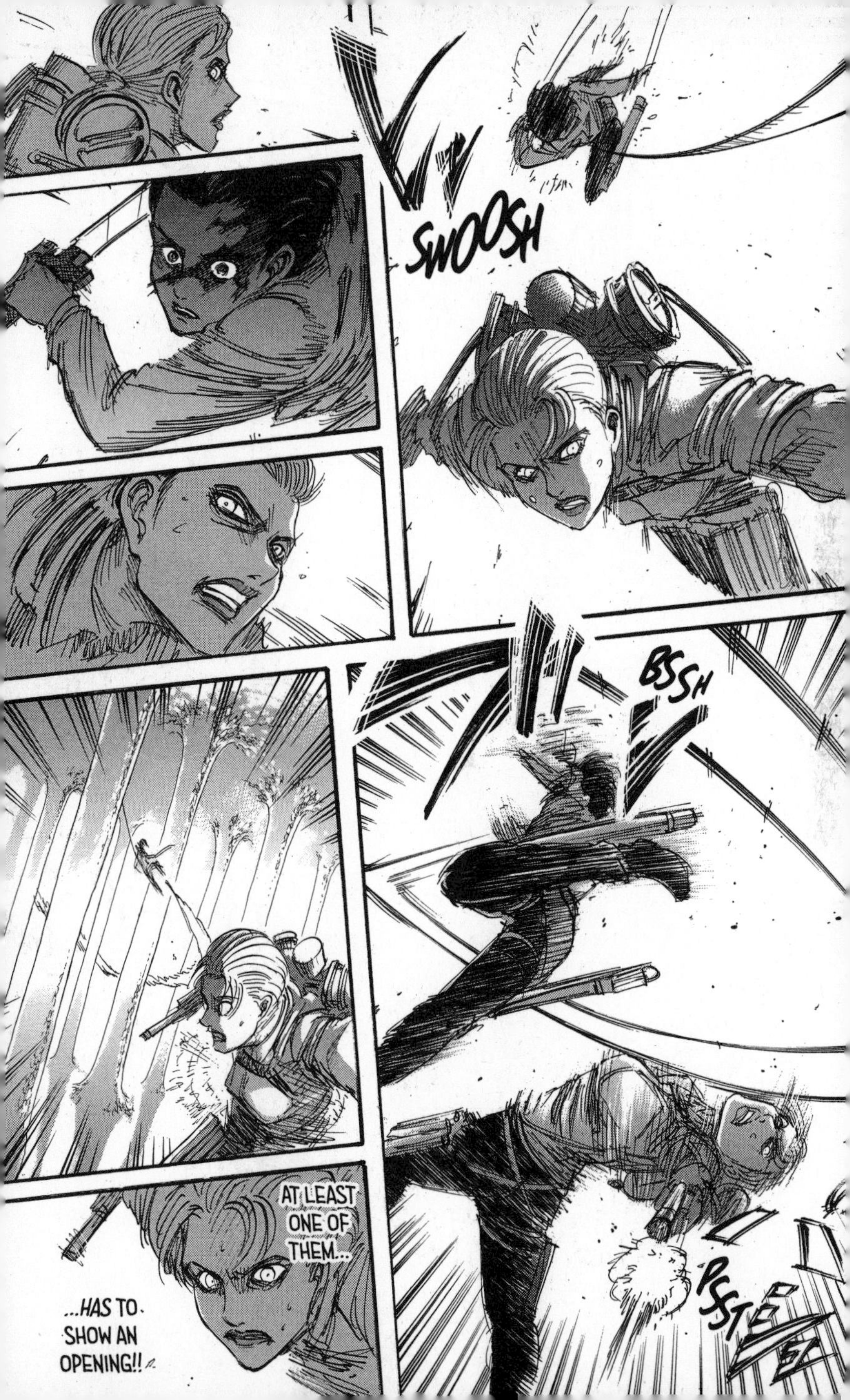
SWOOSH
BSSH
PST
AT LEAST ONE OF THEM...
...HAS TO SHOW AN OPENING!!

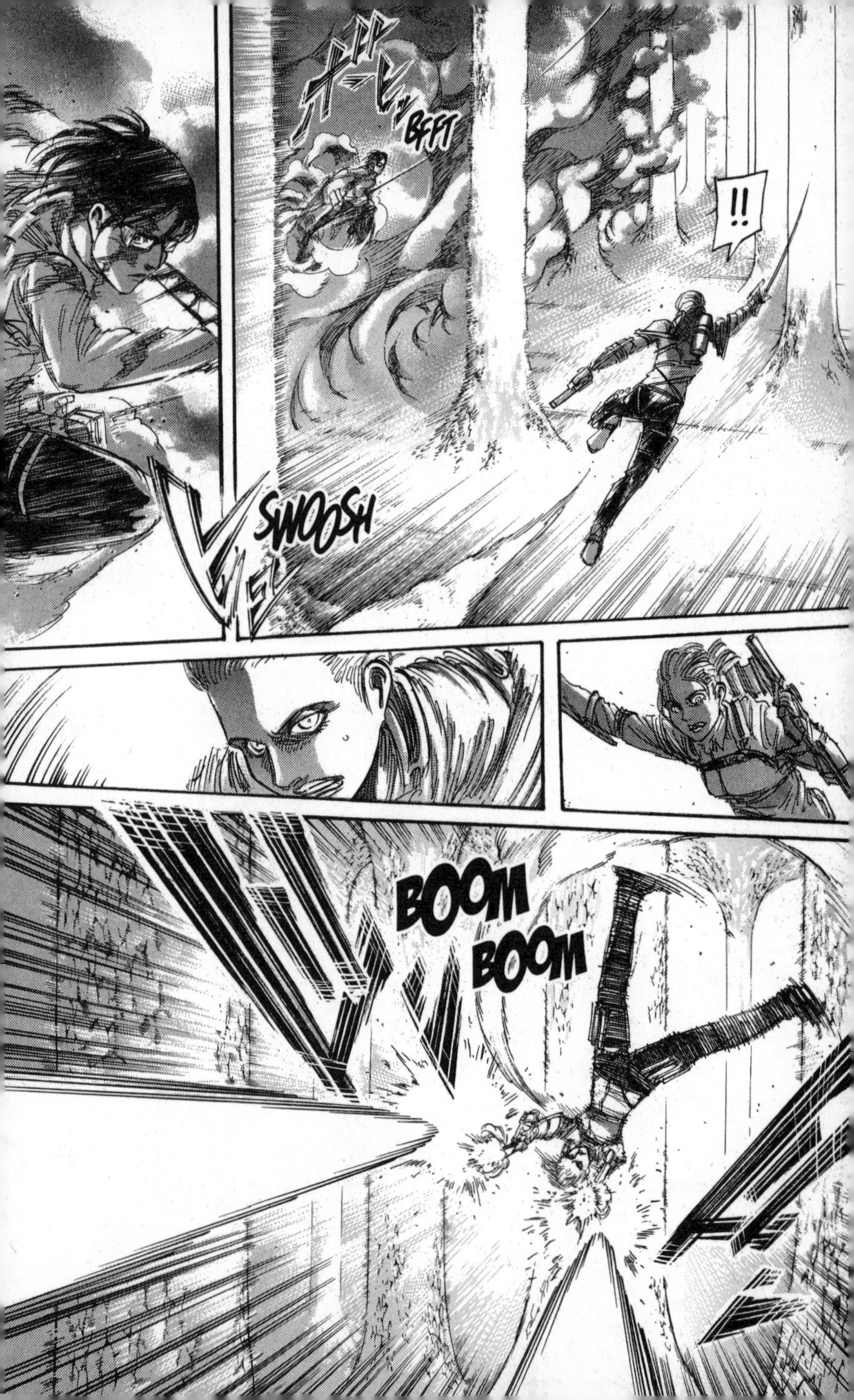
!!
BFFT
SWOOSH
BOOM
BOOM

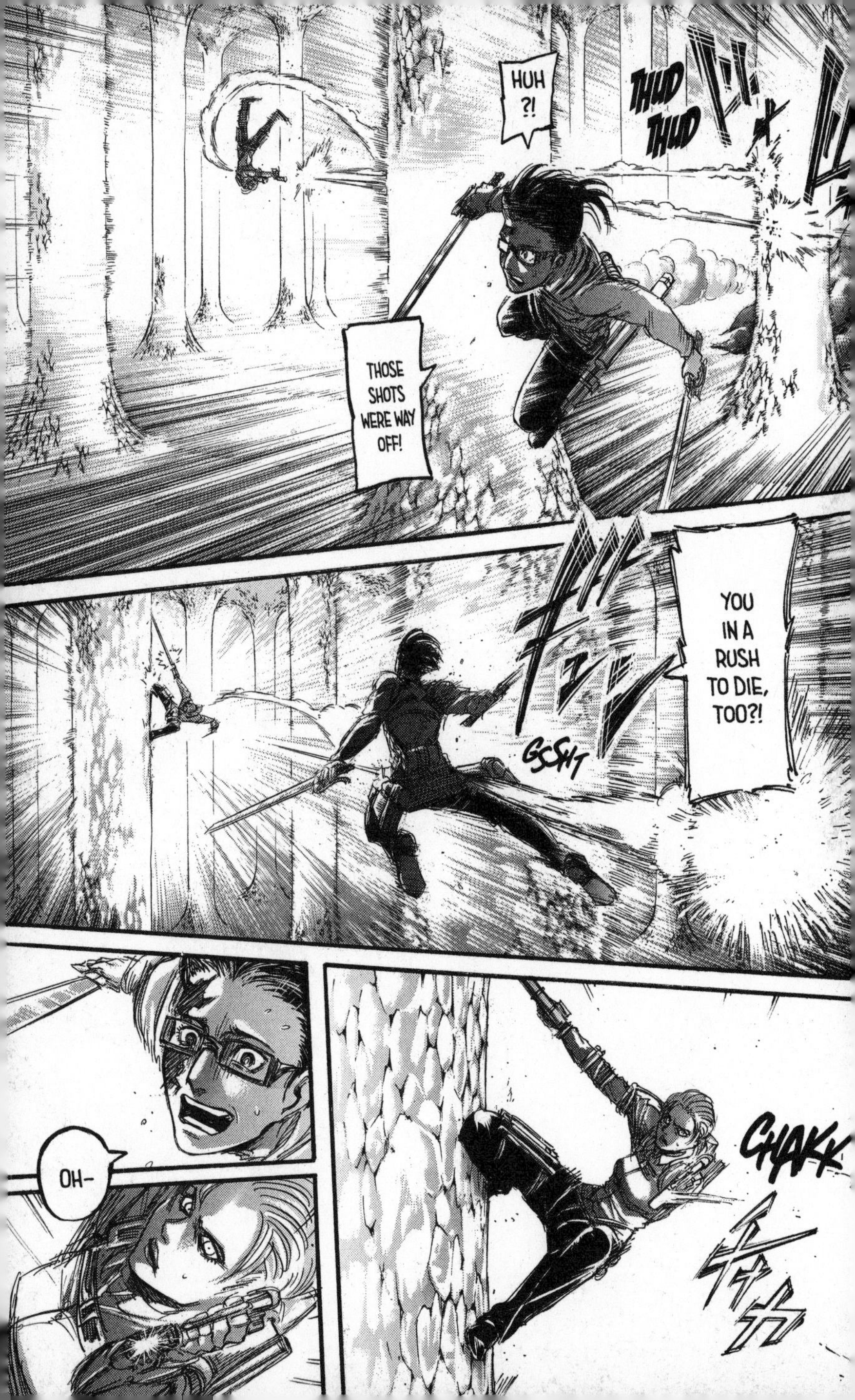
THUD THUD
HUH ?!
THOSE SHOTS WERE WAY OFF!
YOU IN A RUSH TO DIE, TOO?!
GSSHT
CHAKK
OH-

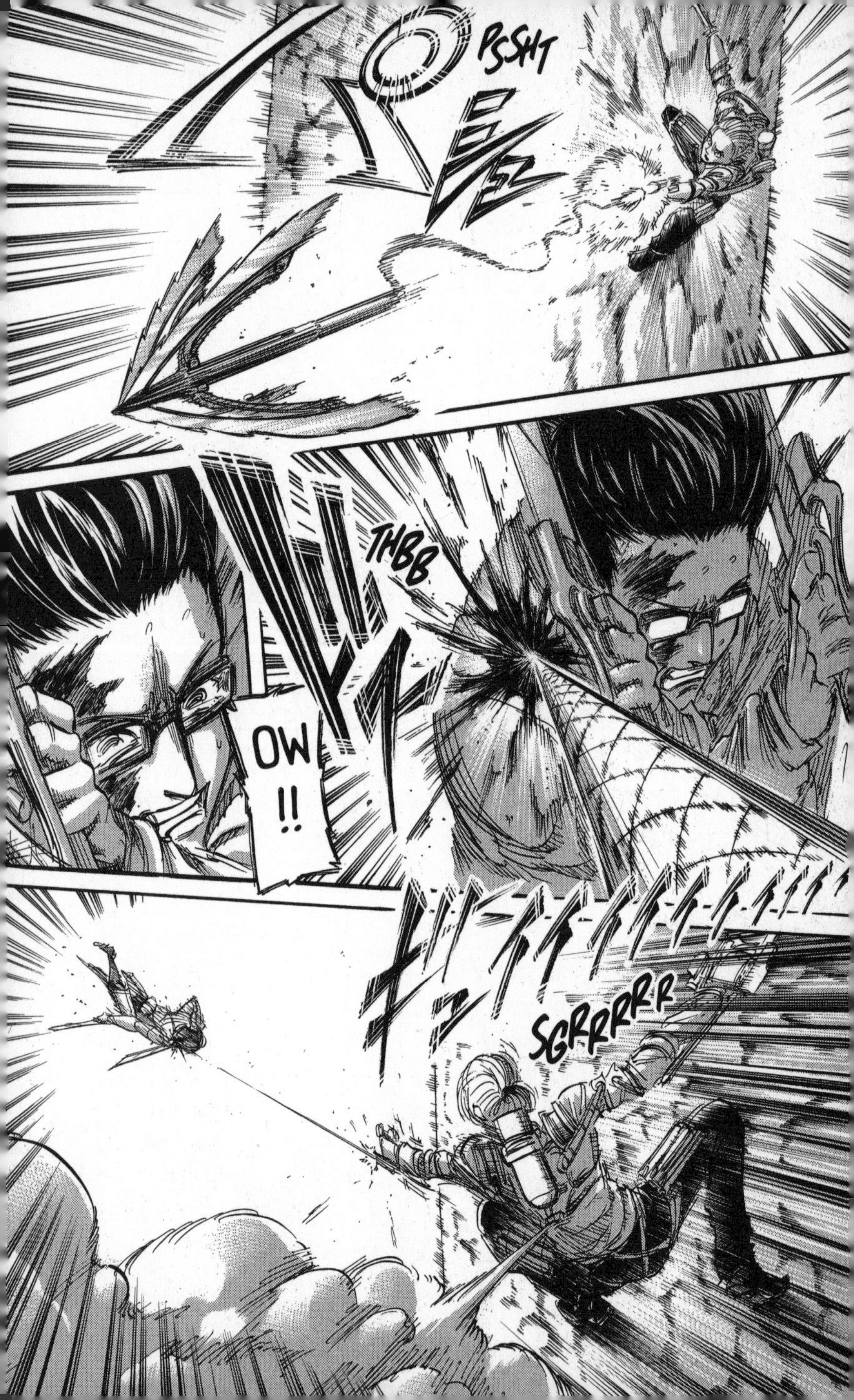
PSSHT
THBB
OW !!
SGRRRRR

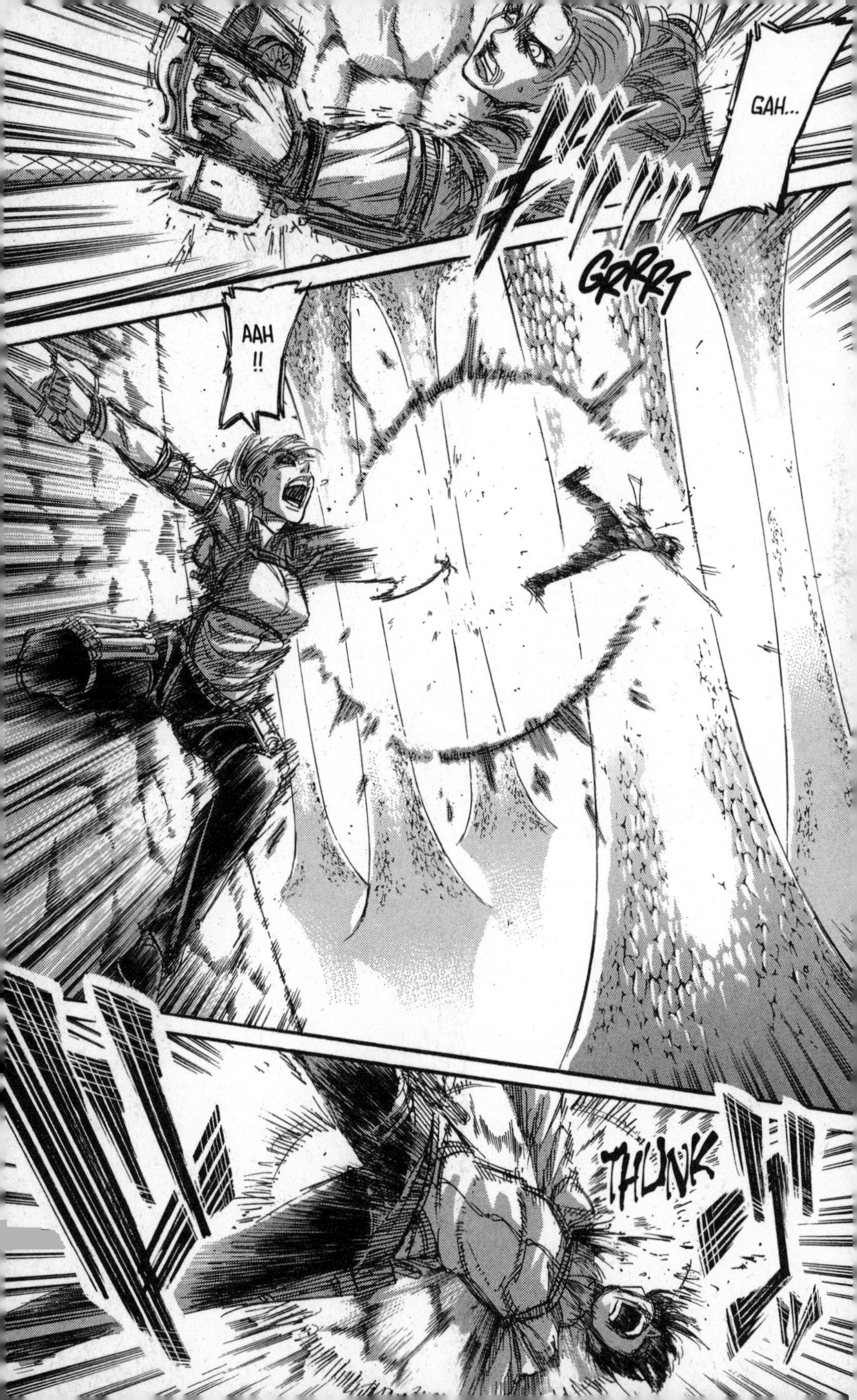
GAH...
GRRR
AAH !!
THUNK

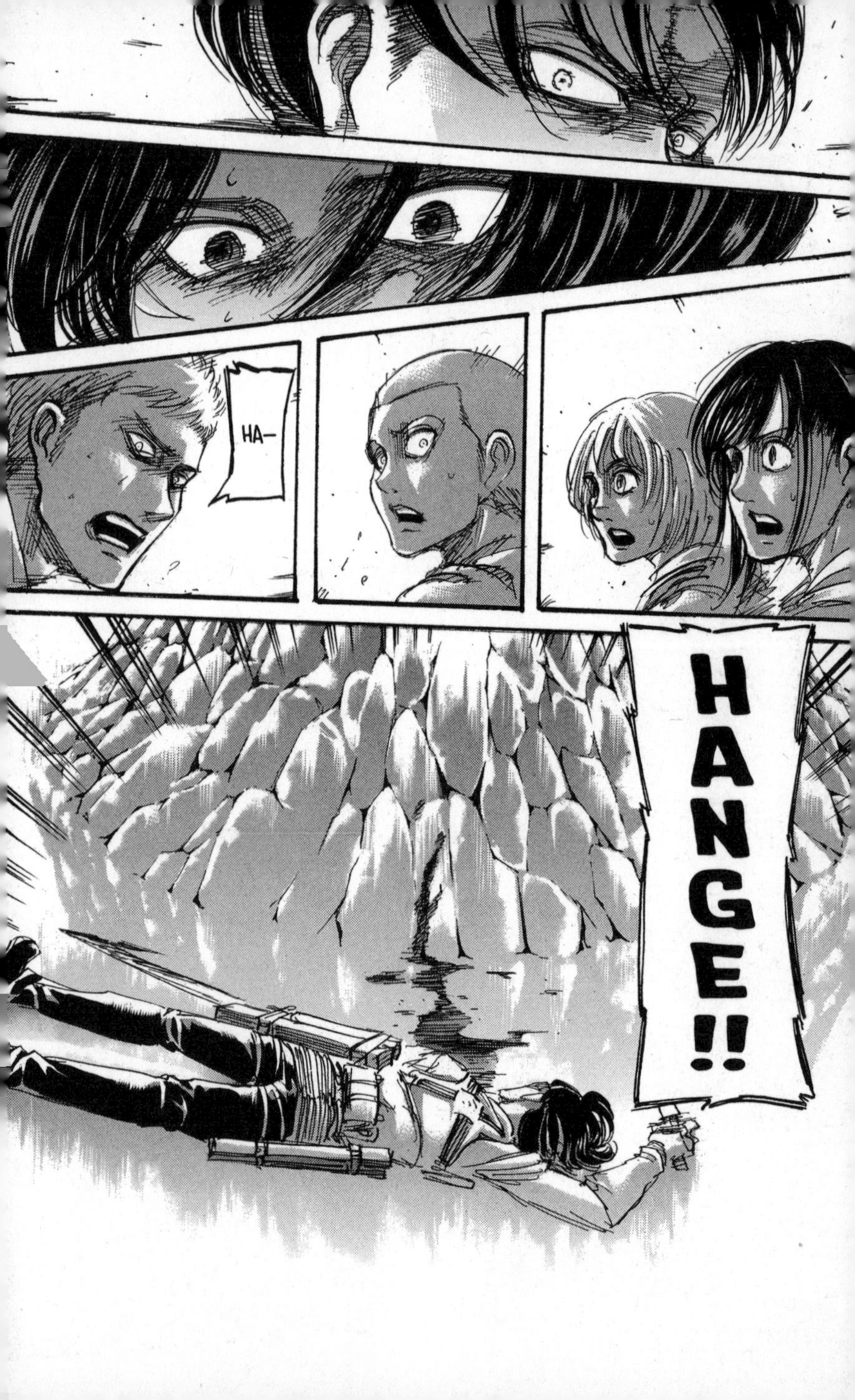
HA-
HANGE!!

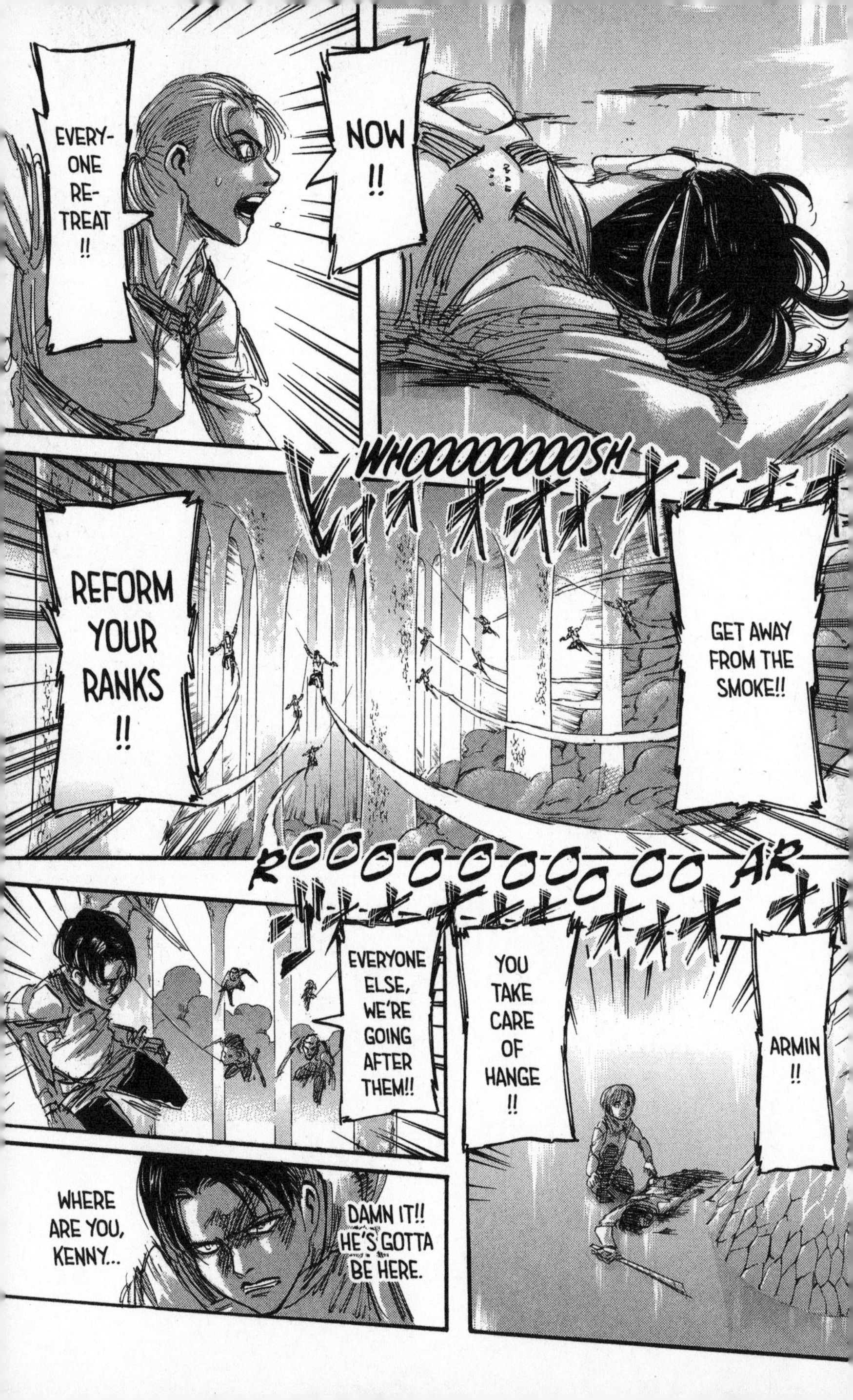
NOW!!
EVERY-ONE RE-TREAT!!
WHOOOOOOOOOSH
GET AWAY FROM THE SMOKE!!
REFORM YOUR RANKS!!
ROOOOOOOOOOOOAR
ARMIN!!
YOU TAKE CARE OF HANGE!!
EVERYONE ELSE, WE'RE GOING AFTER THEM!!
DAMN IT!! HE'S GOTTA BE HERE.
WHERE ARE YOU, KENNY...

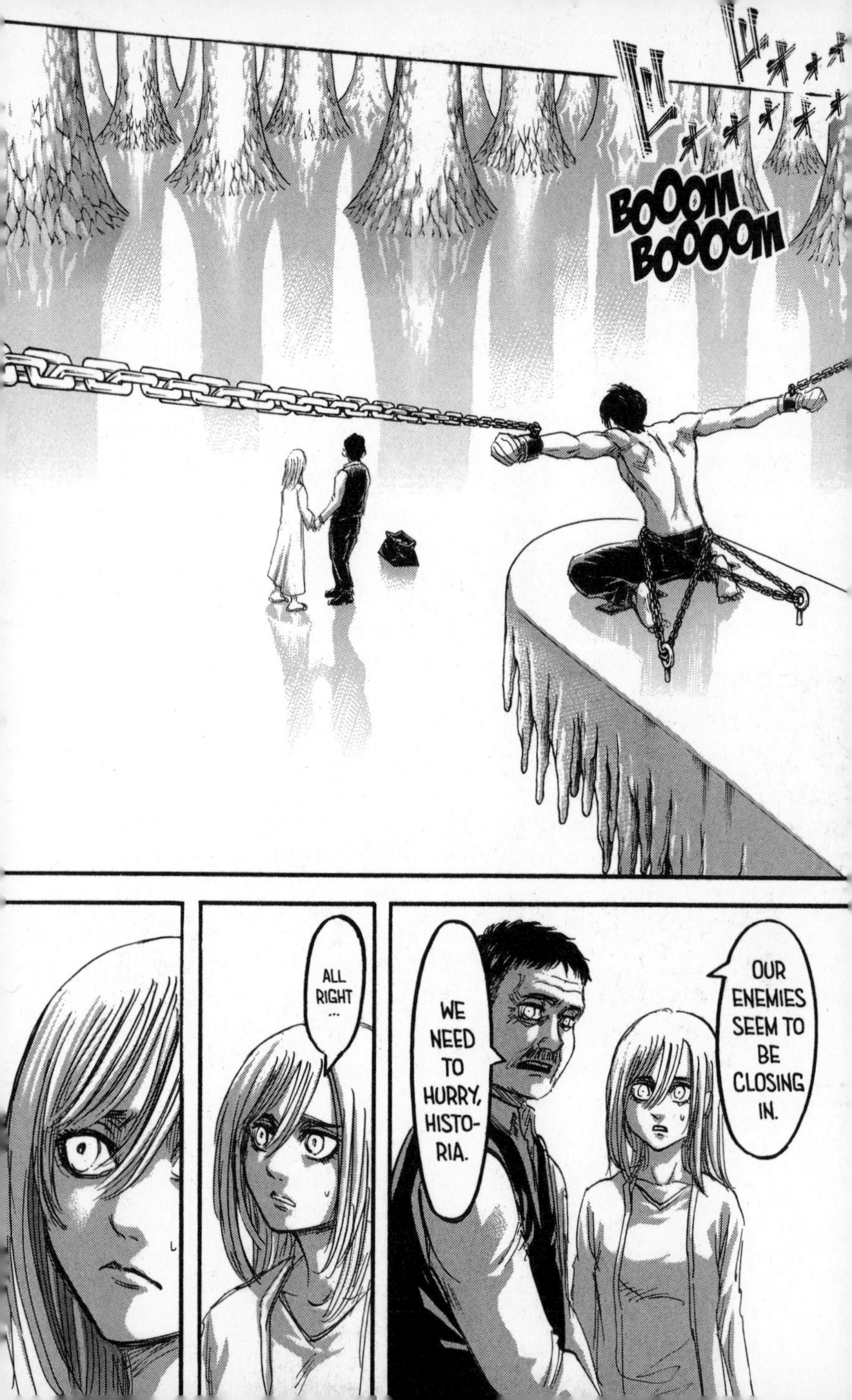
BOOOM
BOOOOM
OUR ENEMIES SEEM TO BE CLOSING IN.
WE NEED TO HURRY, HISTORIA.
ALL RIGHT ...

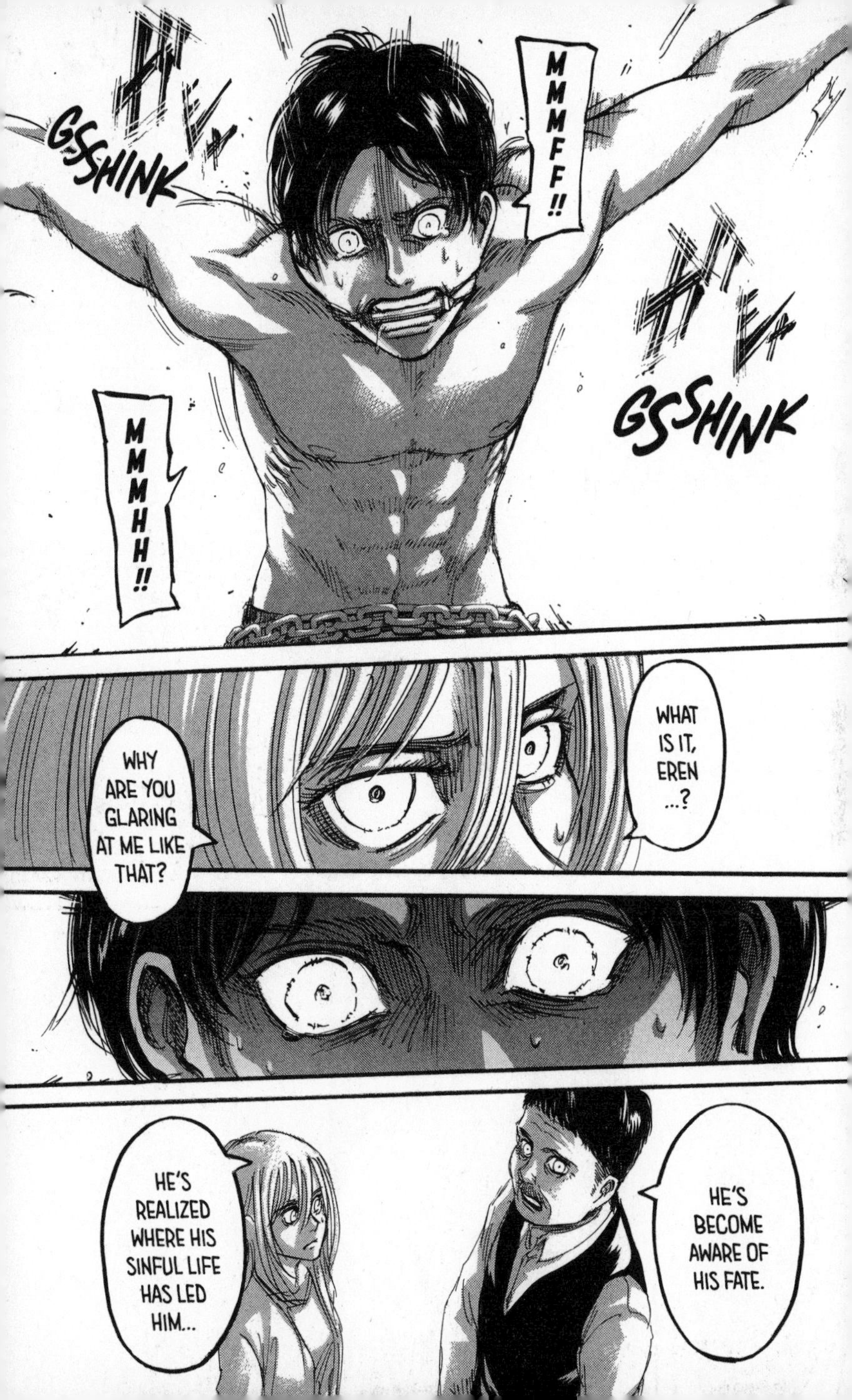
MMMFF!!
GSSHINK
GSSHINK
MMMHH!!
WHAT IS IT, EREN ...?
WHY ARE YOU GLARING AT ME LIKE THAT?
HE'S BECOME AWARE OF HIS FATE.
HE'S REALIZED WHERE HIS SINFUL LIFE HAS LED HIM...

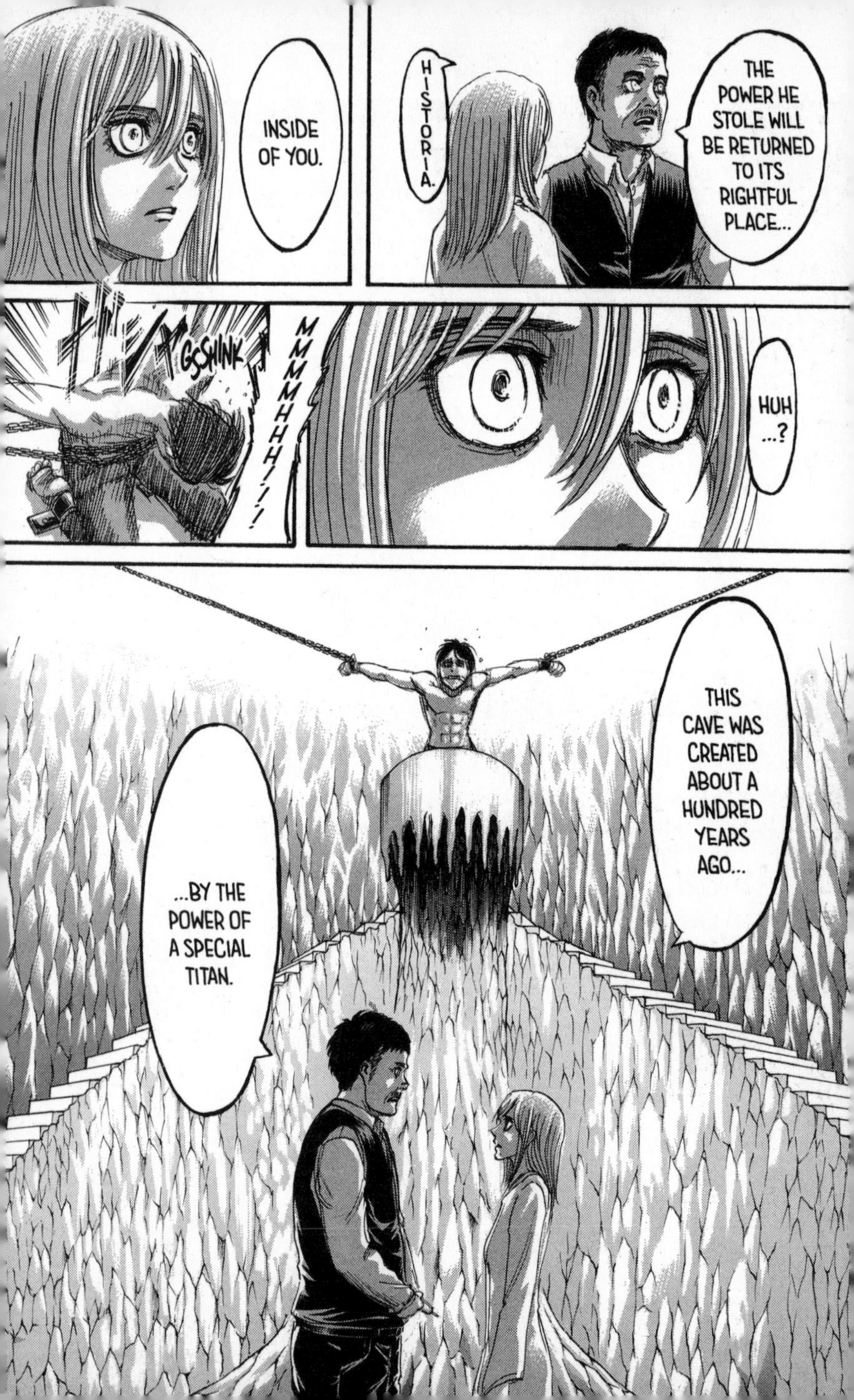
THE POWER HE STOLE WILL BE RETURNED TO ITS RIGHTFUL PLACE...
HISTORIA.
INSIDE OF YOU.
HUH ...?
GSSHINK
MMMMHHH!!!
THIS CAVE WAS CREATED ABOUT A HUNDRED YEARS AGO...
...BY THE POWER OF A SPECIAL TITAN.

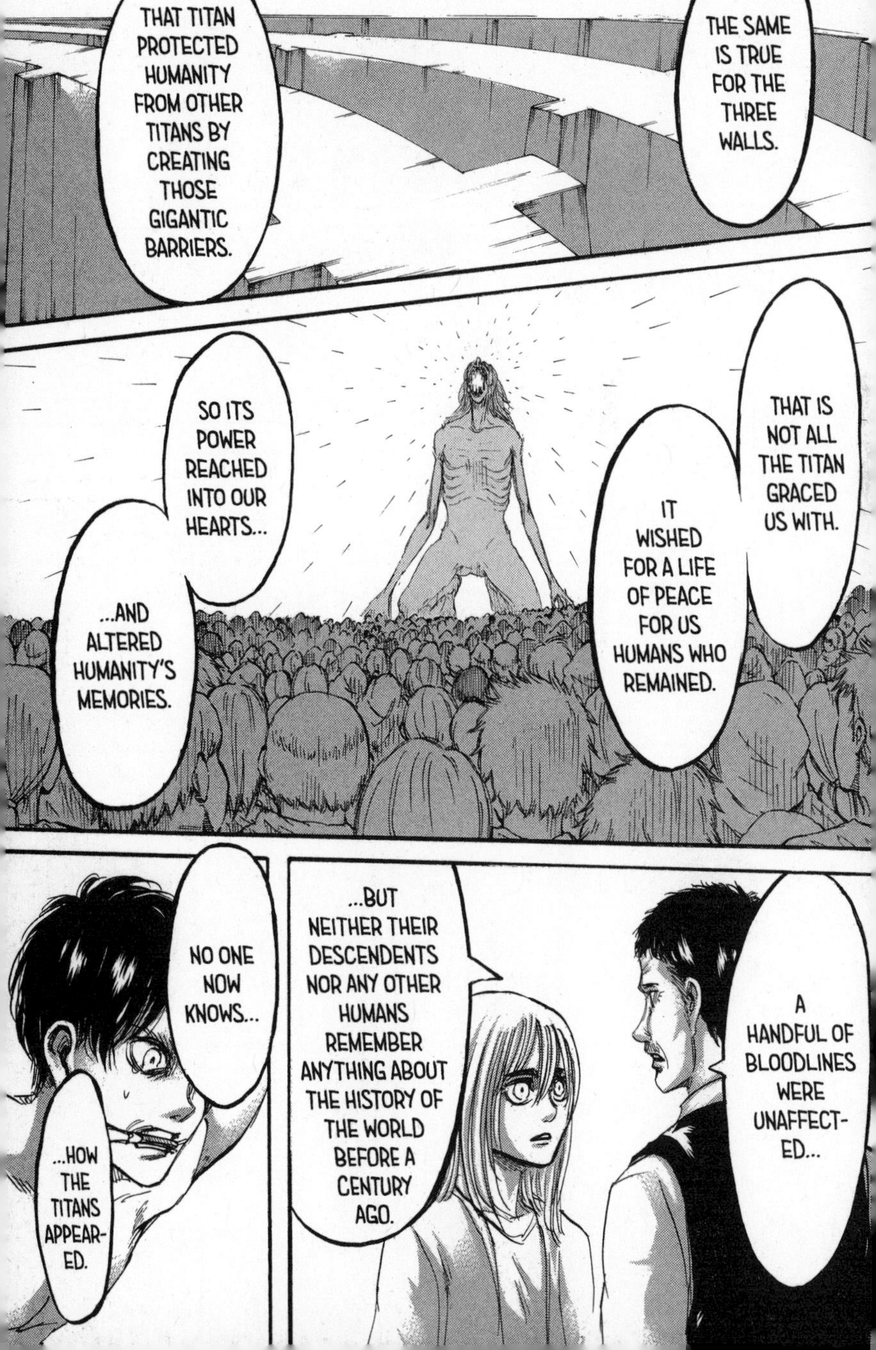
THE SAME IS TRUE FOR THE THREE WALLS.
THAT TITAN PROTECTED HUMANITY FROM OTHER TITANS BY CREATING THOSE GIGANTIC BARRIERS.
THAT IS NOT ALL THE TITAN GRACED US WITH.
IT WISHED FOR A LIFE OF PEACE FOR US HUMANS WHO REMAINED.
SO ITS POWER REACHED INTO OUR HEARTS...
...AND ALTERED HUMANITY'S MEMORIES.
A HANDFUL OF BLOODLINES WERE UNAFFECT-ED...
...BUT NEITHER THEIR DESCENDENTS NOR ANY OTHER HUMANS REMEMBER ANYTHING ABOUT THE HISTORY OF THE WORLD BEFORE A CENTURY AGO.
NO ONE NOW KNOWS...
...HOW THE TITANS APPEAR-ED.

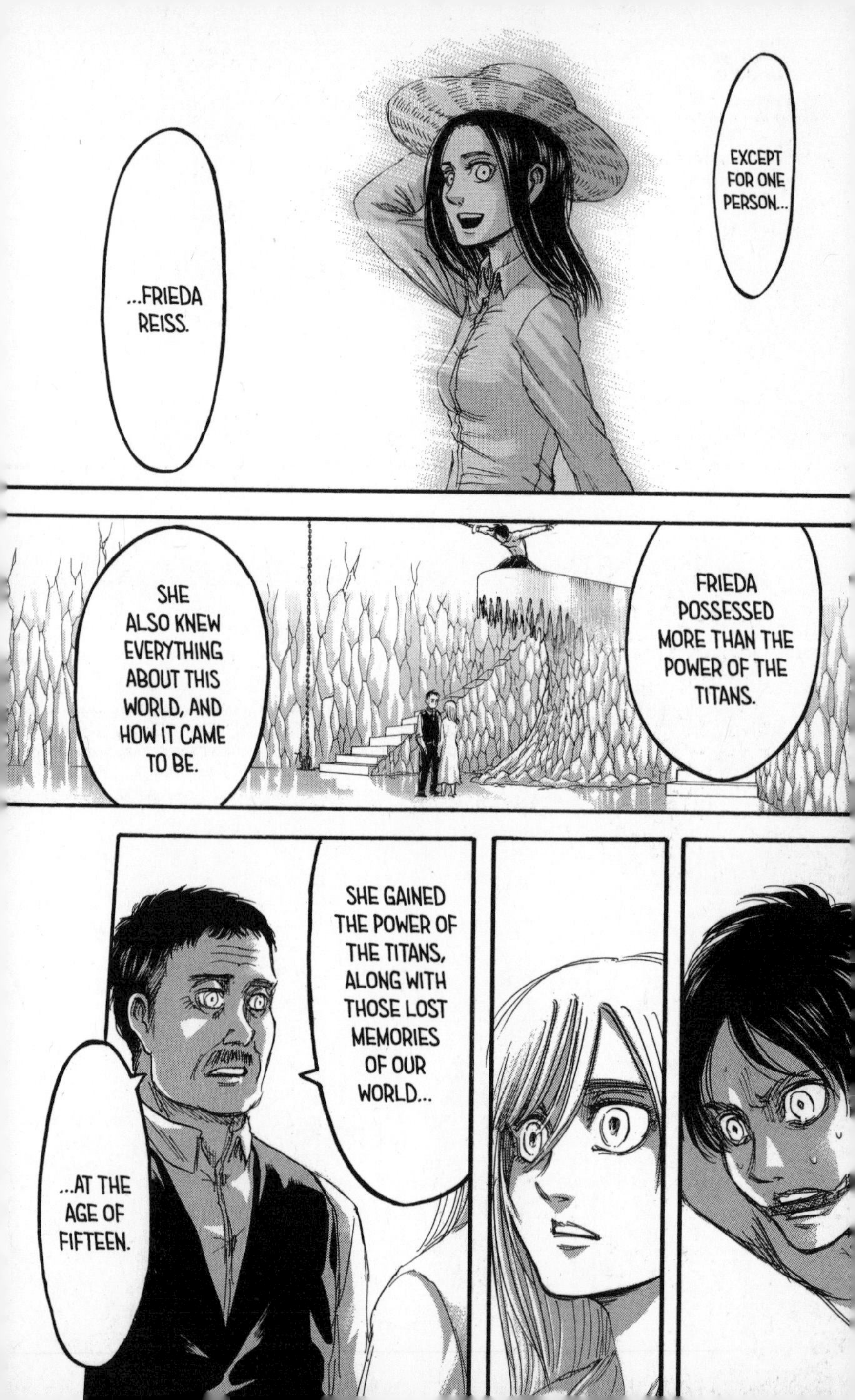
EXCEPT FOR ONE PERSON...
...FRIEDA REISS.
FRIEDA POSSESSED MORE THAN THE POWER OF THE TITANS.
SHE ALSO KNEW EVERYTHING ABOUT THIS WORLD, AND HOW IT CAME TO BE.
SHE GAINED THE POWER OF THE TITANS, ALONG WITH THOSE LOST MEMORIES OF OUR WORLD...
...AT THE AGE OF FIFTEEN.

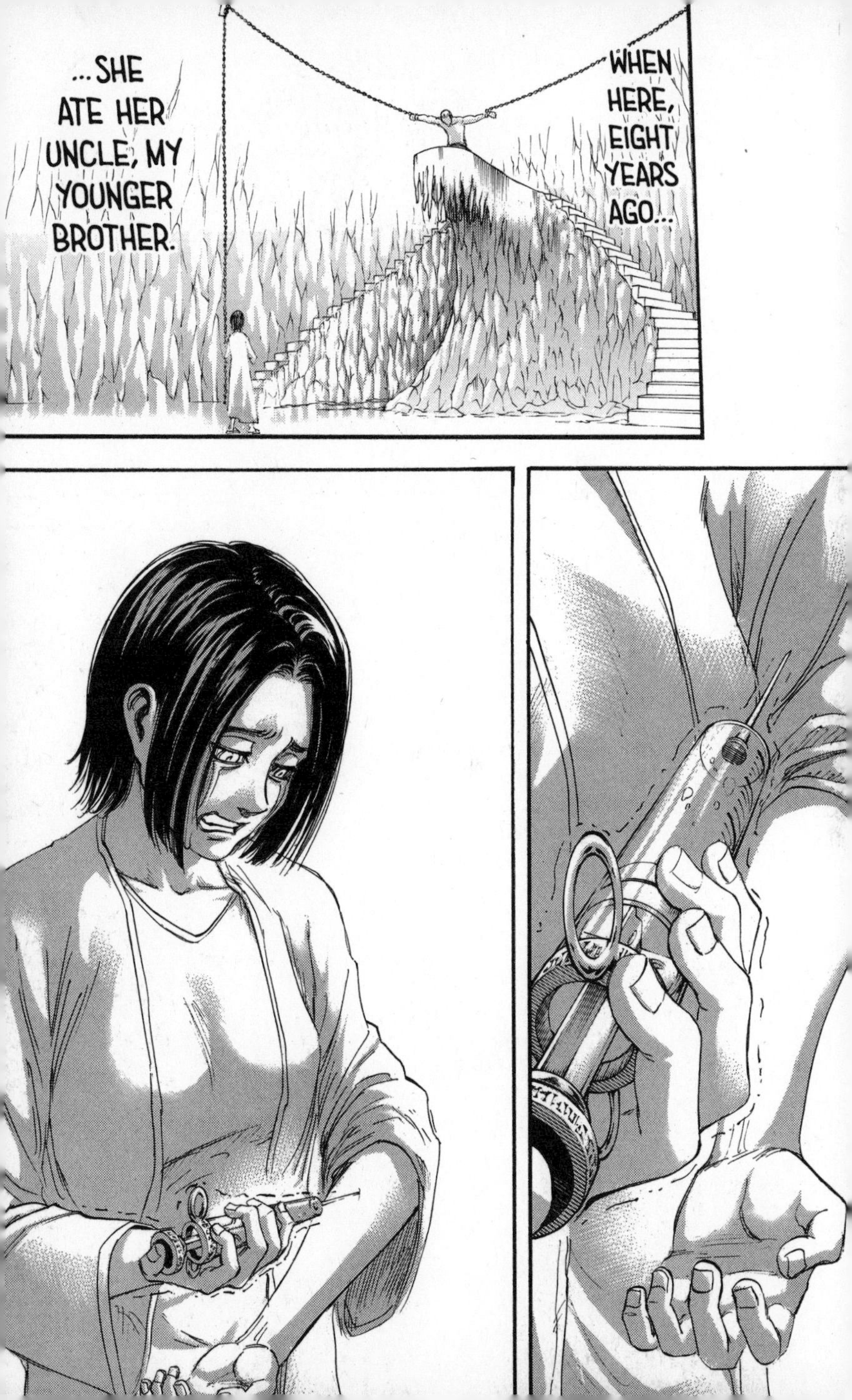
WHEN HERE, EIGHT YEARS AGO...
...SHE ATE HER UNCLE, MY YOUNGER BROTHER.

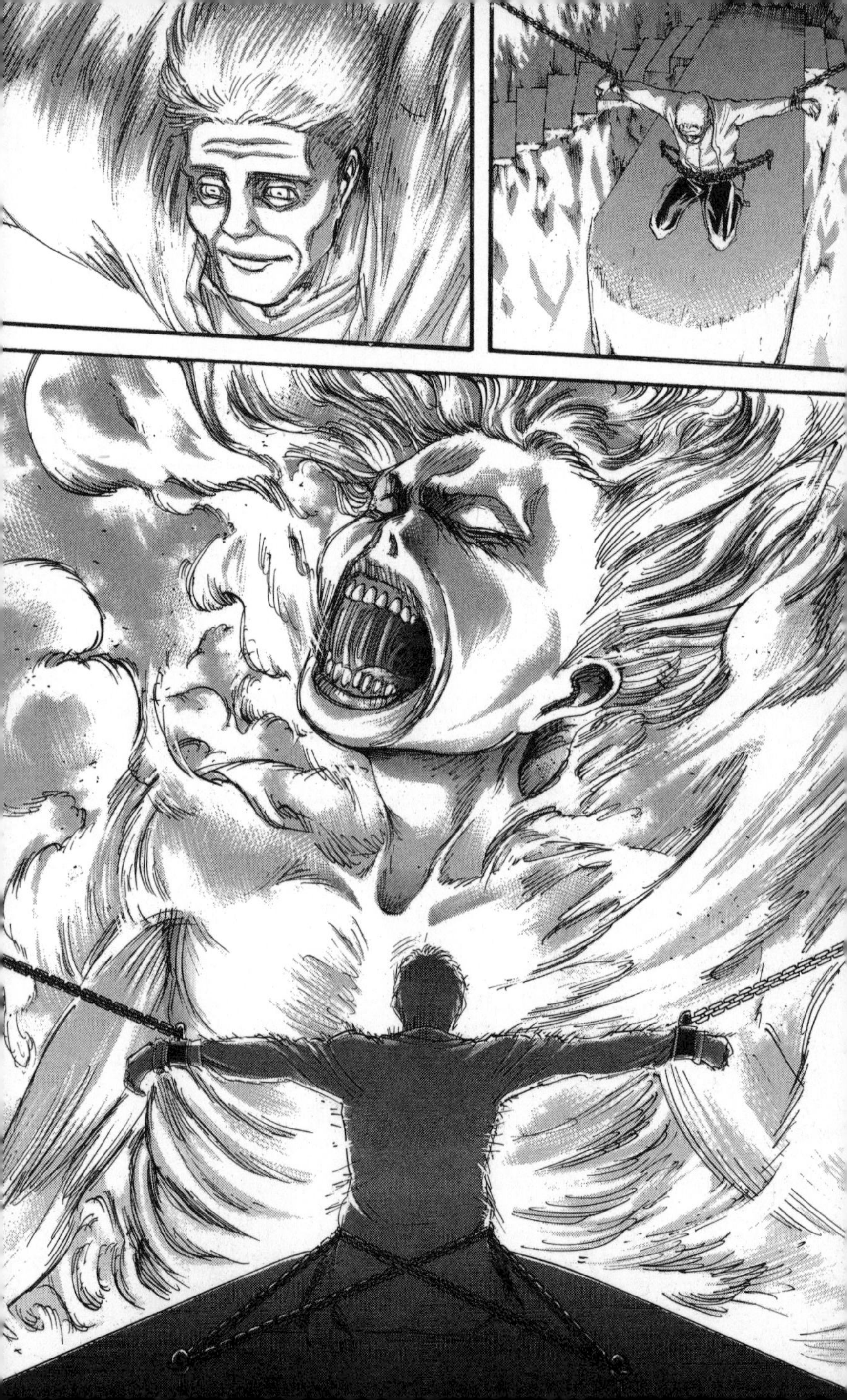

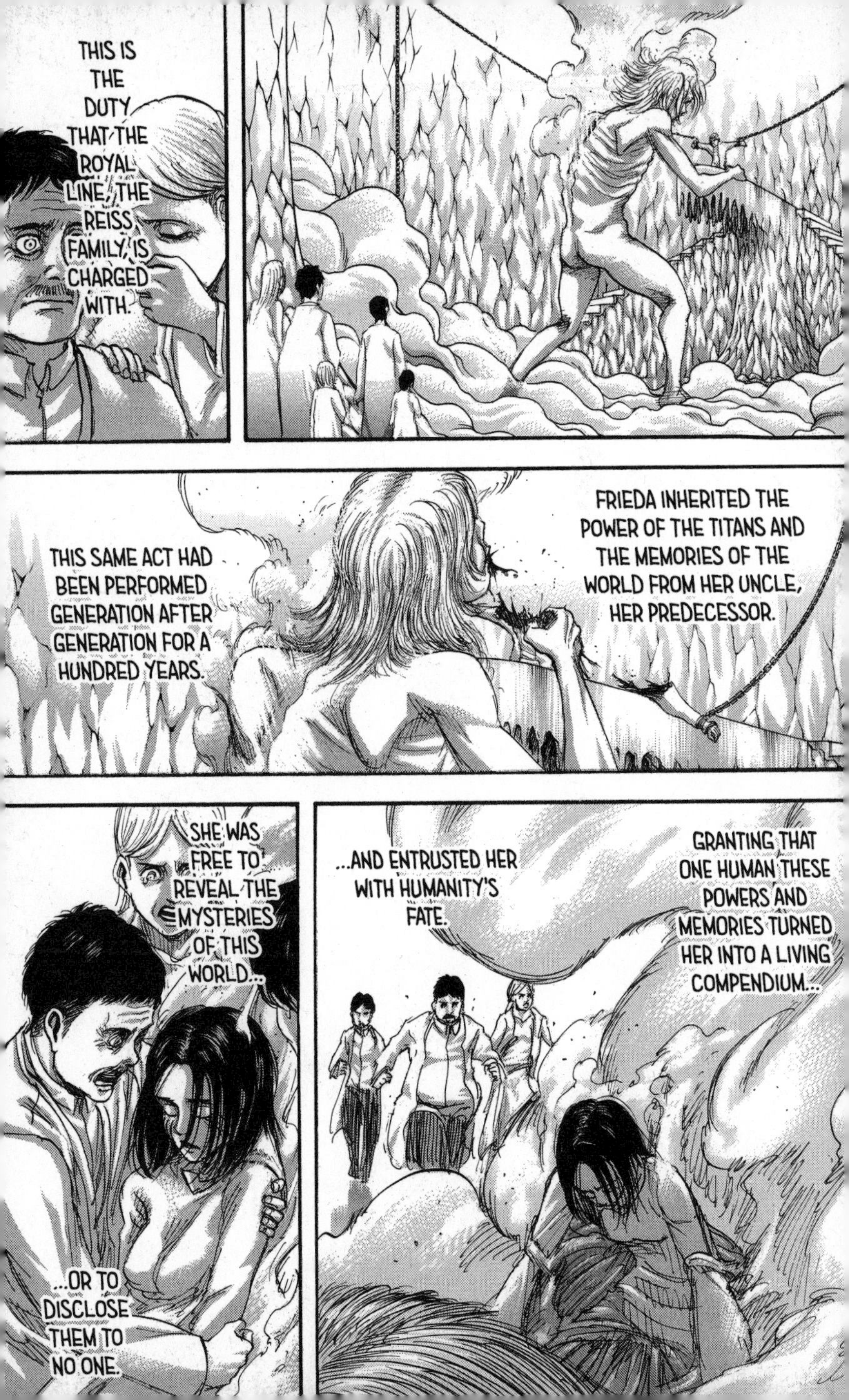
THIS IS THE DUTY THAT THE ROYAL LINE, THE REISS FAMILY, IS CHARGED WITH.
FRIEDA INHERITED THE POWER OF THE TITANS AND THE MEMORIES OF THE WORLD FROM HER UNCLE, HER PREDECESSOR.
THIS SAME ACT HAD BEEN PERFORMED GENERATION AFTER GENERATION FOR A HUNDRED YEARS.
GRANTING THAT ONE HUMAN THESE POWERS AND MEMORIES TURNED HER INTO A LIVING COMPENDIUM...
...AND ENTRUSTED HER WITH HUMANITY'S FATE.
SHE WAS FREE TO REVEAL THE MYSTERIES OF THIS WORLD...
...OR TO DISCLOSE THEM TO NO ONE.

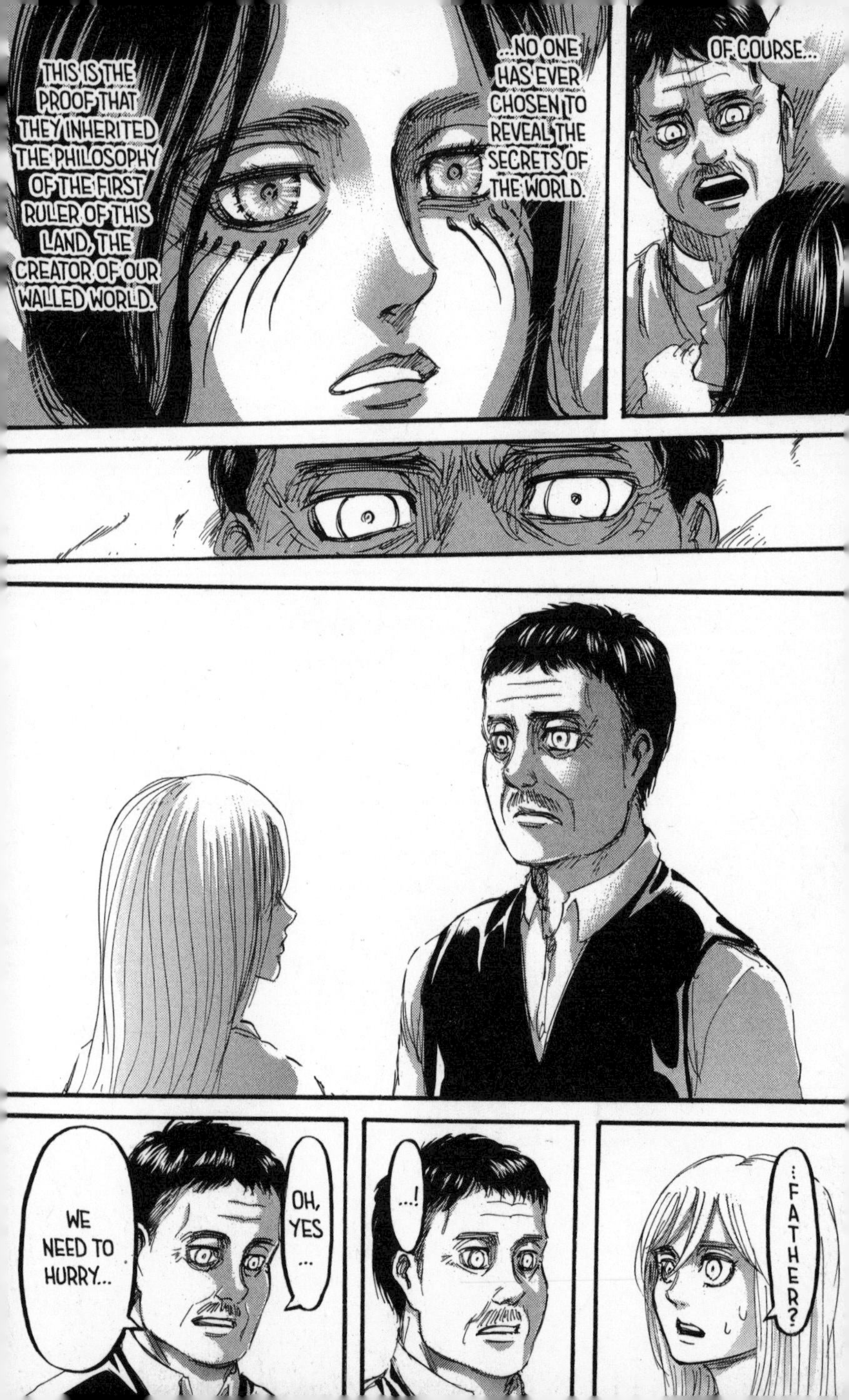
OF COURSE...
...NO ONE HAS EVER CHOSEN TO REVEAL THE SECRETS OF THE WORLD.
THIS IS THE PROOF THAT THEY INHERITED THE PHILOSOPHY OF THE FIRST RULER OF THIS LAND, THE CREATOR OF OUR WALLED WORLD.
...FATHER?
...!
OH, YES ...
WE NEED TO HURRY...

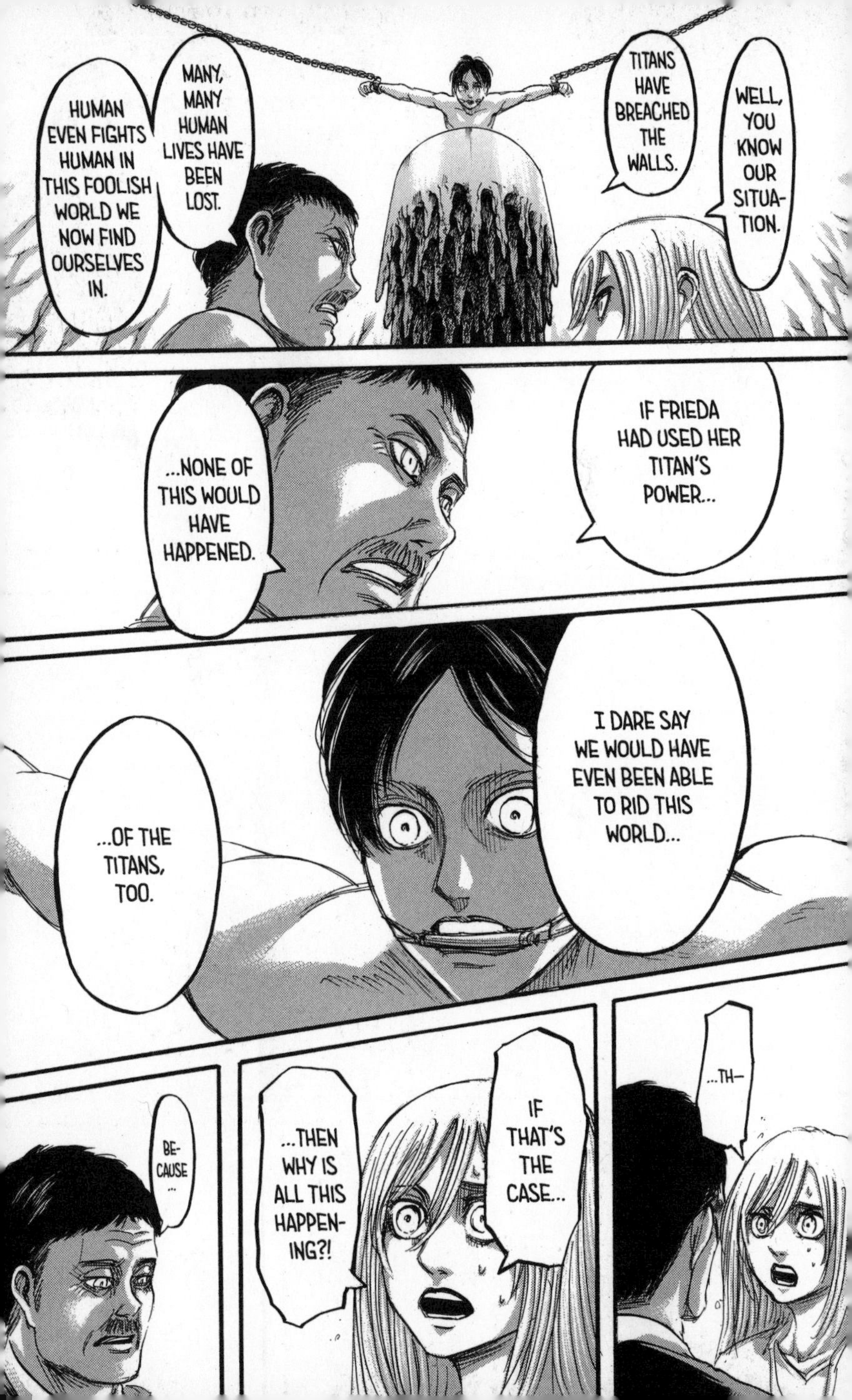
WELL, YOU KNOW OUR SITUATION.
TITANS HAVE BREACHED THE WALLS.
MANY, MANY HUMAN LIVES HAVE BEEN LOST.
HUMAN EVEN FIGHTS HUMAN IN THIS FOOLISH WORLD WE NOW FIND OURSELVES IN.
IF FRIEDA HAD USED HER TITAN'S POWER...
...NONE OF THIS WOULD HAVE HAPPENED.
I DARE SAY WE WOULD HAVE EVEN BEEN ABLE TO RID THIS WORLD...
...OF THE TITANS, TOO.
...TH-
IF THAT'S THE CASE...
...THEN WHY IS ALL THIS HAPPENING?!
BE-CAUSE...

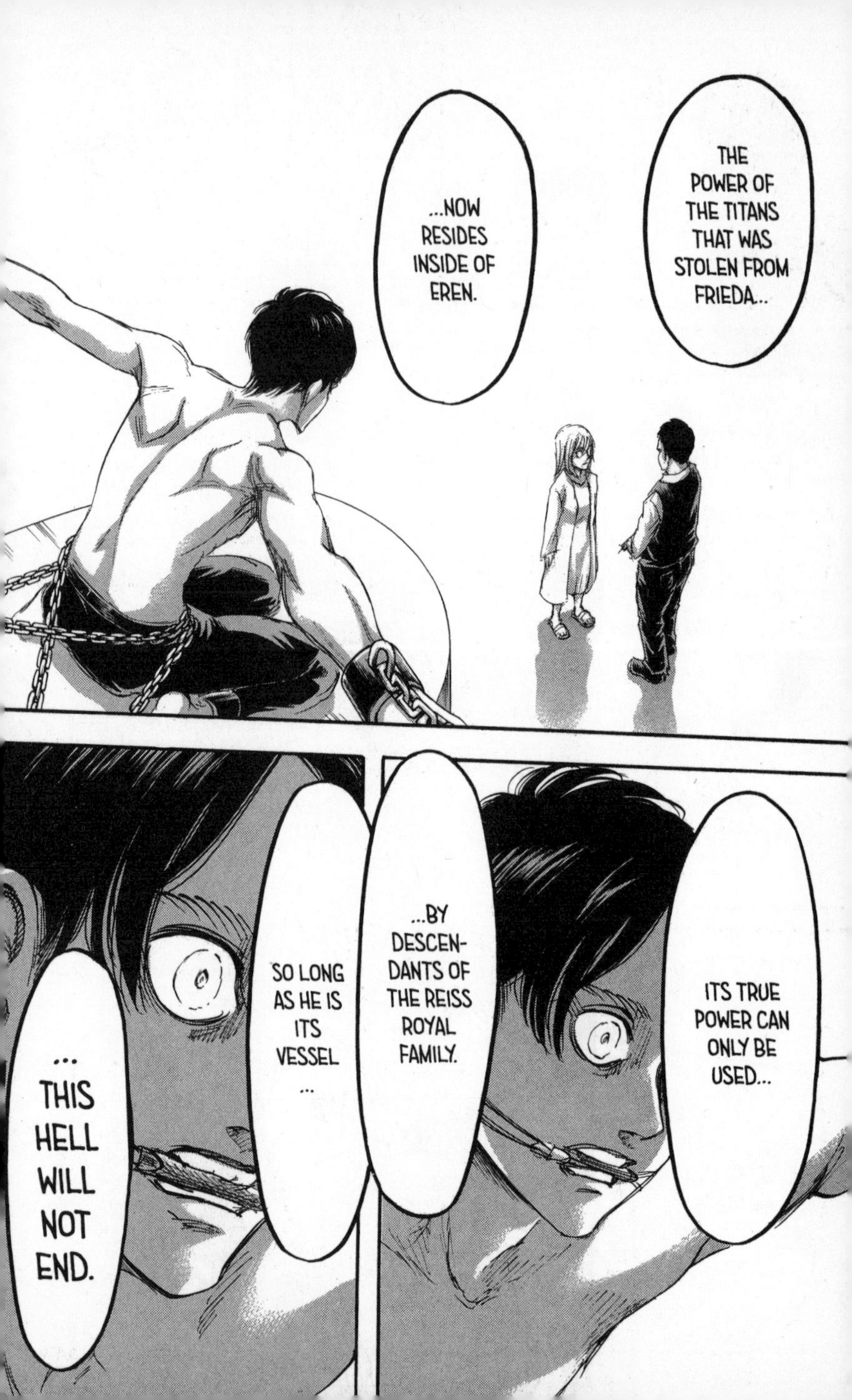
THE POWER OF THE TITANS THAT WAS STOLEN FROM FRIEDA...
...NOW RESIDES INSIDE OF EREN.
ITS TRUE POWER CAN ONLY BE USED...
...BY DESCENDANTS OF THE REISS ROYAL FAMILY.
SO LONG AS HE IS ITS VESSEL...
...THIS HELL WILL NOT END.

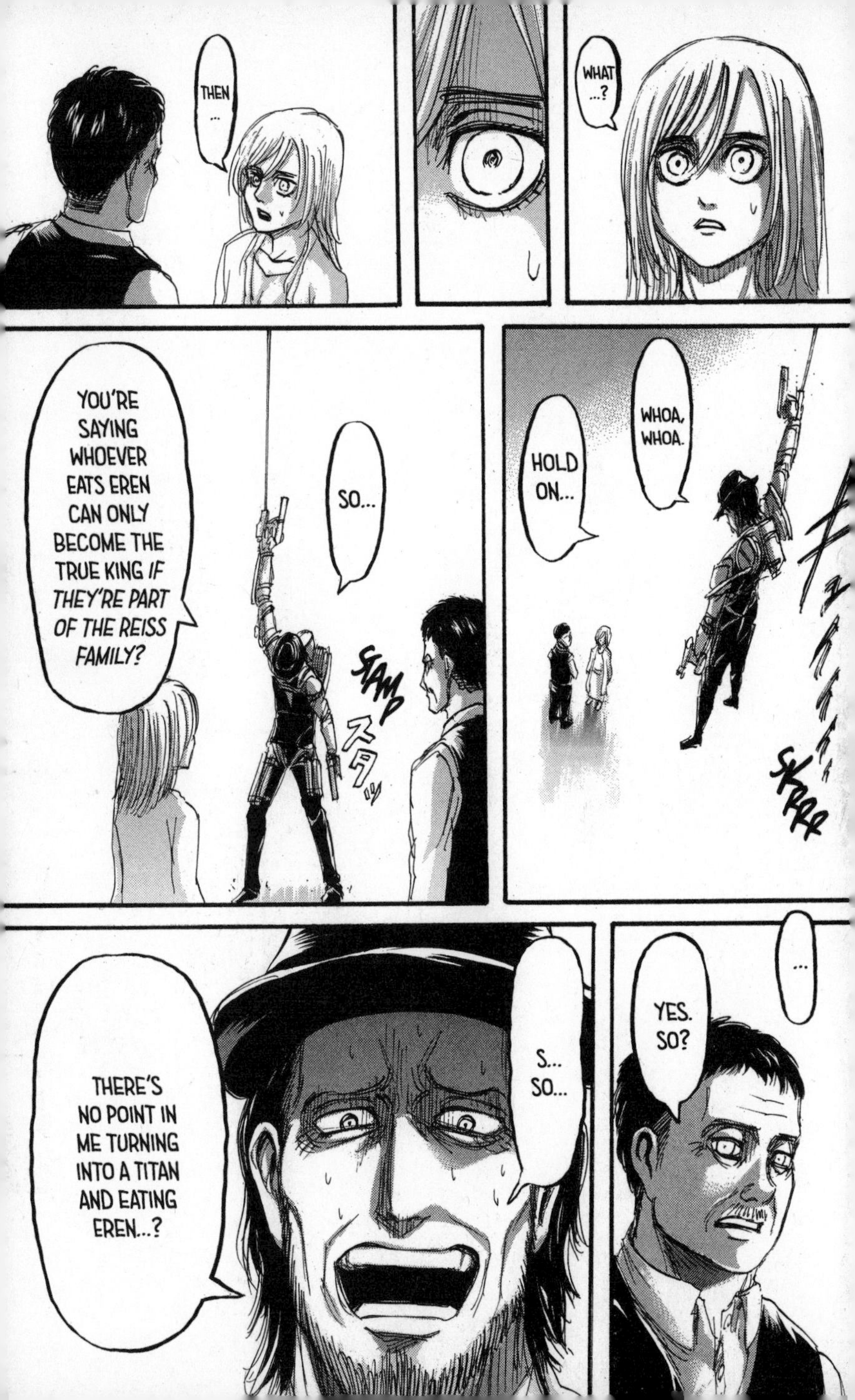
WHAT ...?
THEN ...
WHOA, WHOA.
HOLD ON...
SKRRR
SO...
YOU'RE SAYING WHOEVER EATS EREN CAN ONLY BECOME THE TRUE KING *IF THEY'RE PART OF THE REISS FAMILY?*
SLAM
...
YES. SO?
S... SO...
THERE'S NO POINT IN ME TURNING INTO A TITAN AND EATING EREN...?

ATTACK on TITAN

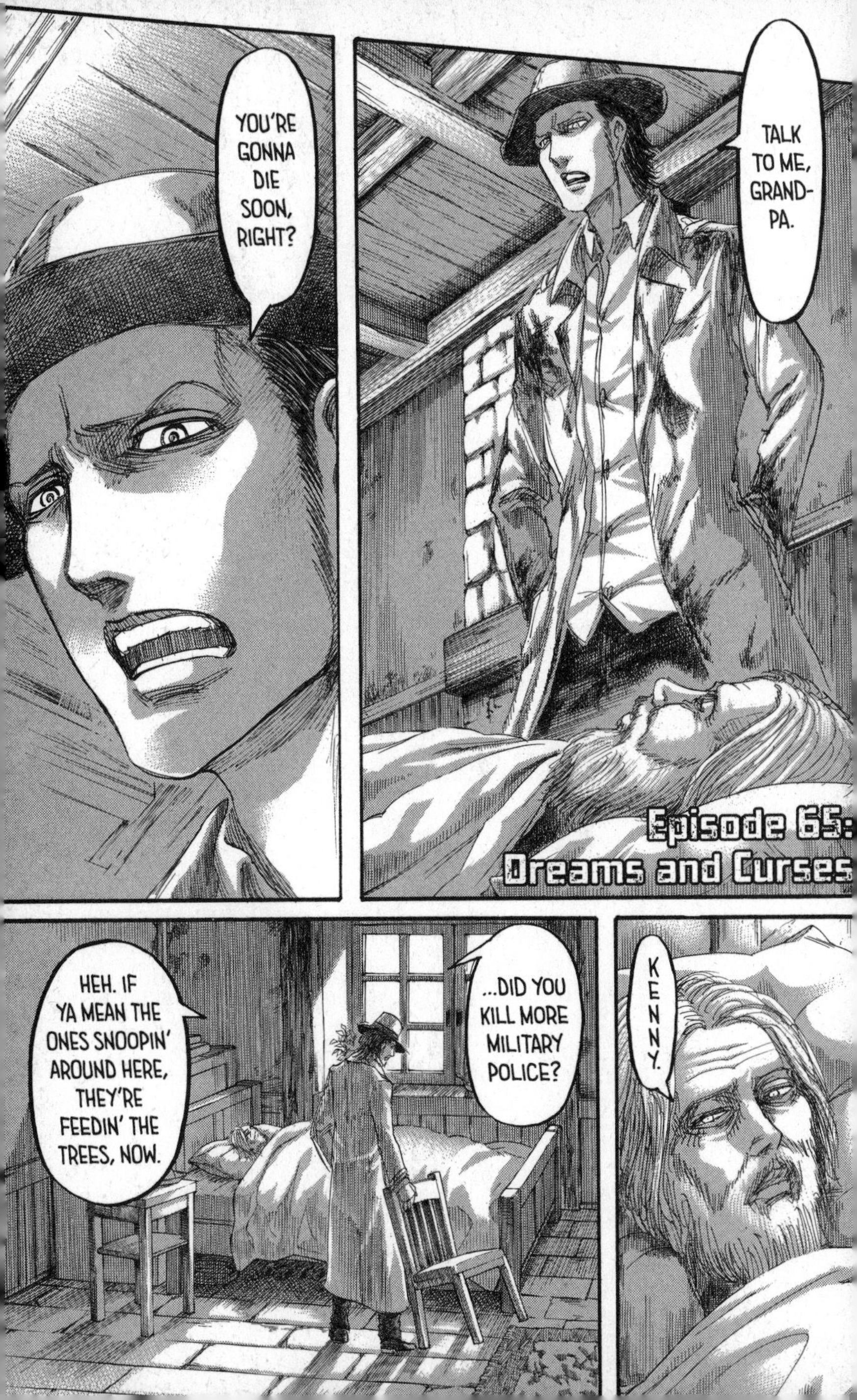
TALK TO ME, GRAND-PA.
Episode 65: Dreams and Curses
YOU'RE GONNA DIE SOON, RIGHT?
KENNY.
...DID YOU KILL MORE MILITARY POLICE?
HEH. IF YA MEAN THE ONES SNOOPIN' AROUND HERE, THEY'RE FEEDIN' THE TREES, NOW.

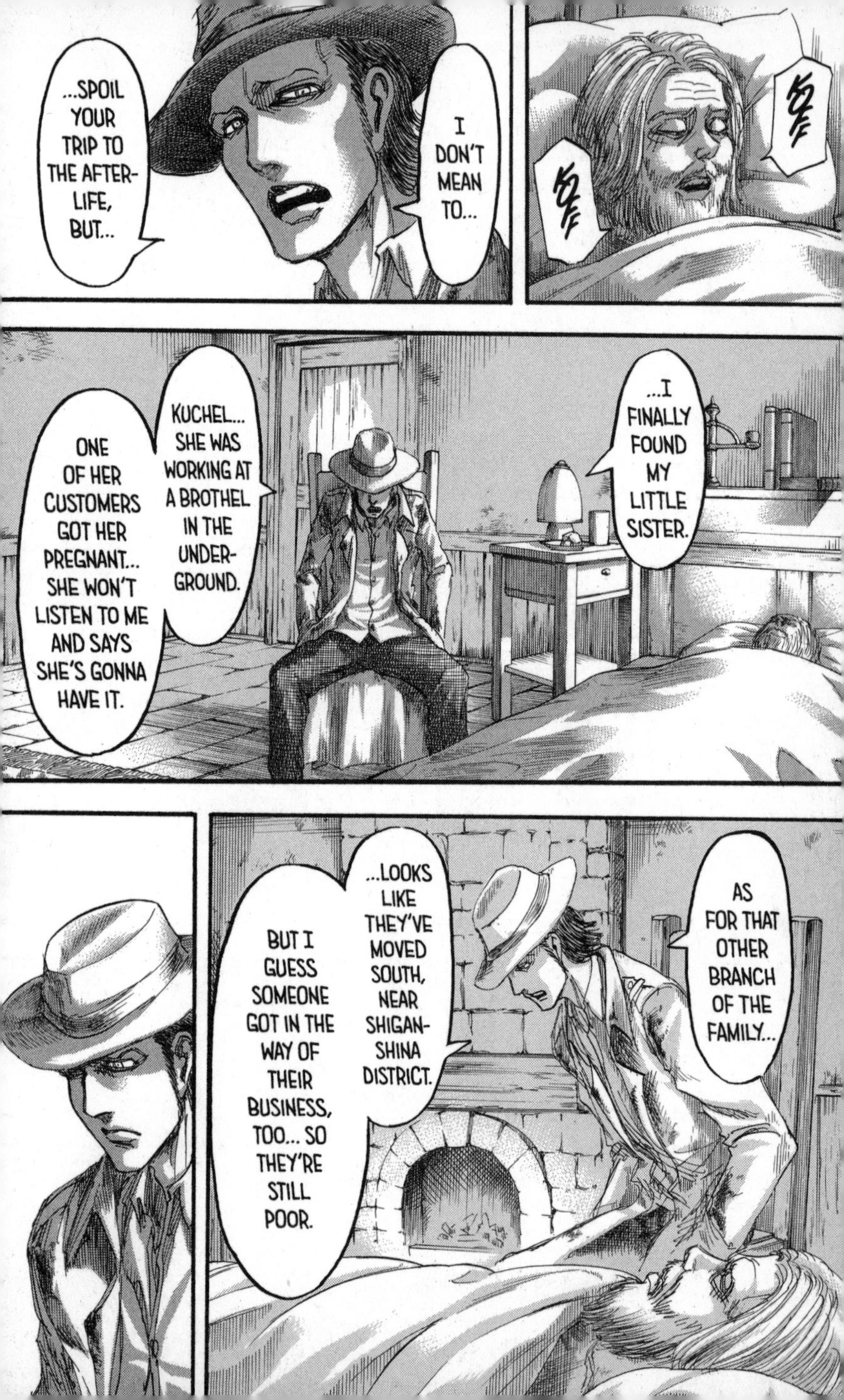
KOFF
KOFF
I DON'T MEAN TO...
...SPOIL YOUR TRIP TO THE AFTER-LIFE, BUT...
...I FINALLY FOUND MY LITTLE SISTER.
KUCHEL... SHE WAS WORKING AT A BROTHEL IN THE UNDER-GROUND.
ONE OF HER CUSTOMERS GOT HER PREGNANT... SHE WON'T LISTEN TO ME AND SAYS SHE'S GONNA HAVE IT.
AS FOR THAT OTHER BRANCH OF THE FAMILY...
...LOOKS LIKE THEY'VE MOVED SOUTH, NEAR SHIGAN-SHINA DISTRICT.
BUT I GUESS SOMEONE GOT IN THE WAY OF THEIR BUSINESS, TOO... SO THEY'RE STILL POOR.

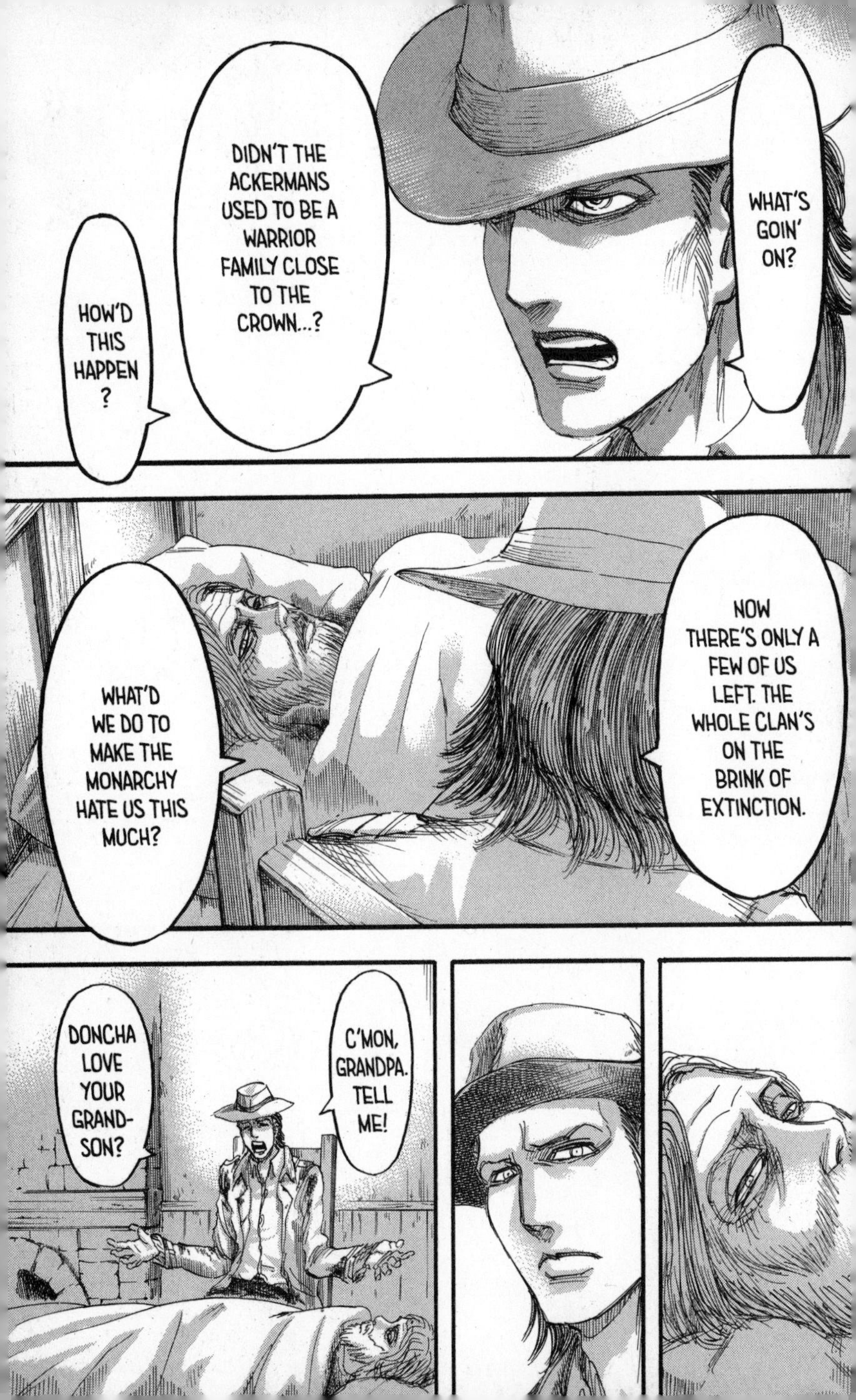
WHAT'S GOIN' ON?
DIDN'T THE ACKERMANS USED TO BE A WARRIOR FAMILY CLOSE TO THE CROWN...?
HOW'D THIS HAPPEN ?
NOW THERE'S ONLY A FEW OF US LEFT. THE WHOLE CLAN'S ON THE BRINK OF EXTINCTION.
WHAT'D WE DO TO MAKE THE MONARCHY HATE US THIS MUCH?
C'MON, GRANDPA. TELL ME!
DONCHA LOVE YOUR GRAND-SON?

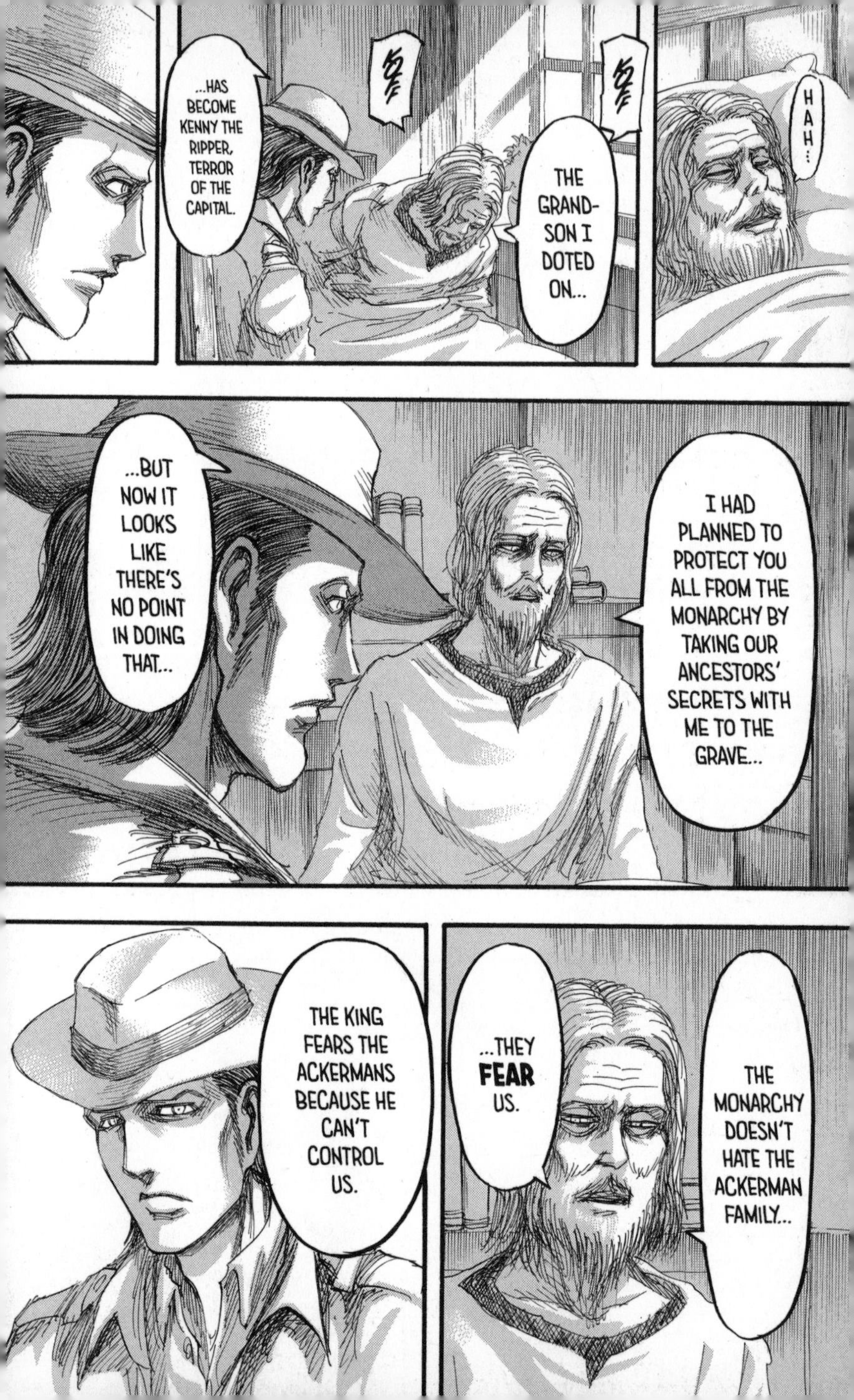
HAH...
THE GRANDSON I DOTED ON...
...HAS BECOME KENNY THE RIPPER, TERROR OF THE CAPITAL.
I HAD PLANNED TO PROTECT YOU ALL FROM THE MONARCHY BY TAKING OUR ANCESTORS' SECRETS WITH ME TO THE GRAVE...
...BUT NOW IT LOOKS LIKE THERE'S NO POINT IN DOING THAT...
THE MONARCHY DOESN'T HATE THE ACKERMAN FAMILY...
...THEY **FEAR** US.
THE KING FEARS THE ACKERMANS BECAUSE HE CAN'T CONTROL US.

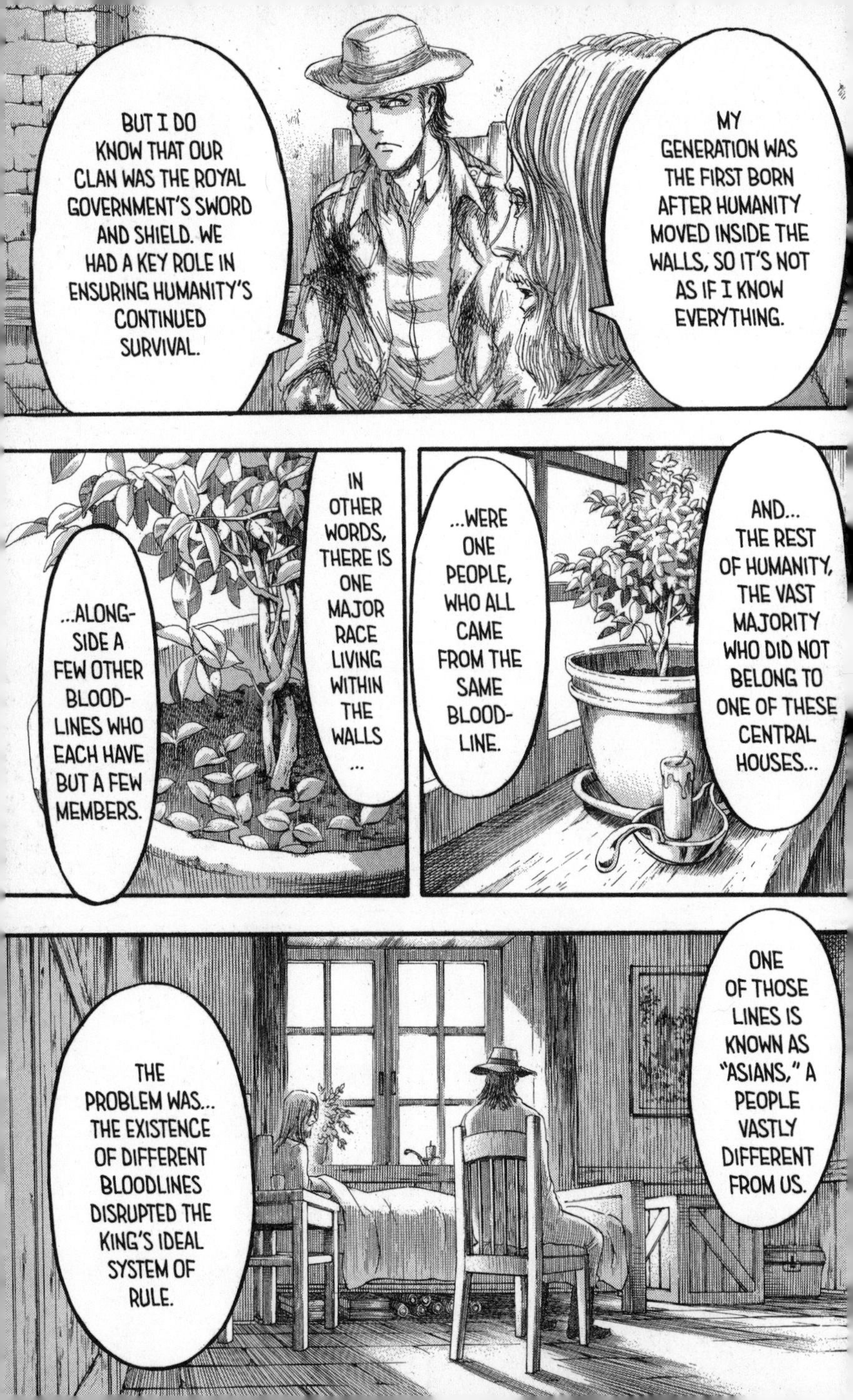
MY GENERATION WAS THE FIRST BORN AFTER HUMANITY MOVED INSIDE THE WALLS, SO IT'S NOT AS IF I KNOW EVERYTHING.
BUT I DO KNOW THAT OUR CLAN WAS THE ROYAL GOVERNMENT'S SWORD AND SHIELD. WE HAD A KEY ROLE IN ENSURING HUMANITY'S CONTINUED SURVIVAL.
AND... THE REST OF HUMANITY, THE VAST MAJORITY WHO DID NOT BELONG TO ONE OF THESE CENTRAL HOUSES...
...WERE ONE PEOPLE, WHO ALL CAME FROM THE SAME BLOOD-LINE.
IN OTHER WORDS, THERE IS ONE MAJOR RACE LIVING WITHIN THE WALLS ...
...ALONG-SIDE A FEW OTHER BLOOD-LINES WHO EACH HAVE BUT A FEW MEMBERS.
ONE OF THOSE LINES IS KNOWN AS "ASIANS," A PEOPLE VASTLY DIFFERENT FROM US.
THE PROBLEM WAS... THE EXISTENCE OF DIFFERENT BLOODLINES DISRUPTED THE KING'S IDEAL SYSTEM OF RULE.

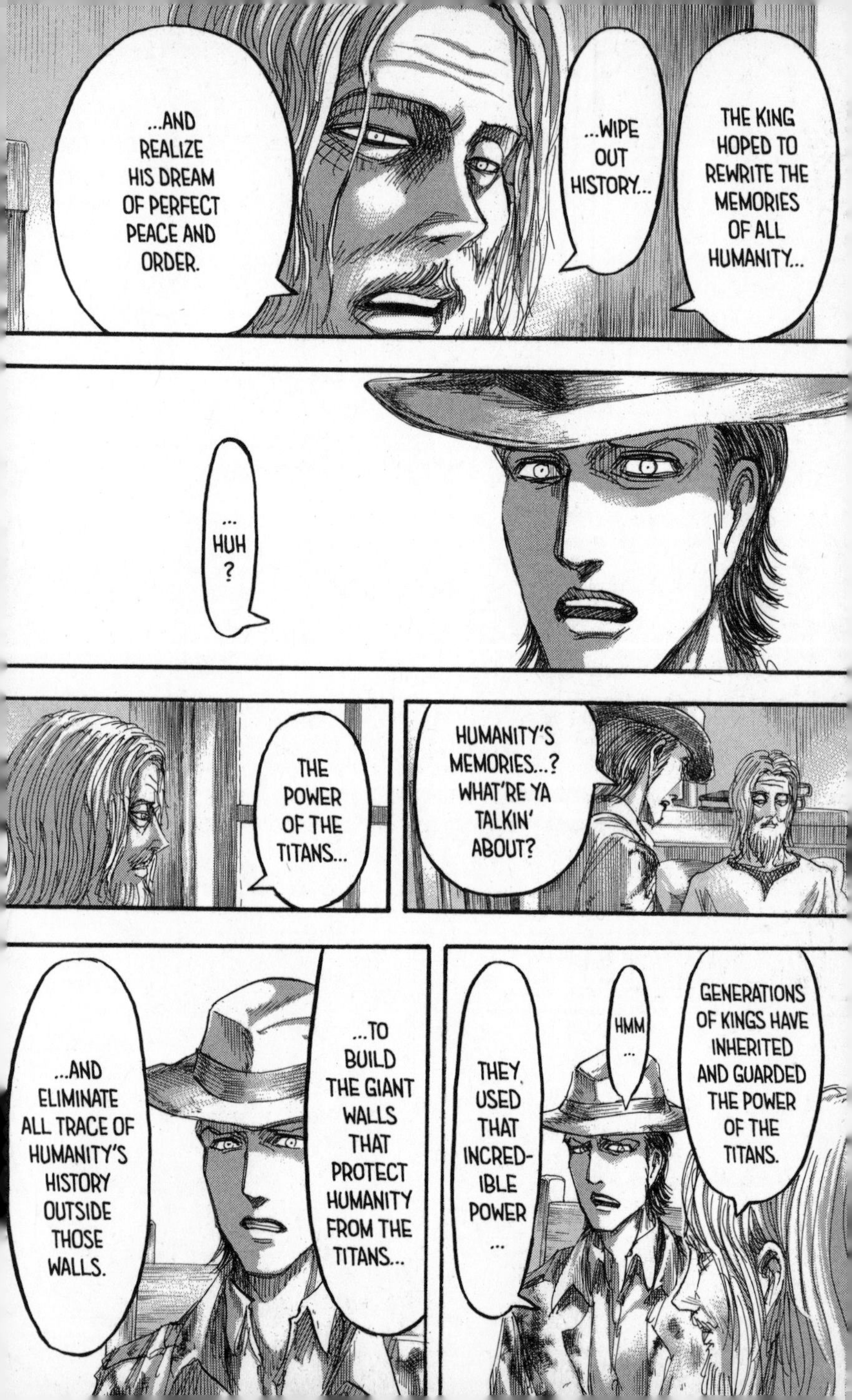
THE KING HOPED TO REWRITE THE MEMORIES OF ALL HUMANITY...
...WIPE OUT HISTORY...
...AND REALIZE HIS DREAM OF PERFECT PEACE AND ORDER.
... HUH ?
HUMANITY'S MEMORIES...? WHAT'RE YA TALKIN' ABOUT?
THE POWER OF THE TITANS...
GENERATIONS OF KINGS HAVE INHERITED AND GUARDED THE POWER OF THE TITANS.
HMM ...
THEY USED THAT INCREDIBLE POWER ...
...TO BUILD THE GIANT WALLS THAT PROTECT HUMANITY FROM THE TITANS...
...AND ELIMINATE ALL TRACE OF HUMANITY'S HISTORY OUTSIDE THOSE WALLS.

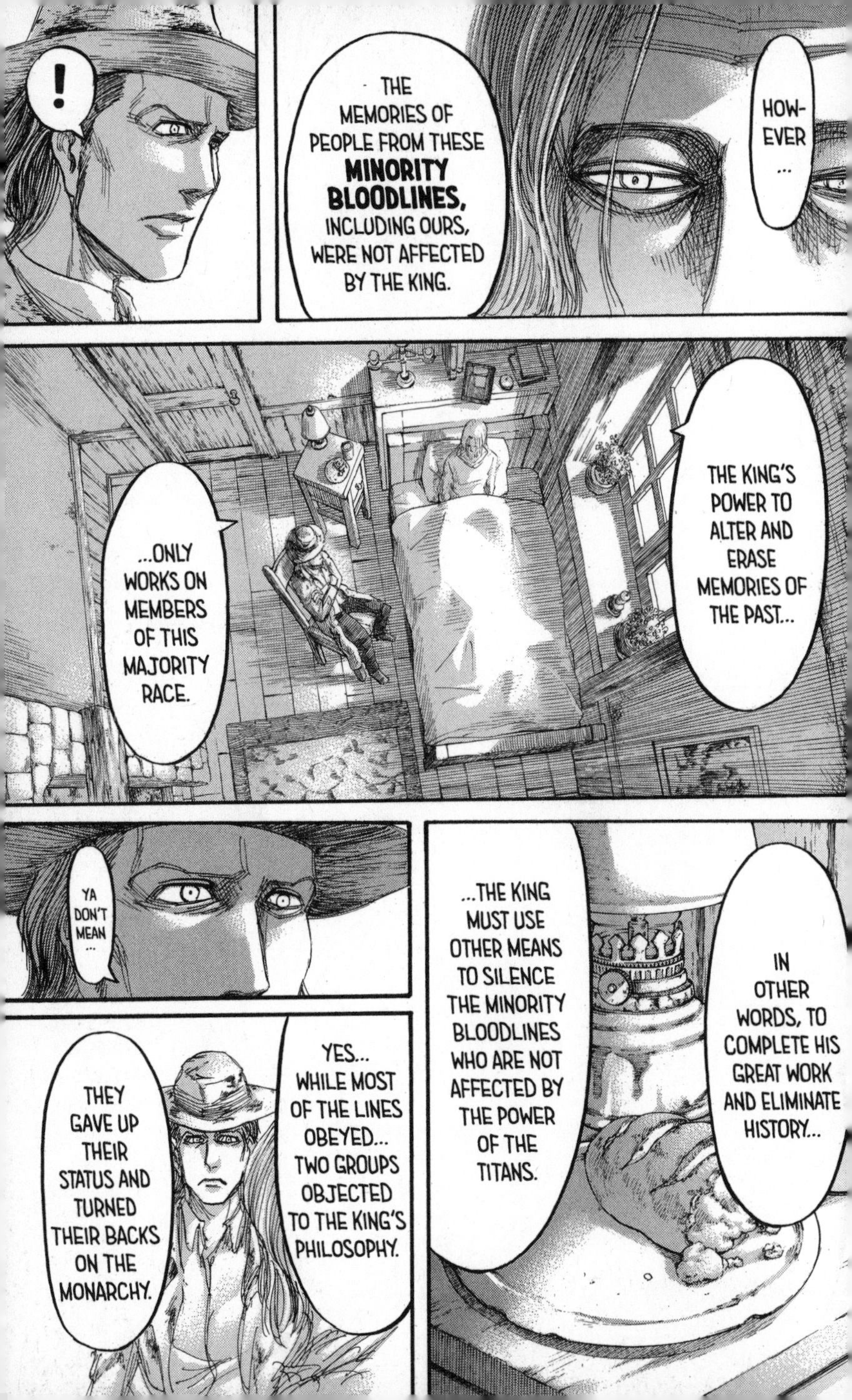
HOW-EVER...
THE MEMORIES OF PEOPLE FROM THESE **MINORITY BLOODLINES,** INCLUDING OURS, WERE NOT AFFECTED BY THE KING.
!
THE KING'S POWER TO ALTER AND ERASE MEMORIES OF THE PAST...
...ONLY WORKS ON MEMBERS OF THIS MAJORITY RACE.
IN OTHER WORDS, TO COMPLETE HIS GREAT WORK AND ELIMINATE HISTORY...
...THE KING MUST USE OTHER MEANS TO SILENCE THE MINORITY BLOODLINES WHO ARE NOT AFFECTED BY THE POWER OF THE TITANS.
YA DON'T MEAN...
YES... WHILE MOST OF THE LINES OBEYED... TWO GROUPS OBJECTED TO THE KING'S PHILOSOPHY.
THEY GAVE UP THEIR STATUS AND TURNED THEIR BACKS ON THE MONARCHY.

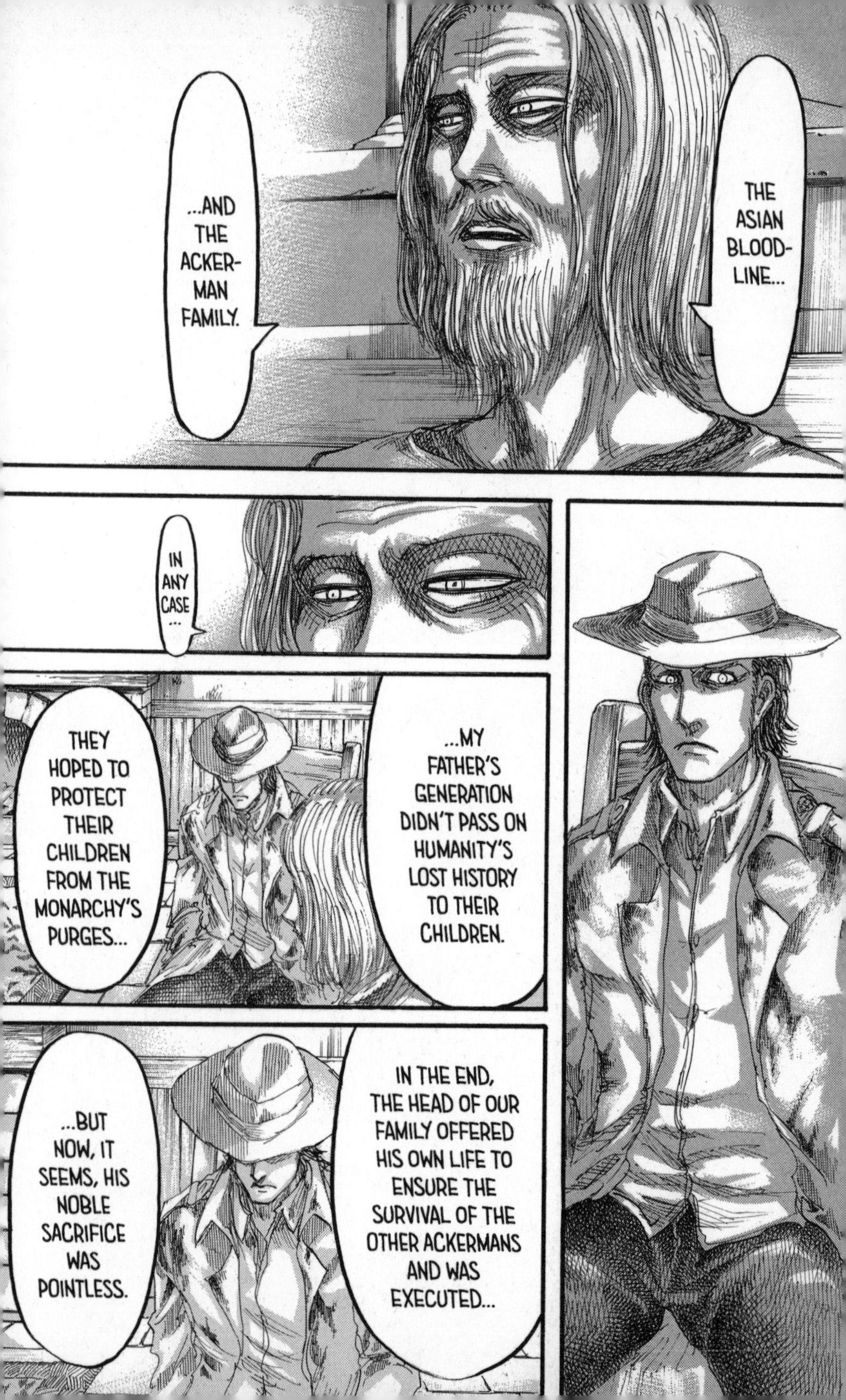
THE ASIAN BLOOD-LINE...
...AND THE ACKER-MAN FAMILY.
IN ANY CASE...
...MY FATHER'S GENERATION DIDN'T PASS ON HUMANITY'S LOST HISTORY TO THEIR CHILDREN.
THEY HOPED TO PROTECT THEIR CHILDREN FROM THE MONARCHY'S PURGES...
IN THE END, THE HEAD OF OUR FAMILY OFFERED HIS OWN LIFE TO ENSURE THE SURVIVAL OF THE OTHER ACKERMANS AND WAS EXECUTED...
...BUT NOW, IT SEEMS, HIS NOBLE SACRIFICE WAS POINTLESS.

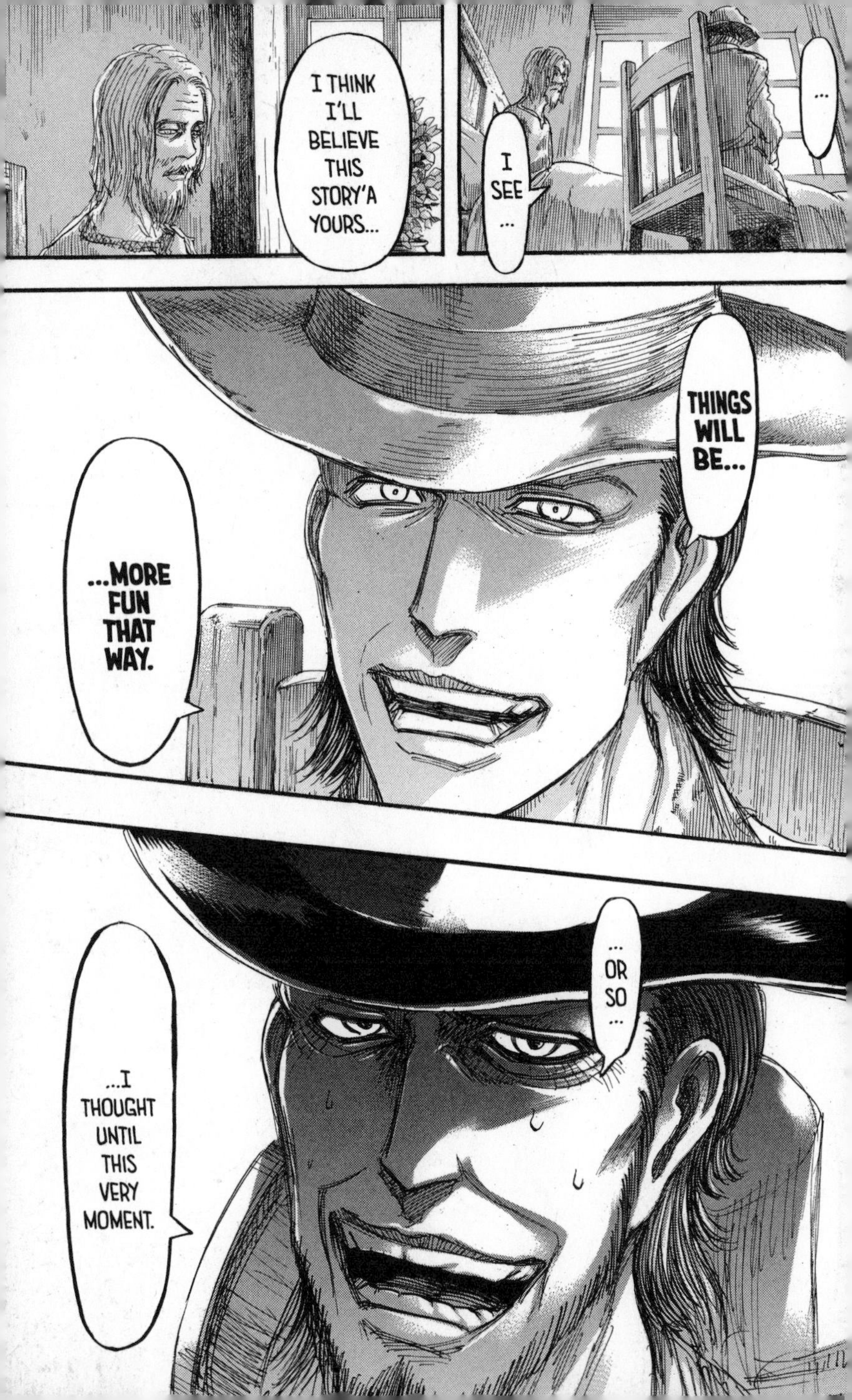
...
I SEE...
I THINK I'LL BELIEVE THIS STORY'A YOURS...
THINGS WILL BE...
...MORE FUN THAT WAY.
...OR SO...
...I THOUGHT UNTIL THIS VERY MOMENT.

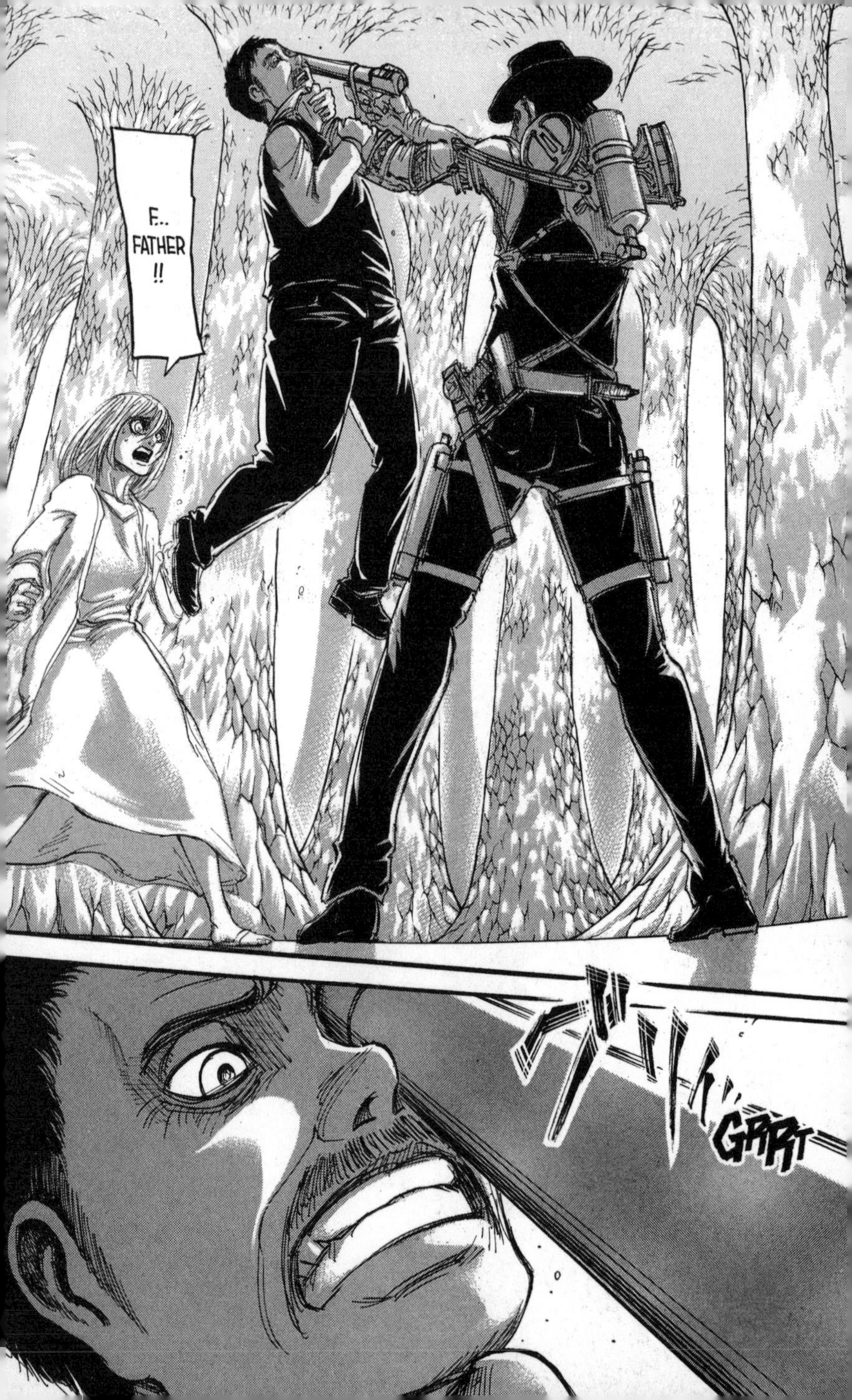
F... FATHER !!
GRRT

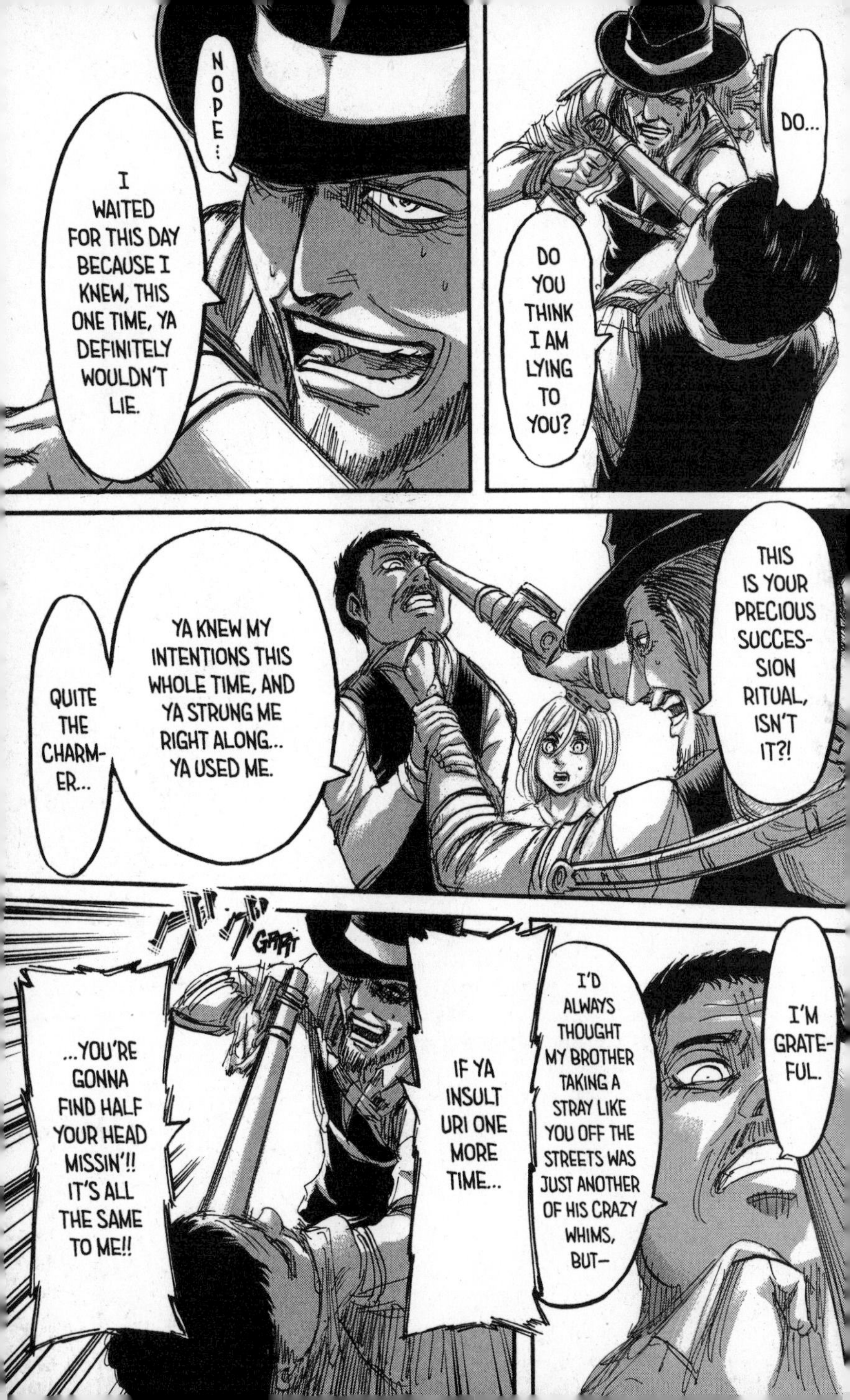
DO...
DO YOU THINK I AM LYING TO YOU?
NOPE...
I WAITED FOR THIS DAY BECAUSE I KNEW, THIS ONE TIME, YA DEFINITELY WOULDN'T LIE.
THIS IS YOUR PRECIOUS SUCCES-SION RITUAL, ISN'T IT?!
YA KNEW MY INTENTIONS THIS WHOLE TIME, AND YA STRUNG ME RIGHT ALONG... YA USED ME.
QUITE THE CHARM-ER...
I'M GRATE-FUL.
I'D ALWAYS THOUGHT MY BROTHER TAKING A STRAY LIKE YOU OFF THE STREETS WAS JUST ANOTHER OF HIS CRAZY WHIMS, BUT—
IF YA INSULT URI ONE MORE TIME...
...YOU'RE GONNA FIND HALF YOUR HEAD MISSIN'!! IT'S ALL THE SAME TO ME!!

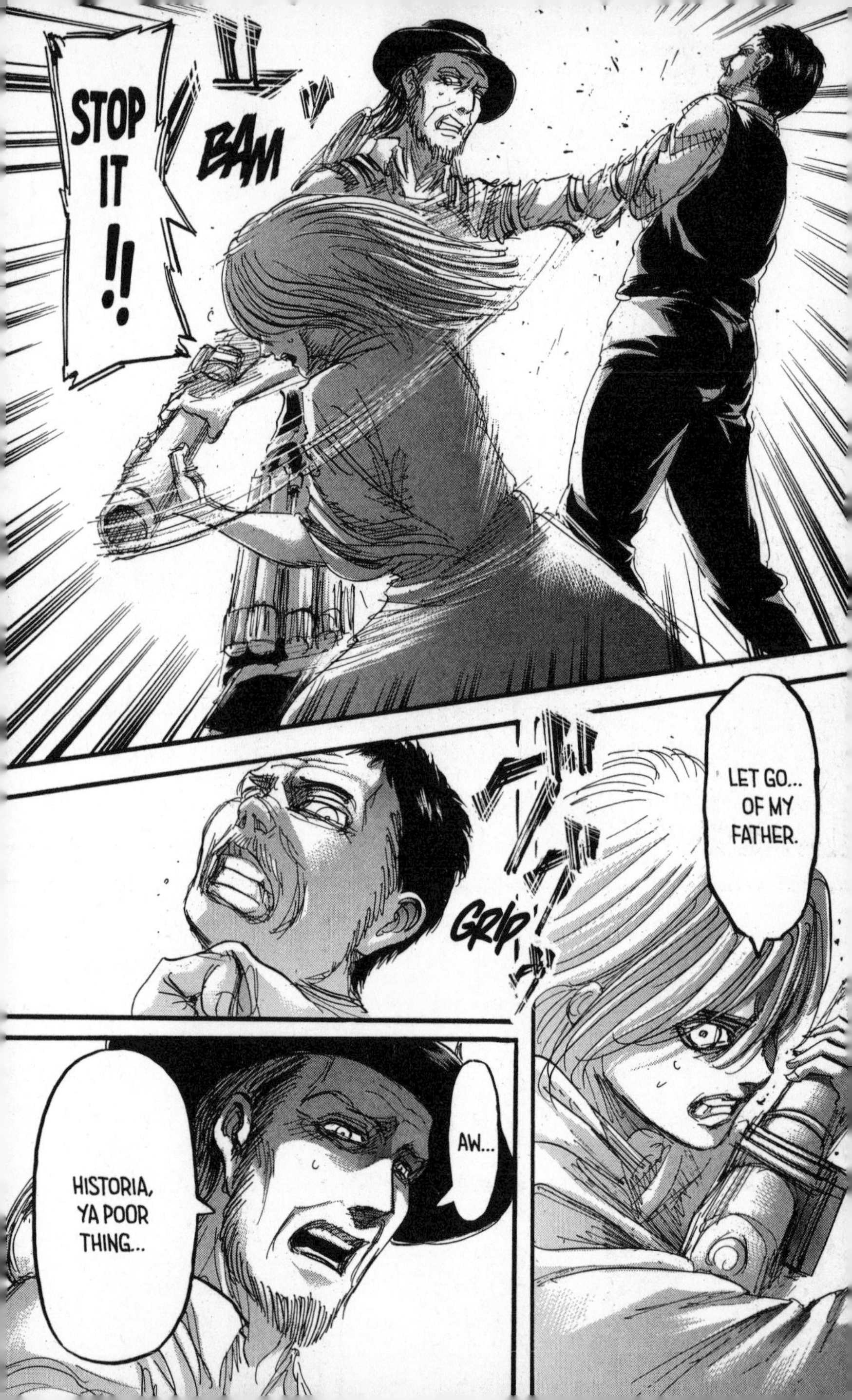
STOP IT !!
BAM
LET GO... OF MY FATHER.
GRIP
AW...
HISTORIA, YA POOR THING...

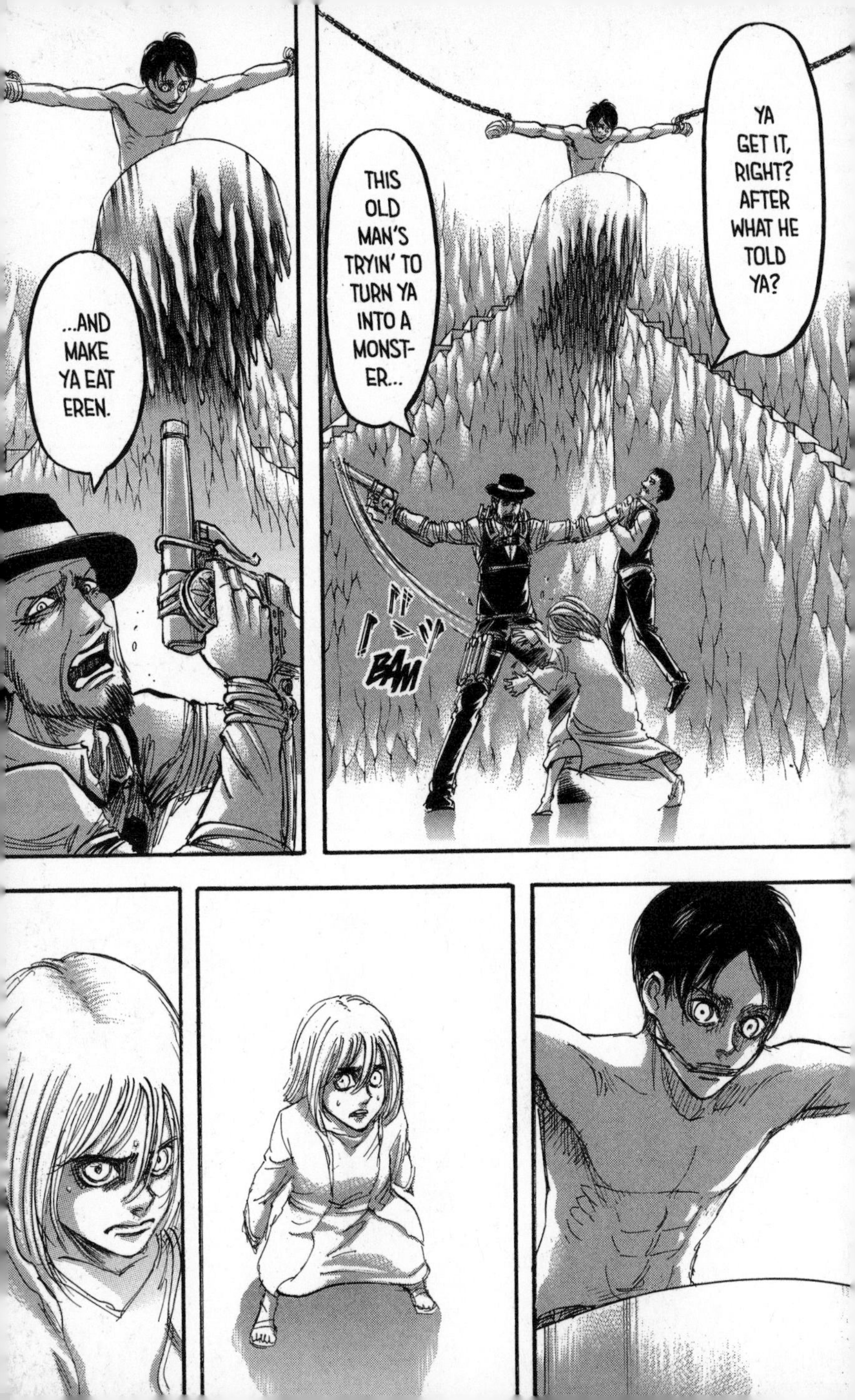
YA GET IT, RIGHT? AFTER WHAT HE TOLD YA?
THIS OLD MAN'S TRYIN' TO TURN YA INTO A MONSTER...
BAM
...AND MAKE YA EAT EREN.

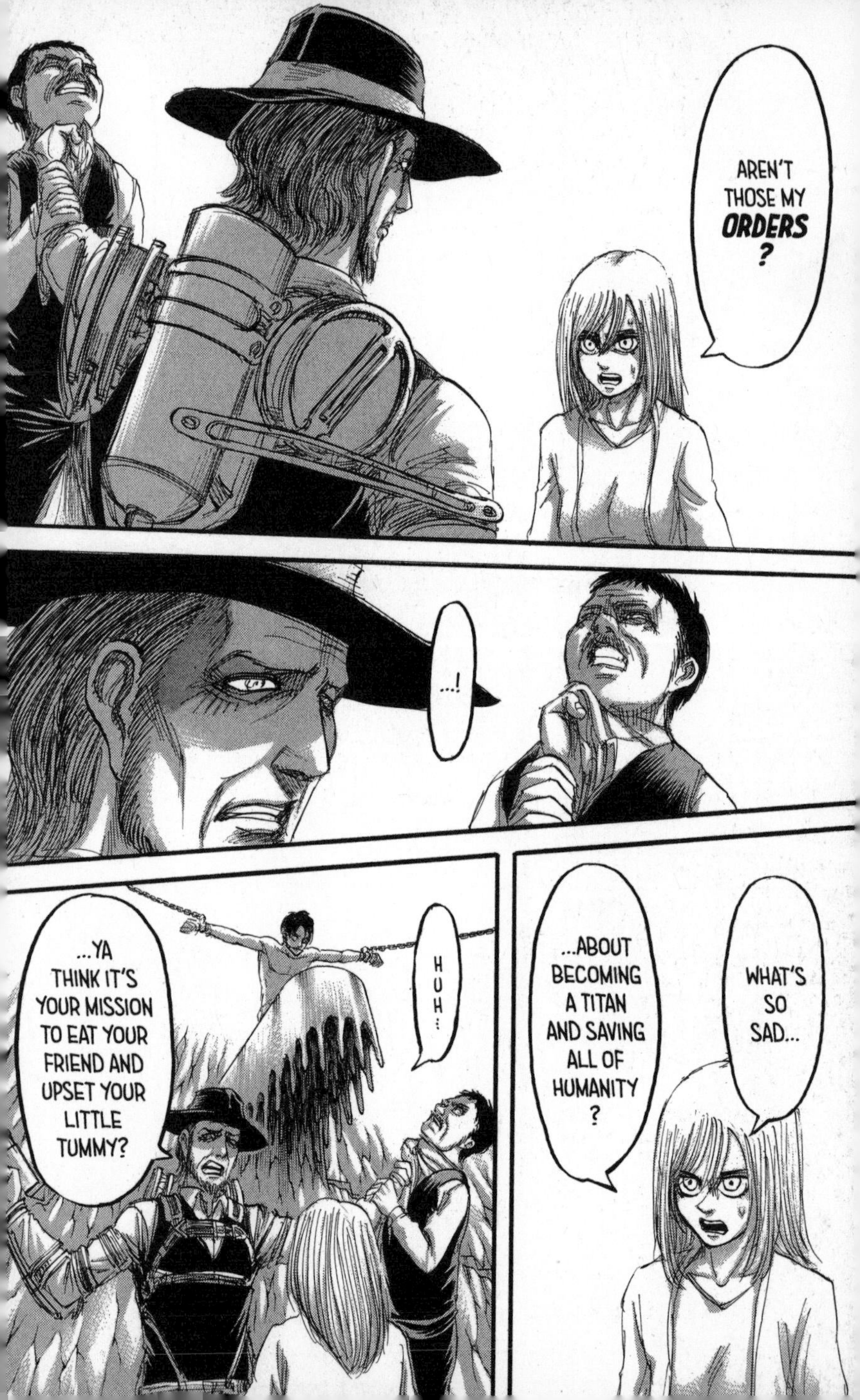
AREN'T THOSE MY **ORDERS**?
...!
WHAT'S SO SAD...
...ABOUT BECOMING A TITAN AND SAVING ALL OF HUMANITY?
HUH...
...YA THINK IT'S YOUR MISSION TO EAT YOUR FRIEND AND UPSET YOUR LITTLE TUMMY?

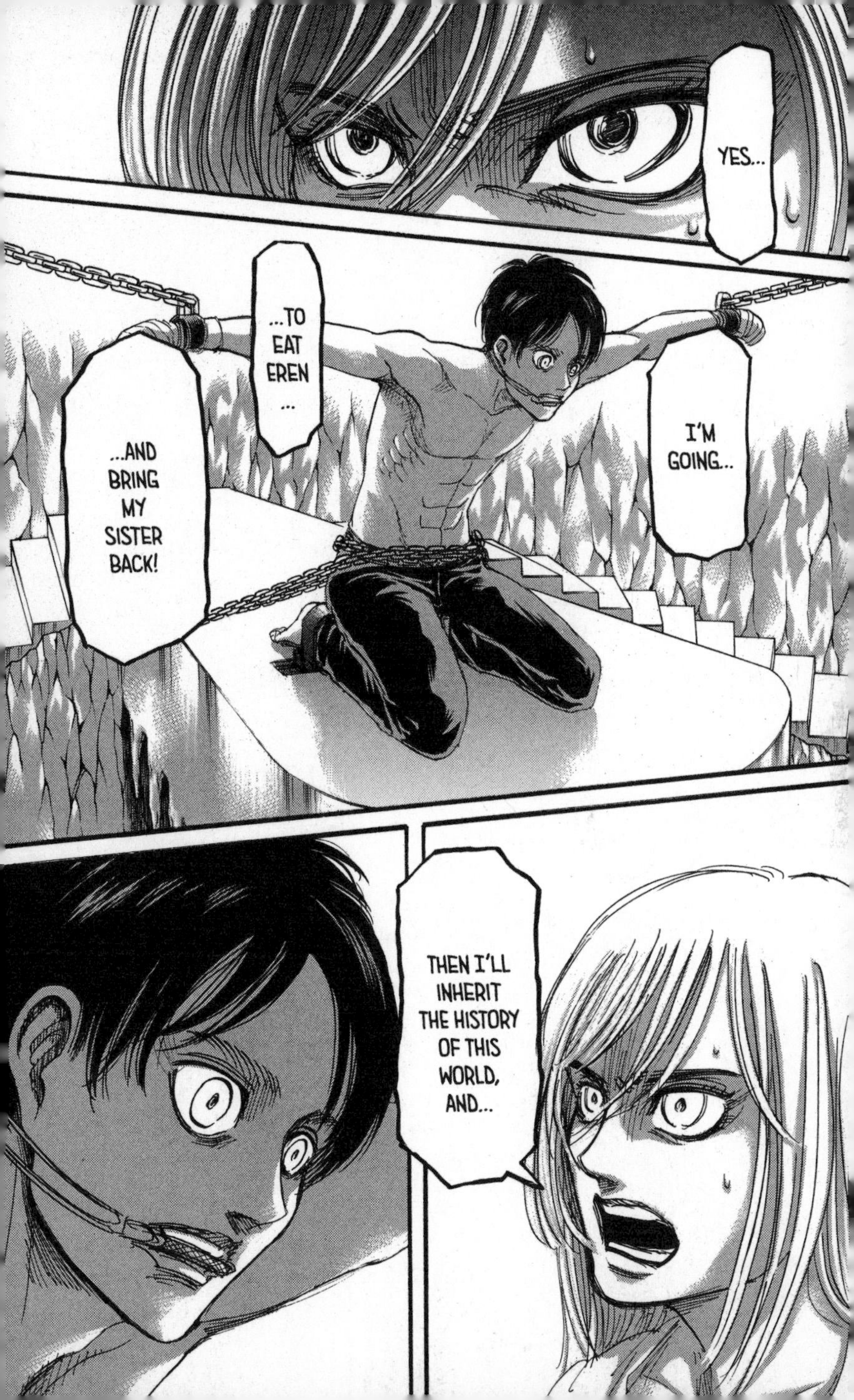
YES...
I'M GOING...
...TO EAT EREN ...
...AND BRING MY SISTER BACK!
THEN I'LL INHERIT THE HISTORY OF THIS WORLD, AND...

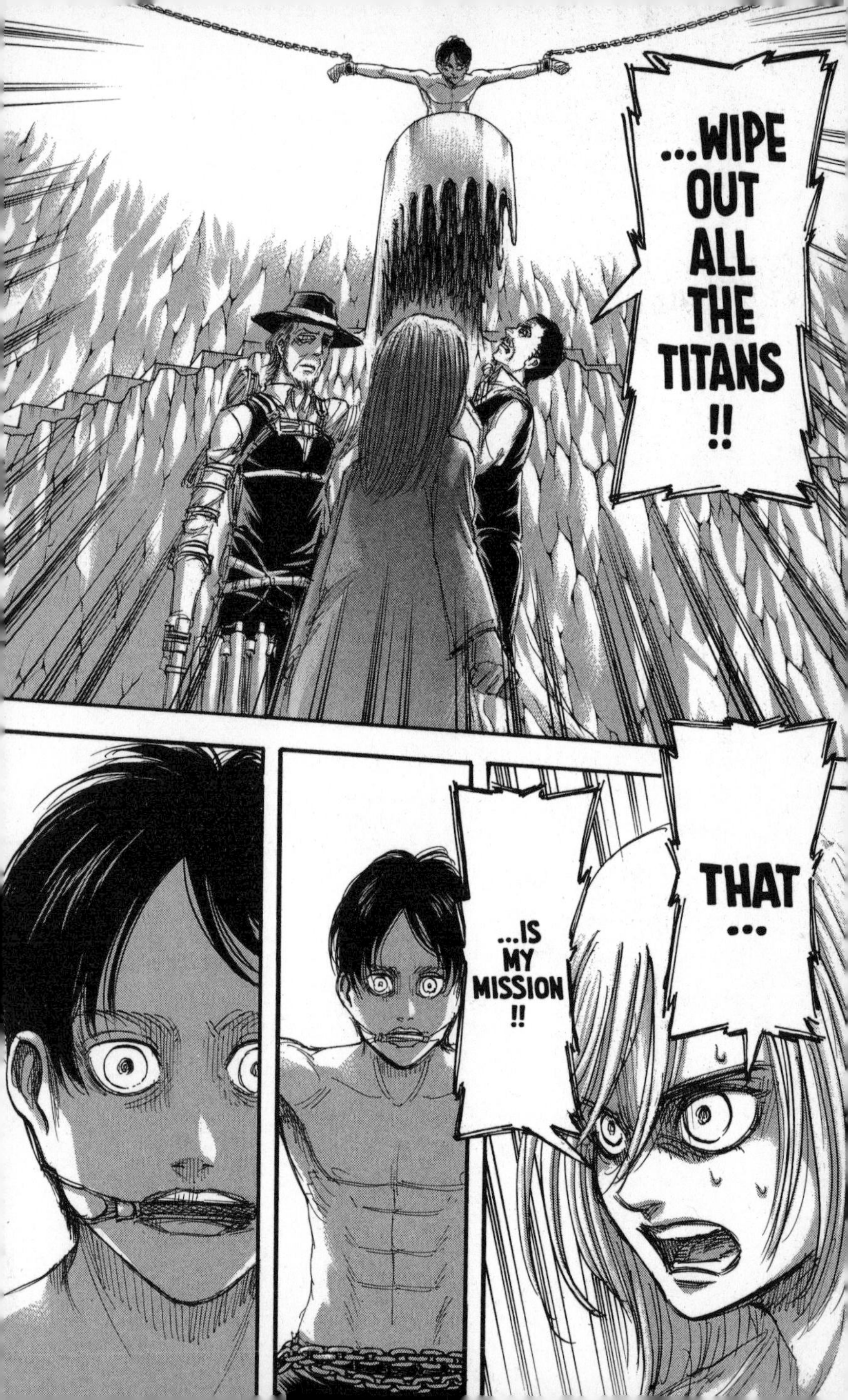
...WIPE OUT ALL THE TITANS !!
THAT ...
...IS MY MISSION !!

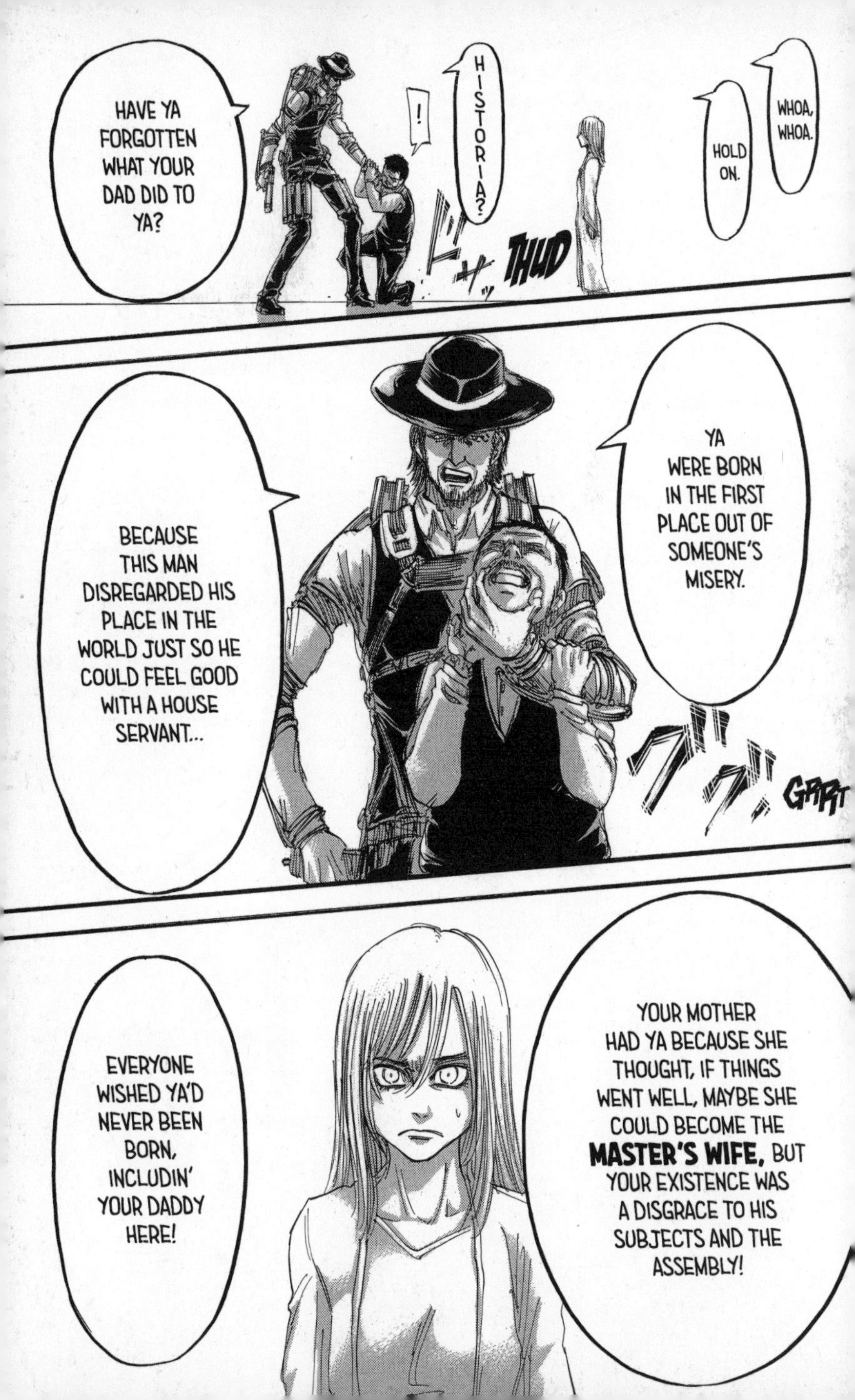
WHOA, WHOA.
HOLD ON.
THUD
HISTORIA?
!
HAVE YA FORGOTTEN WHAT YOUR DAD DID TO YA?
YA WERE BORN IN THE FIRST PLACE OUT OF SOMEONE'S MISERY.
GRRT
BECAUSE THIS MAN DISREGARDED HIS PLACE IN THE WORLD JUST SO HE COULD FEEL GOOD WITH A HOUSE SERVANT...
YOUR MOTHER HAD YA BECAUSE SHE THOUGHT, IF THINGS WENT WELL, MAYBE SHE COULD BECOME THE **MASTER'S WIFE,** BUT YOUR EXISTENCE WAS A DISGRACE TO HIS SUBJECTS AND THE ASSEMBLY!
EVERYONE WISHED YA'D NEVER BEEN BORN, INCLUDIN' YOUR DADDY HERE!

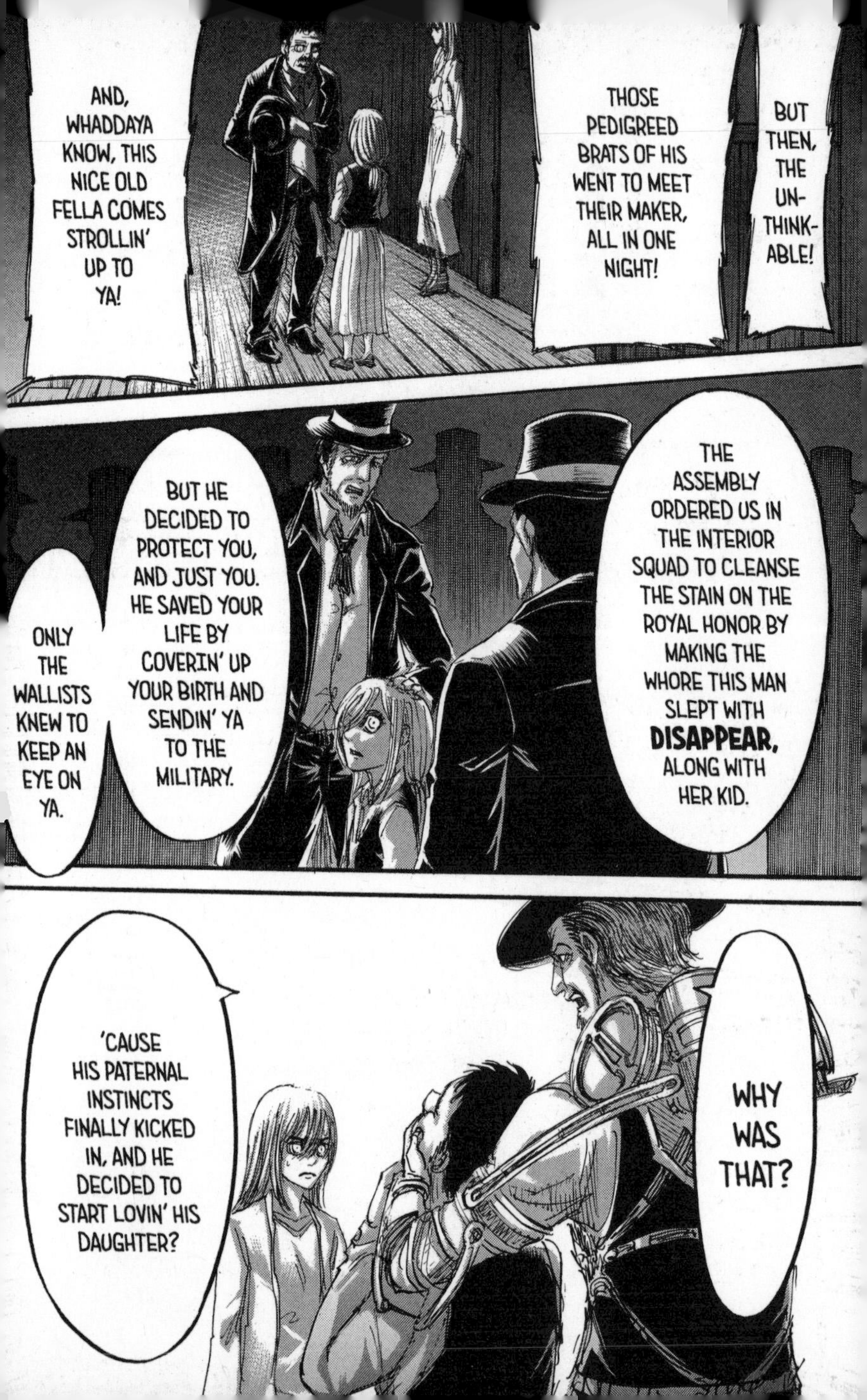
BUT THEN, THE UN-THINKABLE!
THOSE PEDIGREED BRATS OF HIS WENT TO MEET THEIR MAKER, ALL IN ONE NIGHT!
AND, WHADDAYA KNOW, THIS NICE OLD FELLA COMES STROLLIN' UP TO YA!
THE ASSEMBLY ORDERED US IN THE INTERIOR SQUAD TO CLEANSE THE STAIN ON THE ROYAL HONOR BY MAKING THE WHORE THIS MAN SLEPT WITH **DISAPPEAR,** ALONG WITH HER KID.
BUT HE DECIDED TO PROTECT YOU, AND JUST YOU. HE SAVED YOUR LIFE BY COVERIN' UP YOUR BIRTH AND SENDIN' YA TO THE MILITARY.
ONLY THE WALLISTS KNEW TO KEEP AN EYE ON YA.
WHY WAS THAT?
'CAUSE HIS PATERNAL INSTINCTS FINALLY KICKED IN, AND HE DECIDED TO START LOVIN' HIS DAUGHTER?

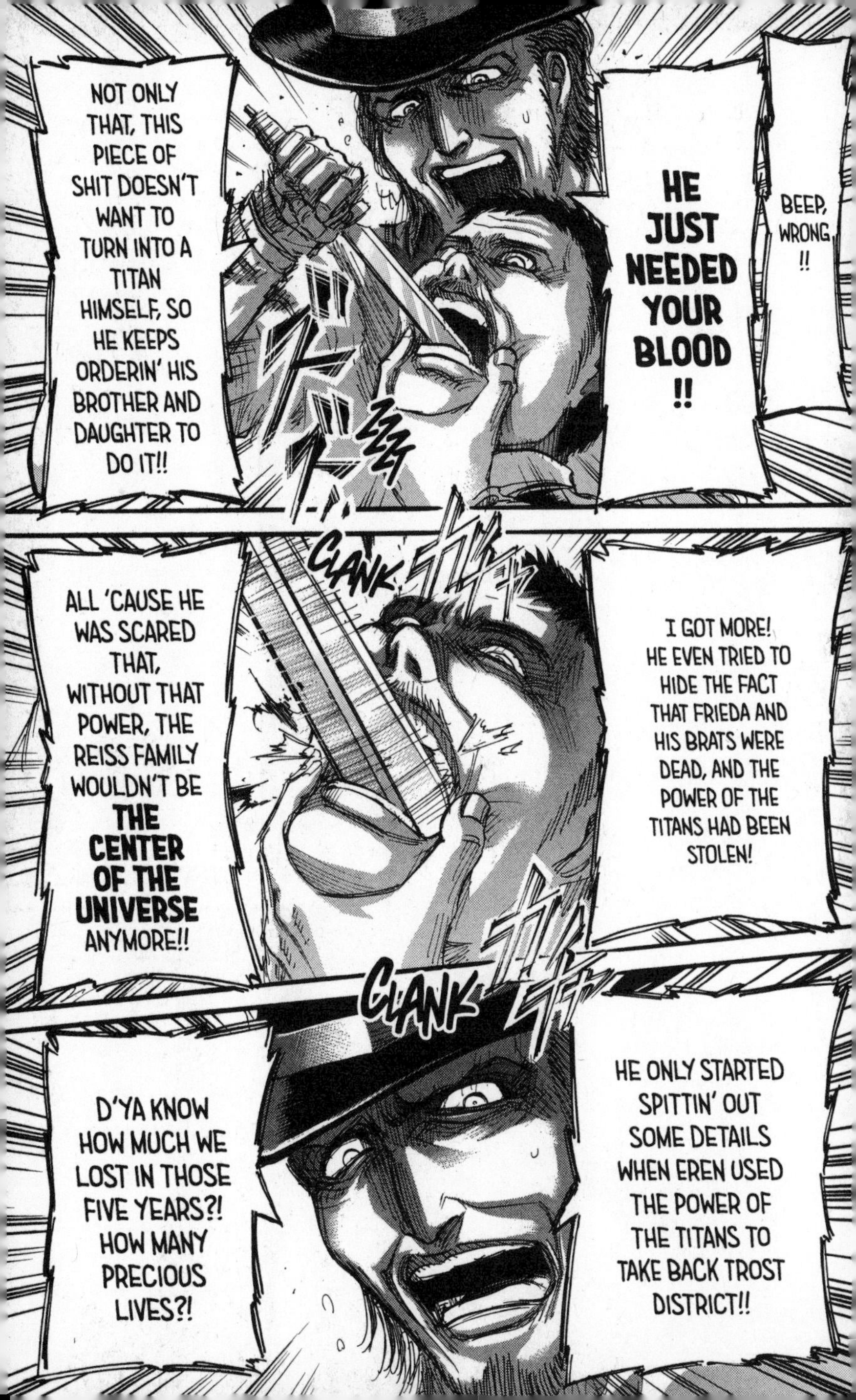
BEEP, WRONG!!
HE JUST NEEDED YOUR BLOOD!!
NOT ONLY THAT, THIS PIECE OF SHIT DOESN'T WANT TO TURN INTO A TITAN HIMSELF, SO HE KEEPS ORDERIN' HIS BROTHER AND DAUGHTER TO DO IT!!
I GOT MORE! HE EVEN TRIED TO HIDE THE FACT THAT FRIEDA AND HIS BRATS WERE DEAD, AND THE POWER OF THE TITANS HAD BEEN STOLEN!
CLANK
ALL 'CAUSE HE WAS SCARED THAT, WITHOUT THAT POWER, THE REISS FAMILY WOULDN'T BE **THE CENTER OF THE UNIVERSE** ANYMORE!!
CLANK
HE ONLY STARTED SPITTIN' OUT SOME DETAILS WHEN EREN USED THE POWER OF THE TITANS TO TAKE BACK TROST DISTRICT!!
D'YA KNOW HOW MUCH WE LOST IN THOSE FIVE YEARS?! HOW MANY PRECIOUS LIVES?!

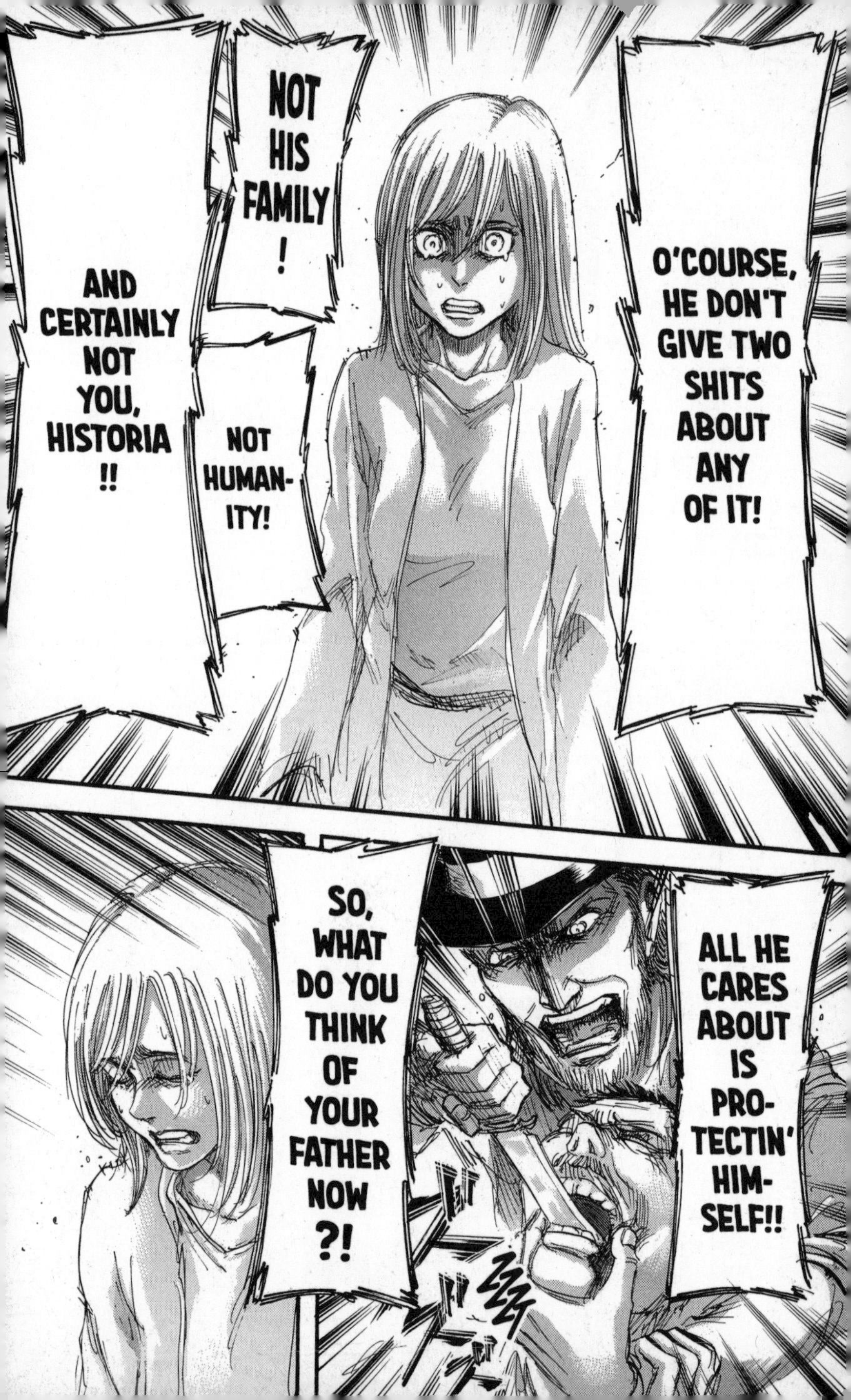
O'COURSE, HE DON'T GIVE TWO SHITS ABOUT ANY OF IT!
NOT HIS FAMILY!
NOT HUMANITY!
AND CERTAINLY NOT YOU, HISTORIA!!
ALL HE CARES ABOUT IS PROTECTIN' HIMSELF!!
SO, WHAT DO YOU THINK OF YOUR FATHER NOW?!

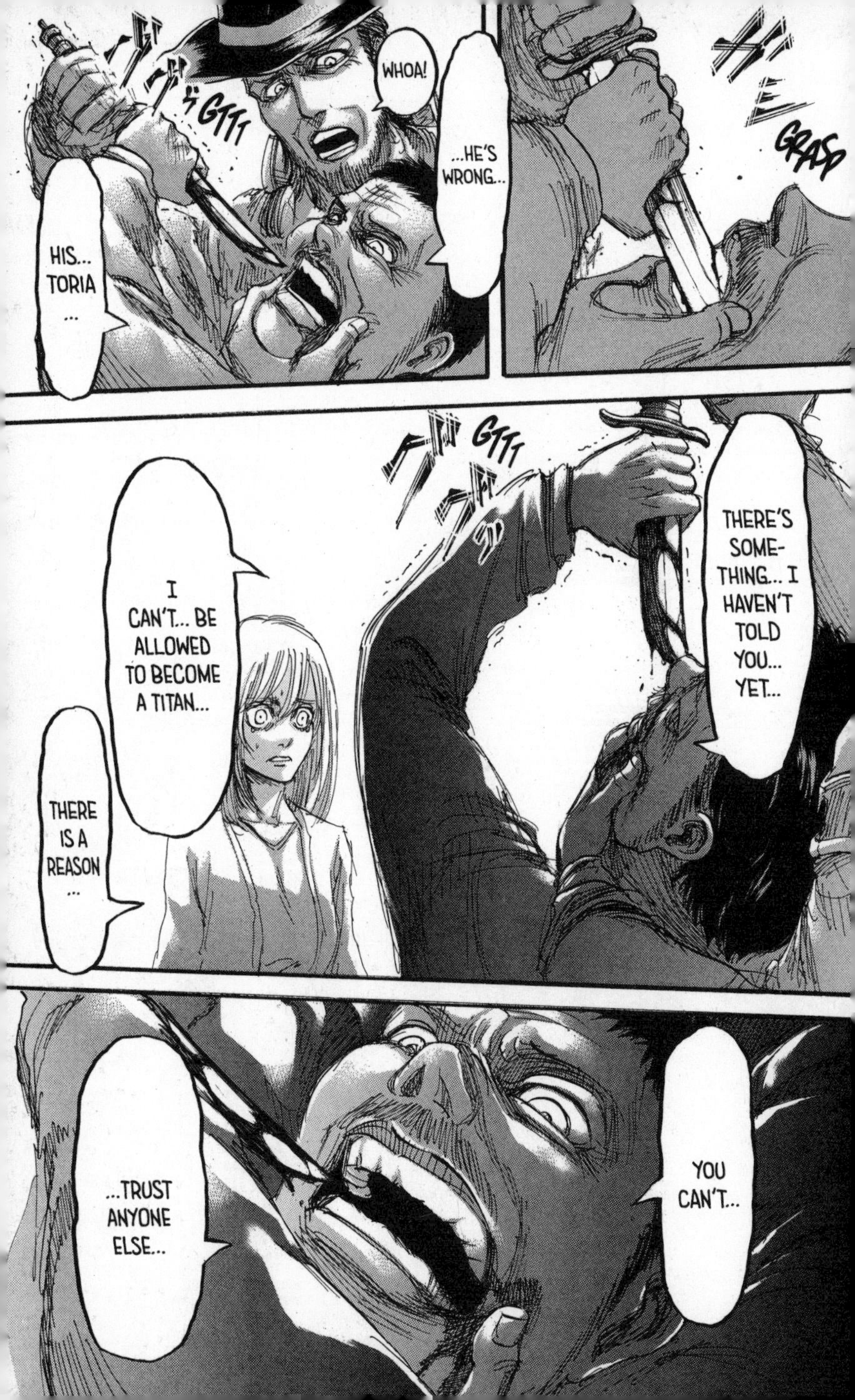
GRASP
WHOA!
...HE'S WRONG...
GTTT
HIS... TORIA ...
THERE'S SOME-THING... I HAVEN'T TOLD YOU... YET...
GTTT
I CAN'T... BE ALLOWED TO BECOME A TITAN...
THERE IS A REASON ...
YOU CAN'T...
...TRUST ANYONE ELSE...

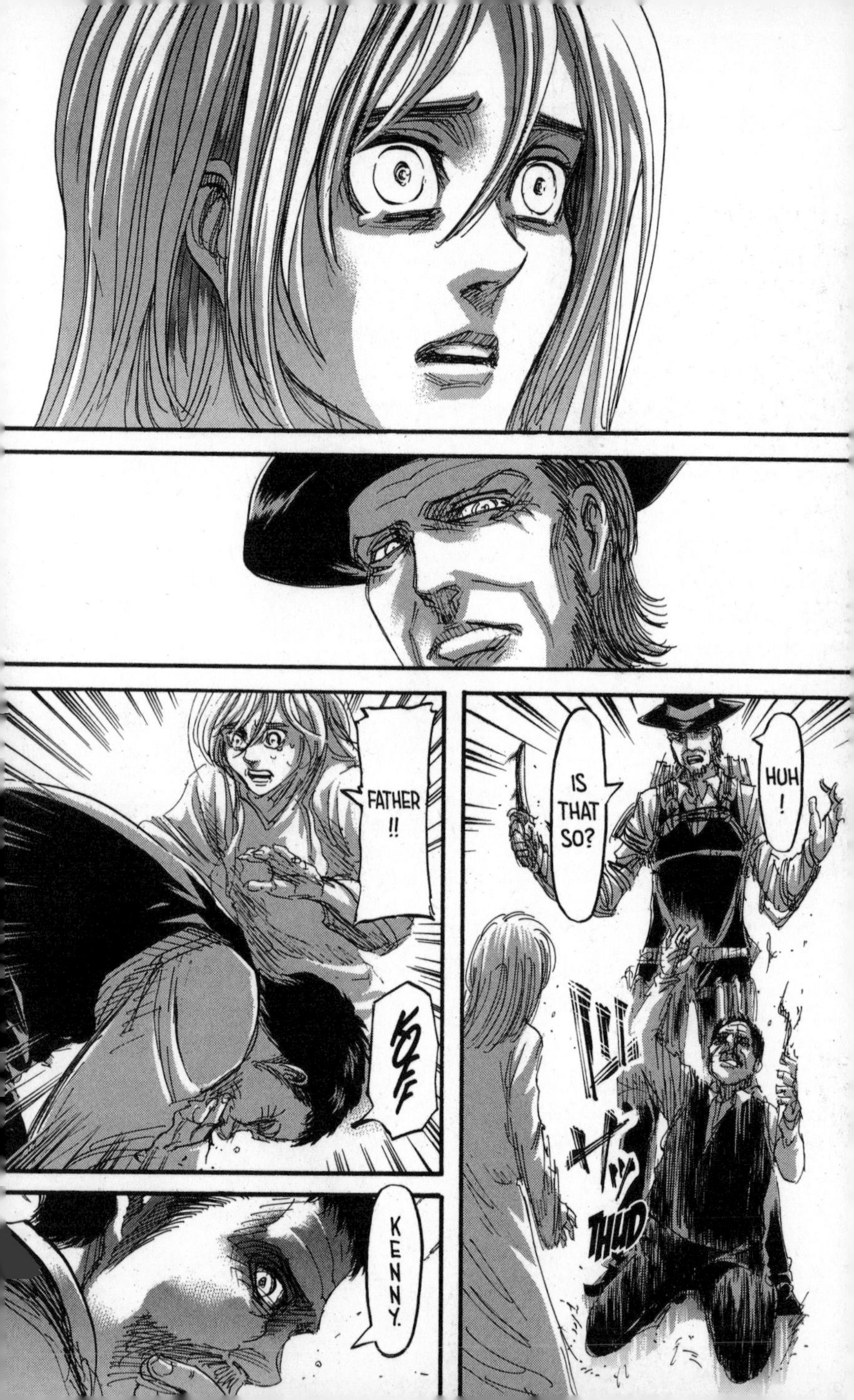
HUH!
IS THAT SO?
THUD
FATHER!!
KOFF
KENNY.

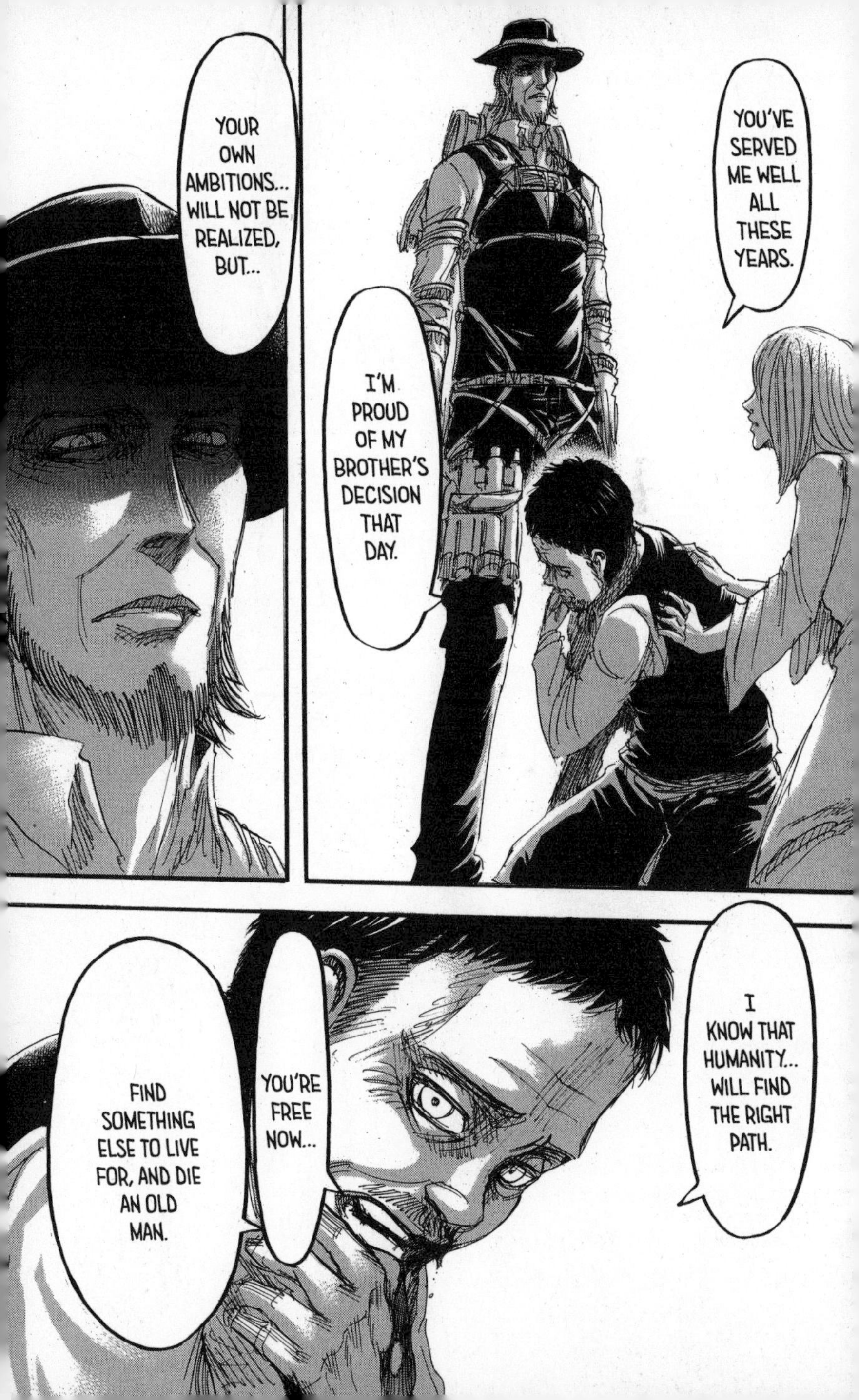
YOU'VE SERVED ME WELL ALL THESE YEARS.
I'M PROUD OF MY BROTHER'S DECISION THAT DAY.
YOUR OWN AMBITIONS... WILL NOT BE REALIZED, BUT...
I KNOW THAT HUMANITY... WILL FIND THE RIGHT PATH.
YOU'RE FREE NOW...
FIND SOMETHING ELSE TO LIVE FOR, AND DIE AN OLD MAN.

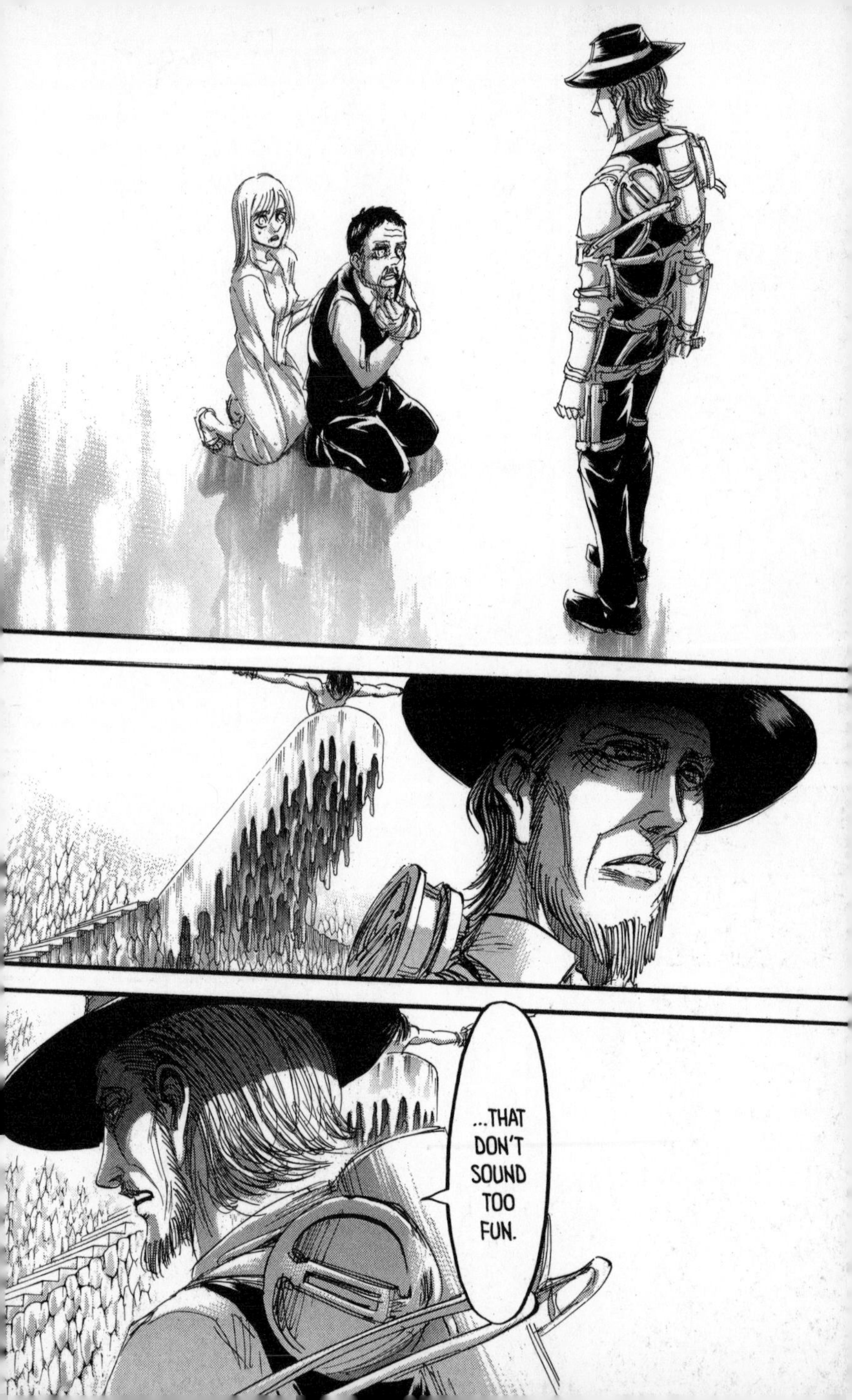
...THAT DON'T SOUND TOO FUN.

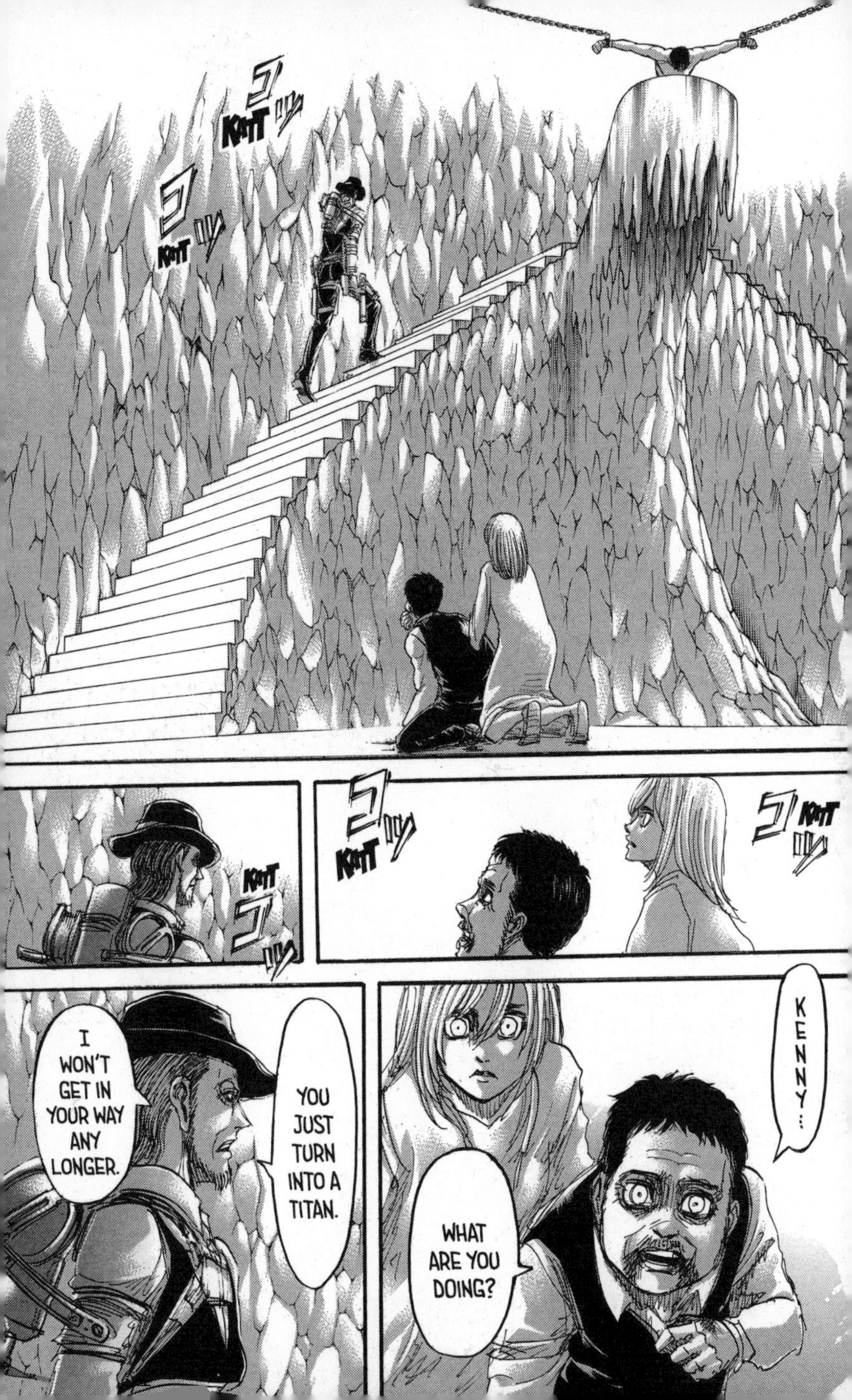
KATT
KATT
KATT
KATT
KATT
KENNY...
WHAT ARE YOU DOING?
YOU JUST TURN INTO A TITAN.
I WON'T GET IN YOUR WAY ANY LONGER.

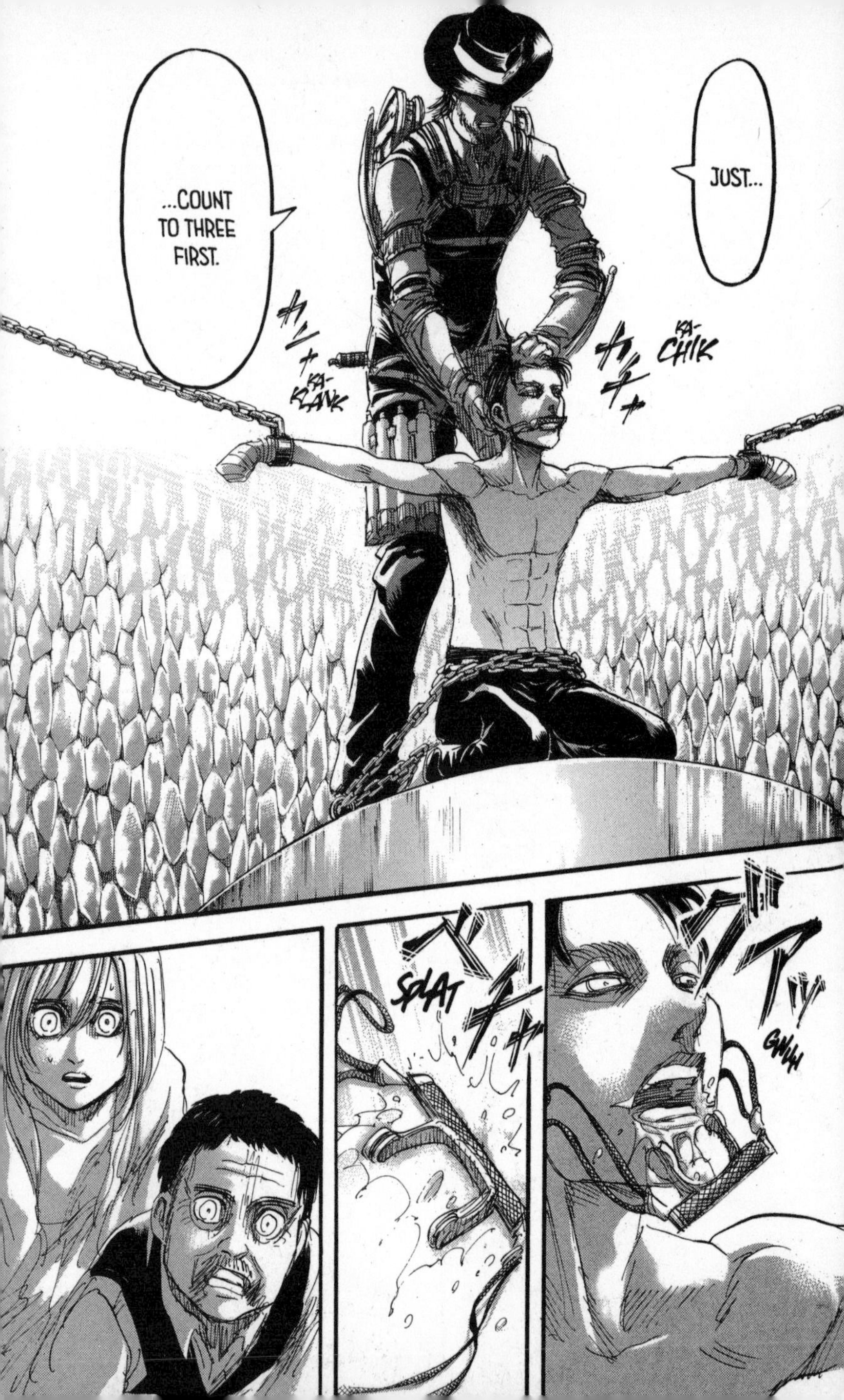
JUST...
...COUNT TO THREE FIRST.
KA-CHIK
KA-KLANK
GWAH
SPLAT

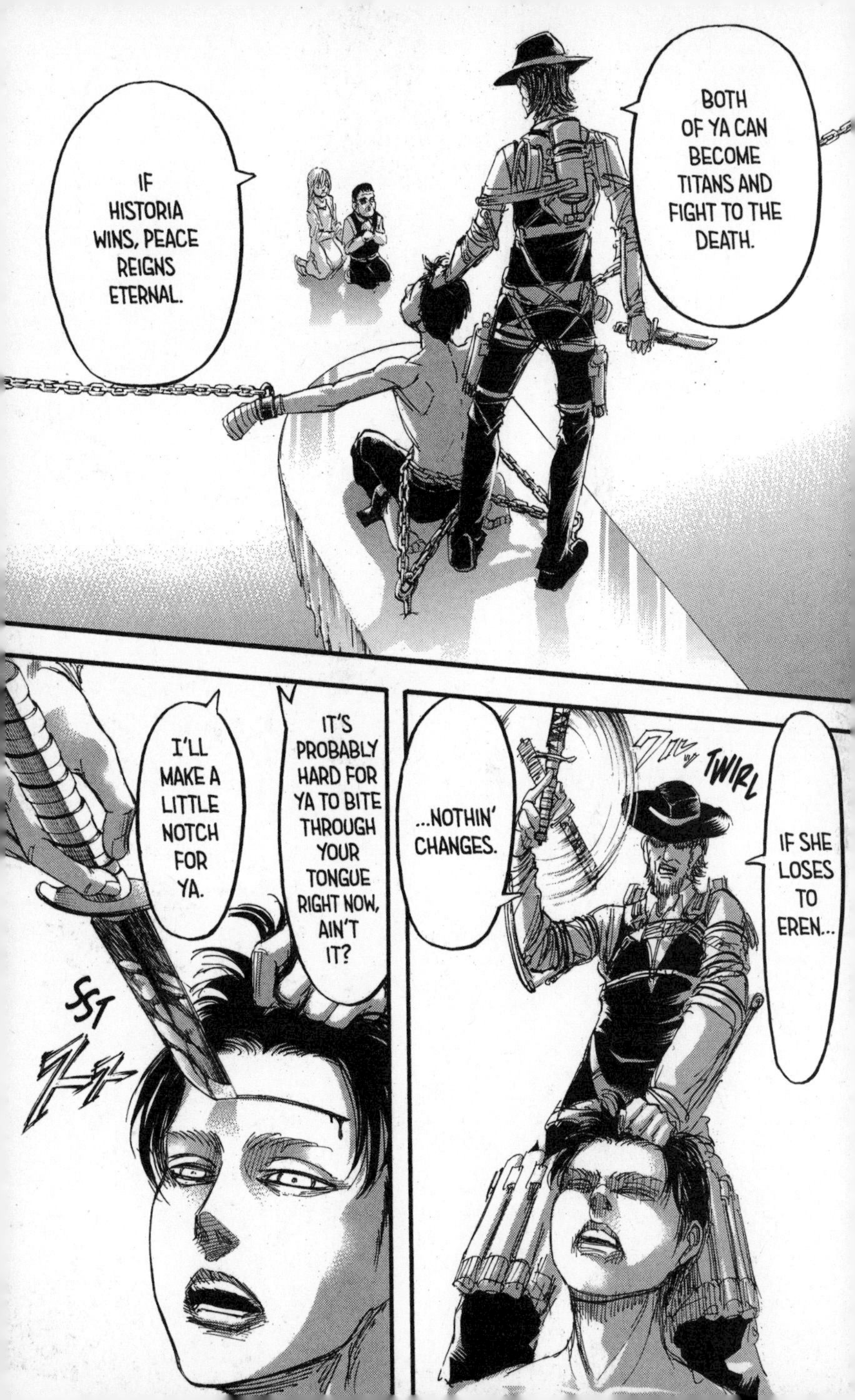
BOTH OF YA CAN BECOME TITANS AND FIGHT TO THE DEATH.
IF HISTORIA WINS, PEACE REIGNS ETERNAL.
IF SHE LOSES TO EREN...
TWIRL
...NOTHIN' CHANGES.
IT'S PROBABLY HARD FOR YA TO BITE THROUGH YOUR TONGUE RIGHT NOW, AIN'T IT?
I'LL MAKE A LITTLE NOTCH FOR YA.

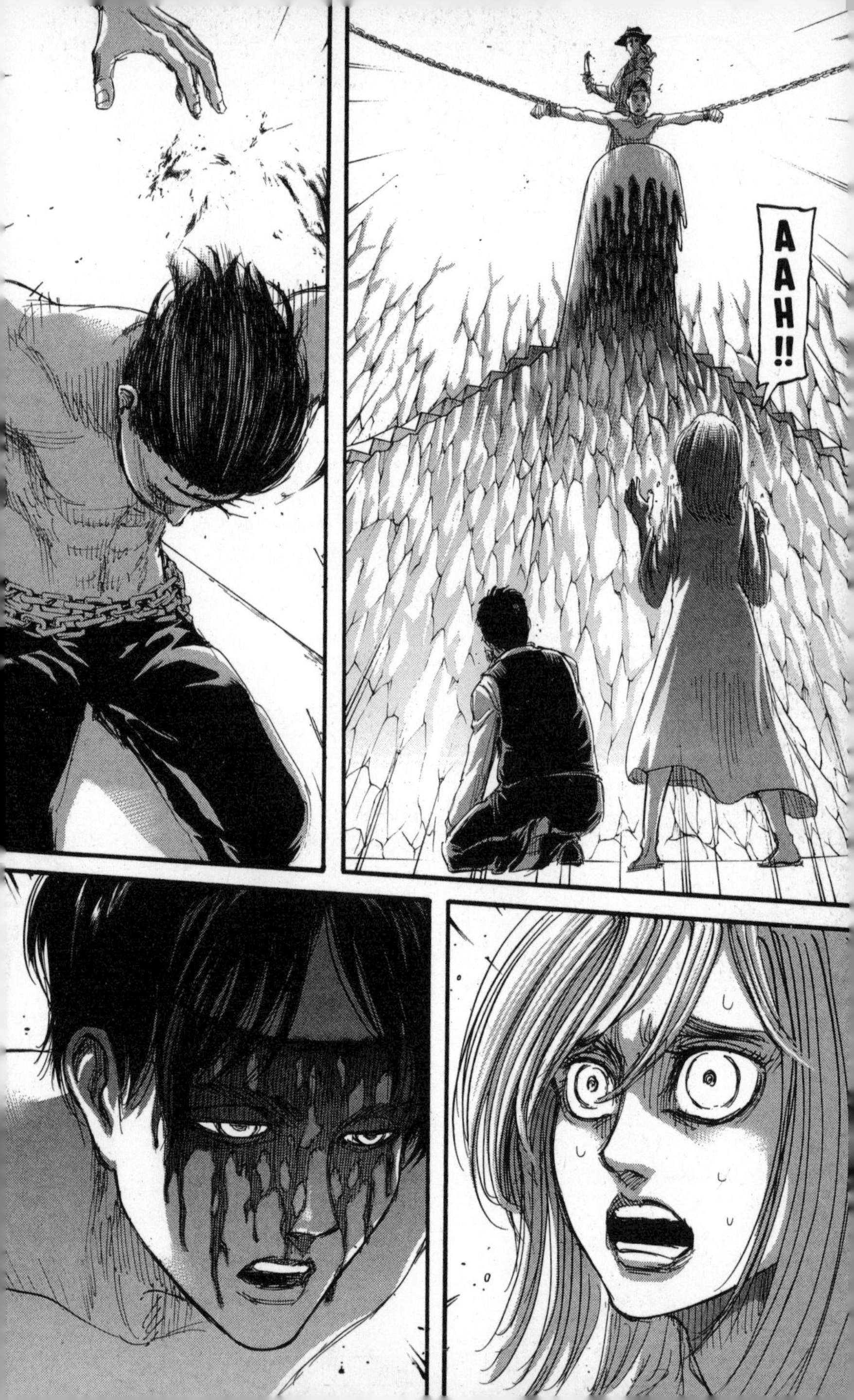
AAH!!

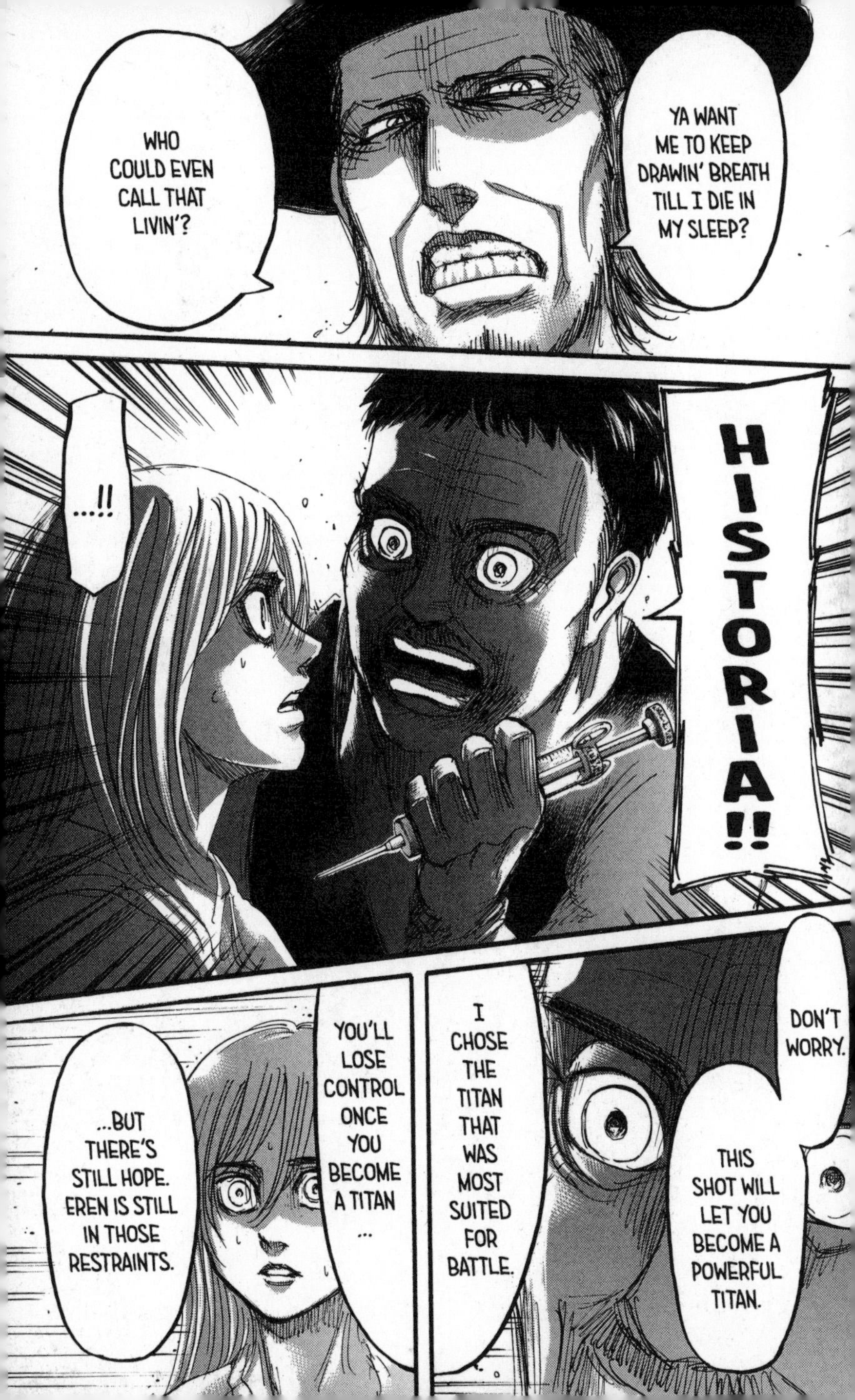
YA WANT ME TO KEEP DRAWIN' BREATH TILL I DIE IN MY SLEEP?
WHO COULD EVEN CALL THAT LIVIN'?
HISTORIA!!
...!!
DON'T WORRY.
THIS SHOT WILL LET YOU BECOME A POWERFUL TITAN.
I CHOSE THE TITAN THAT WAS MOST SUITED FOR BATTLE.
YOU'LL LOSE CONTROL ONCE YOU BECOME A TITAN ...
...BUT THERE'S STILL HOPE. EREN IS STILL IN THOSE RESTRAINTS.

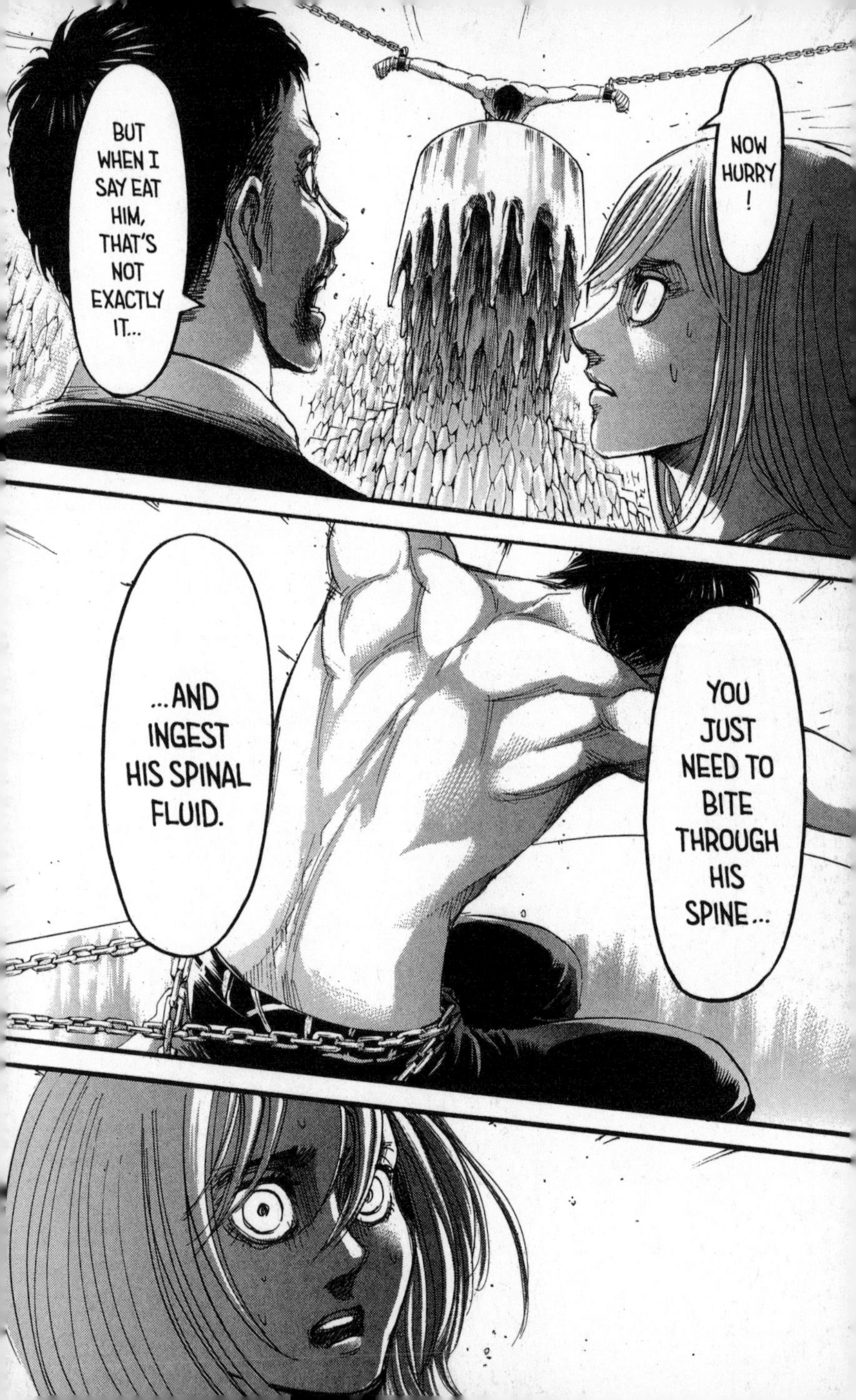
NOW HURRY!
BUT WHEN I SAY EAT HIM, THAT'S NOT EXACTLY IT...
YOU JUST NEED TO BITE THROUGH HIS SPINE...
...AND INGEST HIS SPINAL FLUID.

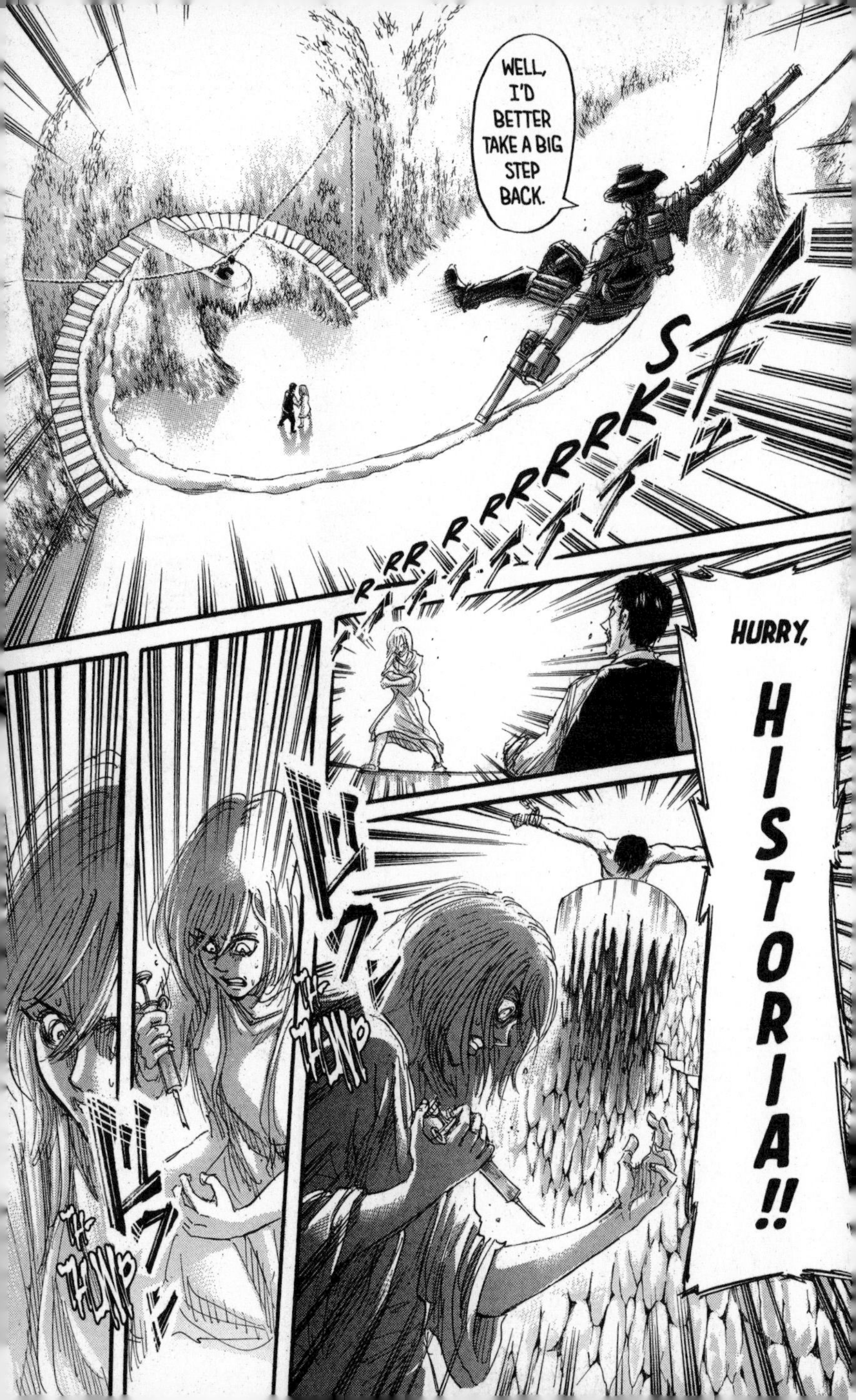
WELL, I'D BETTER TAKE A BIG STEP BACK.
HURRY, HISTORIA!!

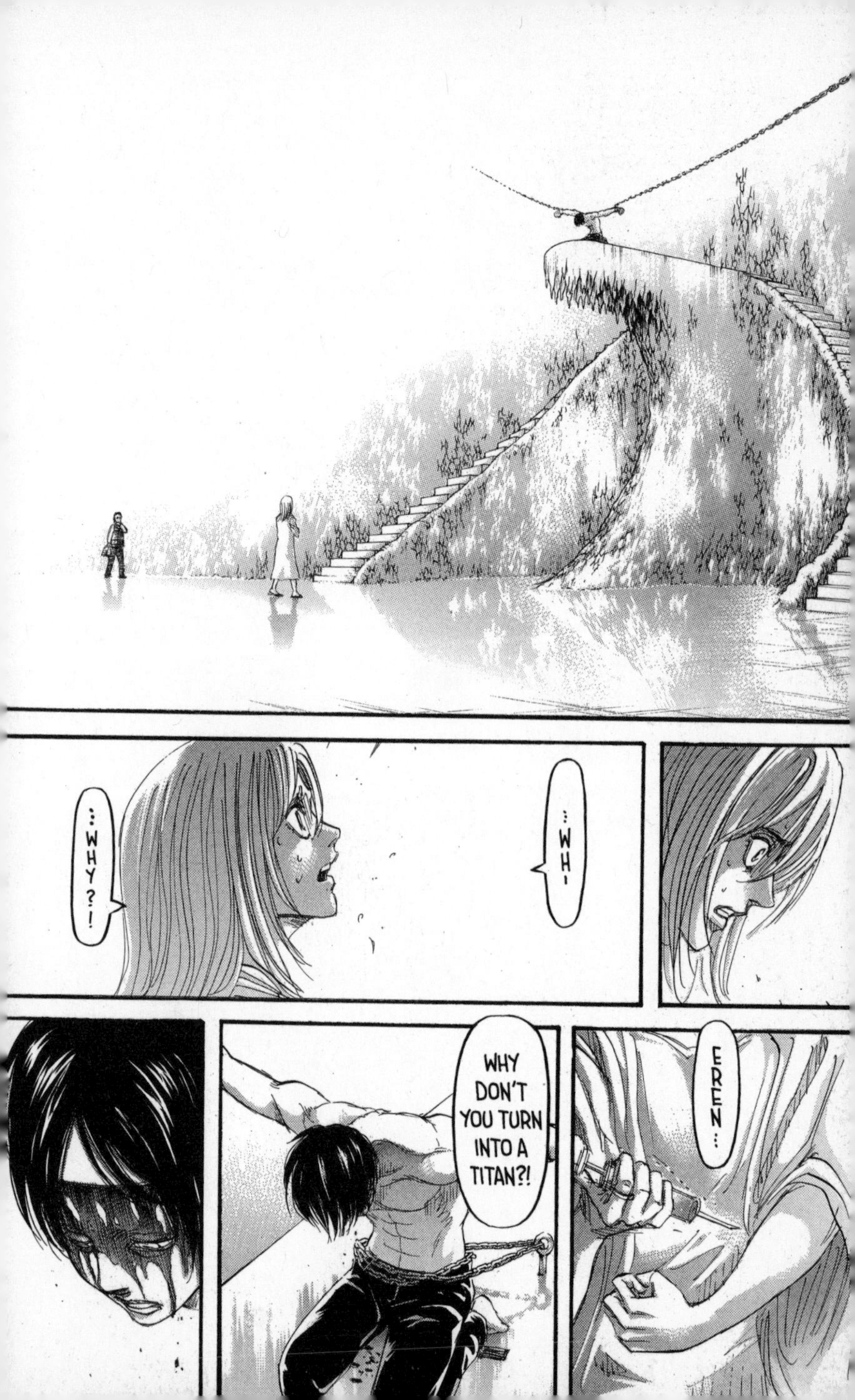
...WH-
...WHY?!
EREN...
WHY DON'T YOU TURN INTO A TITAN?!

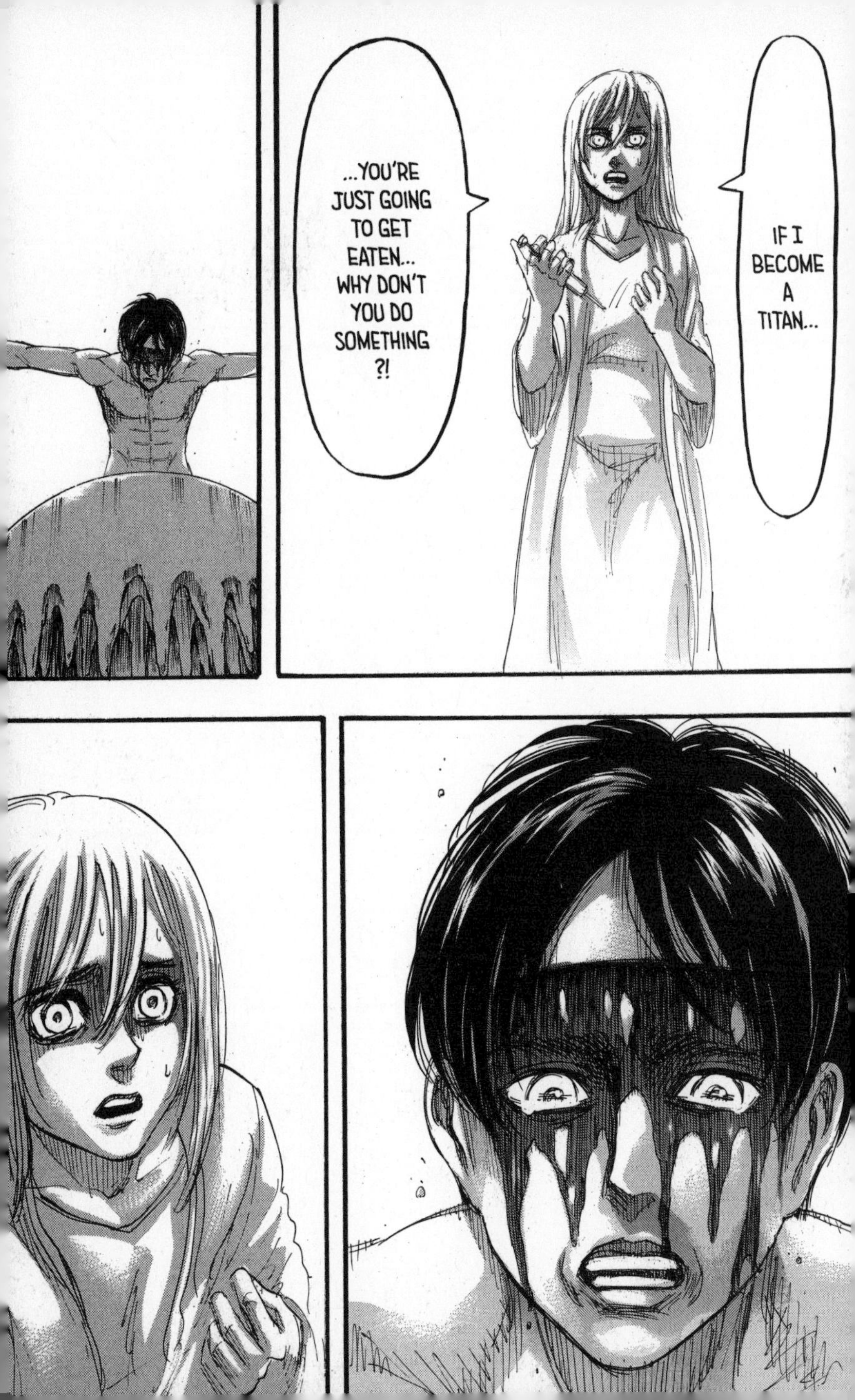
IF I BECOME A TITAN...
...YOU'RE JUST GOING TO GET EATEN... WHY DON'T YOU DO SOMETHING ?!

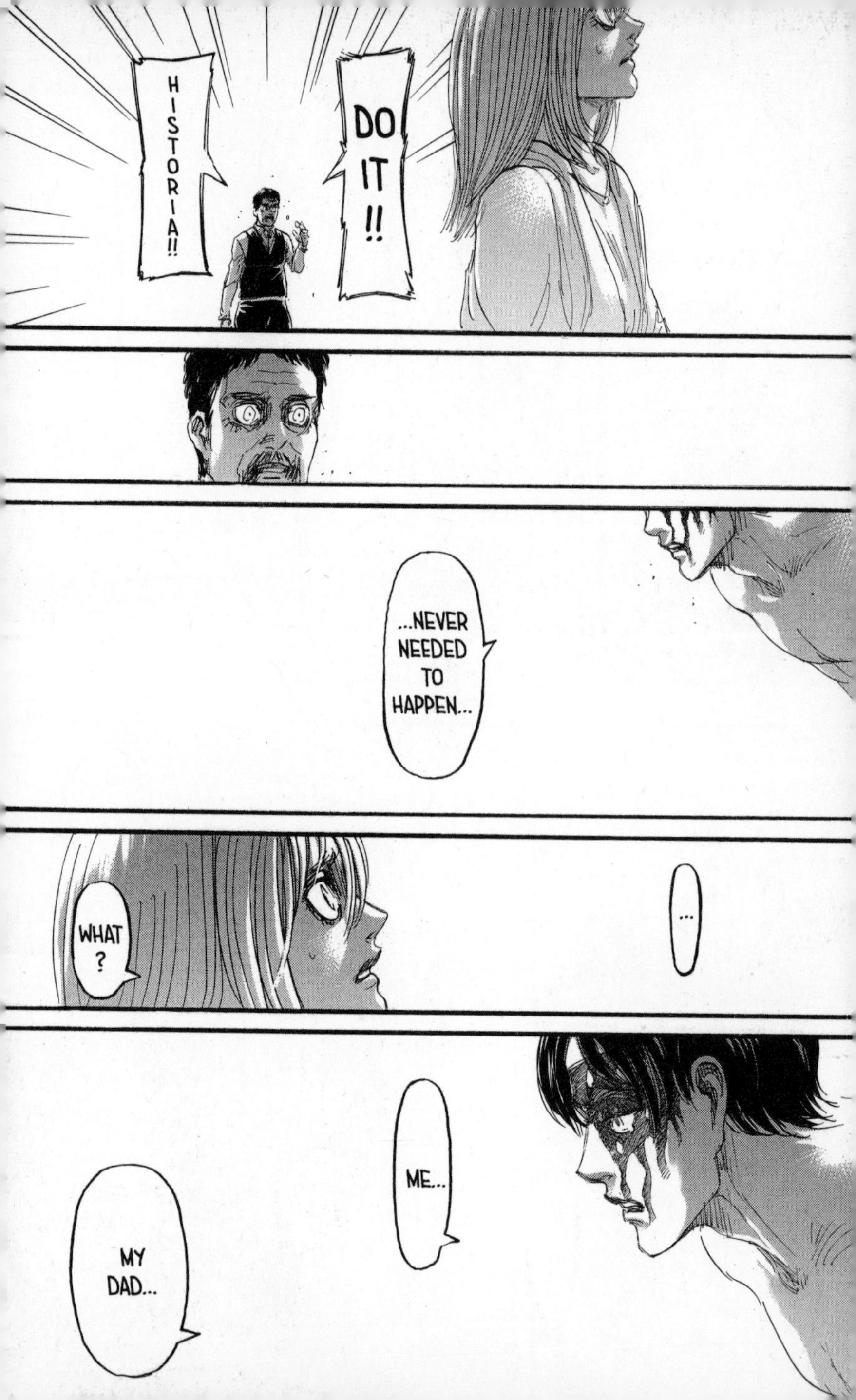
DO IT!!
HISTORIA!!
...NEVER NEEDED TO HAPPEN...
...
WHAT?
ME...
MY DAD...

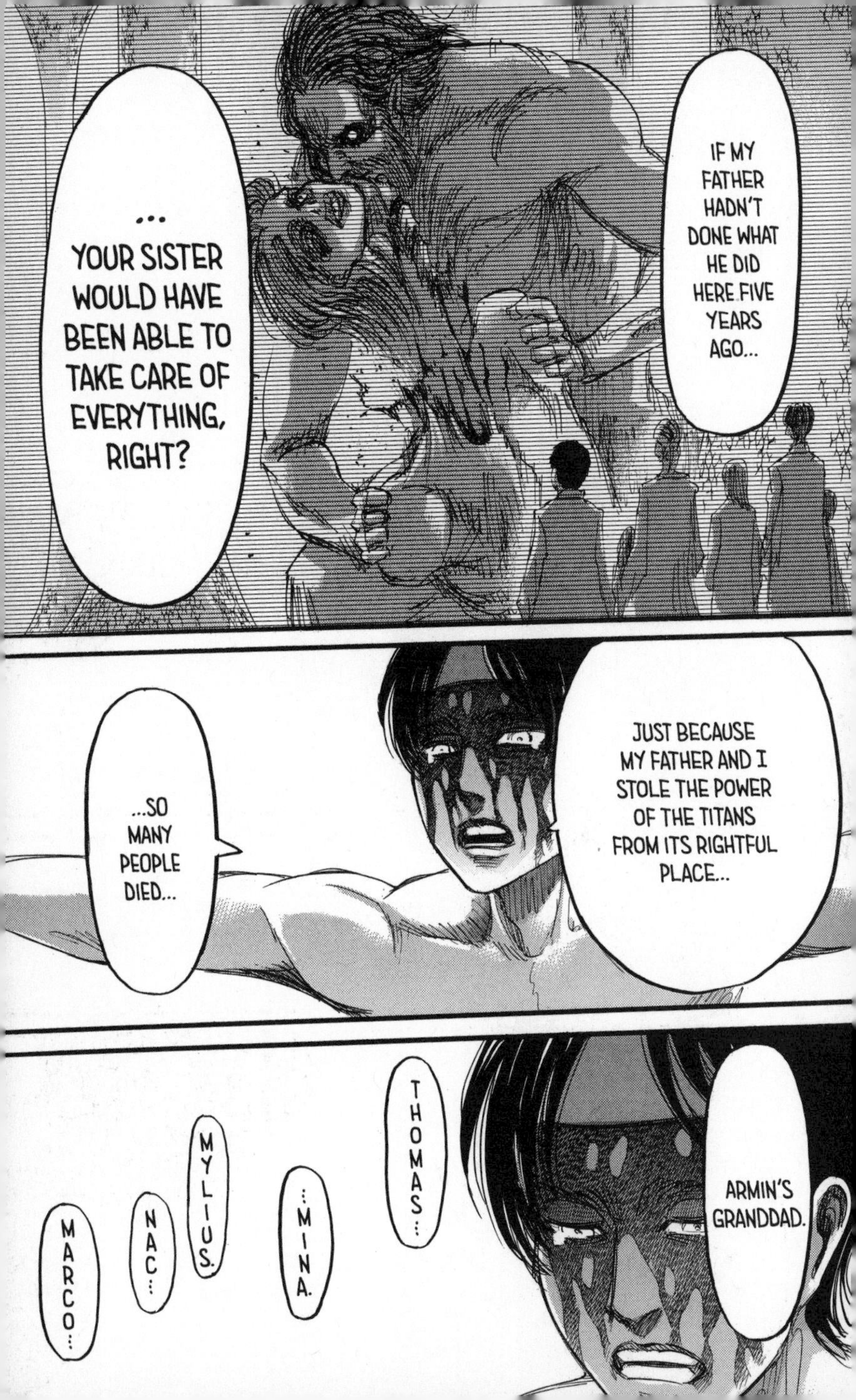
IF MY FATHER HADN'T DONE WHAT HE DID HERE FIVE YEARS AGO...
... YOUR SISTER WOULD HAVE BEEN ABLE TO TAKE CARE OF EVERYTHING, RIGHT?
JUST BECAUSE MY FATHER AND I STOLE THE POWER OF THE TITANS FROM ITS RIGHTFUL PLACE...
...SO MANY PEOPLE DIED...
ARMIN'S GRANDDAD.
THOMAS...
...MINA.
MYLIUS.
NAC...
MARCO...

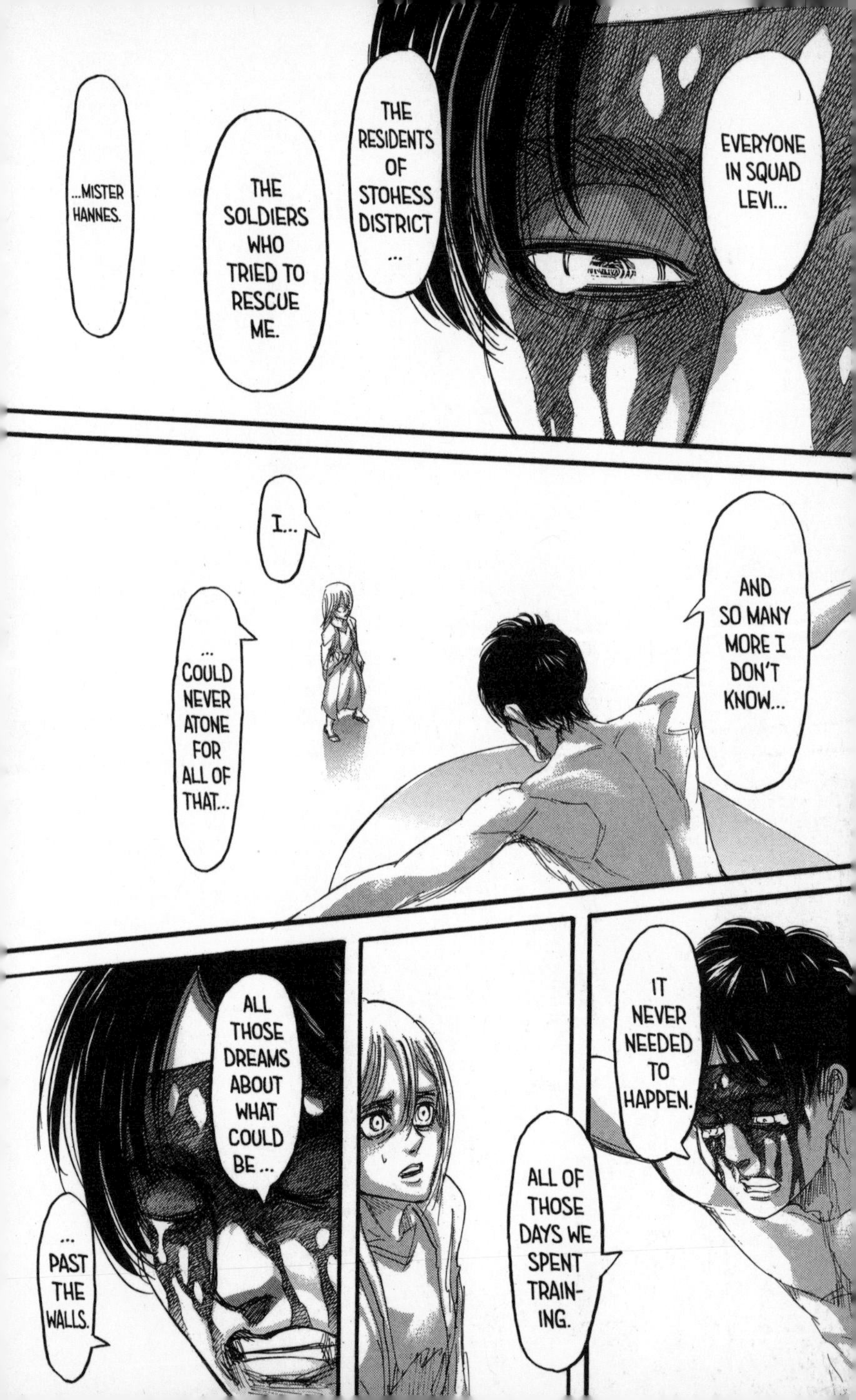
EVERYONE IN SQUAD LEVI...
THE RESIDENTS OF STOHESS DISTRICT ...
THE SOLDIERS WHO TRIED TO RESCUE ME.
...MISTER HANNES.
AND SO MANY MORE I DON'T KNOW...
I...
... COULD NEVER ATONE FOR ALL OF THAT...
IT NEVER NEEDED TO HAPPEN.
ALL OF THOSE DAYS WE SPENT TRAIN-ING.
ALL THOSE DREAMS ABOUT WHAT COULD BE ...
... PAST THE WALLS.

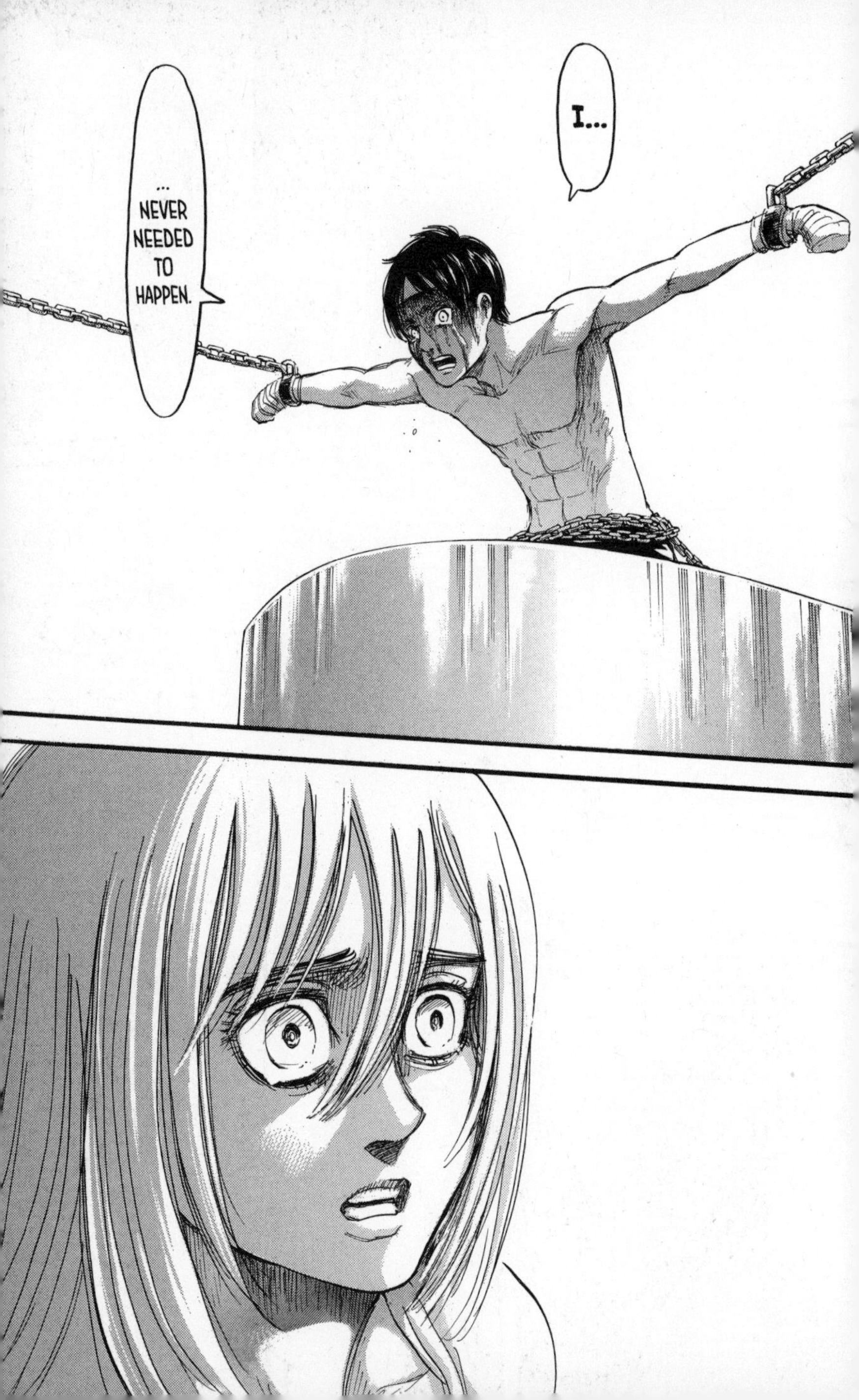
I...
... NEVER NEEDED TO HAPPEN.

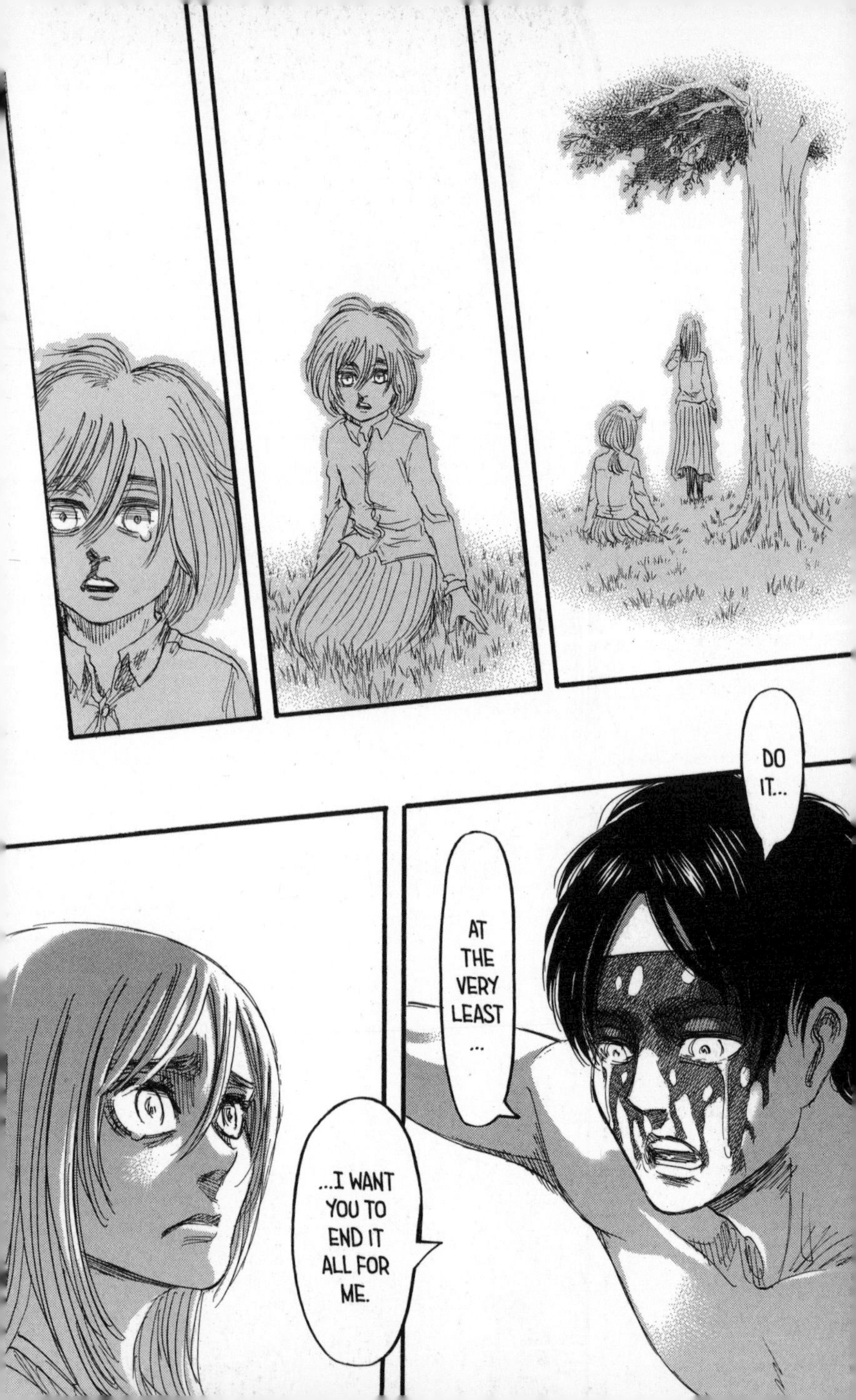
DO IT...
AT THE VERY LEAST ...
...I WANT YOU TO END IT ALL FOR ME.

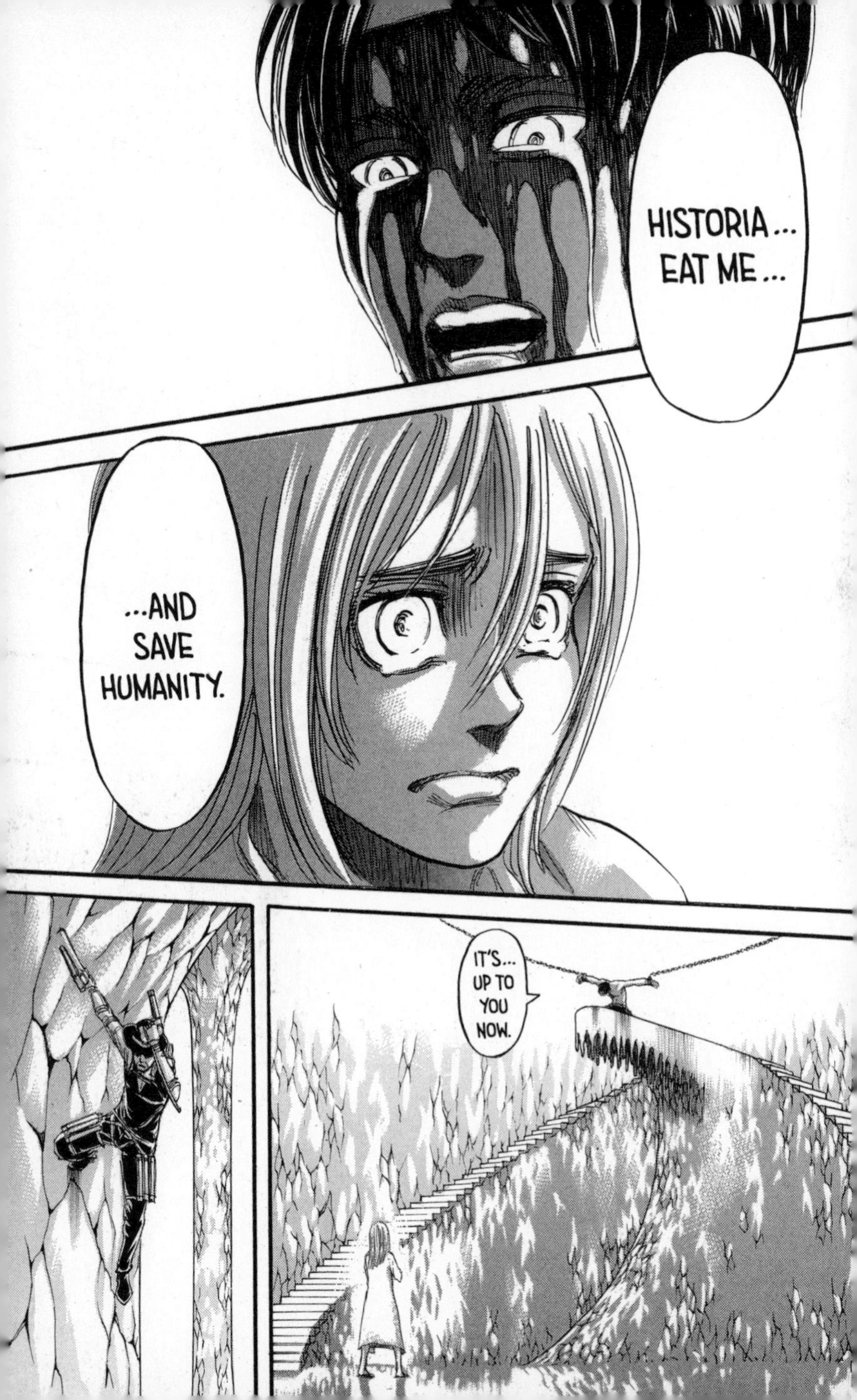
HISTORIA... EAT ME...
...AND SAVE HUMANITY.
IT'S... UP TO YOU NOW.

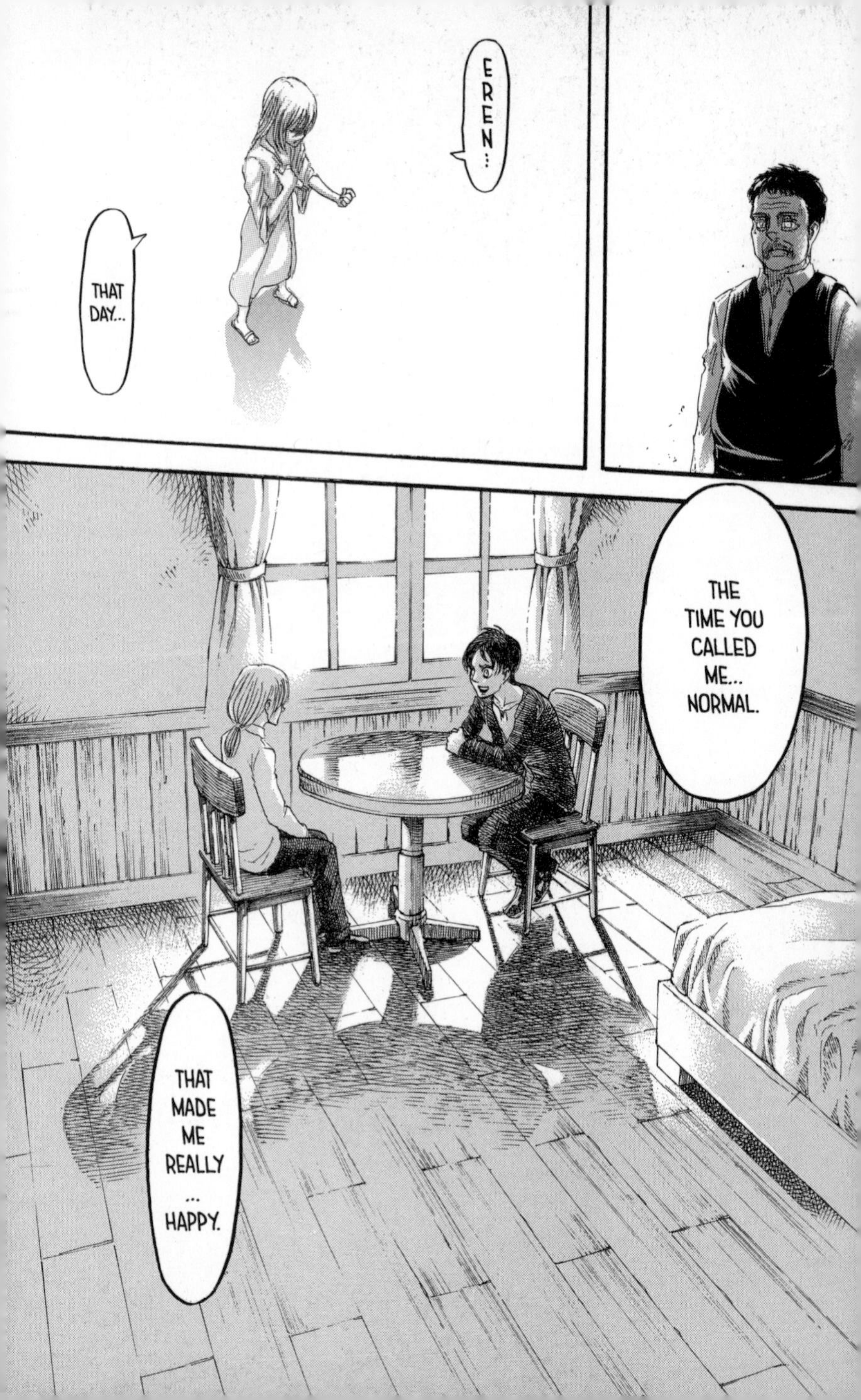
EREN...
THAT DAY...
THE TIME YOU CALLED ME... NORMAL.
THAT MADE ME REALLY ... HAPPY.

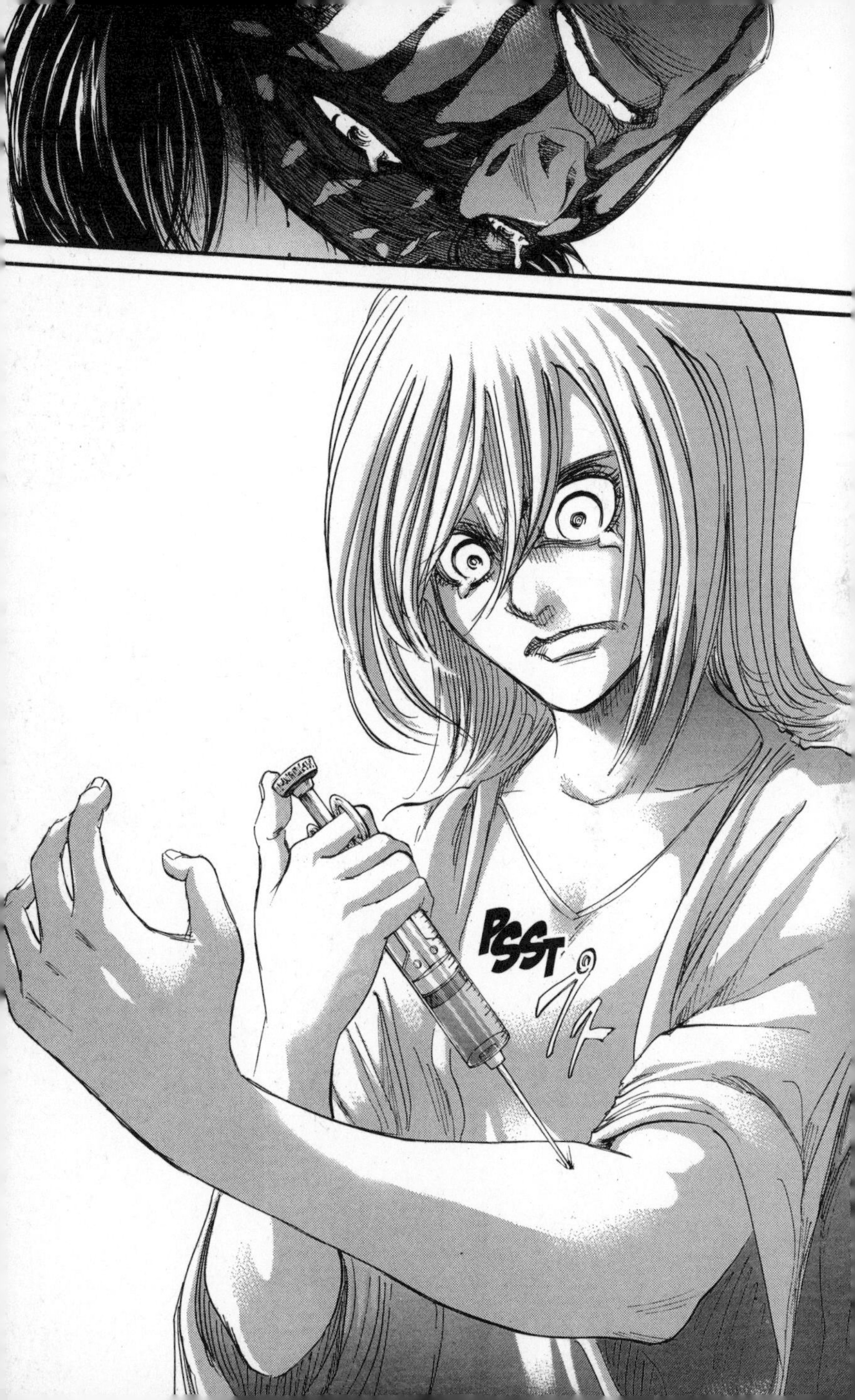
PSST

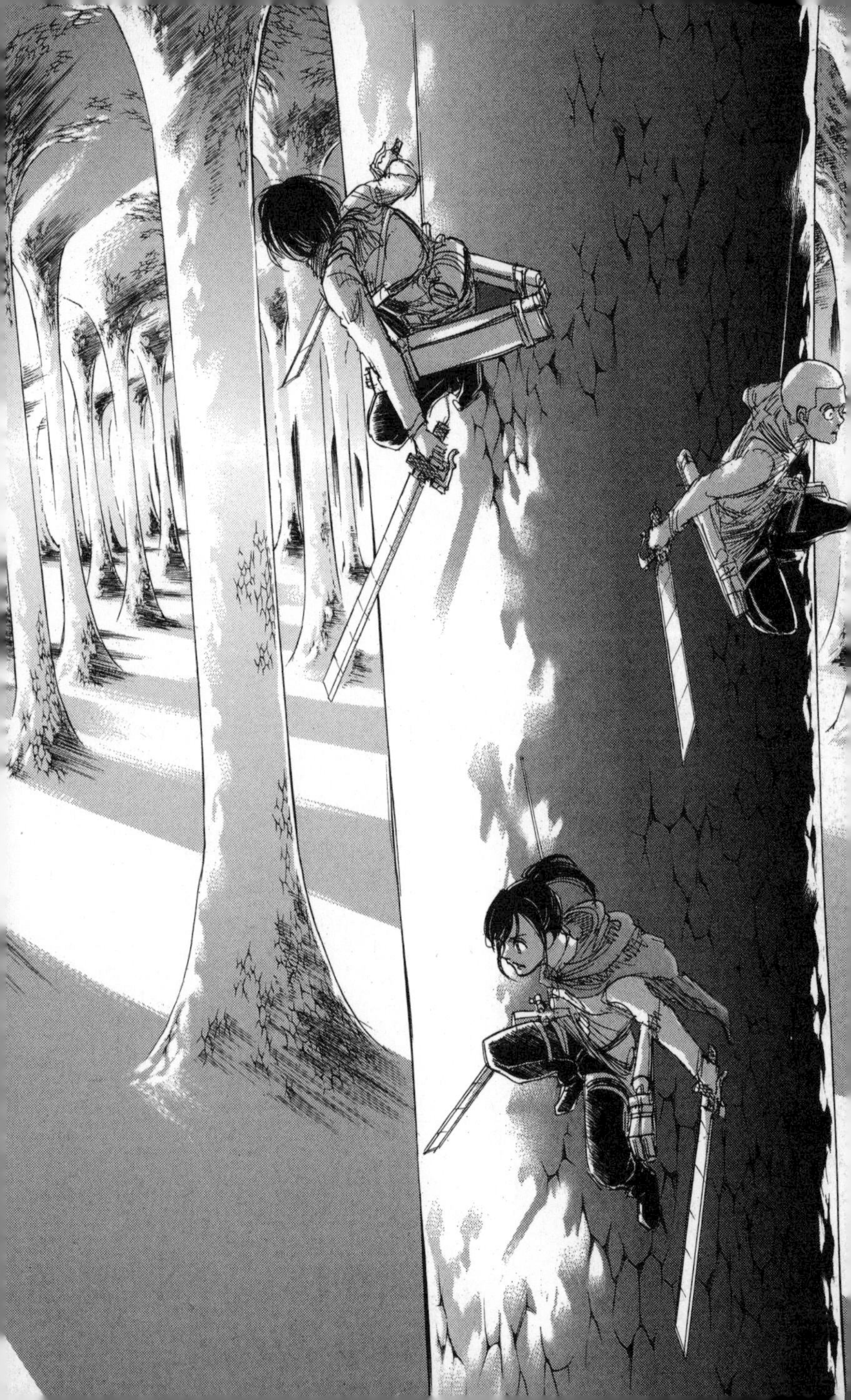

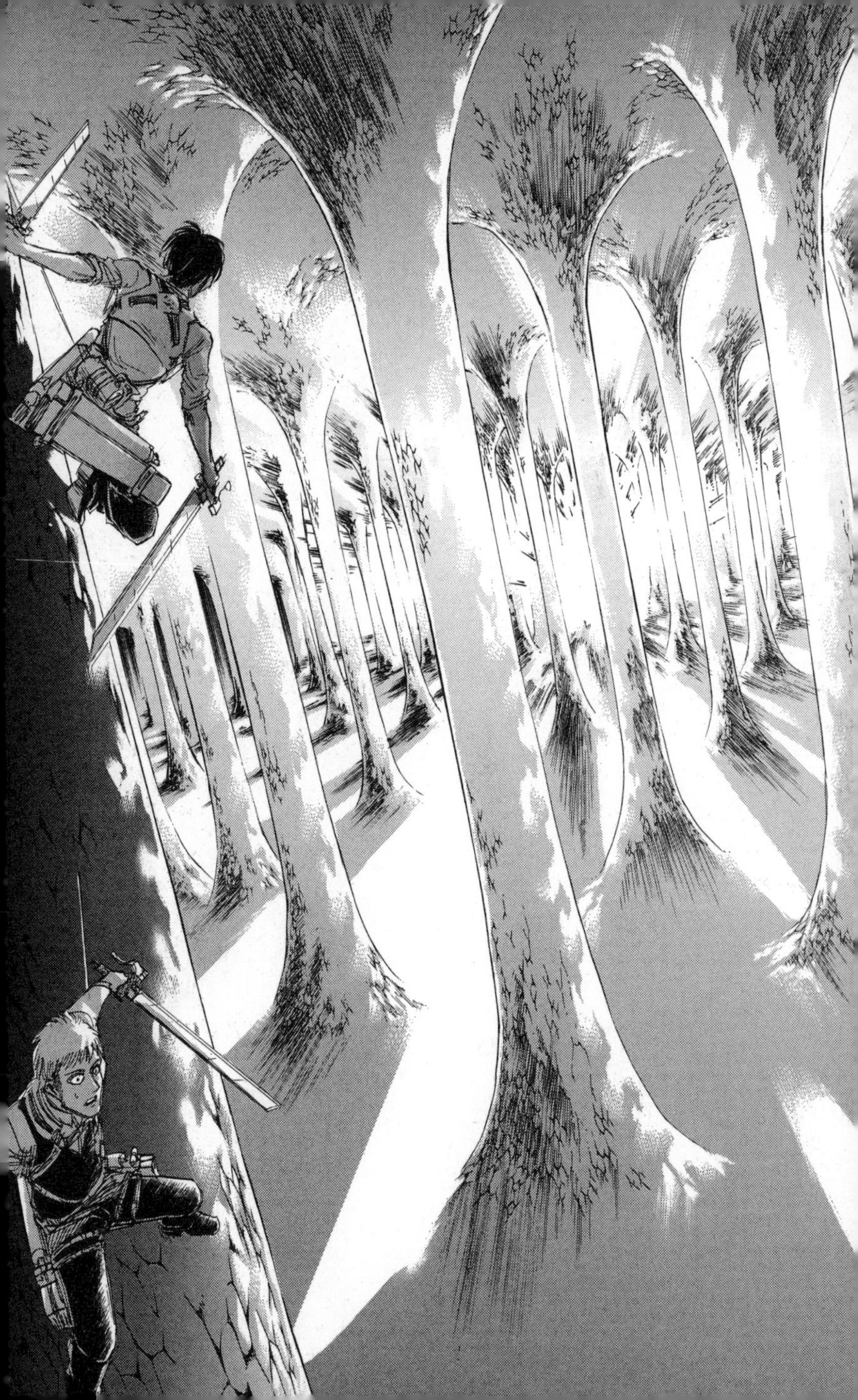

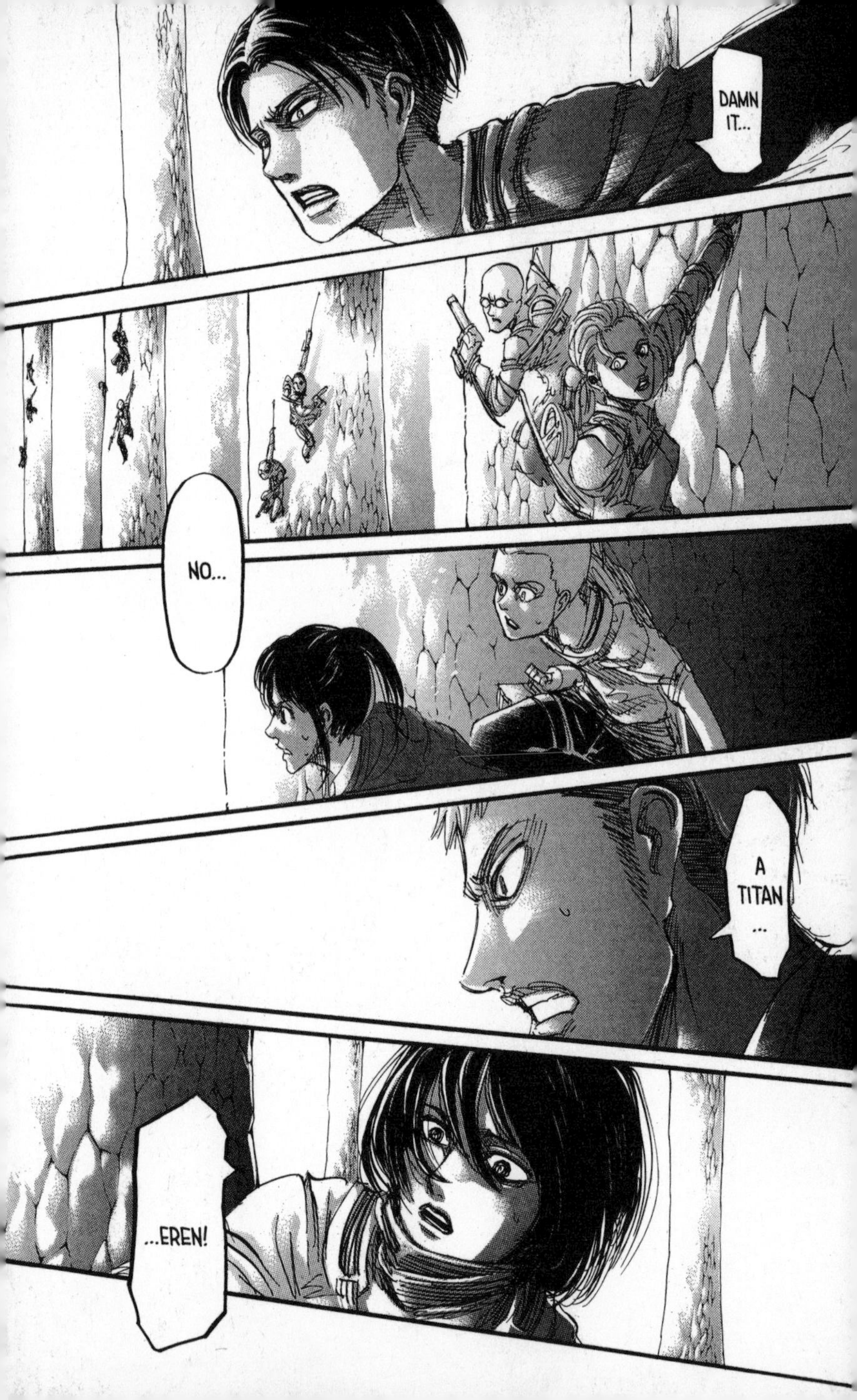
DAMN IT...
NO...
A TITAN ...
...EREN!

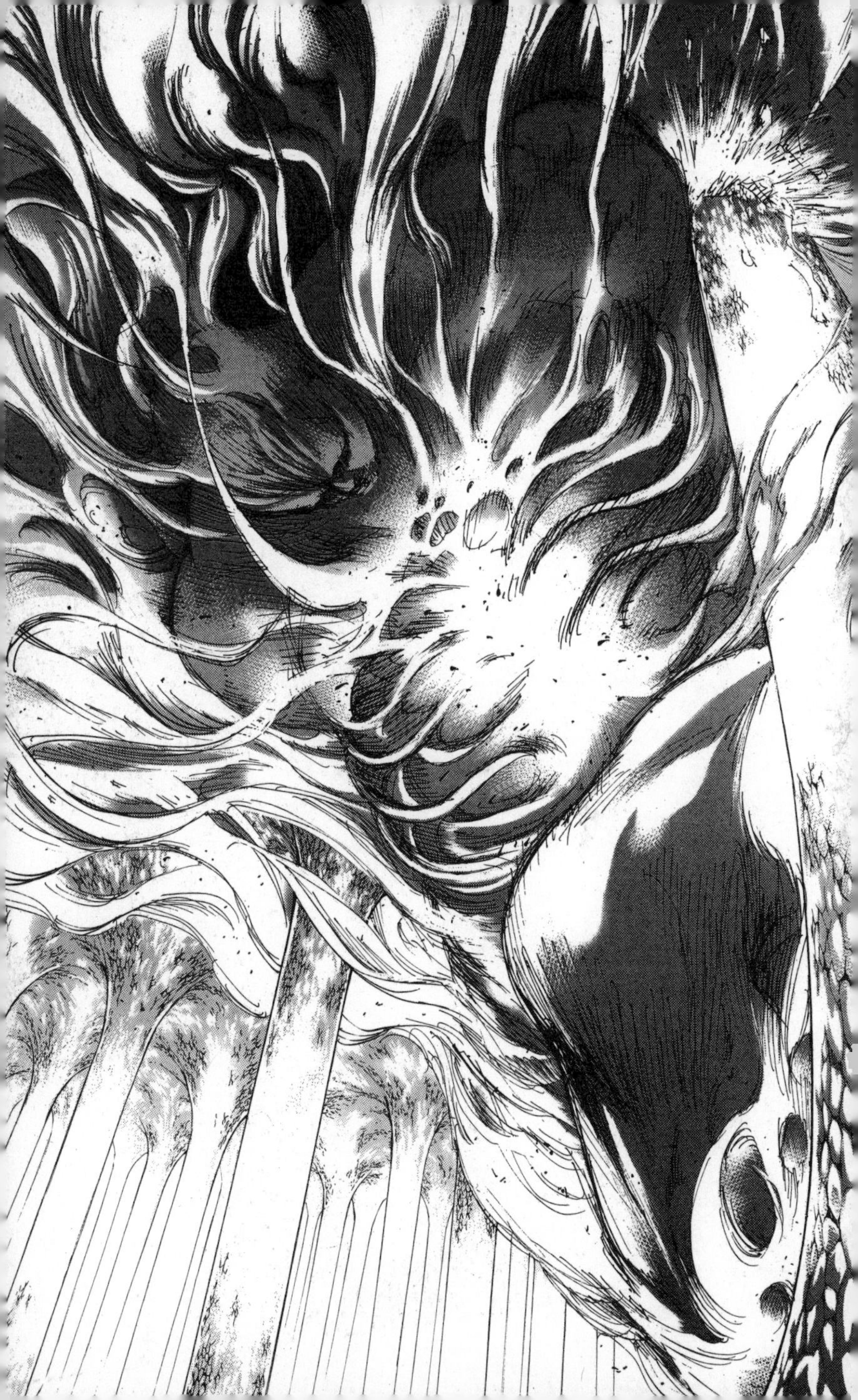

ATTACK on TITAN

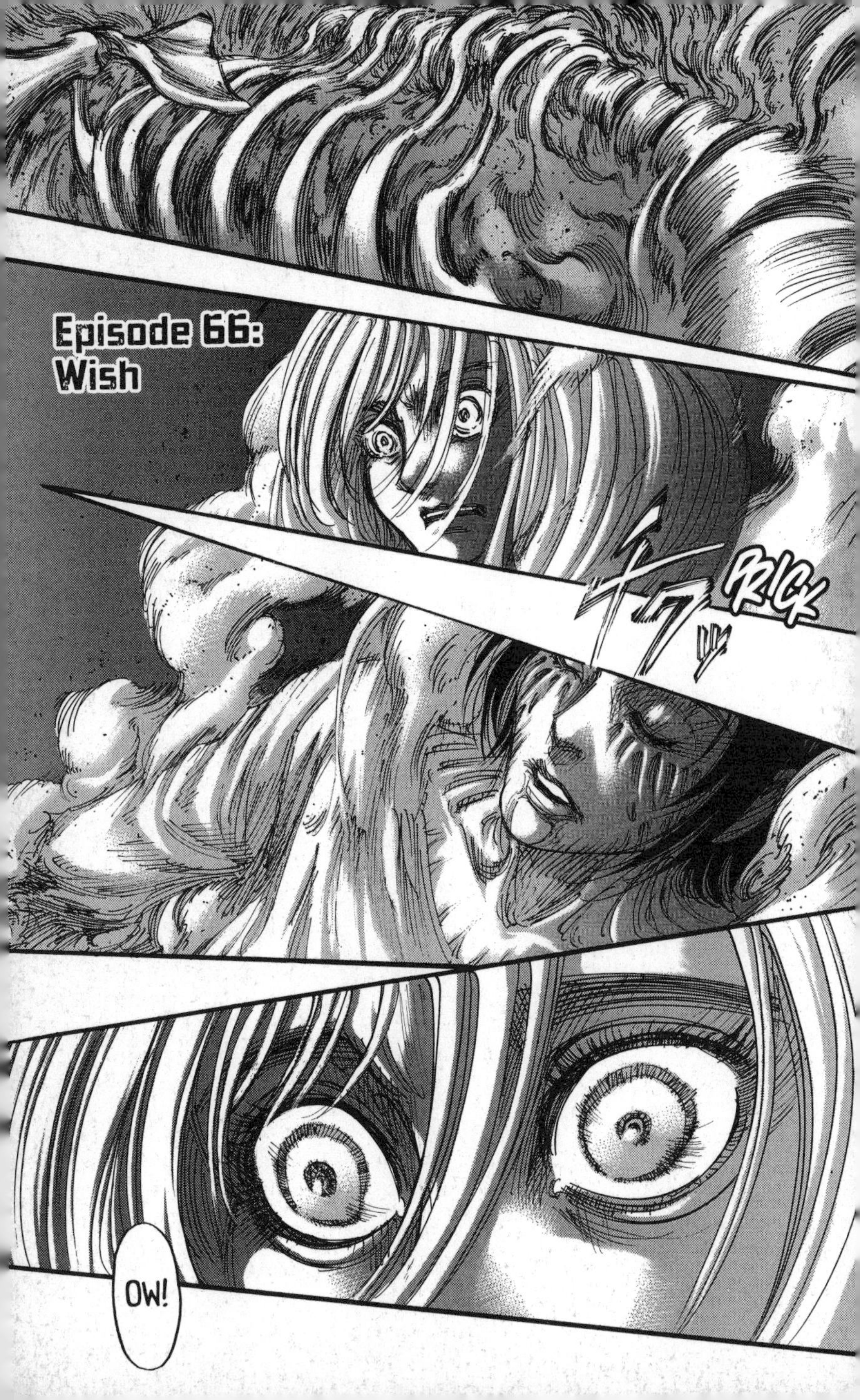
Episode 66:
Wish
PRICK
OW!

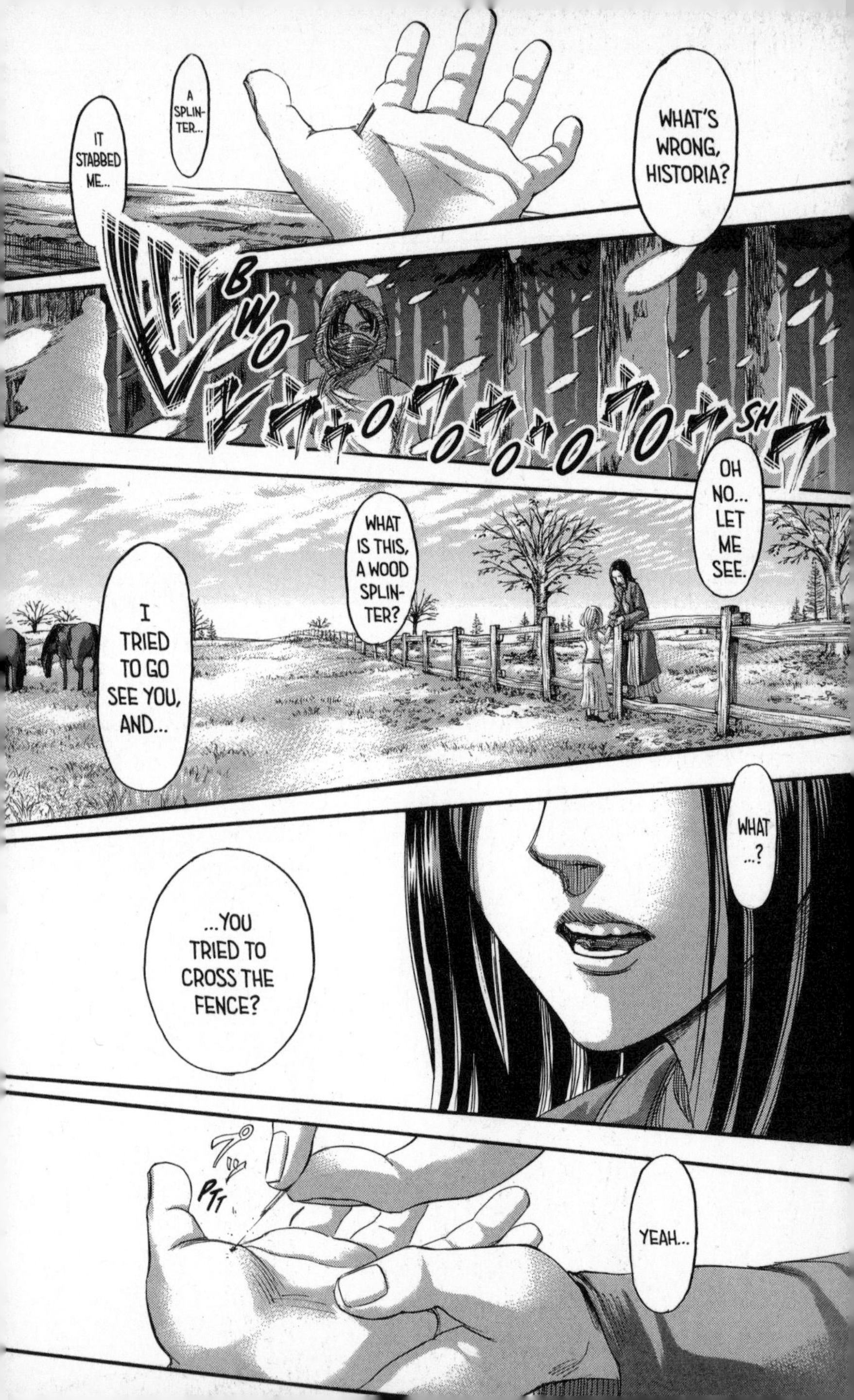
WHAT'S WRONG, HISTORIA?
A SPLINTER...
IT STABBED ME...
OH NO... LET ME SEE.
WHAT IS THIS, A WOOD SPLINTER?
I TRIED TO GO SEE YOU, AND...
WHAT ...?
...YOU TRIED TO CROSS THE FENCE?
YEAH...
PTT

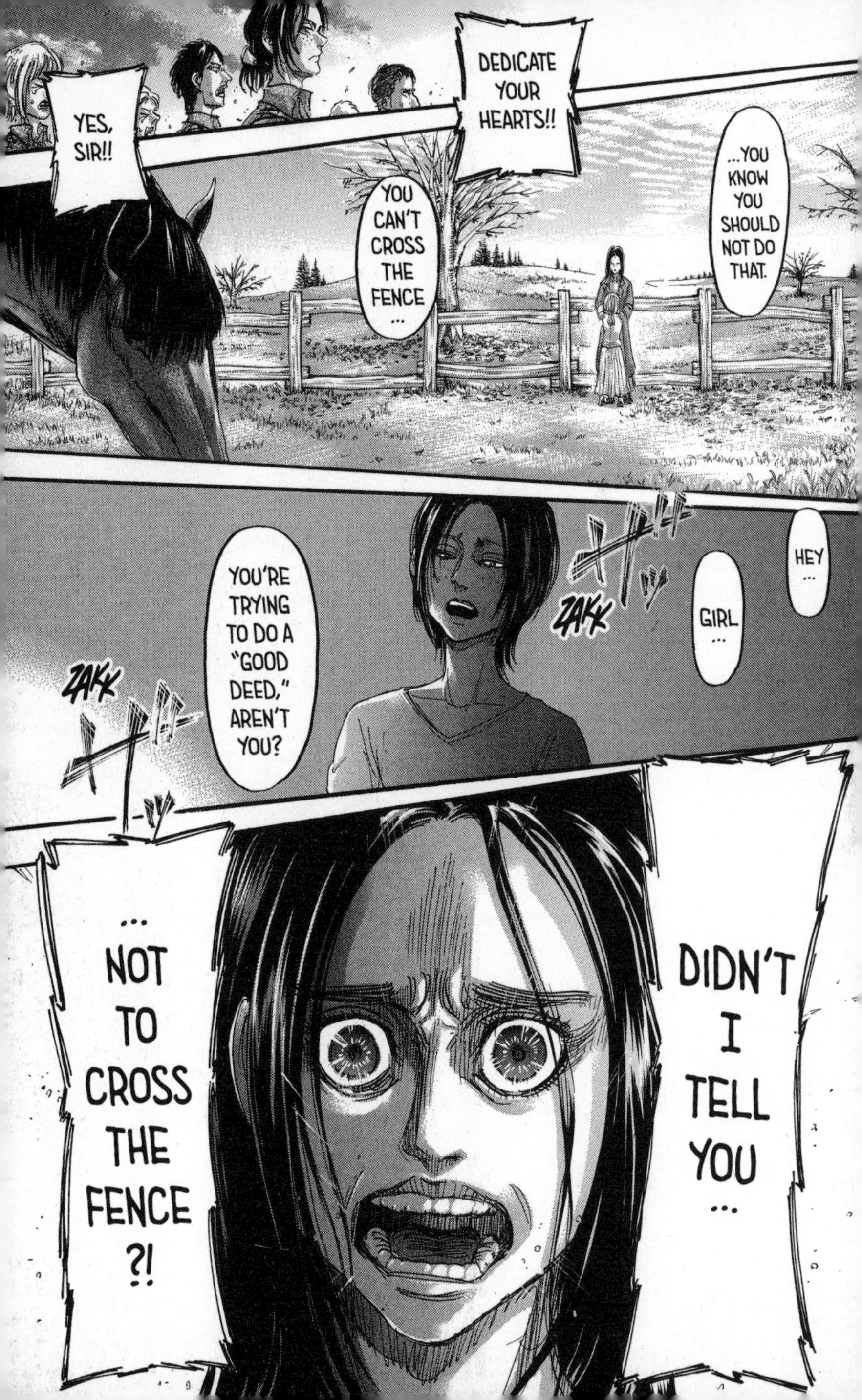
DEDICATE YOUR HEARTS!!
YES, SIR!!
...YOU KNOW YOU SHOULD NOT DO THAT.
YOU CAN'T CROSS THE FENCE...
HEY...
GIRL...
ZAKK
YOU'RE TRYING TO DO A "GOOD DEED," AREN'T YOU?
ZAKK
DIDN'T I TELL YOU...
...NOT TO CROSS THE FENCE?!

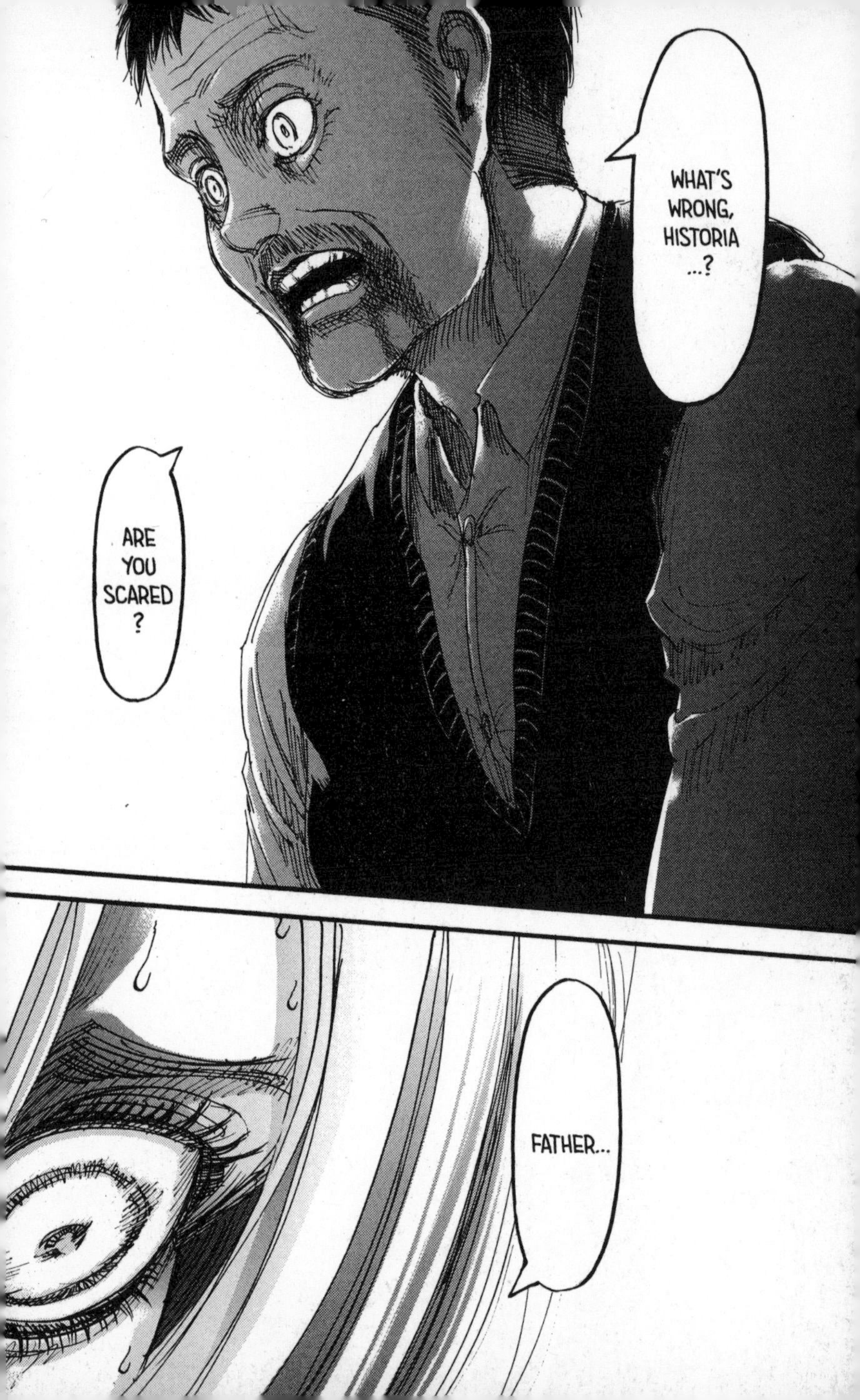
WHAT'S WRONG, HISTORIA ...?
ARE YOU SCARED ?
FATHER...

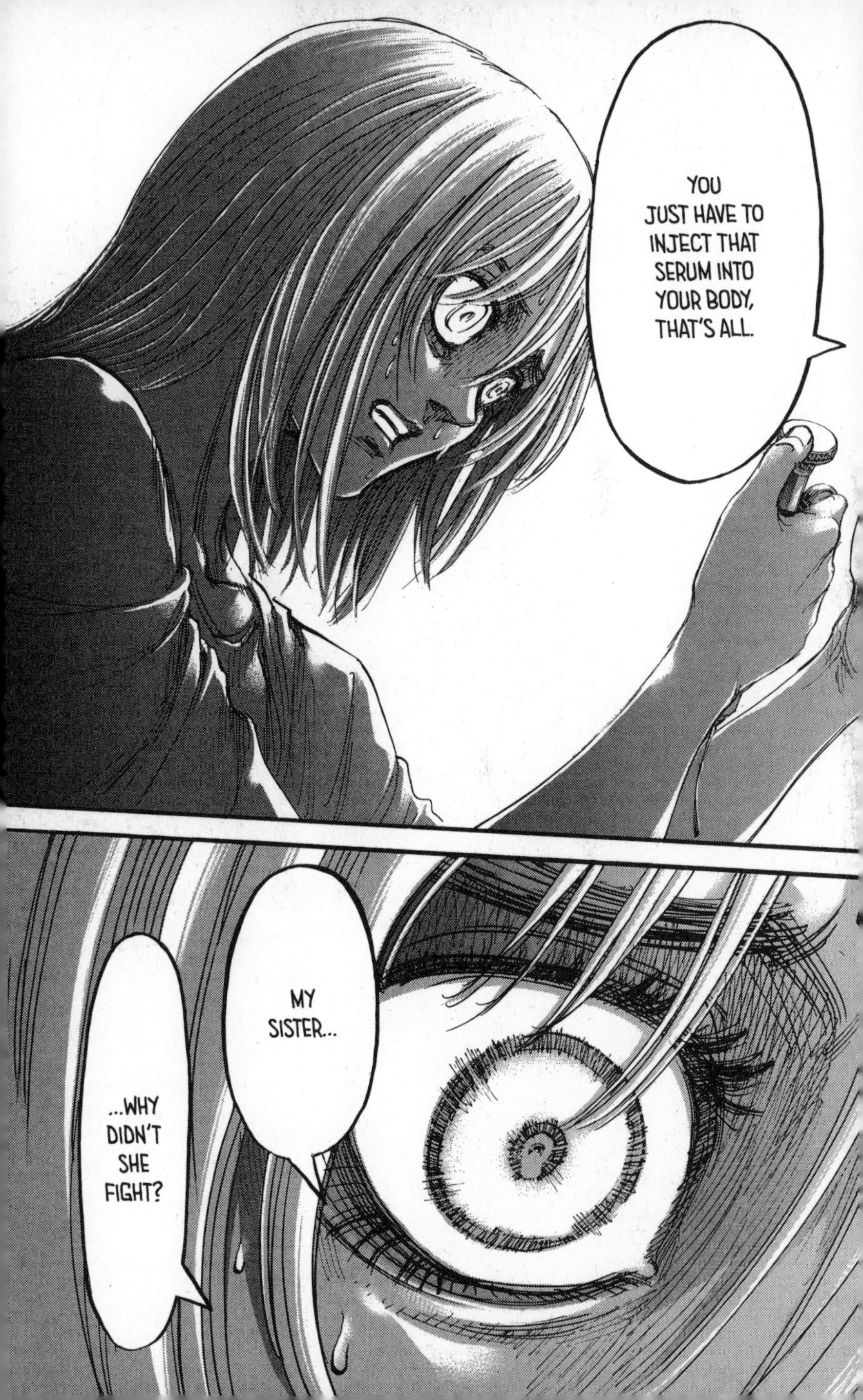
YOU JUST HAVE TO INJECT THAT SERUM INTO YOUR BODY, THAT'S ALL.
MY SISTER...
...WHY DIDN'T SHE FIGHT?

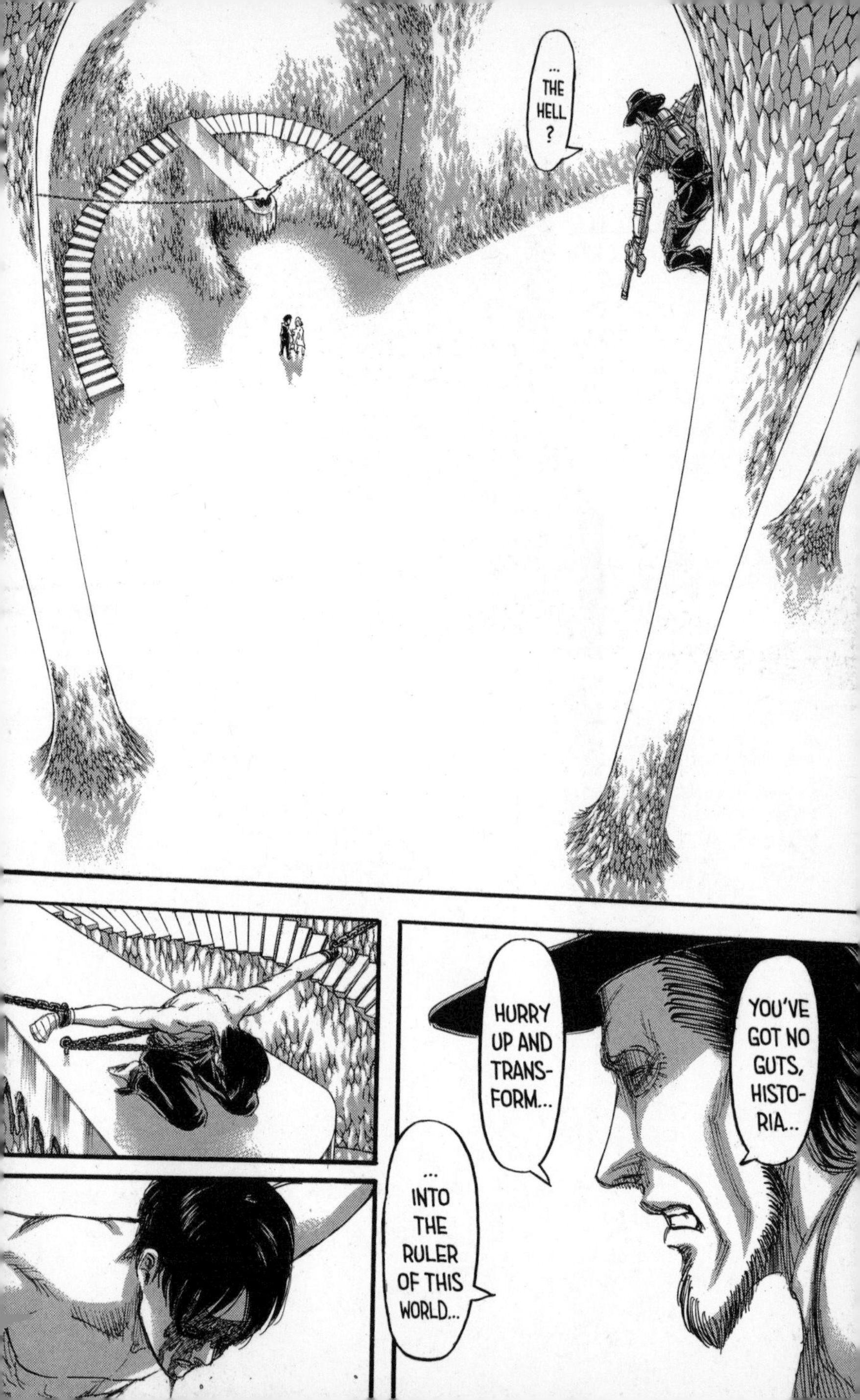
... THE HELL ?
YOU'VE GOT NO GUTS, HISTORIA...
HURRY UP AND TRANSFORM...
... INTO THE RULER OF THIS WORLD...

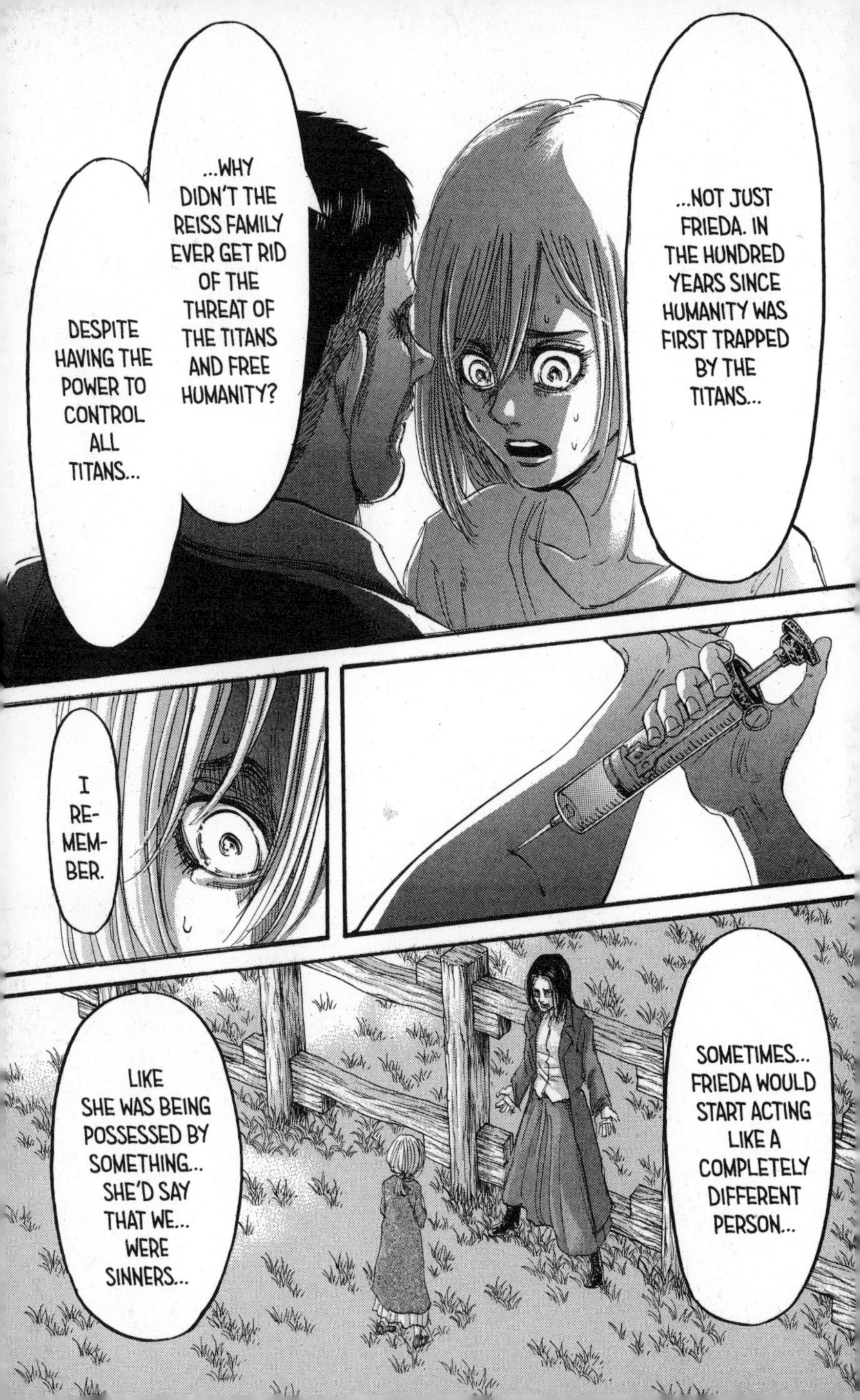
...NOT JUST FRIEDA. IN THE HUNDRED YEARS SINCE HUMANITY WAS FIRST TRAPPED BY THE TITANS...
...WHY DIDN'T THE REISS FAMILY EVER GET RID OF THE THREAT OF THE TITANS AND FREE HUMANITY?
DESPITE HAVING THE POWER TO CONTROL ALL TITANS...
I RE-MEM-BER.
SOMETIMES... FRIEDA WOULD START ACTING LIKE A COMPLETELY DIFFERENT PERSON...
LIKE SHE WAS BEING POSSESSED BY SOMETHING... SHE'D SAY THAT WE... WERE SINNERS...

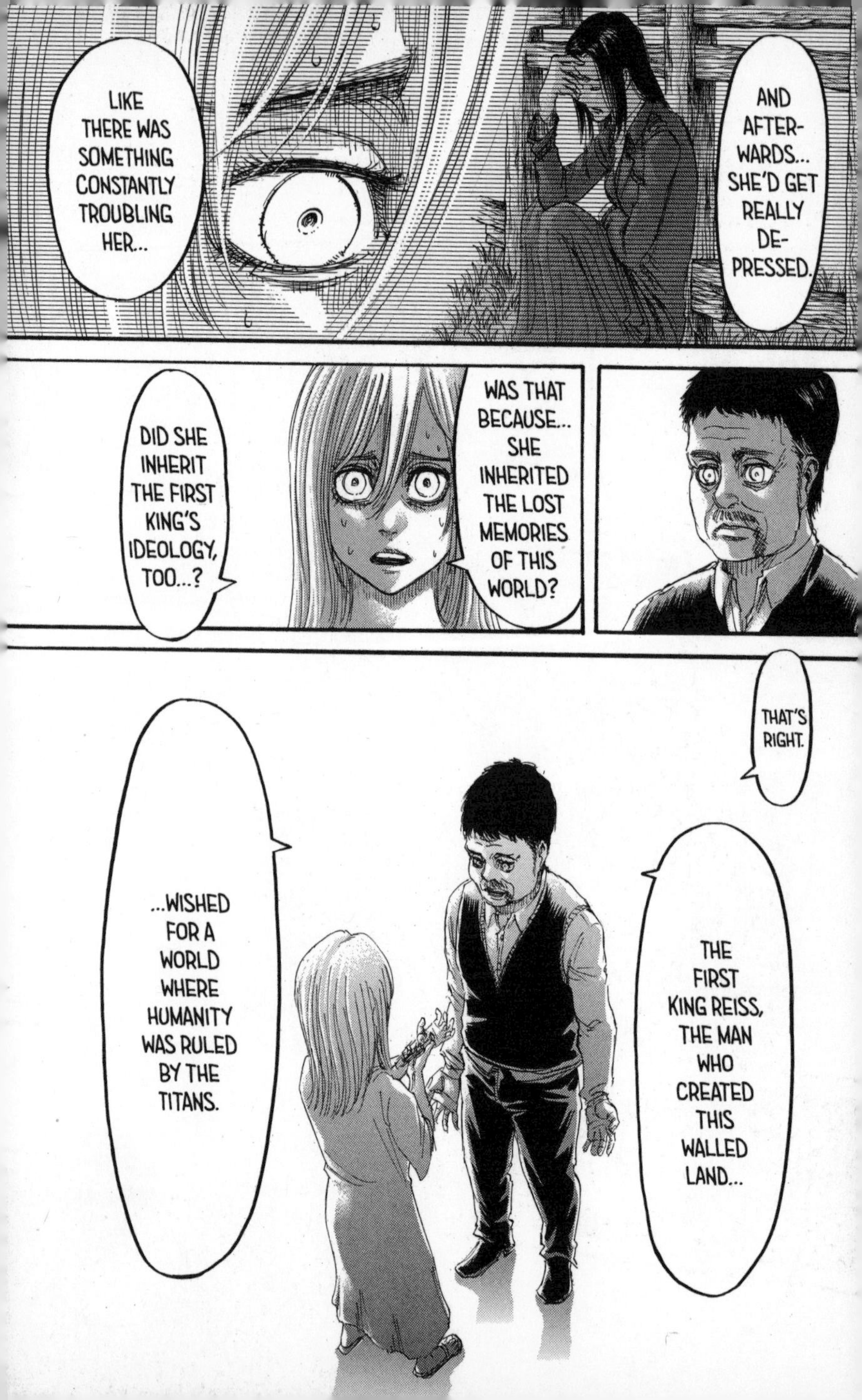
AND AFTER-WARDS... SHE'D GET REALLY DE-PRESSED.
LIKE THERE WAS SOMETHING CONSTANTLY TROUBLING HER...
WAS THAT BECAUSE... SHE INHERITED THE LOST MEMORIES OF THIS WORLD?
DID SHE INHERIT THE FIRST KING'S IDEOLOGY, TOO...?
THAT'S RIGHT.
THE FIRST KING REISS, THE MAN WHO CREATED THIS WALLED LAND...
...WISHED FOR A WORLD WHERE HUMANITY WAS RULED BY THE TITANS.

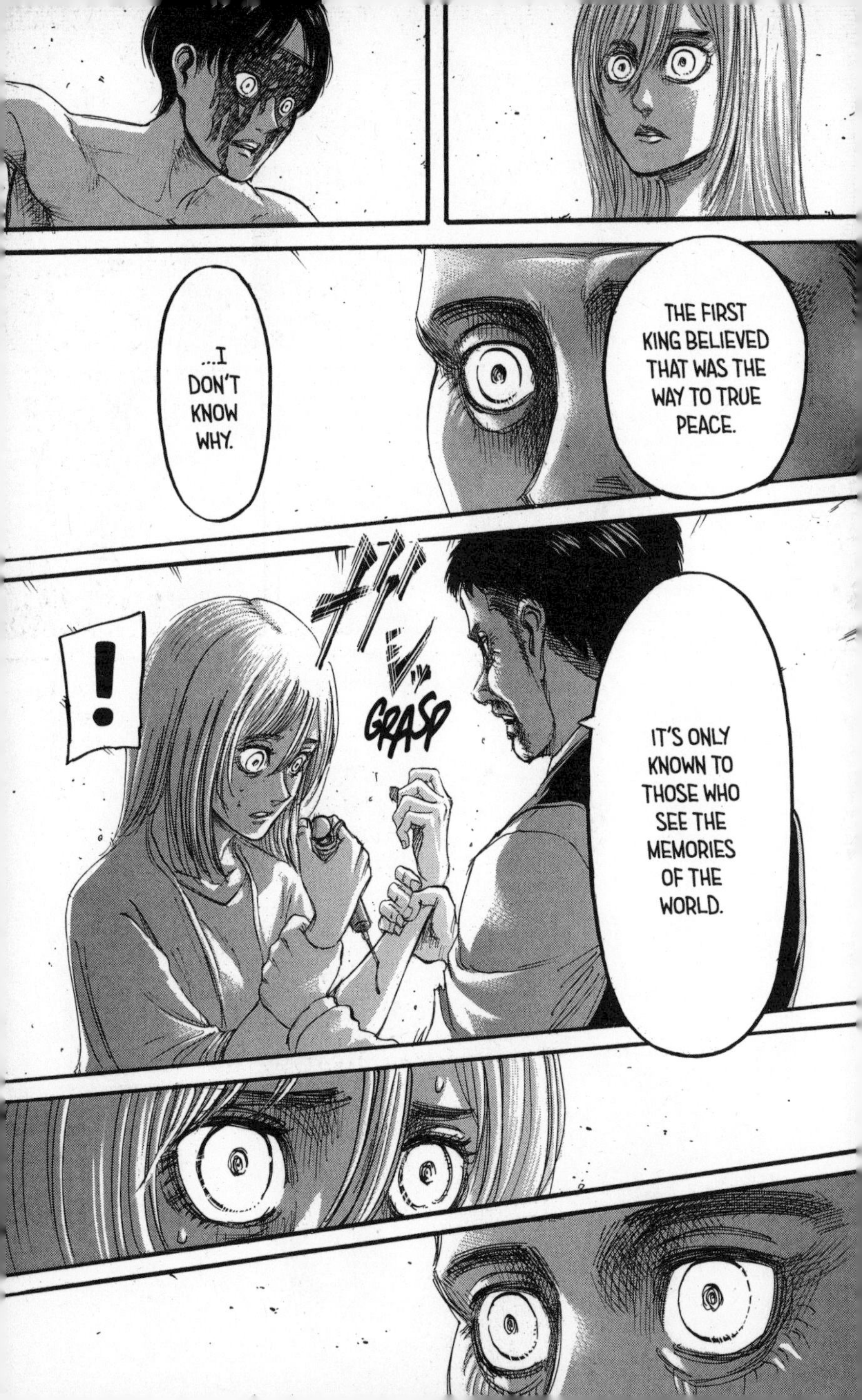
THE FIRST KING BELIEVED THAT WAS THE WAY TO TRUE PEACE.
...I DON'T KNOW WHY.
IT'S ONLY KNOWN TO THOSE WHO SEE THE MEMORIES OF THE WORLD.
GRASP
!

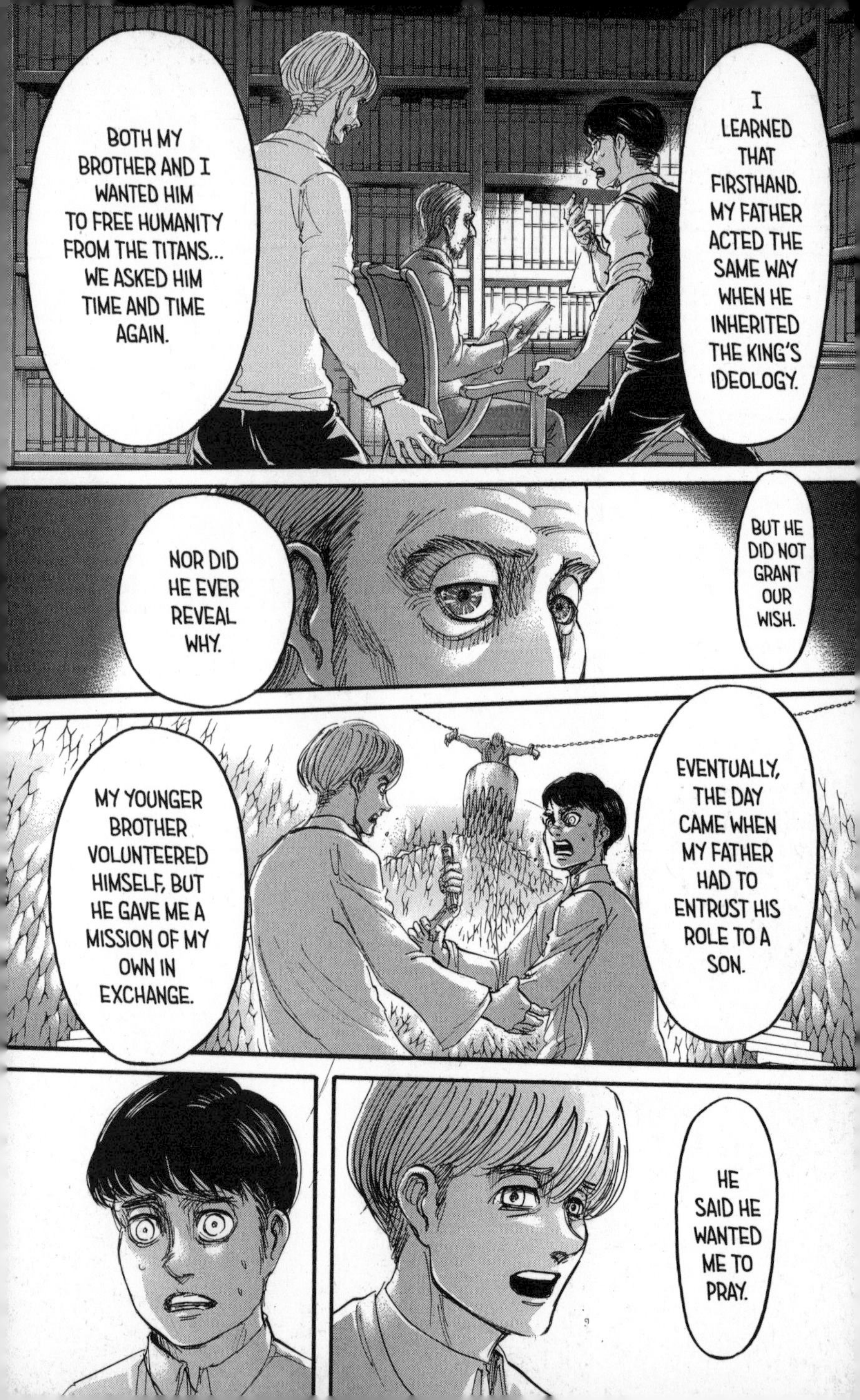
I LEARNED THAT FIRSTHAND. MY FATHER ACTED THE SAME WAY WHEN HE INHERITED THE KING'S IDEOLOGY.
BOTH MY BROTHER AND I WANTED HIM TO FREE HUMANITY FROM THE TITANS... WE ASKED HIM TIME AND TIME AGAIN.
BUT HE DID NOT GRANT OUR WISH.
NOR DID HE EVER REVEAL WHY.
EVENTUALLY, THE DAY CAME WHEN MY FATHER HAD TO ENTRUST HIS ROLE TO A SON.
MY YOUNGER BROTHER VOLUNTEERED HIMSELF, BUT HE GAVE ME A MISSION OF MY OWN IN EXCHANGE.
HE SAID HE WANTED ME TO PRAY.

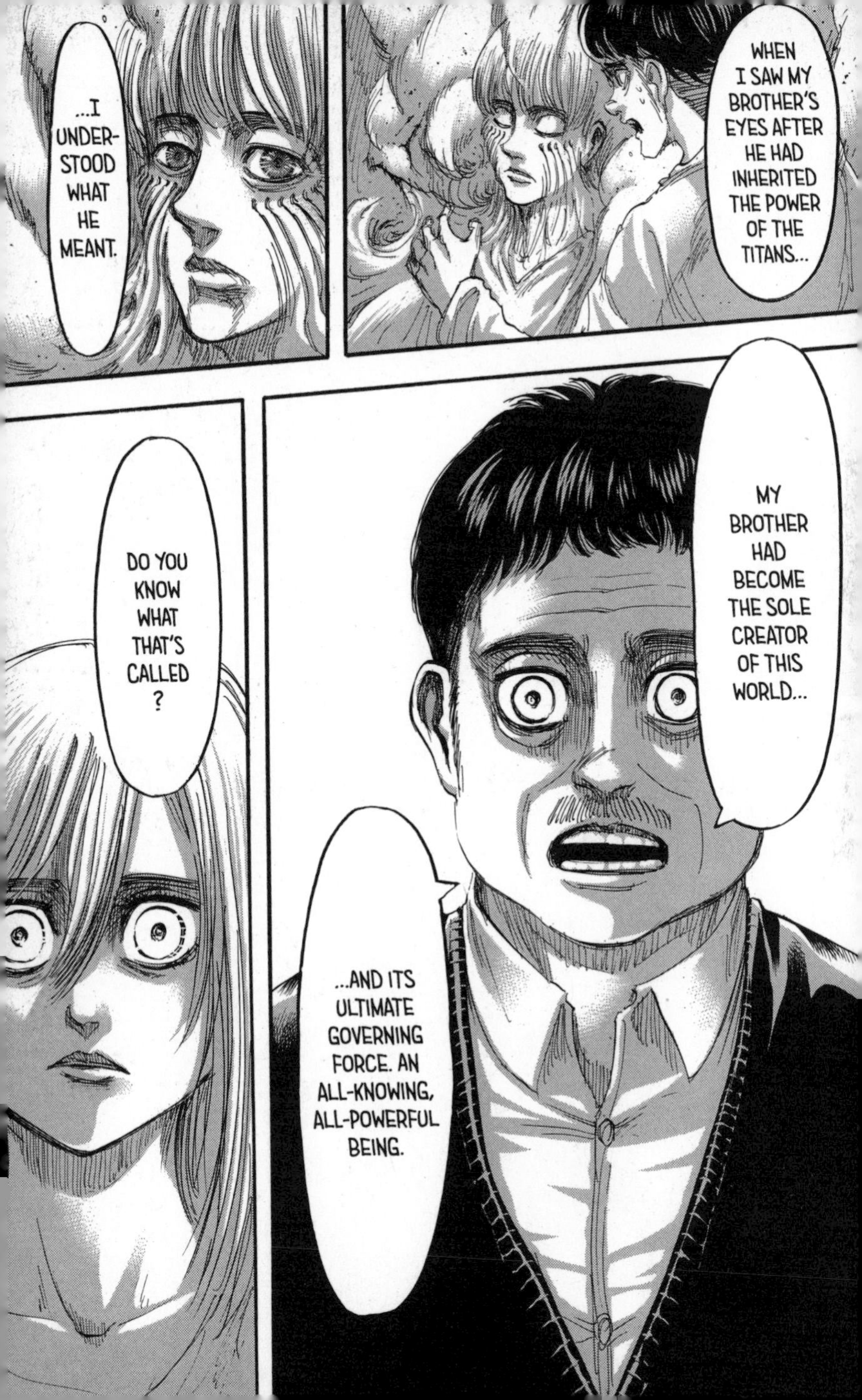
WHEN I SAW MY BROTHER'S EYES AFTER HE HAD INHERITED THE POWER OF THE TITANS...
...I UNDER-STOOD WHAT HE MEANT.
MY BROTHER HAD BECOME THE SOLE CREATOR OF THIS WORLD...
...AND ITS ULTIMATE GOVERNING FORCE. AN ALL-KNOWING, ALL-POWERFUL BEING.
DO YOU KNOW WHAT THAT'S CALLED ?

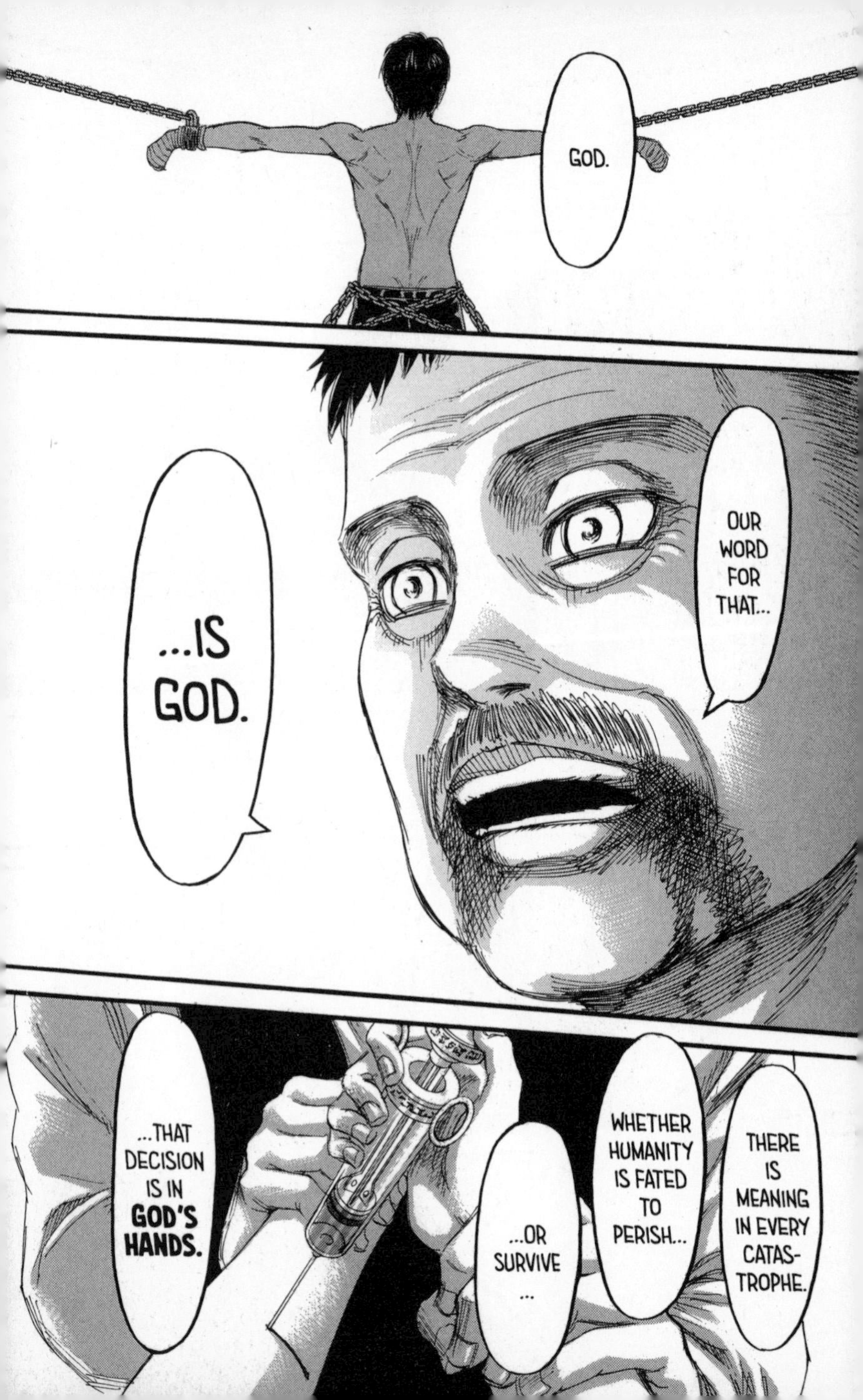
GOD.
OUR WORD FOR THAT...
...IS GOD.
THERE IS MEANING IN EVERY CATAS-TROPHE.
WHETHER HUMANITY IS FATED TO PERISH...
...OR SURVIVE ...
...THAT DECISION IS IN **GOD'S HANDS.**

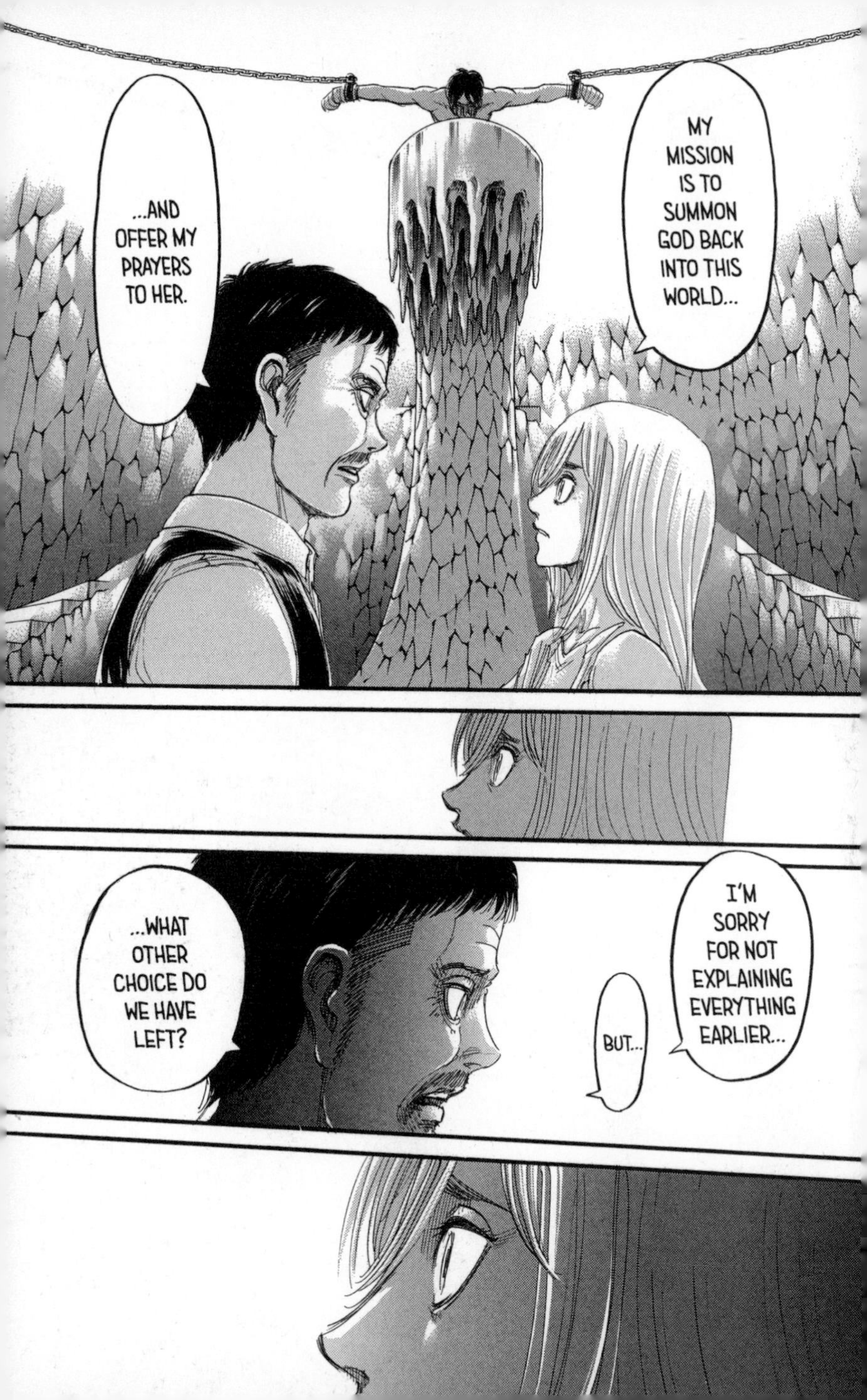
MY MISSION IS TO SUMMON GOD BACK INTO THIS WORLD...
...AND OFFER MY PRAYERS TO HER.
I'M SORRY FOR NOT EXPLAINING EVERYTHING EARLIER...
BUT...
...WHAT OTHER CHOICE DO WE HAVE LEFT?

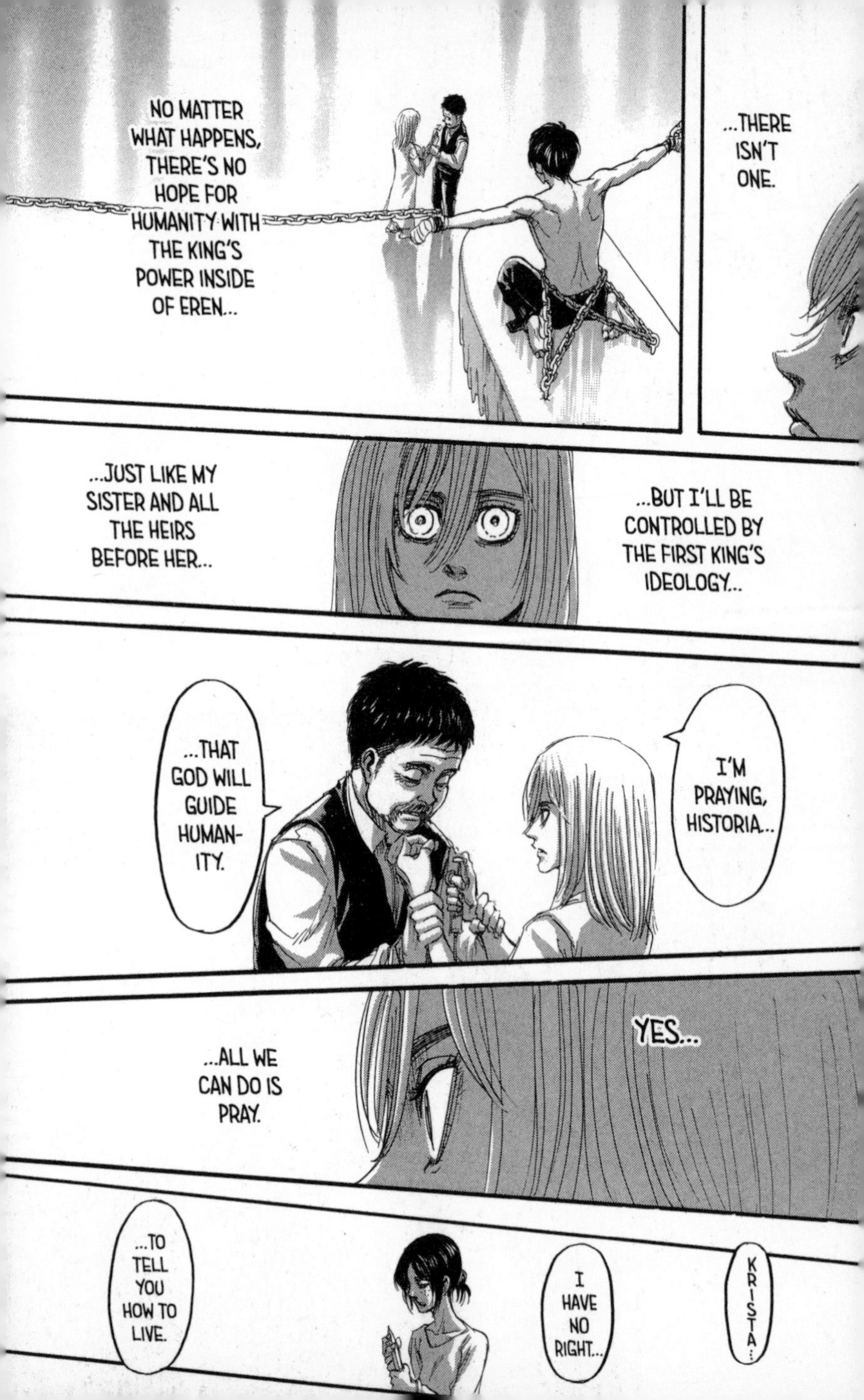
...THERE ISN'T ONE.
NO MATTER WHAT HAPPENS, THERE'S NO HOPE FOR HUMANITY WITH THE KING'S POWER INSIDE OF EREN...
...BUT I'LL BE CONTROLLED BY THE FIRST KING'S IDEOLOGY...
...JUST LIKE MY SISTER AND ALL THE HEIRS BEFORE HER...
I'M PRAYING, HISTORIA...
...THAT GOD WILL GUIDE HUMAN-ITY.
YES...
...ALL WE CAN DO IS PRAY.
KRISTA...
I HAVE NO RIGHT...
...TO TELL YOU HOW TO LIVE.

I MUST LET GOD DWELL WITHIN ME...

THAT IS MY MISSION...

...A WISH OF MINE.

SO THIS IS JUST...

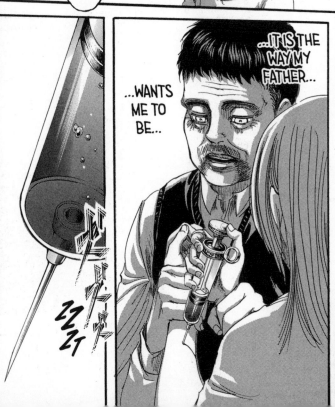

...IT IS THE WAY MY FATHER...

...WANTS ME TO BE...

AND... SO...

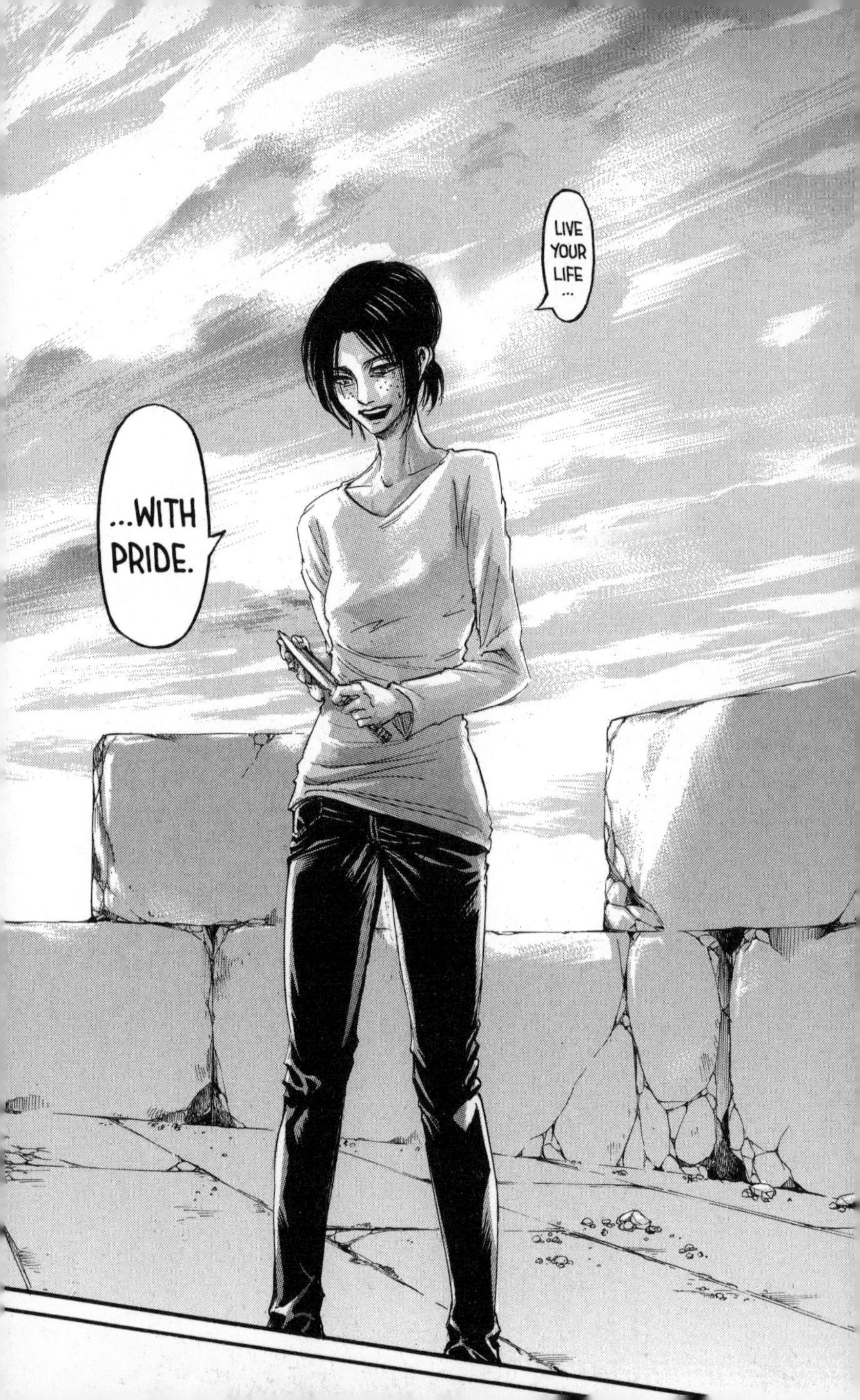
LIVE YOUR LIFE ...
...WITH PRIDE.

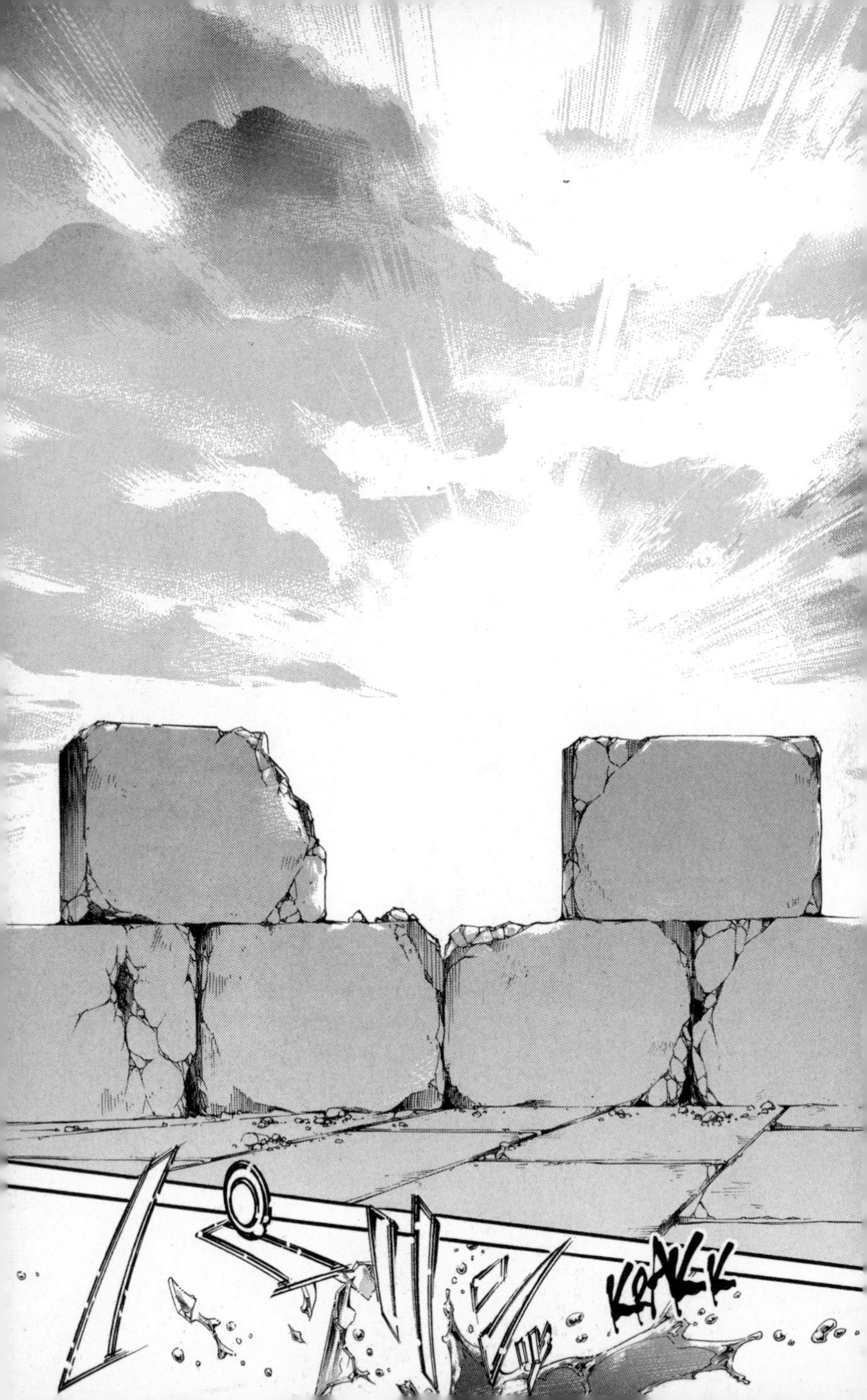
KRAKK

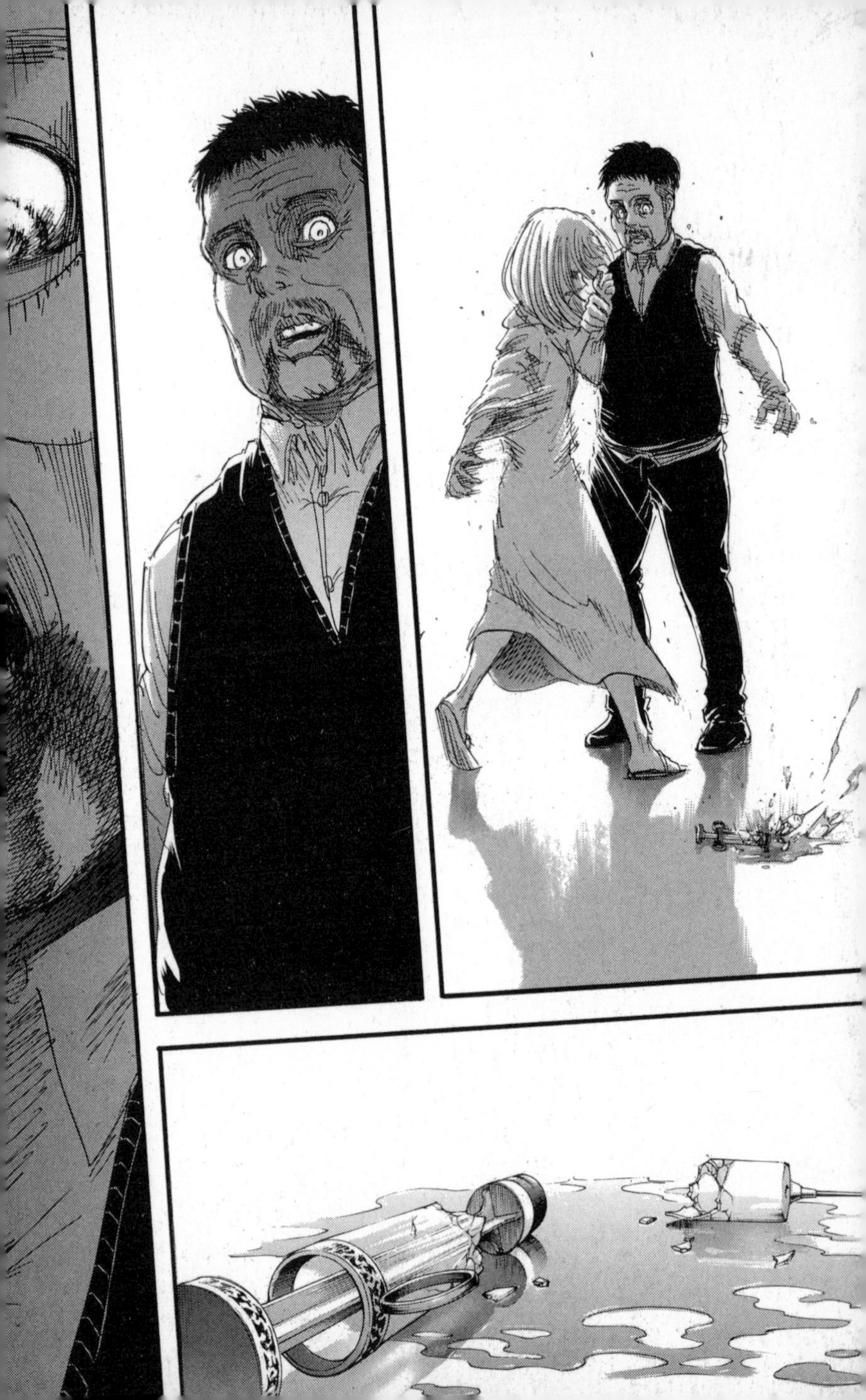

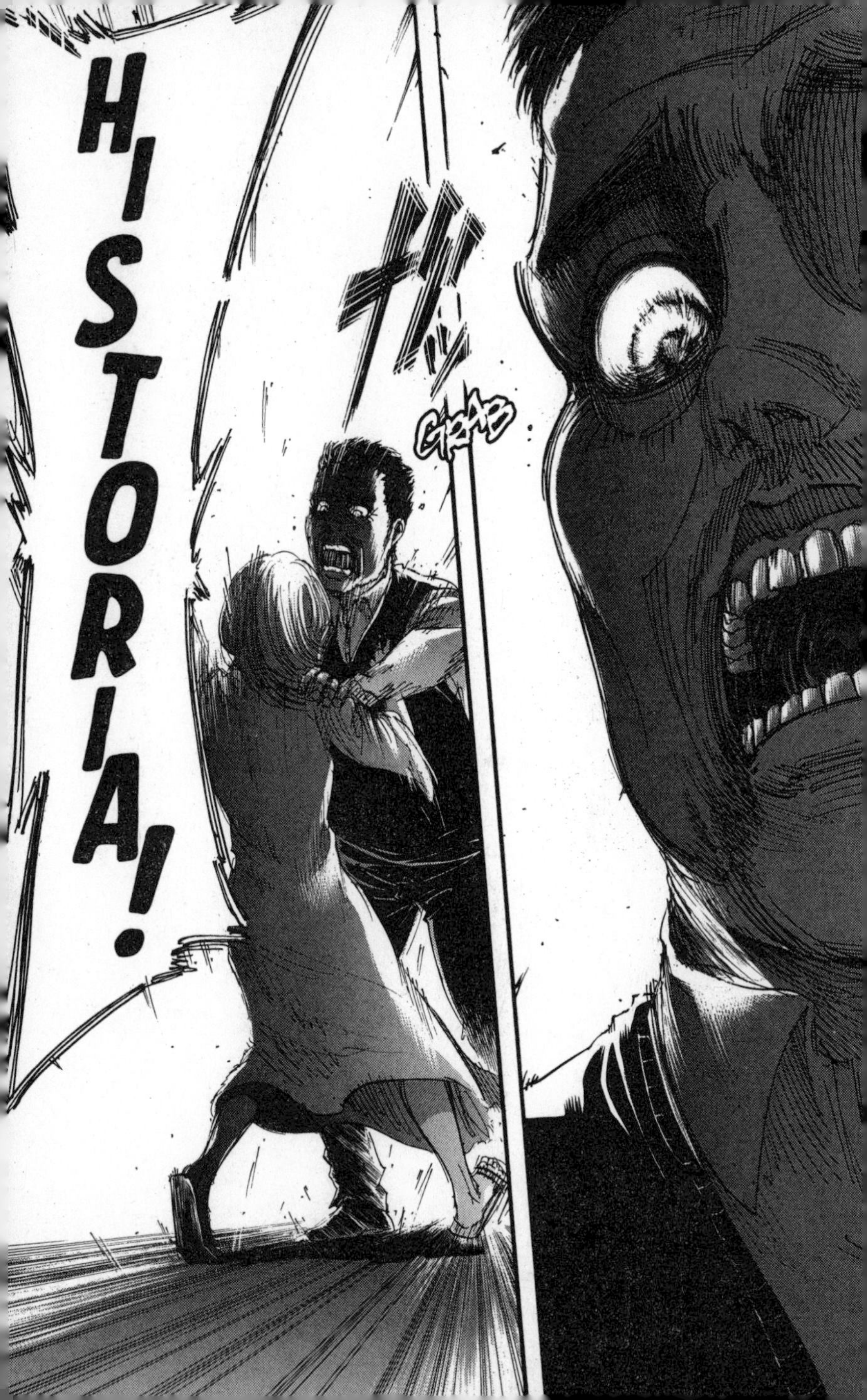
HISTORIA!
GRAB

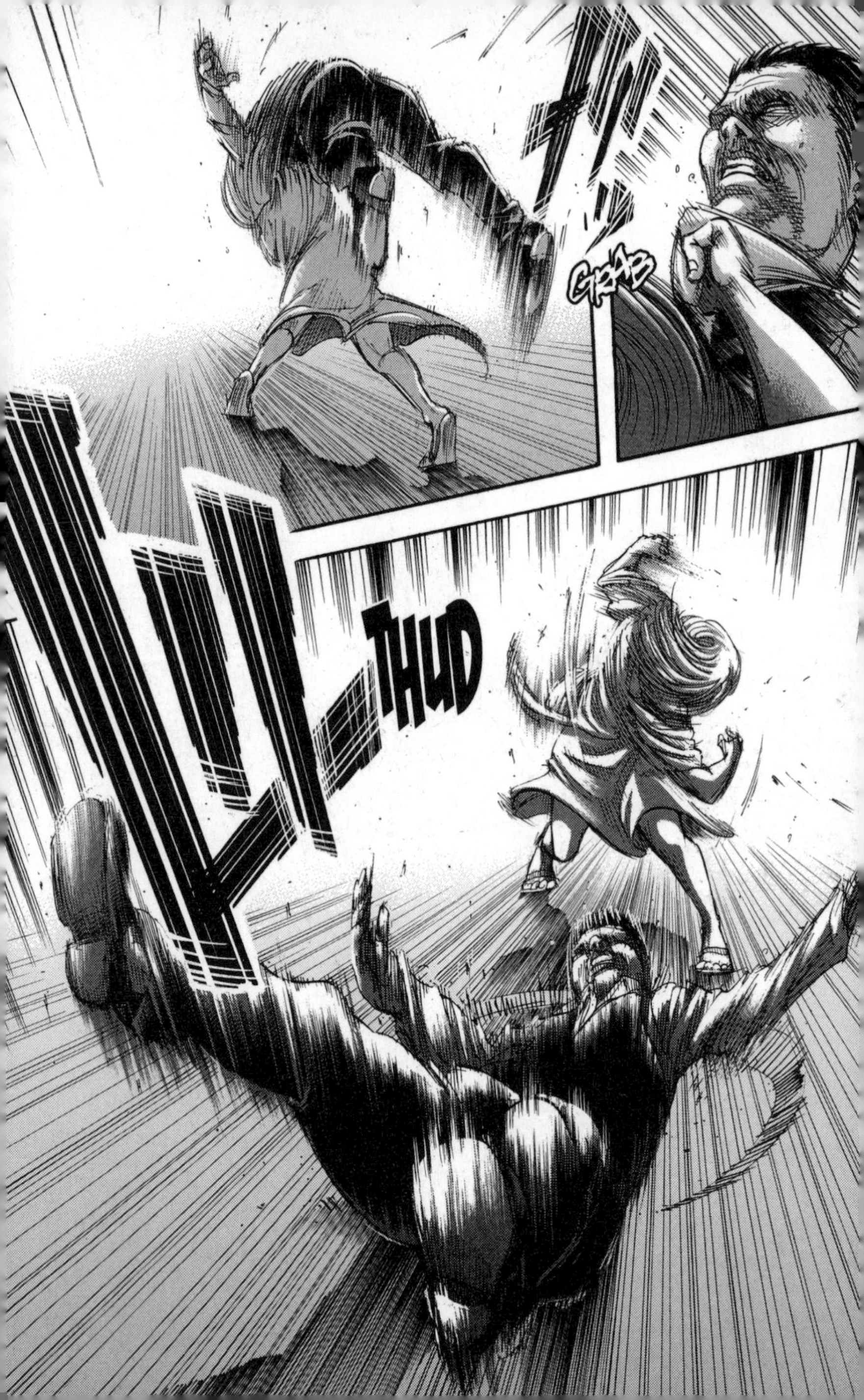
GRAB
THUD

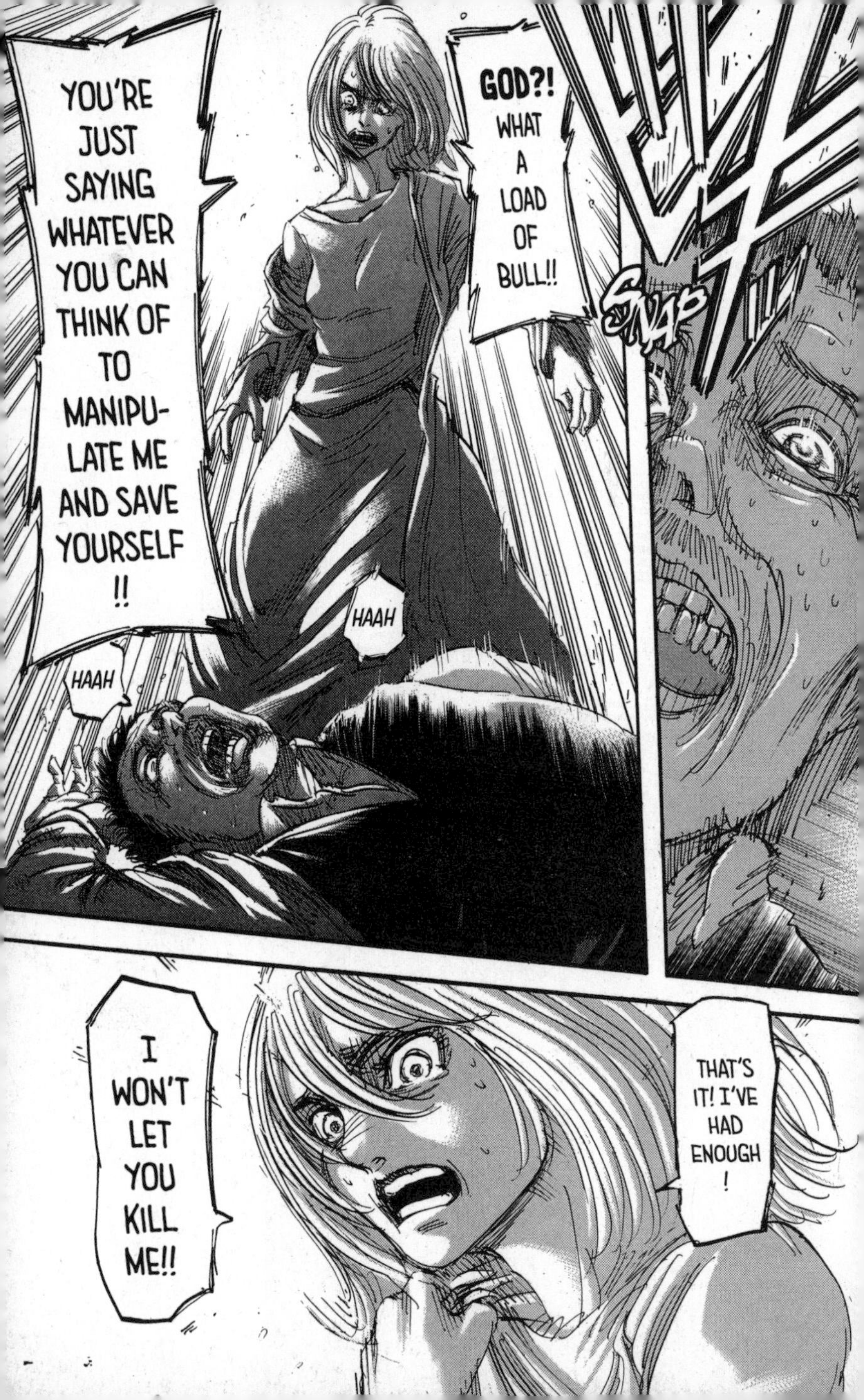
SNAP
GOD?! WHAT A LOAD OF BULL!!
YOU'RE JUST SAYING WHATEVER YOU CAN THINK OF TO MANIPU-LATE ME AND SAVE YOURSELF!!
HAAH
HAAH
THAT'S IT! I'VE HAD ENOUGH!
I WON'T LET YOU KILL ME!!

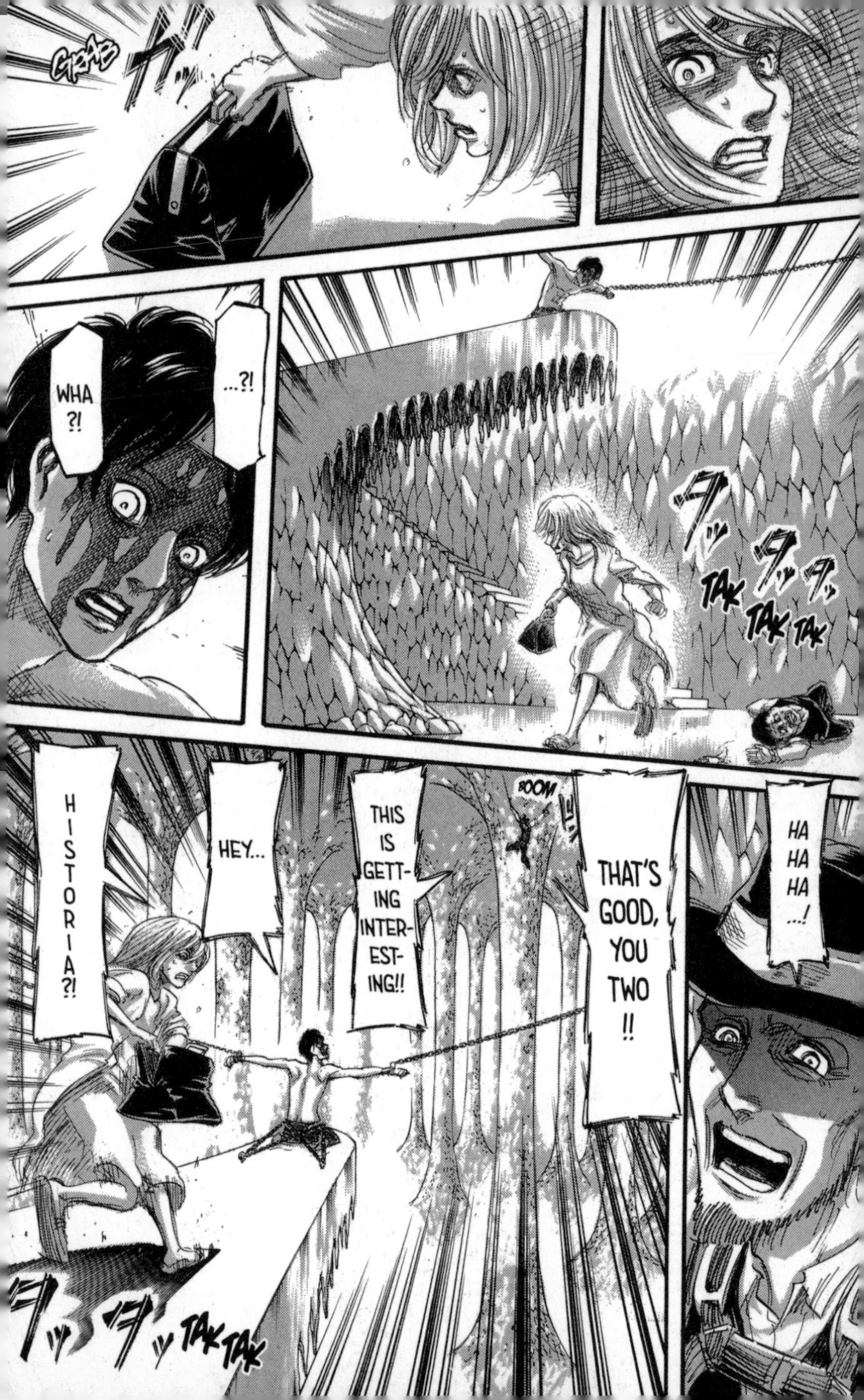
GRAB
TAK TAK TAK TAK
...?!
WHA ?!
HA HA HA ...!
THAT'S GOOD, YOU TWO !!
BOOM
THIS IS GETT-ING INTER-EST-ING!!
HEY...
HISTORIA?!
TAK TAK

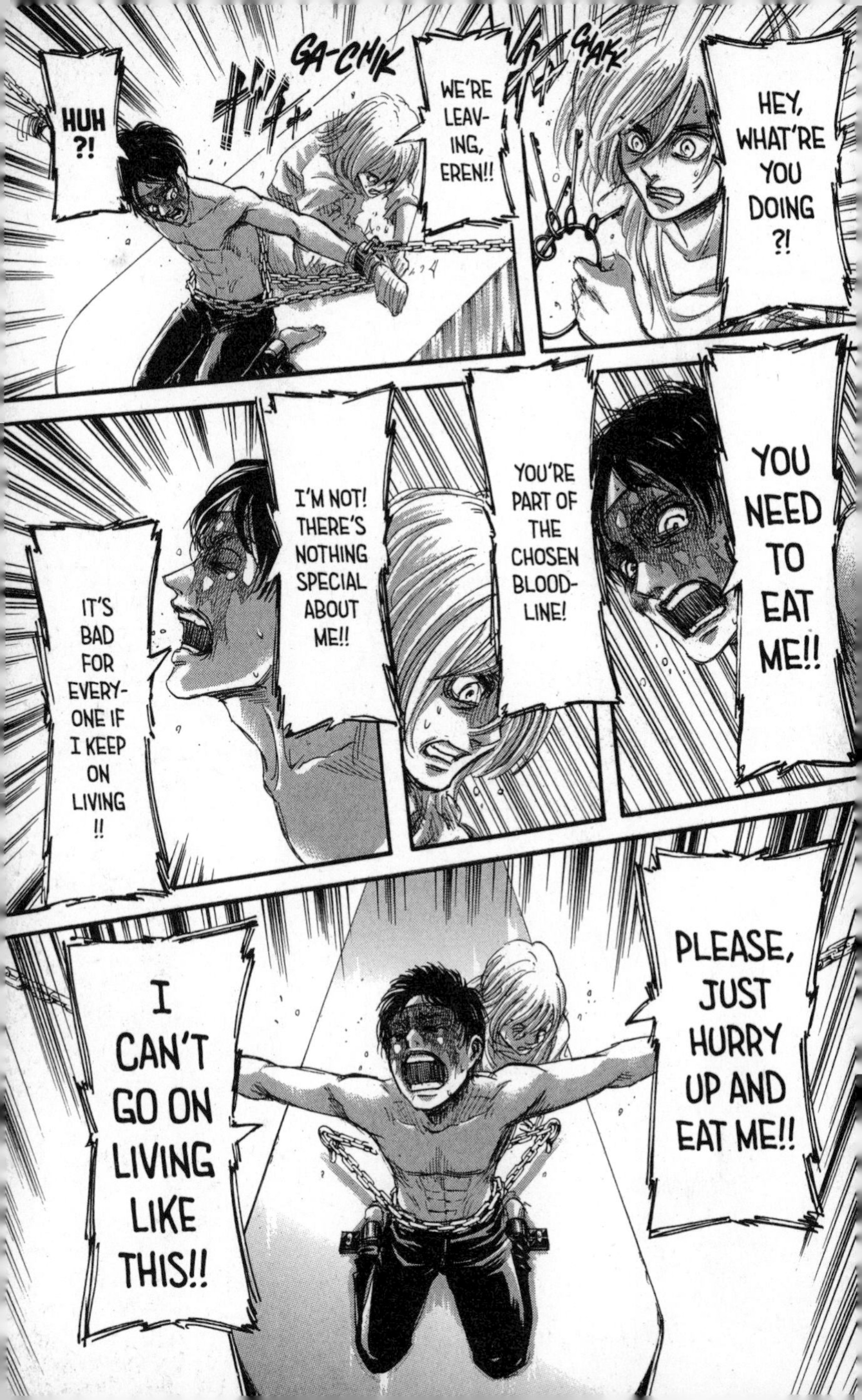
CHAKK
HEY, WHAT'RE YOU DOING ?!
WE'RE LEAV-ING, EREN!!
GA-CHIK
HUH ?!
YOU NEED TO EAT ME!!
YOU'RE PART OF THE CHOSEN BLOOD-LINE!
I'M NOT! THERE'S NOTHING SPECIAL ABOUT ME!!
IT'S BAD FOR EVERY-ONE IF I KEEP ON LIVING !!
PLEASE, JUST HURRY UP AND EAT ME!!
I CAN'T GO ON LIVING LIKE THIS!!

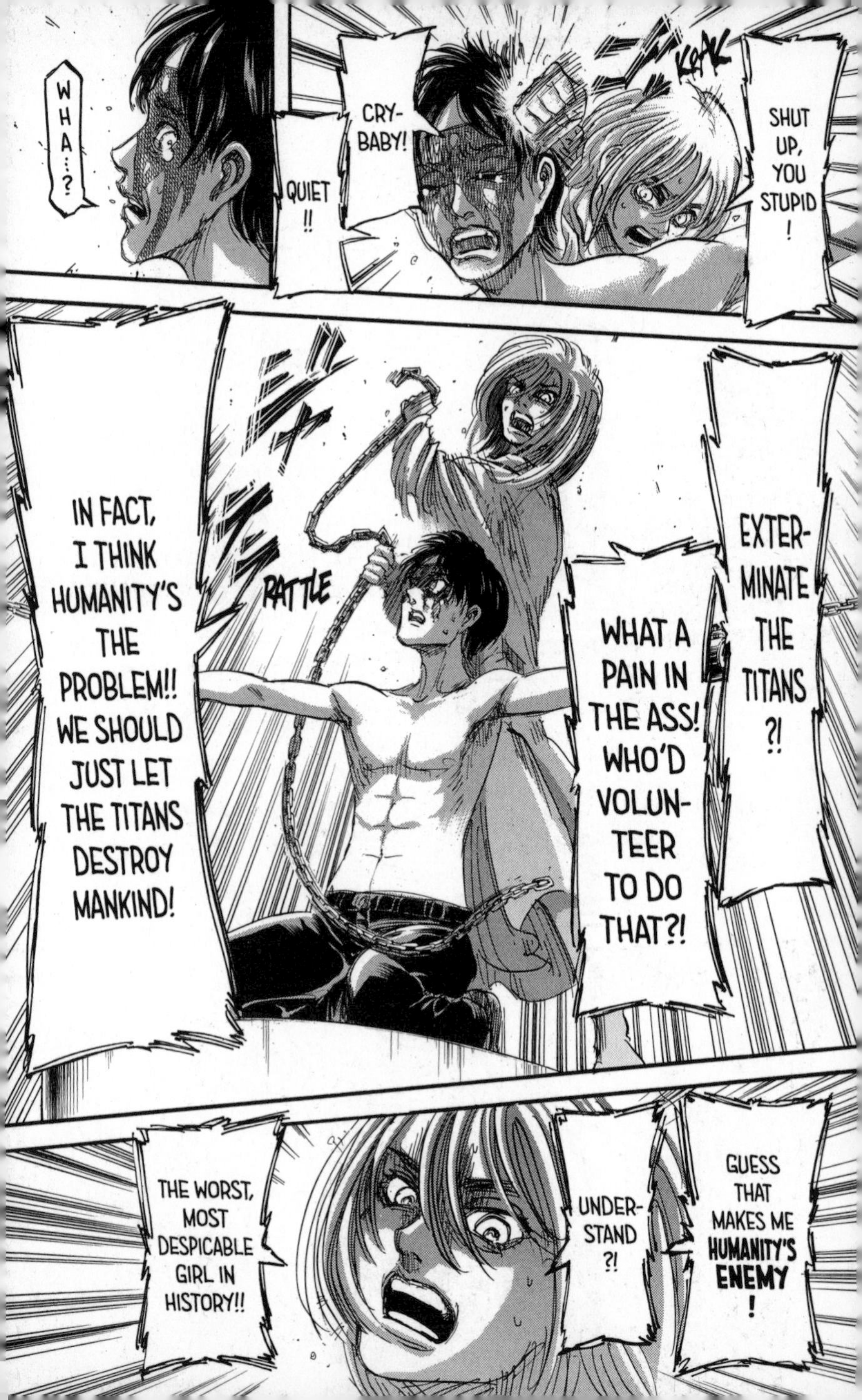
KRAK
SHUT UP, YOU STUPID!
CRY-BABY!
QUIET!!
WHA...?
EXTER-MINATE THE TITANS?!
WHAT A PAIN IN THE ASS! WHO'D VOLUN-TEER TO DO THAT?!
RATTLE
IN FACT, I THINK HUMANITY'S THE PROBLEM!! WE SHOULD JUST LET THE TITANS DESTROY MANKIND!
GUESS THAT MAKES ME **HUMANITY'S ENEMY**!
UNDER-STAND?!
THE WORST, MOST DESPICABLE GIRL IN HISTORY!!

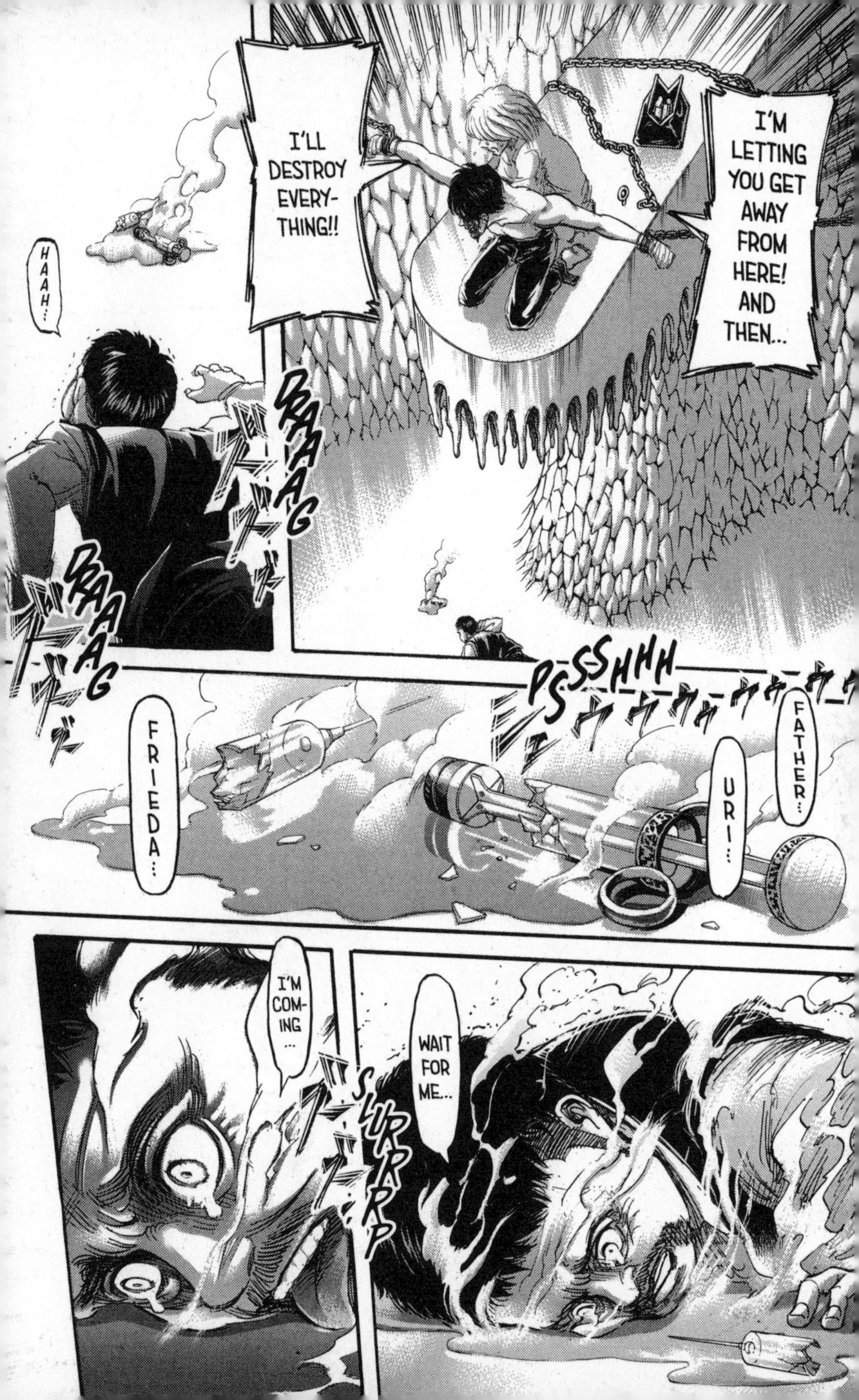
I'M LETTING YOU GET AWAY FROM HERE! AND THEN...
I'LL DESTROY EVERYTHING!!
HAAAH...
DRAAAAG
DRAAAAG
PSSSHHH
FATHER...
URI...
FRIEDA...
WAIT FOR ME...
SLURRRP
I'M COMING...

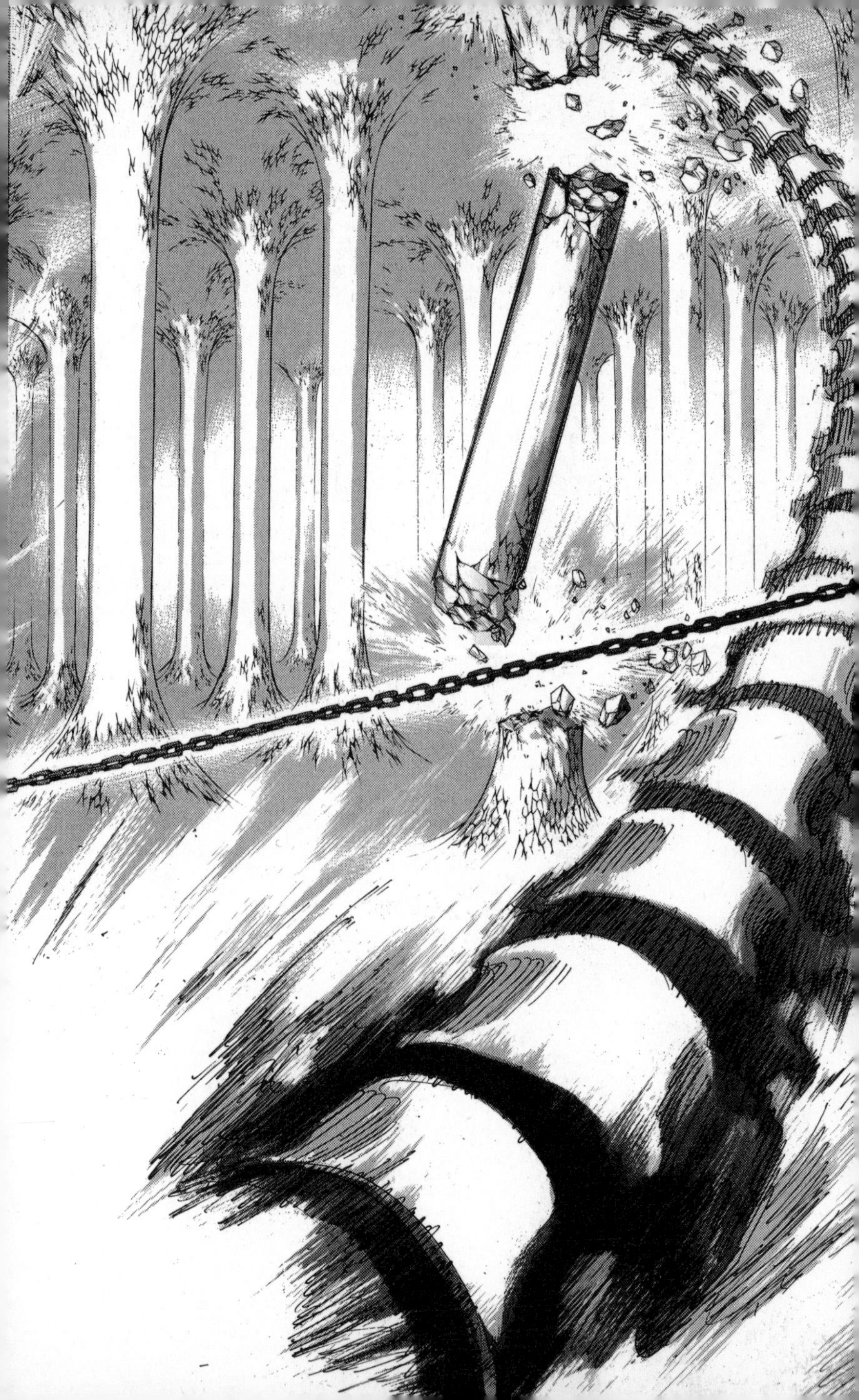

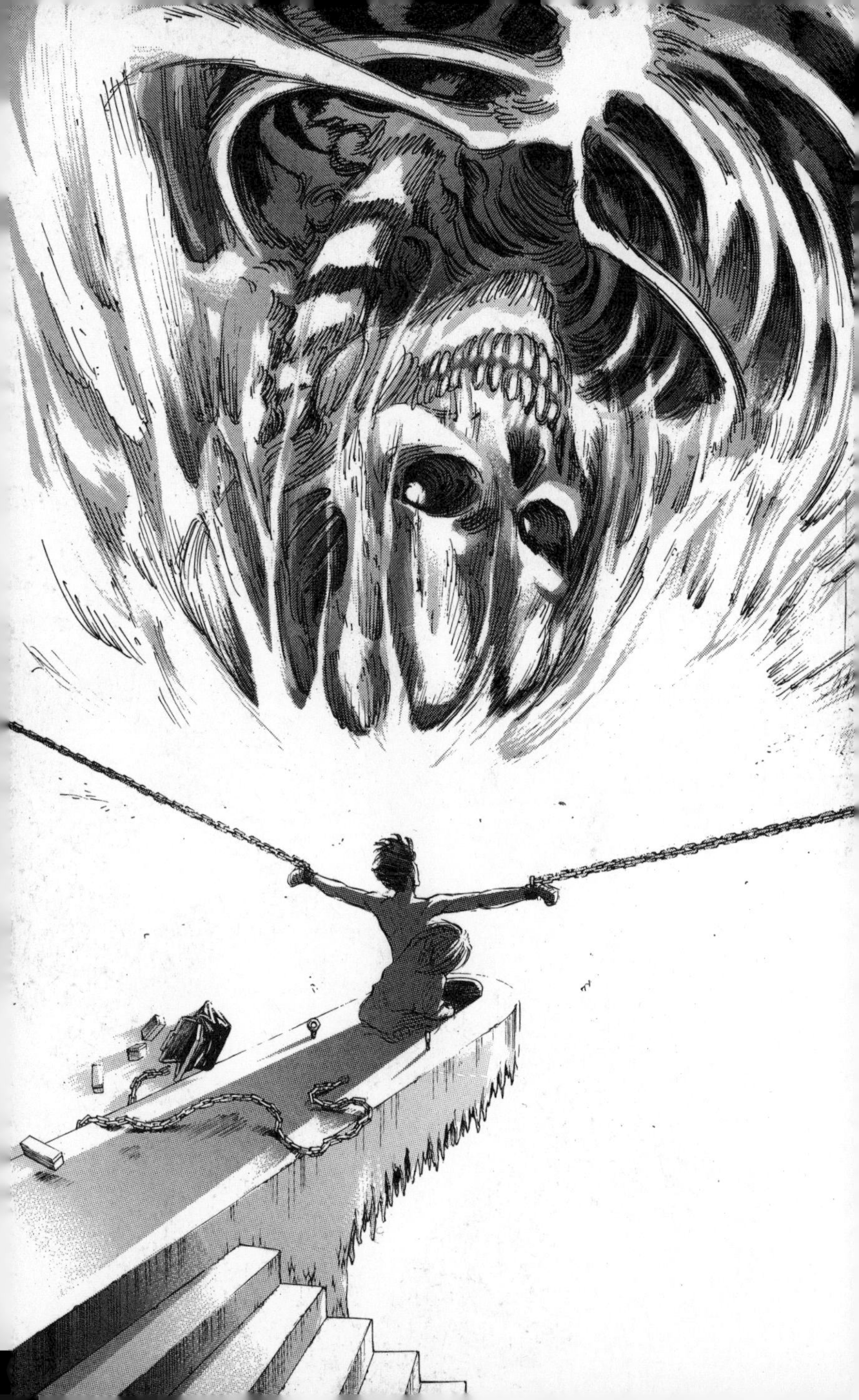

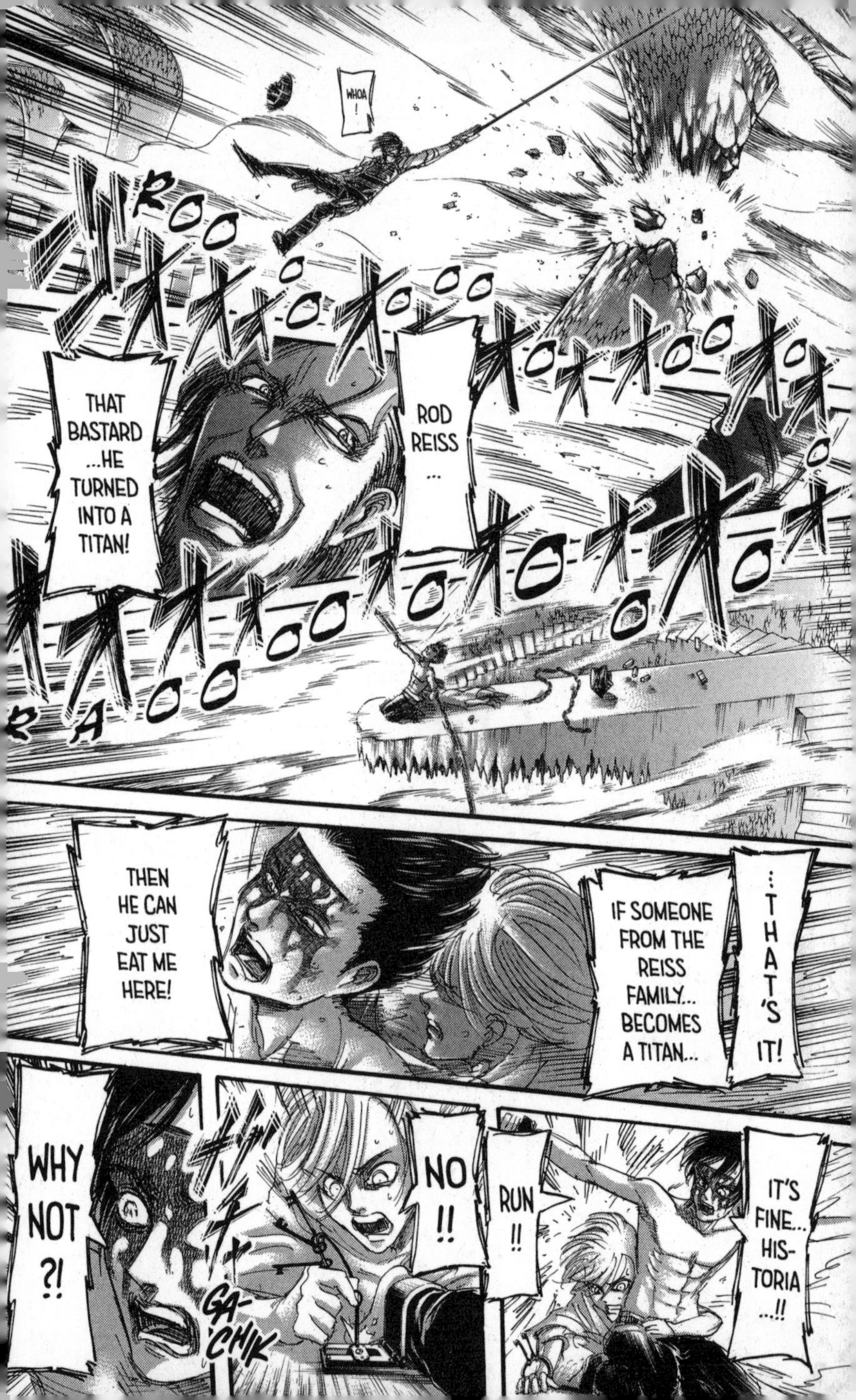
WHOA !
ROOOOOOOOOOO
ROD REISS ...
THAT BASTARD ...HE TURNED INTO A TITAN!
RAOOOOOOOOO
...THAT'S IT!
IF SOMEONE FROM THE REISS FAMILY... BECOMES A TITAN...
THEN HE CAN JUST EAT ME HERE!
IT'S FINE... HIS-TORIA ...!!
RUN !!
NO !!
GA-CHIK
WHY NOT ?!

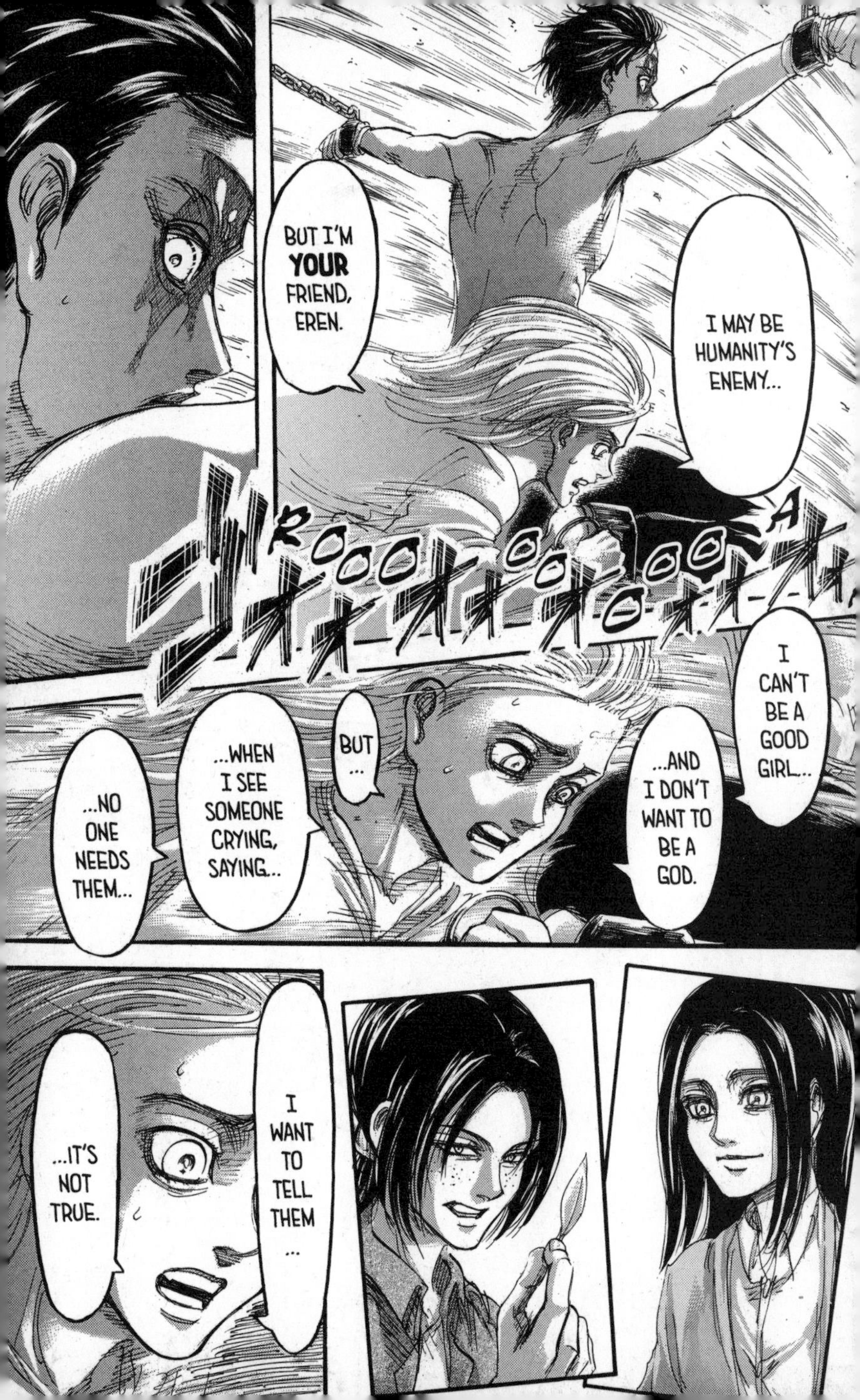
I MAY BE HUMANITY'S ENEMY...
BUT I'M YOUR FRIEND, EREN.
ROOOOOOOOOOA
I CAN'T BE A GOOD GIRL...
...AND I DON'T WANT TO BE A GOD.
BUT...
...WHEN I SEE SOMEONE CRYING, SAYING...
...NO ONE NEEDS THEM...
I WANT TO TELL THEM...
...IT'S NOT TRUE.

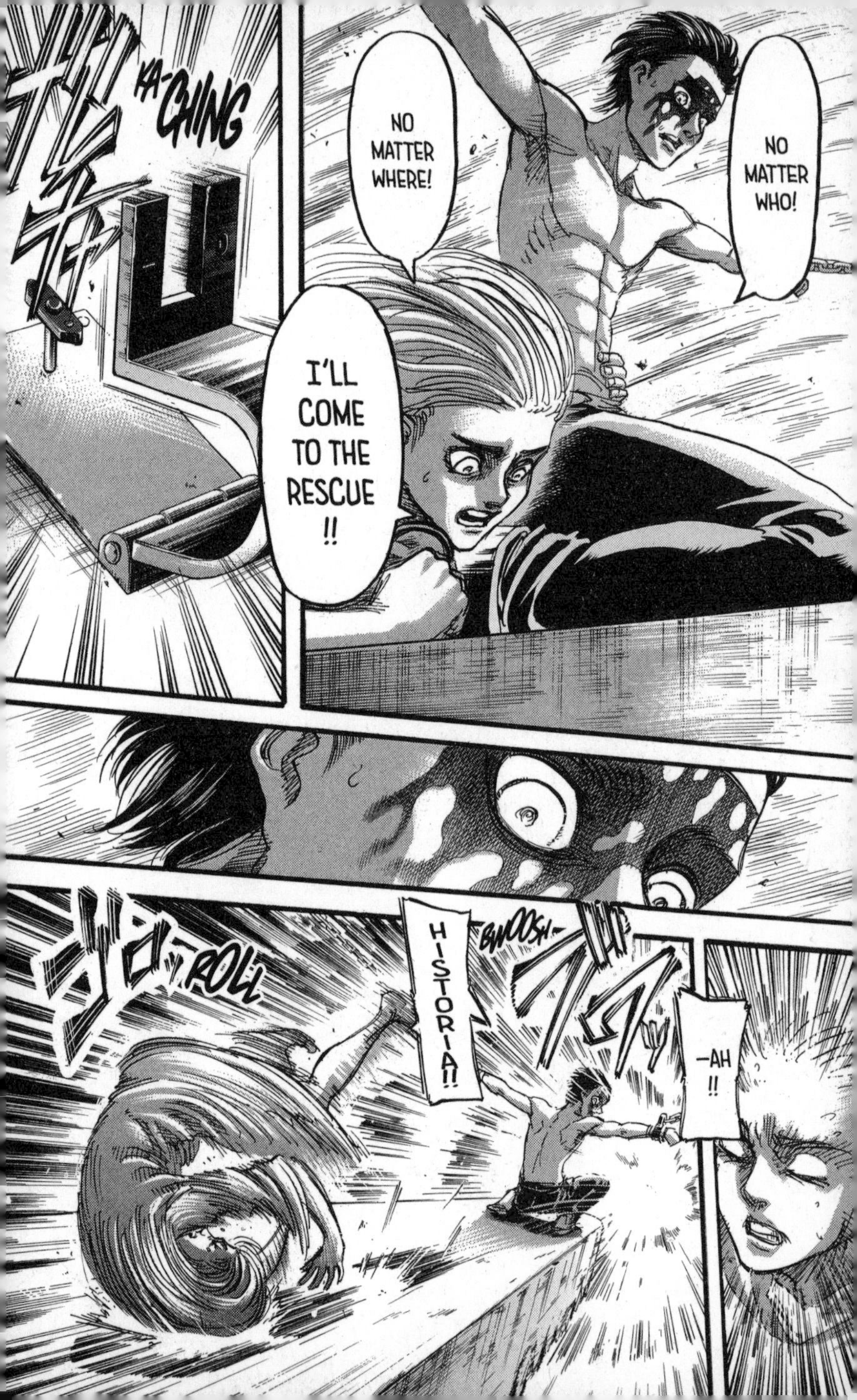
NO MATTER WHO!
NO MATTER WHERE!
I'LL COME TO THE RESCUE !!
KA-CHING
—AH !!
BWOOSH
HISTORIA!!
ROLL

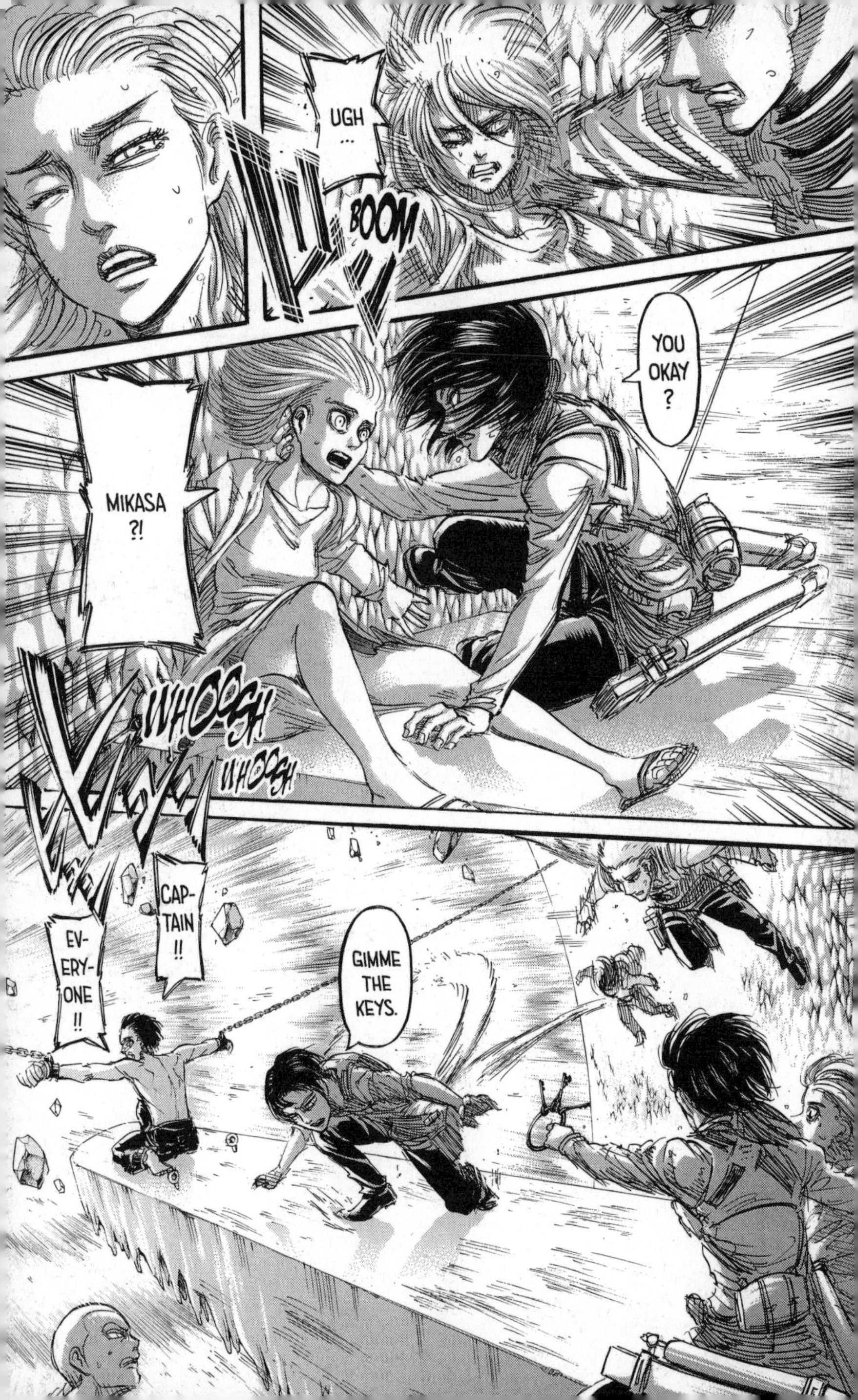
UGH ...
BOOM
YOU OKAY ?
MIKASA ?!
WHOOSH
WHOOSH
GIMME THE KEYS.
CAP-TAIN !!
EV-ERY-ONE !!

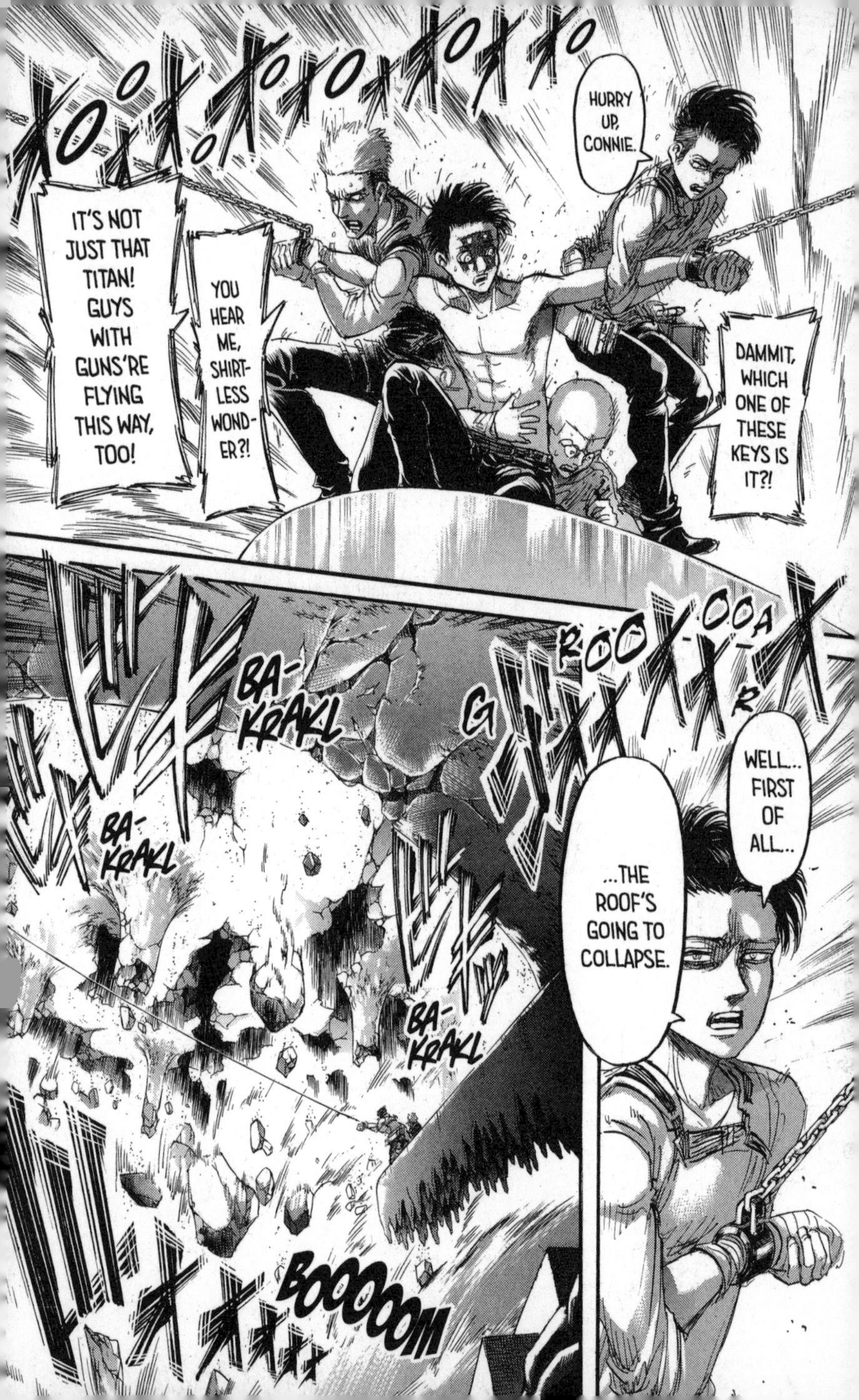
HURRY UP, CONNIE.
DAMMIT, WHICH ONE OF THESE KEYS IS IT?!
YOU HEAR ME, SHIRTLESS WONDER?!
IT'S NOT JUST THAT TITAN! GUYS WITH GUNS'RE FLYING THIS WAY, TOO!
GROOOOAR
BA-KRAKL
WELL... FIRST OF ALL...
...THE ROOF'S GOING TO COLLAPSE.
BA-KRAKL
BA-KRAKL
BOOOOOM

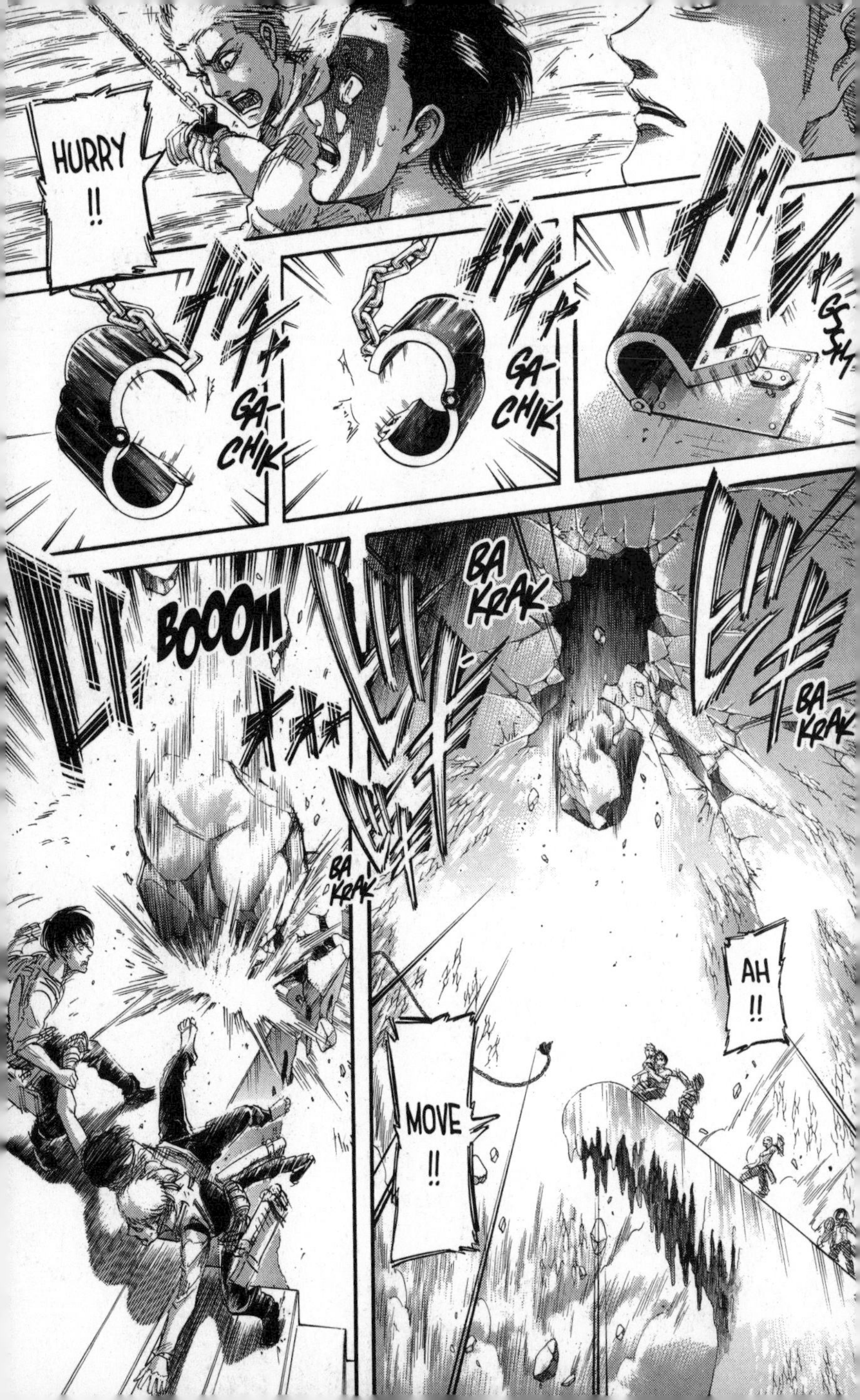
HURRY !!
GA-CHIK
GA-CHIK
BA KRAK
BA KRAK
BOOOM
BA KRAK
AH !!
MOVE !!

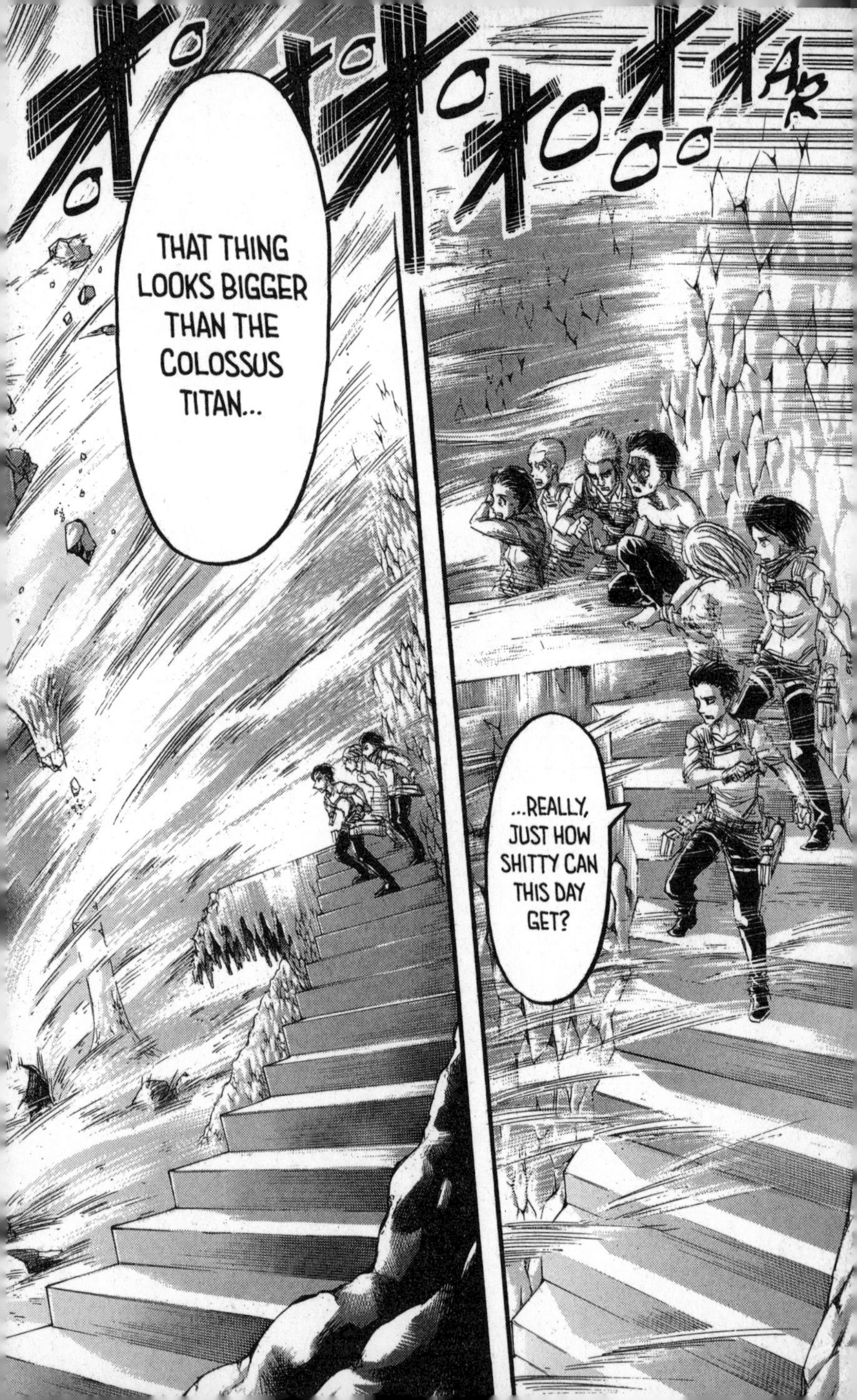
...REALLY, JUST HOW SHITTY CAN THIS DAY GET?
THAT THING LOOKS BIGGER THAN THE COLOSSUS TITAN...

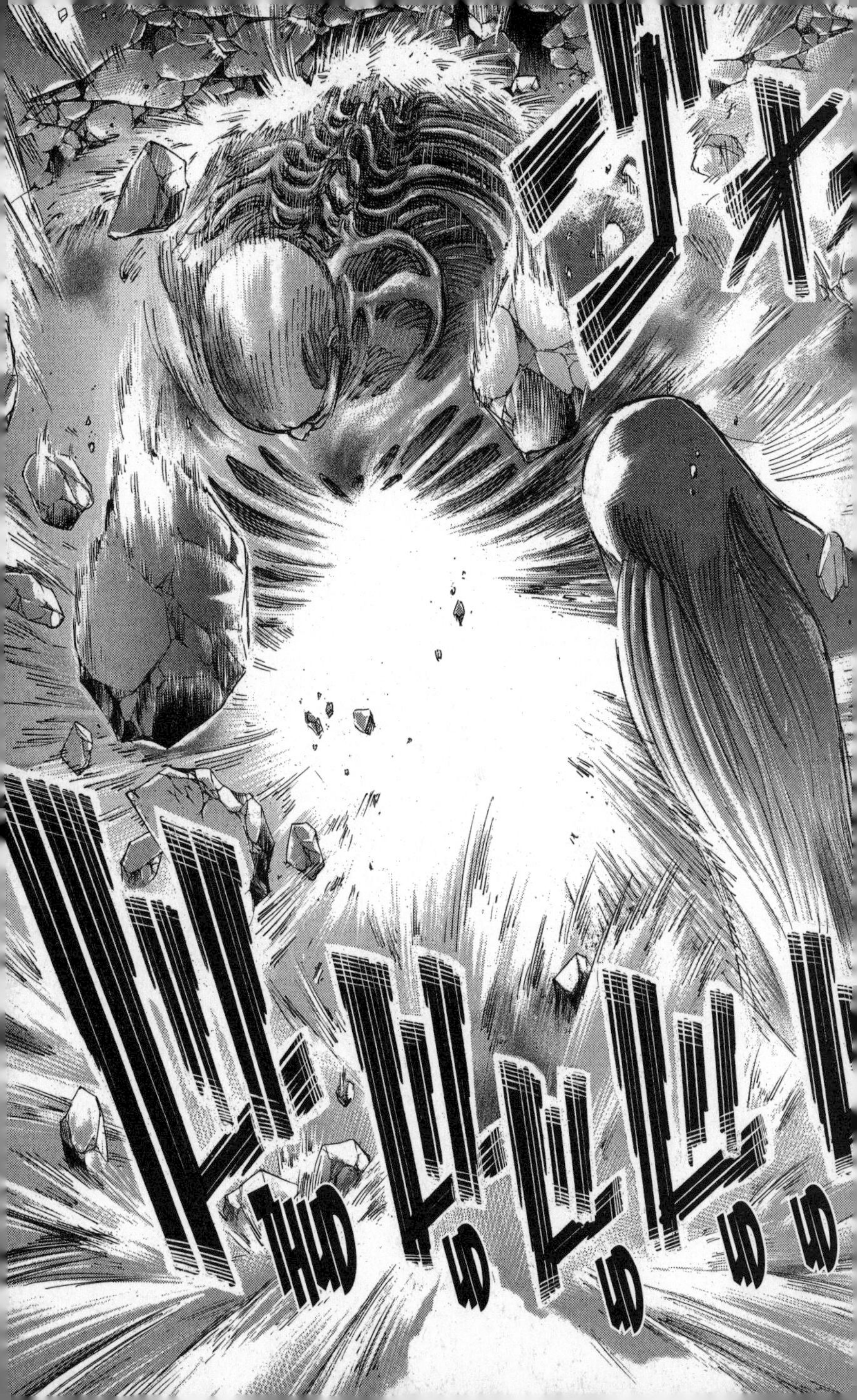
THUD
UD
UD
UD
UD

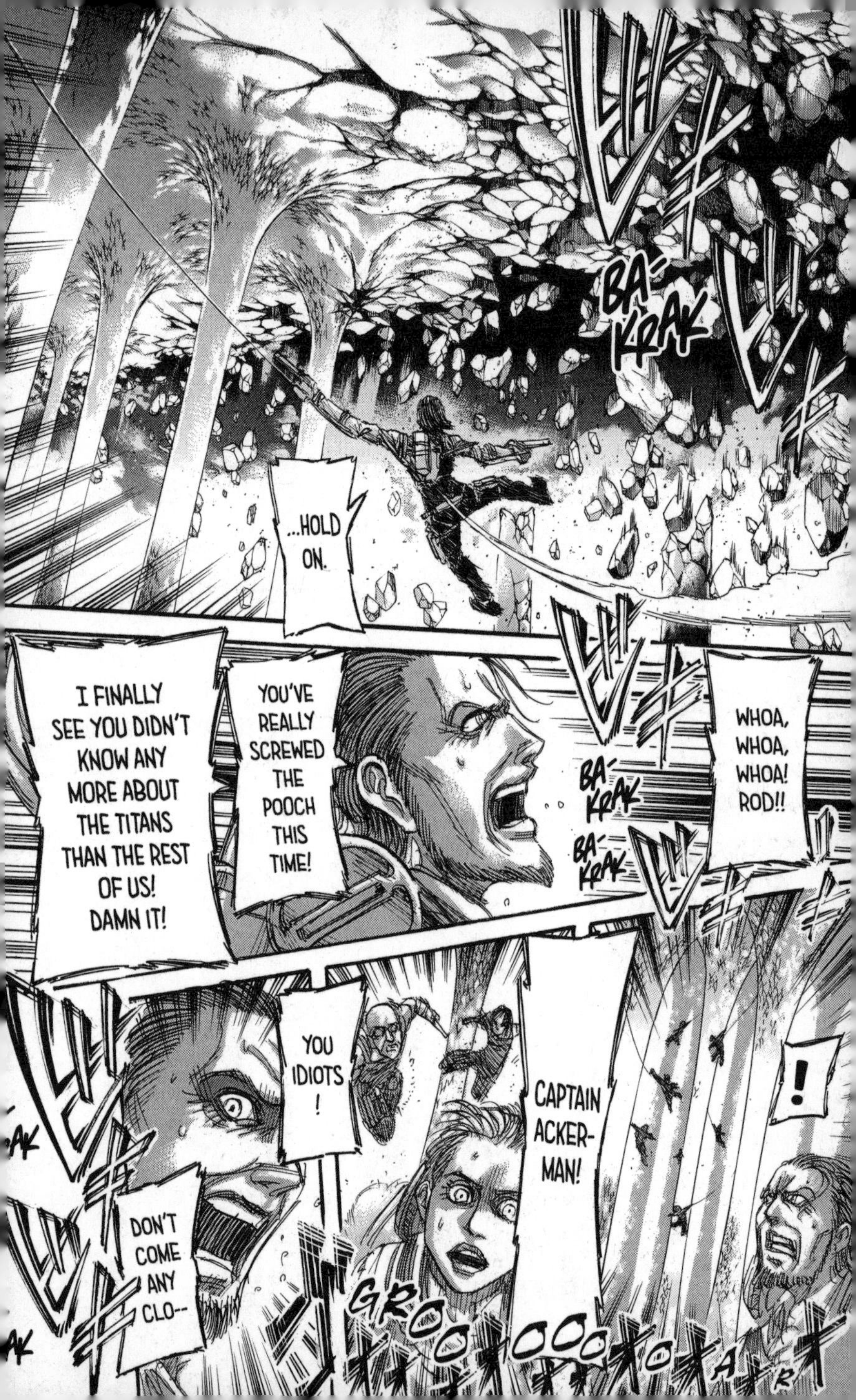
BA-KRAK
...HOLD ON.
WHOA, WHOA, WHOA! ROD!!
BA-KRAK
BA-KRAK
YOU'VE REALLY SCREWED THE POOCH THIS TIME!
I FINALLY SEE YOU DIDN'T KNOW ANY MORE ABOUT THE TITANS THAN THE REST OF US! DAMN IT!
!
CAPTAIN ACKERMAN!
YOU IDIOTS!
DON'T COME ANY CLO--
GROOOOOOOAR

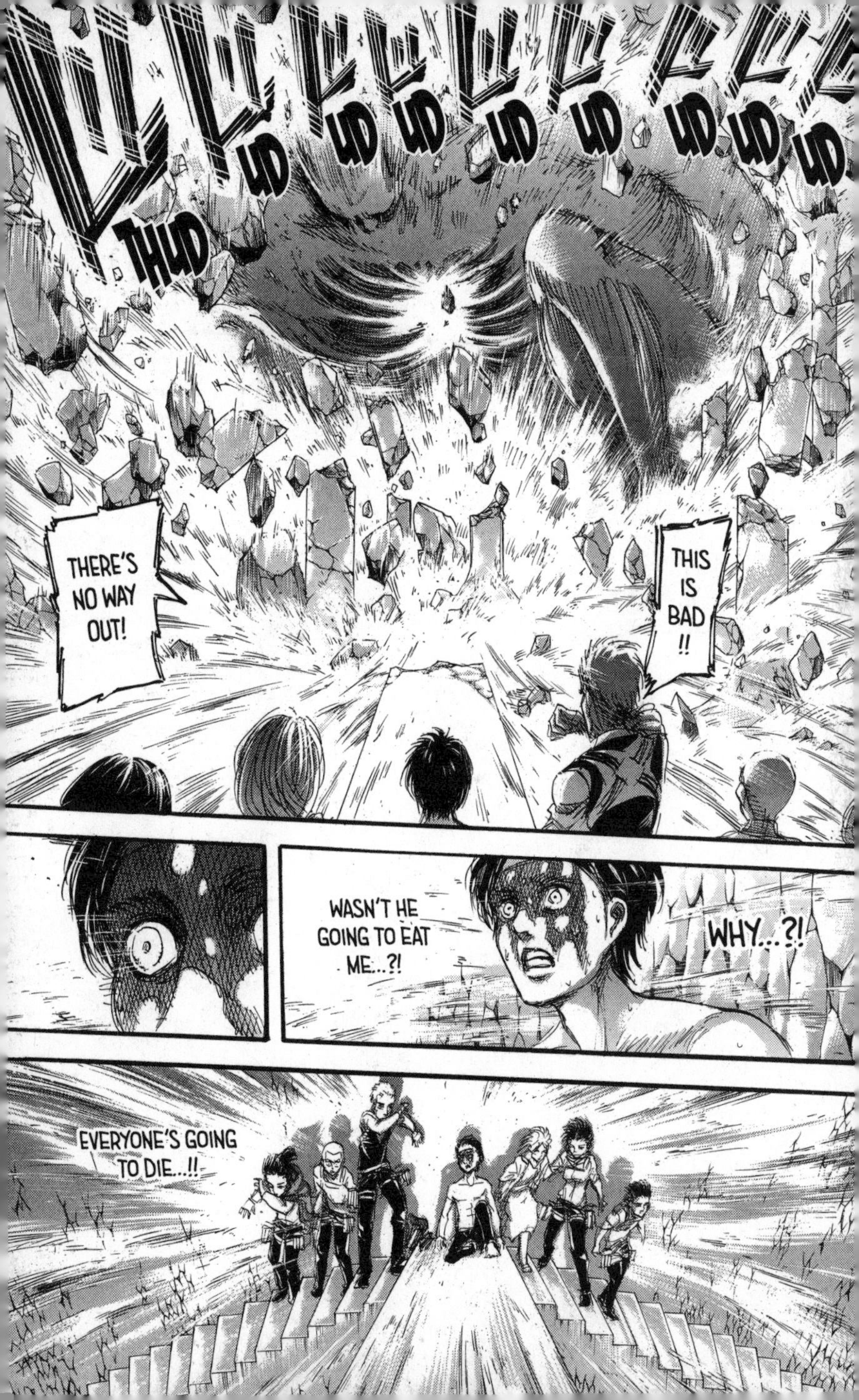
THUD UD UD UD UD UD UD UD UD UD
THIS IS BAD!!
THERE'S NO WAY OUT!
WHY...?!
WASN'T HE GOING TO EAT ME...?!
EVERYONE'S GOING TO DIE...!!

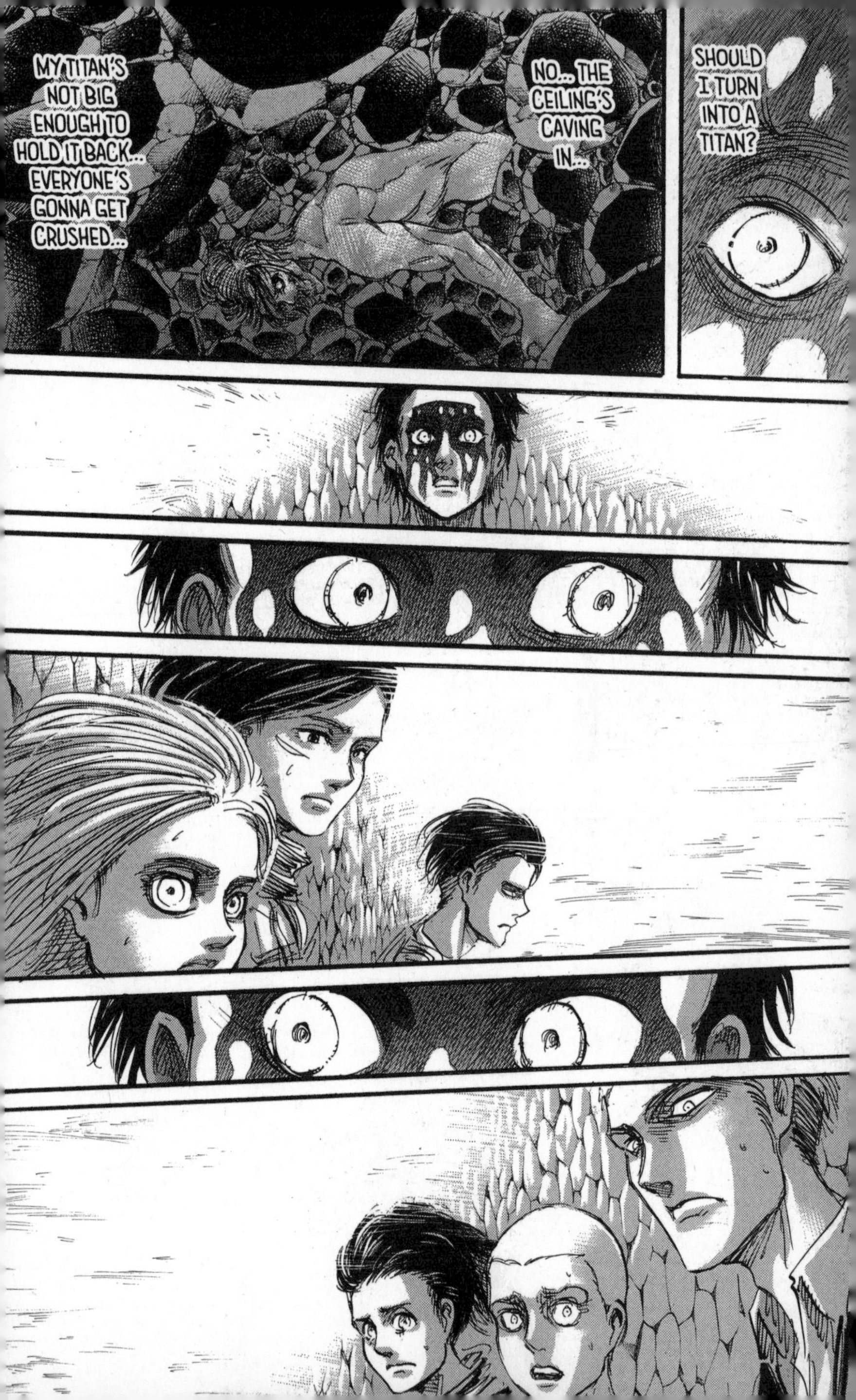
SHOULD I TURN INTO A TITAN?
NO... THE CEILING'S CAVING IN...
MY TITAN'S NOT BIG ENOUGH TO HOLD IT BACK... EVERYONE'S GONNA GET CRUSHED...

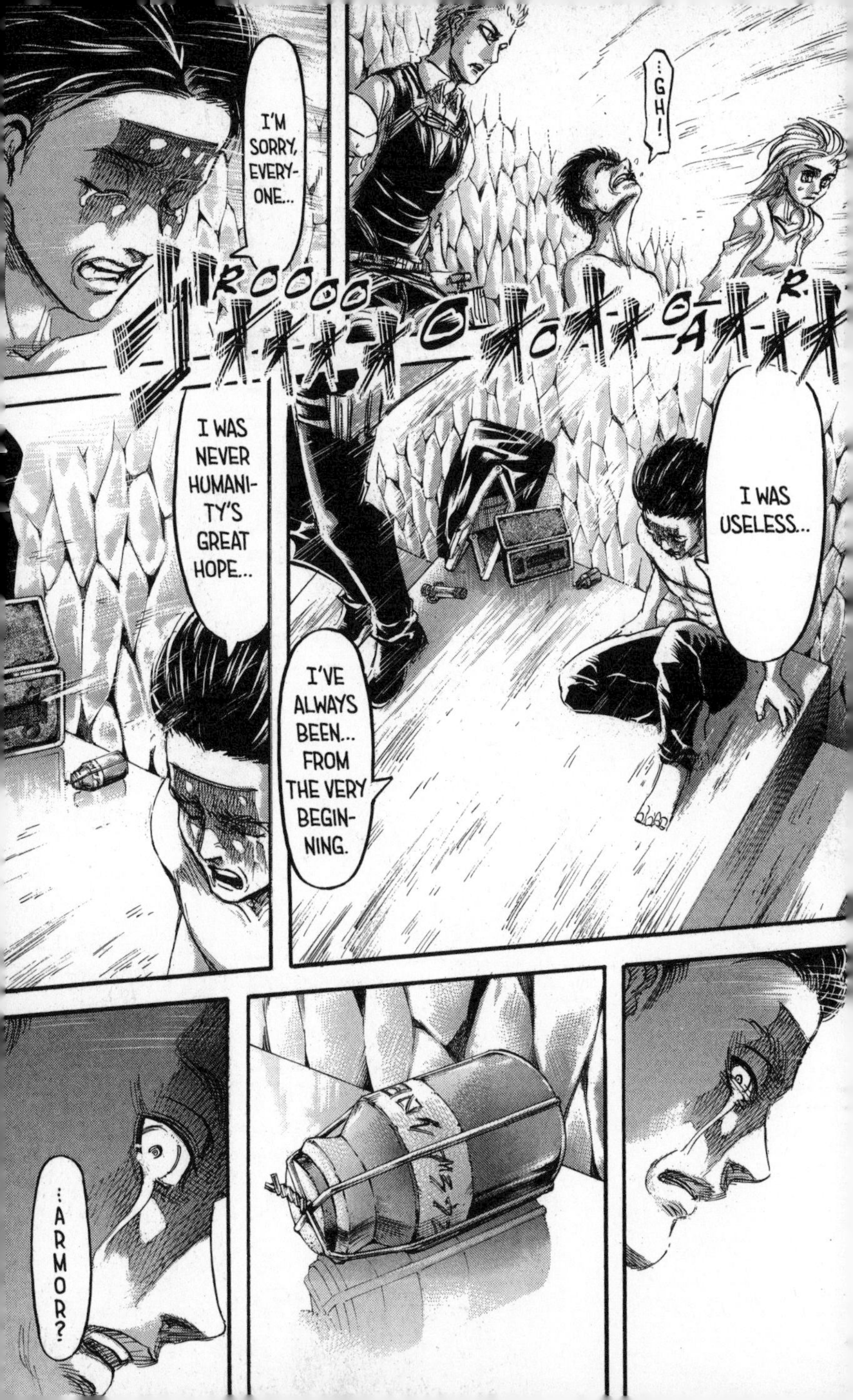
...GH!
I'M SORRY, EVERYONE...
ROOOOOOAR
I WAS USELESS...
I'VE ALWAYS BEEN... FROM THE VERY BEGINNING.
I WAS NEVER HUMANITY'S GREAT HOPE...
...ARMOR?

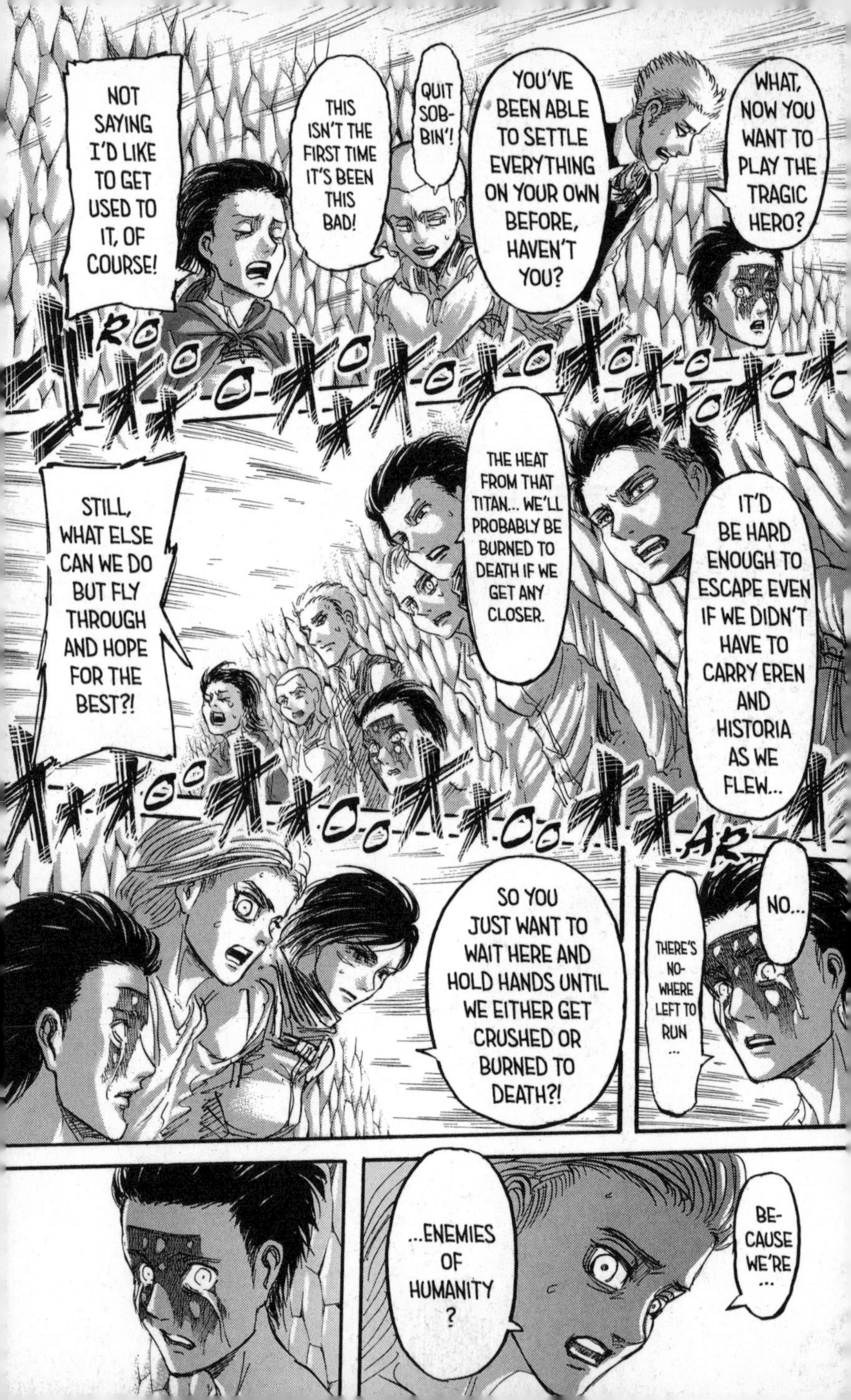
WHAT, NOW YOU WANT TO PLAY THE TRAGIC HERO?
YOU'VE BEEN ABLE TO SETTLE EVERYTHING ON YOUR OWN BEFORE, HAVEN'T YOU?
QUIT SOB-BIN'!
THIS ISN'T THE FIRST TIME IT'S BEEN THIS BAD!
NOT SAYING I'D LIKE TO GET USED TO IT, OF COURSE!
ROOOOOOOOOO
IT'D BE HARD ENOUGH TO ESCAPE EVEN IF WE DIDN'T HAVE TO CARRY EREN AND HISTORIA AS WE FLEW...
THE HEAT FROM THAT TITAN... WE'LL PROBABLY BE BURNED TO DEATH IF WE GET ANY CLOSER.
STILL, WHAT ELSE CAN WE DO BUT FLY THROUGH AND HOPE FOR THE BEST?!
OOOOOOAR
NO...
THERE'S NO-WHERE LEFT TO RUN ...
SO YOU JUST WANT TO WAIT HERE AND HOLD HANDS UNTIL WE EITHER GET CRUSHED OR BURNED TO DEATH?!
BE-CAUSE WE'RE ...
...ENEMIES OF HUMANITY ?

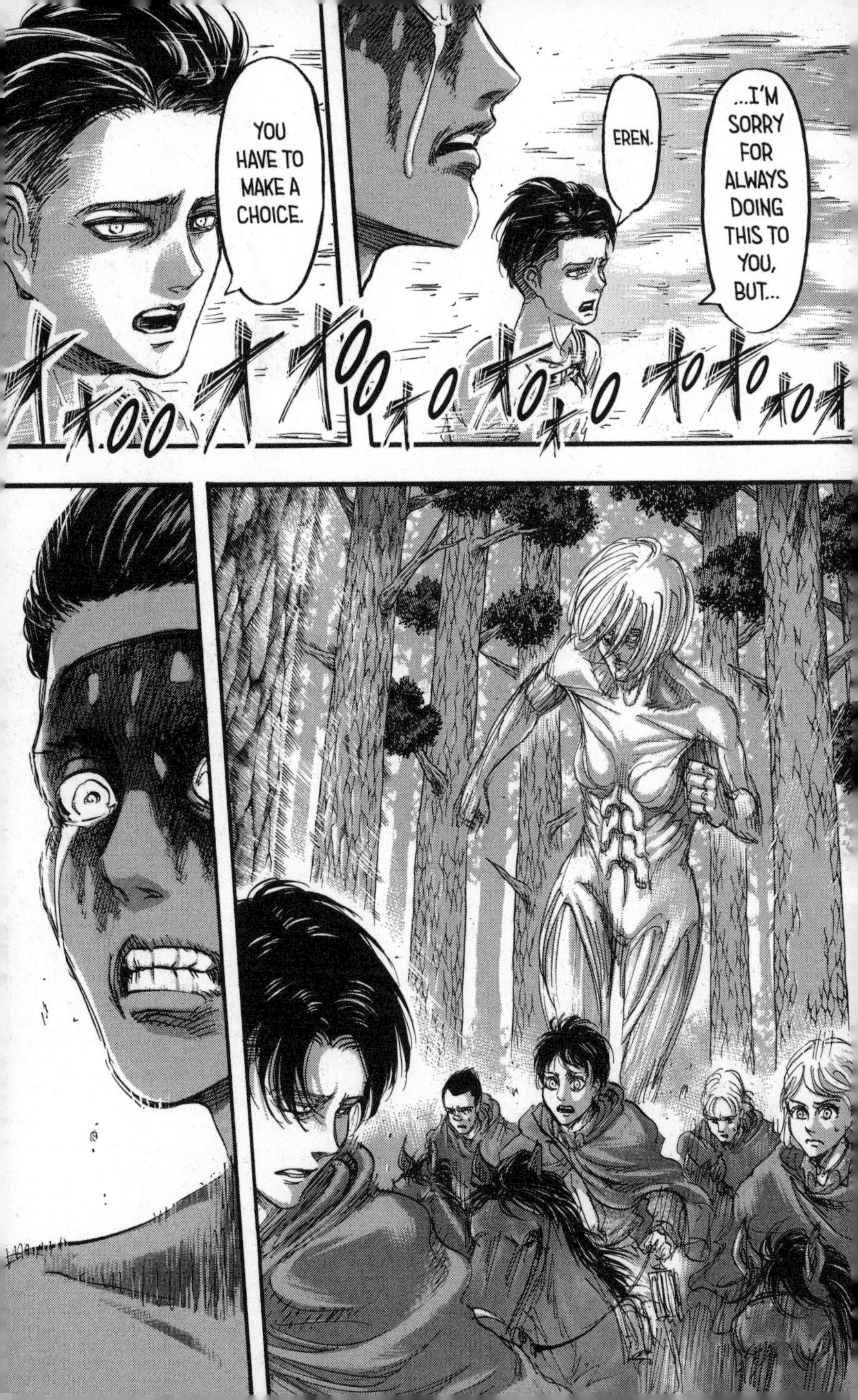
...I'M SORRY FOR ALWAYS DOING THIS TO YOU, BUT...
EREN.
YOU HAVE TO MAKE A CHOICE.

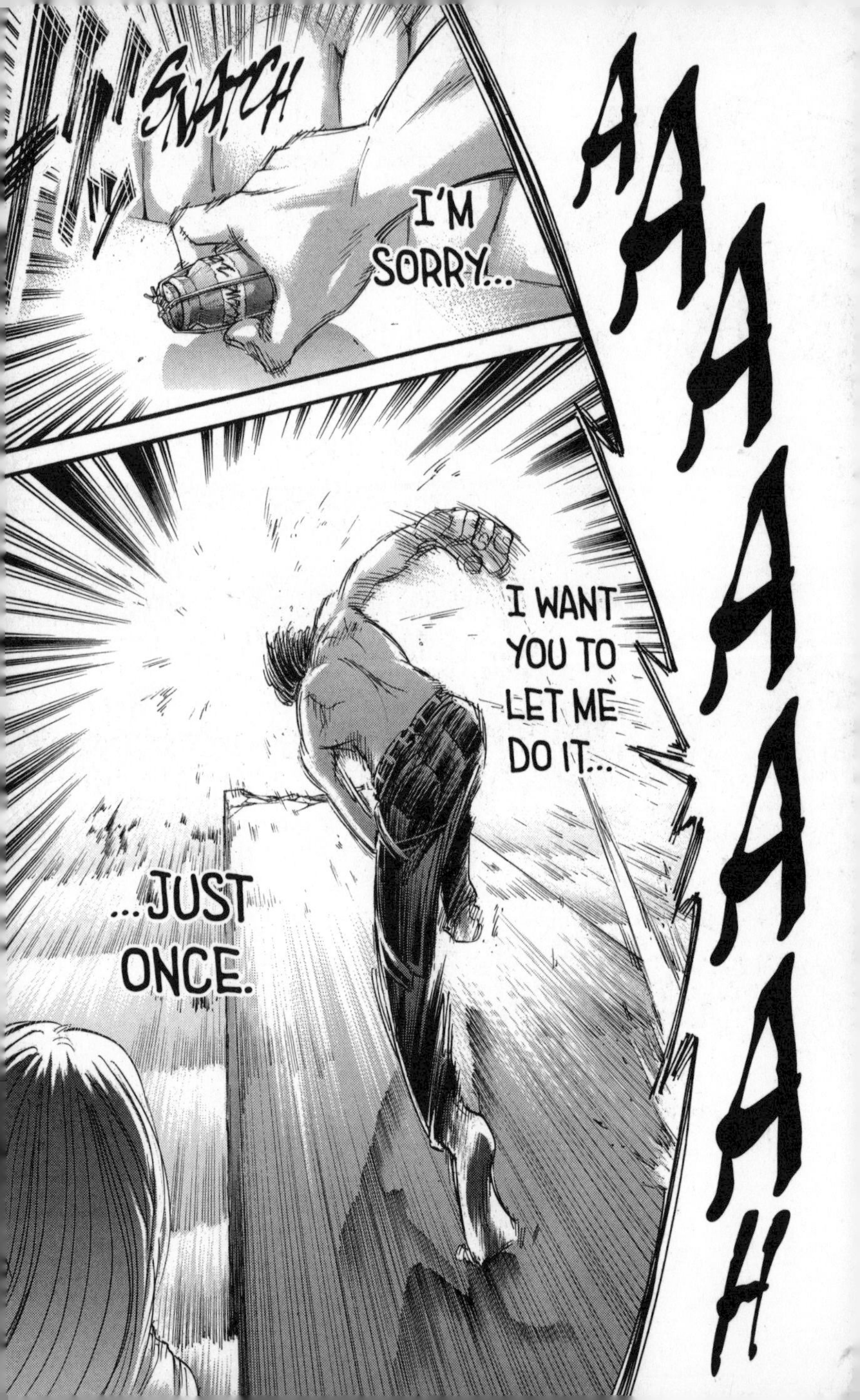
SNATCH
I'M SORRY...
AAAAAAAH
I WANT YOU TO LET ME DO IT...
...JUST ONCE.

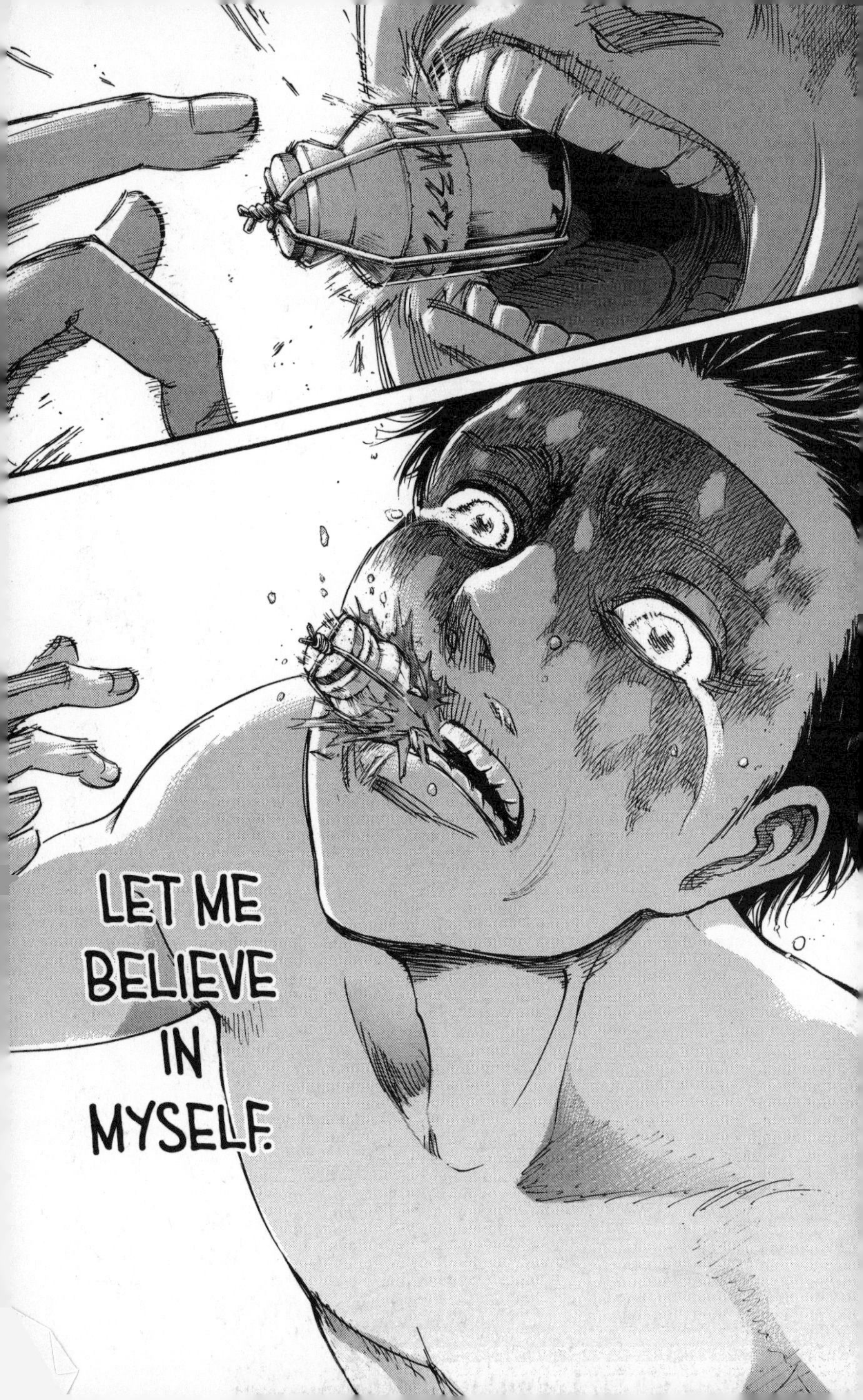
LET ME BELIEVE IN MYSELF.

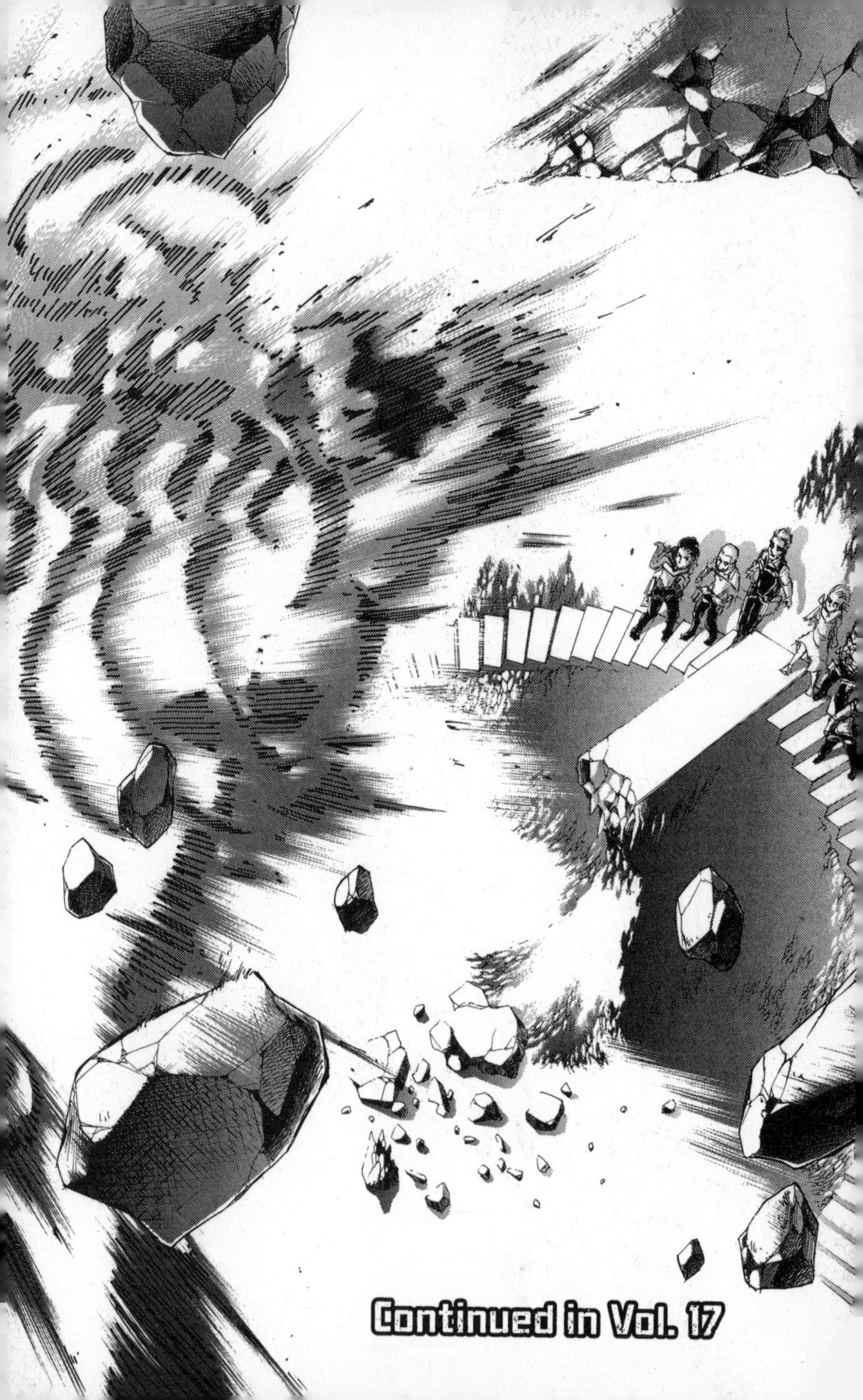
Continued in Vol. 17

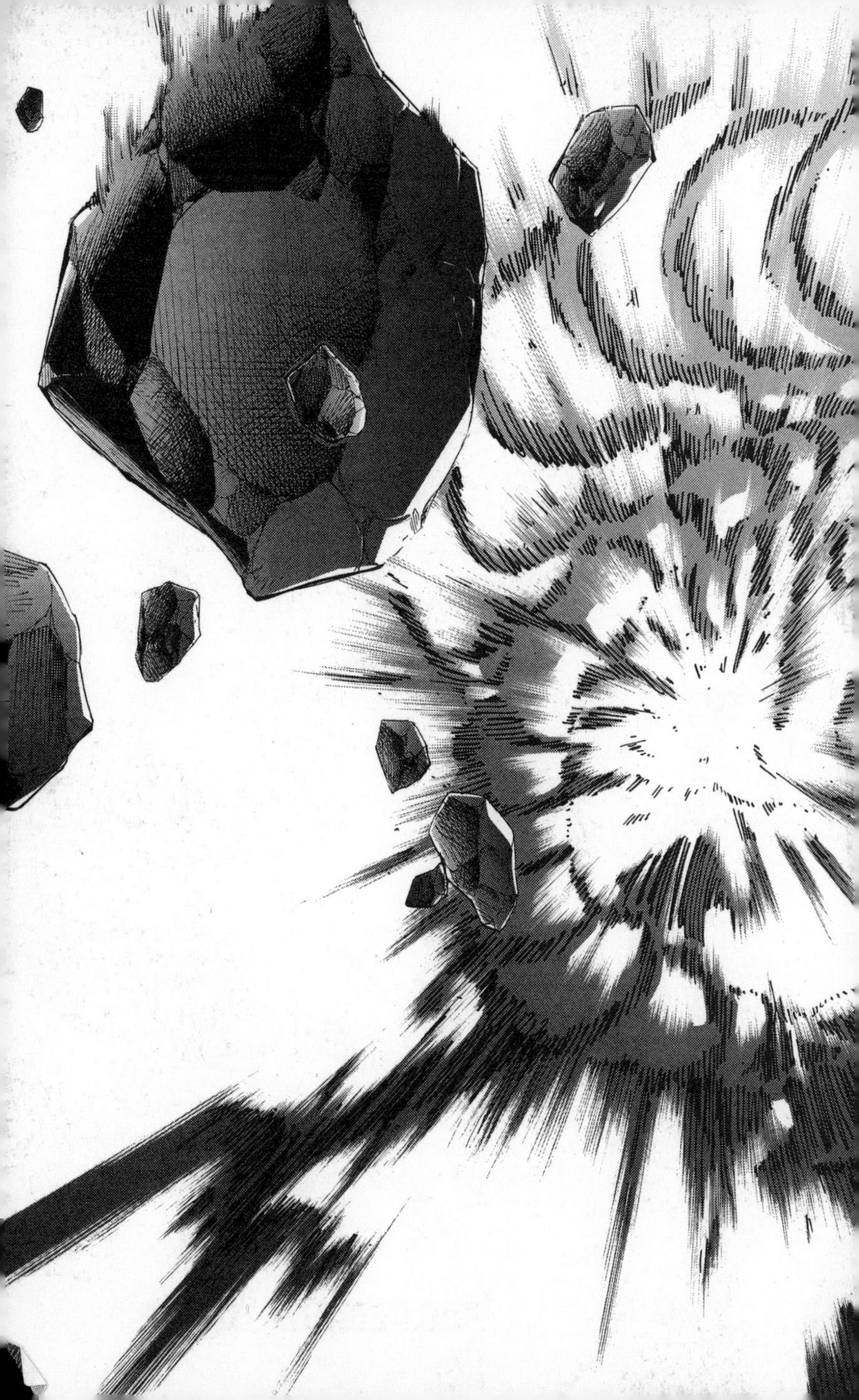

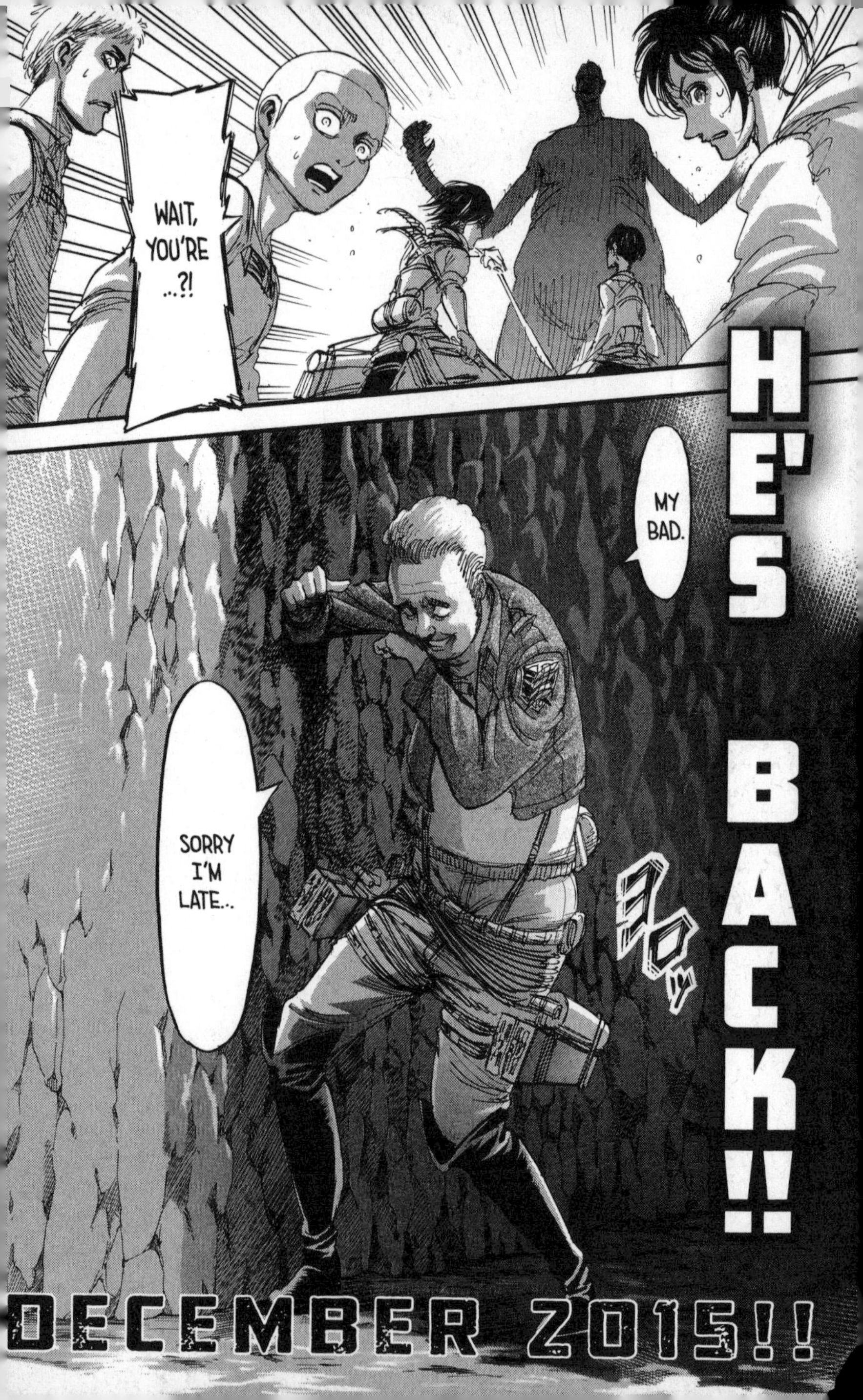
WAIT, YOU'RE ...?!
HE'S BACK!!
MY BAD.
SORRY I'M LATE...
DECEMBER 2015!!

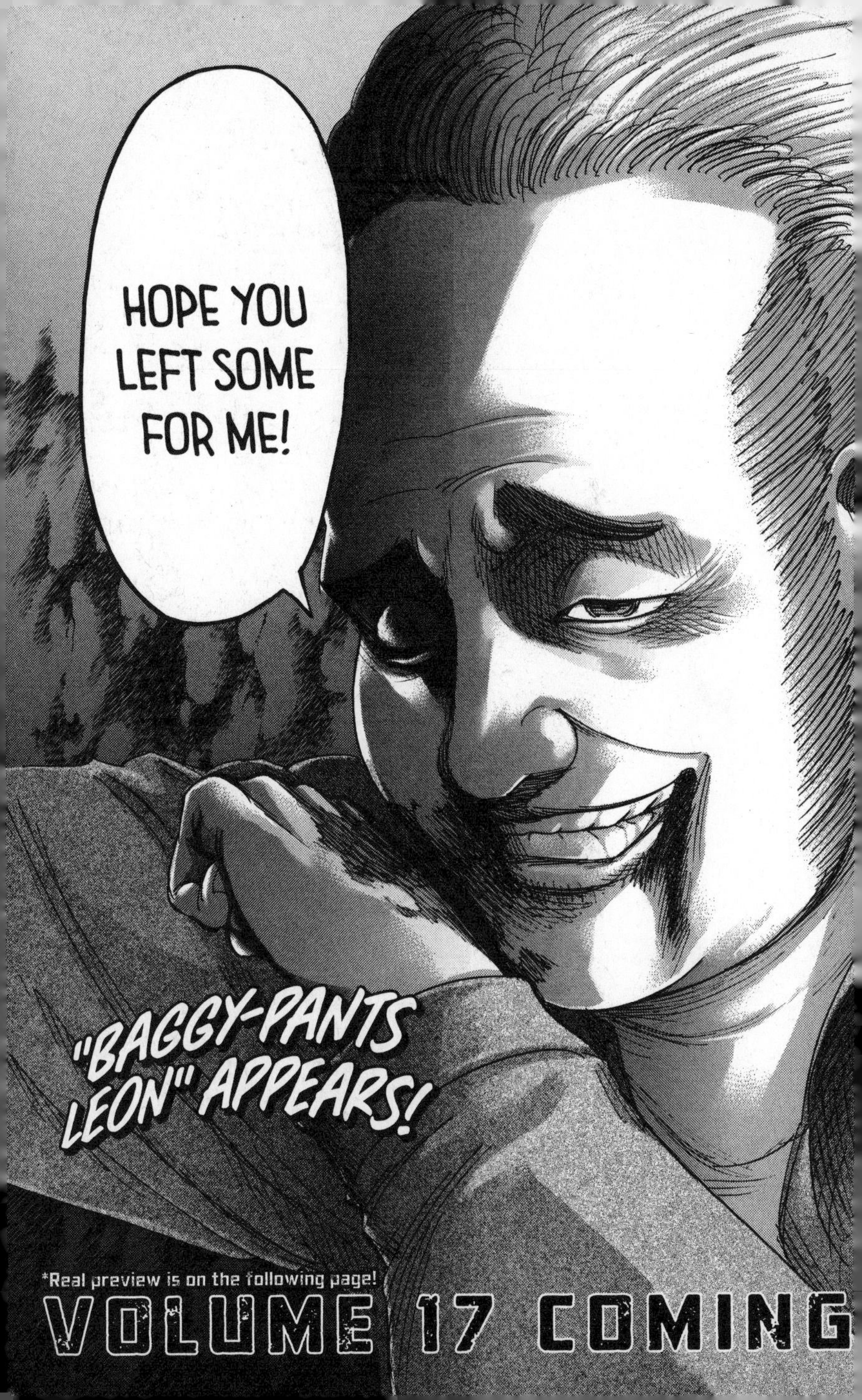
HOPE YOU LEFT SOME FOR ME!
"BAGGY-PANTS LEON" APPEARS!
*Real preview is on the following page!
VOLUME 17 COMING

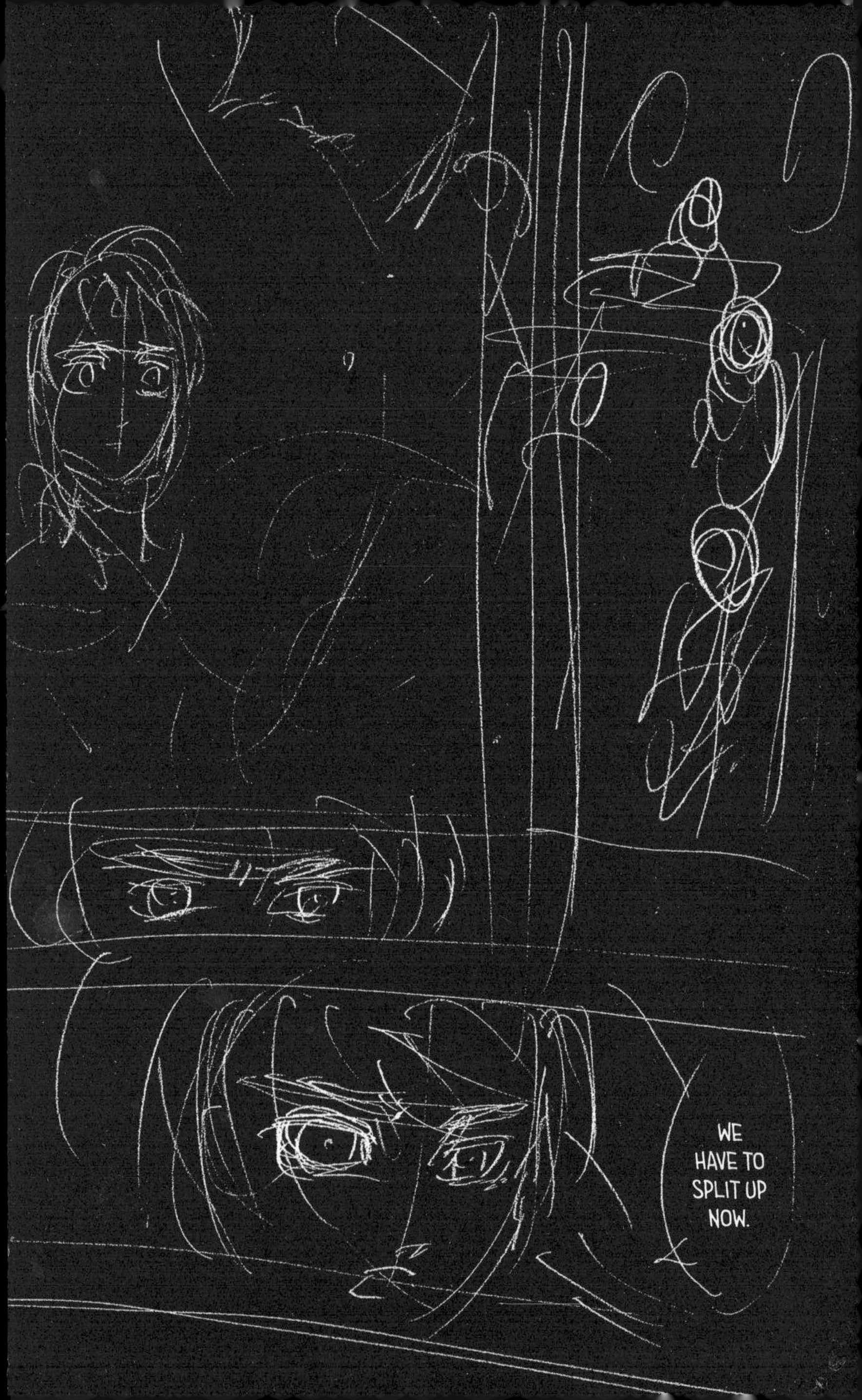
WE HAVE TO SPLIT UP NOW.

HISTORIA, EREN, THE 104th... THE WALL THEY FACE IS UNSCALABLE UNLESS THEY EACH MAKE THEIR OWN DECISIONS.

Attack on Titan volume 16 is a work of fiction. Names, characters, places, and incidents are the products of the author's imagination or are used fictitiously. Any resemblance to actual events, locales, or persons, living or dead, is entirely coincidental.

A Kodansha Comics Trade Paperback Original

Published in the United States by Kodansha Comics, an imprint of Kodansha USA Publishing, LLC, New York.

Publication rights for this English edition arranged through Kodansha Ltd, Tokyo.

First published in Japan in 2015 by Kodansha Ltd., Tokyo as *Shingeki no Kyojin*, volume 16.

ISBN 978-1-61262-980-3

Original cover design by Takashi Shimoyama (Red Rooster)

Printed in the United States of America.

www.kodanshacomics.com

9 8 7 6 5 4 3 2
Translation: Ko Ransom
Lettering: Steve Wands
Editing: Ben Applegate
Kodansha Comics edition cover design by Phil Balsman